OXFORD ISLAMIC LEGAL STUDIES

Series Editors:
Anver M. Emon, Clark B. Lombardi, and Lynn Welchman

SHARĪ'A AND MUSLIM MINORITIES

OXFORD ISLAMIC LEGAL STUDIES

Series Editors:
Anver M. Emon, Clark B. Lombardi, and Lynn Welchman

Satisfying the growing interest in Islam and Islamic law, the *Oxford Islamic Legal Studies* series speaks to both specialists and those interested in the study of a legal tradition that shapes lives and societies across the globe. Islamic law operates at several levels. It shapes private decision making, binds communities, and it is also imposed by states as domestic positive law. The series features innovative and interdisciplinary studies that explore Islamic law as it operates at each of these levels. The series also sheds new light on the history and jurisprudence of Islamic law and provides for a richer understanding of the state of Islamic law in the contemporary Muslim world, including parts of the world where Muslims are minorities.

Sharī'a and Muslim Minorities

The wasaṭī *and* salafī *approaches to* fiqh al-aqalliyyāt al-Muslima

URIYA SHAVIT

OXFORD
UNIVERSITY PRESS

OXFORD
UNIVERSITY PRESS

Great Clarendon Street, Oxford, OX2 6DP,
United Kingdom

Oxford University Press is a department of the University of Oxford.
It furthers the University's objective of excellence in research, scholarship,
and education by publishing worldwide. Oxford is a registered trade mark of
Oxford University Press in the UK and in certain other countries

First Edition published in 2015

Published in the United States of America by Oxford University Press
198 Madison Avenue, New York, NY 10016, United States of America

British Library Cataloguing in Publication Data
Data available

Library of Congress Control Number: 2015953463

ISBN 978-0-19-875723-8

To the memory of Joseph Kostiner,
a teacher, a friend, a noble soul

Series Editors' Preface

Sharīʿa and Muslim Minorities is a work of intellectual history that offers a sustained analysis of two competing approaches to Islamic legal interpretation among contemporary Muslims. Focusing on the *fiqh al-aqalliyyāt al-Muslima*, or the *fiqh* of Muslim minorities, Uriya Shavit lays bare the contours of both the *wasaṭiyya* and *salafiyya* approaches to interpretation, and explores their substantive disagreement regarding legal issues facing Muslim minorities in Europe and North America. Drawing upon both fieldwork and an extensive (and often difficult to locate) archive of publications, Shavit cautions readers against making simple assumptions about what Sharīʿa is or what Muslims believe. A work of intellectual history, *Sharīʿa and Muslim Minorities* illuminates the internal debates, conflicts, and disagreements that have led to these distinct intellectual approaches that reflect on law and religion in the modern state. Shavit has laid an important foundation for future research on a number of topics of great interest to the academy today.

Anver M. Emon
Clark B. Lombardi
Lynn Welchman

Acknowledgments

I take great pleasure in paying tribute to the individuals and organizations whose support and assistance made the writing of this book possible. In nine years of research, I met dozens of imāms, mosque-attendees, and owners of Islamic bookstores across Europe and the United States, who shared with me their insights, offered assistance, and provided me with important texts. I am particularly indebted to Ḥusayn Ḥalāwa, Secretary General of the European Council for Fatwa and Research, Dublin, 'Umar Jāmāykī, imām of the Ibnu Taymeeyah Brixton Mosque, London, Bilāl Davis (Abū Ḥakīm), the Salafi Mosque and Islamic Centre, Birmingham, Maḥbūb al-Raḥman, imām of the Islamic Cultural Center, Norway, Muḥammad Naved Johari, Islamische Information und Serviceleistungen (IIS mosque), Frankfurt am Main, and Nāṣir al-'Īsā, imām of al-Nūr mosque, Berlin, for their gracious hospitality and kindness.

The Israel Science Foundation supported the research for this book (grant 627.11). I thank the foundation's staff for their generosity which made the writing of the book possible.

Dr. Ofir Winter, my research assistant through much of this project, located dozens of religious decisions and treatises, transliterated the Arabic names and terms, compiled the bibliography, and contributed important observations. Carl Yonker edited the manuscript, improved it beyond recognition, and greatly assisted in facilitating its publication. Kfir Gross meticulously proofread the transliterations and bibliographical information, and prepared the index. I am deeply thankful for their encouragement and friendship. I also want to thank Teresa Harings, Andrew Esensten, Marion Gliksberg, and Sören Andresen for their assistance. My friend Iyād Zaḥālqa, Qāḍī of Jerusalem, taught me a lot about Islam, Islamic law, and Muslim minorities. My brother Avner greatly assisted in my studies in French mosques. My sister Noga supplied me with important information about online resources. I am also indebted to David Shavit, Avital Regev-Shoshani, and Avi Shoshani for their invaluable advice.

I am grateful to Prof. Eyal Zisser, Dean of Humanities at Tel Aviv University, for his advice and generous support, and to Prof. Joseph Klafter, President of the university, for his encouragement, without which this study could not have been written.

The support and advice of Prof. Shlomo Biderman, Prof. Yishai Peled, Dr. Nehama Verbin, Prof. Asher Susser, Prof. Ron Margolin, Prof. Camila Adang, and Prof. Ephraim Yaar, Tel Aviv University, was invaluable. I am also thankful to Prof. David S. Powers, Cornell University; Prof. David Thomas, University of Birmingham; Prof. Amikam Nachmani, Bar-Ilan University; Prof. Itzchak Weismann, Haifa University; and Prof. Ursula Apitzsch, University of Frankfurt, for their good advice and encouragement.

My parents, Zohar and Yaacov Shavit, and my friends Hakan Yar, Robert Litae, Frederic Wiesenbach, Eli Novershtern, Joav Toker, Oliver Stuchel, Felicia Herrschaft, Aviad Beit-Halachmi, Efrat Deutsch, Jalal Banna, Yoram Pajand, and Yazan al-Khatib contributed to my understanding of the issues examined in this study.

I feel fortunate to have taught so many creative and brilliant graduate and undergraduate students at Tel Aviv University. Several of the participants in my classes on Islamic law located, as part of their final papers, religious decisions which were incorporated in this study.

I am profoundly indebted to the team at Oxford University Press: Alex Flach, Commissioning Editor, Academic Law; Natasha Flemming, Product Development Editor; and Elinor Shields, Assistant Commissioning Editor, for their good advice, patience, and encouragement. I am grateful to Jeremy Langworthy for his meticulous and wise copy-editing, and to Scott Greenway for his splendid design of the cover. I also want to thank the editors of Oxford Islamic Legal Studies Series, Prof. Anver Emon, Prof. Clark Lombardi, and Prof. Lynn Welchman, for their insightful comments and directions, which greatly improved this study.

Contents

Note on Transliterations

Book titles, institutions, and authors referenced from English-language sources appear in the references as in the original texts. Thus, a number of names appear in various transliterations.

Introduction to *Sharīʿa and Muslim Minorities*

The *hijra*, or migration, constitutes the defining moment in Muslim history. It marks the beginning of the Muslim calendar and the crossroads between persecution and ascendance. The Prophet Muḥammad was forced to leave his hometown of Mecca in AD 622 with a group of several dozen supporters and settle in a new territory, Yathrib, which he renamed al-Madīna and from where he continued to spread Allah's final message. Throughout Muslim history, both before and after the *hijra*, there have been numerous instances of Muslims residing under non-Islamic rule: the migration of some one hundred Muslims to Ethiopia in 615–16, where they found shelter under a Christian king; the continued presence of some Muslims in Mecca after the Prophet established a new community in al-Madīna; and periods where millions of Muslims resided in lands that were occupied as a result of Christian military campaigns, from the *Reconquista* to modern imperialism.

While migration constitutes the formative myth of Islam, and while the condition of Muslims living as a minority is not a novelty in Islamic history, the movement of millions of Muslims to Western lands since the end of the Second World War presented jurists with a new conceptual challenge. The Muslims who migrated to Ethiopia did so when no Muslim state existed and with the blessing of the Prophet. The *hijra* led by the Prophet transferred believers from one infidel society to another, where their prospects were better. The Muslims who remained in Mecca after the *hijra* were natives of the town and had the Prophet's consent. Muslims who continued to live under Christian occupiers clung to ancestral lands and some had no alternative but to stay put. Post-Second World War migration to the West was the first time in history in which masses of

Muslims voluntarily and individually left Muslim lands and settled in non-Muslim lands, in most cases for the purpose of improving their economic situation. Thus, their choice created an unprecedented theological-juristic challenge of legitimacy.

Adding to this fundamental difficulty were those migrants' encounters with numerous modern and post-modern norms that appeared to conflict with Islamic norms. These ranged from the permissibility of naturalization in secular Western states to that of celebrating Valentine's Day, to that of eschewing fasting during Ramaḍān to pursue careers as professional athletes. Some religio-juristic difficulties resulted from attacks on multiculturalism and from anti-Muslim sentiments that proliferated in the West, particularly during the 2000s. Some resulted from cultural divides between integrated second-generation Muslim migrants and the first generation. Still other challenges resulted from financial hardships encountered by Muslims in the West, many of who came from modest backgrounds. Westerners who converted, or considered converting to Islam, also generated new and complicated opportunities and hurdles.

The field of jurisprudence that examines the legitimacy of voluntary, modern migration to and residence in non-Muslim societies and addresses specific, everyday challenges that Muslim minorities confront is called *fiqh al-aqalliyyāt al-Muslima*. This field draws from the religio-juristic heritage that developed in relation to previous minority conditions while struggling to resolve dilemmas that have not been treated by jurists of the past.

Based on a comparative analysis of several thousand religio-juristic treatises and *fatwās*, this book examines the origins, evolution, ideologies, methodologies, and *fatwās* of two preeminent and contesting contemporary approaches to *fiqh al-aqalliyyāt al-Muslima*—the *wasaṭī*, associated with al-Azhar graduates, led by the Egyptian Qatar-based Yūsuf al-Qaraḍāwī and institutionalized through the Dublin-based European Council for Fatwa and Research, and the *salafī*, associated with Saudi Arabia's religious establishment, led by the late ʿAbd al-ʿAzīz b. ʿAbdallāh b. Bāz and the late Muḥammad b. Ṣāliḥ al-ʿUthaymīn, and promoted in the West through dozens of loosely connected and at times rival associations, publishers, and mosques.

The main thesis of the book is that the *wasaṭī* and *salafī* approaches to the religious law of Muslim minorities constitute extensions of the competing ideologies and methodologies that *wasaṭīs* and *salafīs* promote in contemporary majority Muslim societies and reflect, in a dialectic manner in some cases, the general disagreements and disputes between these approaches. Because some challenges Muslim minorities encounter are uniquely complicated and unprecedented, the treatment of these challenges by *wasaṭī* and *salafī* jurists is instructive in measuring the extent of the flexibility and creativity allowed by the two approaches and how they balance between conflicting objectives and ambitions. Both *wasaṭīs* and *salafīs* primarily legitimize Muslim residence in non-Muslim societies by considering Muslim residence as a means to proselytize and bring about the eventual Islamization of the West. Yet, *wasaṭīs* accept other justifications and suggest that Muslims are not only allowed but should be encouraged to create a permanent presence in Western lands, while *salafī* legitimizations are more reluctant and narrow. *Wasaṭī fiqh al-aqalliyyāt al-Muslima* connects two ideological objectives that are central also to the general *wasaṭī* approach: *al-taysīr fī al-fatwā wal-tabshīr fī al-daʿwa*, or facilitation in issuing religious laws and proselytizing by gentle means and in a gradualist manner. To promote these objectives *wasaṭīs* broadly apply *maṣlaḥa* (safeguarding primary objectives of the *sharīʿa*) and cross-searching within and beyond the four schools of law. The most significant innovation of *wasaṭī fiqh al-aqalliyyāt al-Muslima* is its regard of *daʿwa* as a *maṣlaḥa* that justifies radical accommodations of religious laws. In contrast, *salafīs* argue that neither the unique difficulties that individual Muslims encounter in non-Muslim societies nor the prospect of converting non-Muslims to Islam justifies adjustments of religious laws. Drawing from their general approach, *salafīs* stress the necessity of strict, steadfast adherence to Allah's laws, as they interpret them, regardless of geographic location or any individual hardships experienced. *Salafī* opinions rely heavily on their conceptualization of *al-walāʾ wal-barāʾ* (loyalty and disavowal), which prohibits extending loyalty or friendship to infidels as well as imitating them. However, coinciding with their general approach, *salafīs* demonstrate a measure of flexibility when treating the relationship of Muslim minorities with state institutions.

The competing agendas promulgated by *wasaṭīs* and *salafīs* resulted in the evolution of two corpuses of *fatwās* for Muslim minorities that sharply differ on several vital issues. *Salafīs* vehemently reject *wasaṭī* conditional legitimizations of mortgages, continuation of marriages between female converts and non-Muslim husbands, receiving the inheritance of non-Muslim parents, greeting Christians on their holidays, breaking the Ramaḍān fast to pursue a career, serving in military forces that fight against Muslims, and taking off the *ḥijāb* when required by law. On other issues, including naturalization and electoral participation, *wasaṭīs* and some *salafīs* have found more common ground between their respective approaches.

The majority of Muslim minorities live in non-Western lands. In India alone, the number of Muslims is larger than the total number of Muslims in Western countries. *Wasaṭīs* and *salafīs* have not directed their views of *fiqh al-aqalliyyāt al-Muslima* exclusively to Muslims living in the West. Nevertheless, the focus of their theorizing on the general permissibility of living in a non-Muslim country, as demonstrated by a majority of their *fatwās*, is the Muslims of the West. Several reasons explain this focus. First, *wasaṭīs* and *salafīs* are preoccupied with the West. Indeed, they consider it to be the greatest threat to the future of Islam; an economically, scientifically, and technologically advanced civilization that presently leads the world and cannot be ignored, and a sum of negative moral values that is decaying and will eventually collapse and embrace Islam. Thus, the future of Muslims in Western Europe and North America is of the greatest interest to them. Second, voluntary migration (rather than residence under non-Muslim occupiers) and the doubts regarding its permissibility led to the formulation of *wasaṭī* and *salafī* conceptualizations of *fiqh al-aqalliyyāt al-Muslima*. At present, the majority of voluntary Muslim migrants live in the West. Third, while the *wasaṭī* and *salafī* corpuses on *fiqh al-aqalliyyāt al-Muslima* were not composed exclusively by Arabs, a majority of the jurists who were involved in their composition were Arab jurists based in the Arab world or in Western countries, who focused on the concerns of Muslims originating from Arab countries and residing in the West.

While the corpuses studied in this book are profoundly important to a minority of Muslims in the West, they should in no way be confused as affecting the majority. As noted by March, "the downside of focusing on this discourse [*fiqh al-aqalliyyāt al-Muslima*] is that it runs the risk of privileging and overemphasizing the contributions of scholars in the Arab world at the expense of the quotidian practices and attitudes of Muslims actually living under Western secularism."[1] *Sharīʿa*, to quote Mathias Rohe, does not affect the lives of a majority of Muslims living in the West, who "simply accept the prevailing secular legal and social frameworks without reflection."[2] Tariq Ramadan, a Swiss-based Muslim political philosopher and a prolific theorist and commentator on Islam in the West, estimated that most Muslim Westerners—some 75 to 80 percent—"do not practice their religion regularly and experience no specific 'religious' problems in their daily lives."[3] Patterns of behavior that are at times spontaneously identified by observers as being based on the systematic internalization by individuals of a set, or sets, of *sharʿī* norms—for example, certain dress-codes—often reflect a more general and sporadic desire to incorporate traditions without considering religious law a binding or exclusive framework. Furthermore, Muslims who do strive to regulate their lives based on Islamic law as an exclusive framework do not necessarily abide by *wasaṭī or salafī* interpretations; they may not even be aware of the existence of these distinct corpuses. And, as will be demonstrated in this book, even in the cases of those who do demonstrate a preference for one of the two approaches, *fatwās* are not distributed through hierarchical processes; rather, they are subject to debates and negotiations, which are sometimes ongoing. Thus, while jurists from the two approaches speak in the name of Islam, their efforts should not be confused as representing Muslims in the West.

While it is a relatively new field, various aspects of *fiqh al-aqalliyyāt al-Muslima*, primarily its *wasaṭī* articulations, have been analyzed by a number of scholars. These include Wasif Shadid and Sjoerd van Koningsveld, who were among the first to survey contemporary conceptualizations

[1] Andrew March, "Are Secularism and Neutrality Attractive to Religious Minorities? Islamic Discussions of Western Secularism in the 'Jurisprudence of Muslim Minorities' (Fiqh al-Aqalliyyāt) Discourse," *Cardozo Law Review* 30, 6 (2009), 2827.

[2] Mathias Rohe, "Islam and the Law in Europe," *Orient* 51, 2 (2010), 31.

[3] Tariq Ramadan, *What I Believe* (Oxford and New York: Oxford University Press, 2010), 46–7.

of the legitimacy of Muslim presence in the West by Muslim jurists, as well as a range of *fatwās* predominantly pertaining to the relations between Muslim minorities and their state institutions;[4] Alexandre Caeiro, who offered the most detailed studies on the ideology, methodology, mechanisms of operation, and demographic composition of the European Council for Fatwa and Research, as well as analyzed in depth a number of the Council's decisions;[5] Andrew March, who analyzed juristic deliberations, primarily *wasaṭī*, on the legitimacy of Muslim residence in non-Muslim lands, and the relations between Muslim minorities and non-Muslim societies and state institutions, and reflected on their ethical implications;[6] Shammai Fishman, who analyzed *fiqh al-aqalliyyāt al-Muslima* as a combined effort of Ṭaha Jābir al-'Alwānī and Yūsuf al-Qaraḍāwī;[7] Tauseef Ahmad Parray, who highlighted the criticism of al-'Alwānī's and al-Qaraḍāwī's concept of *taysīr*;[8] Ralph Ghadban, who offered a succinct examination of their conceptualization of *fiqh al-aqalliyyāt al-Muslima* and

[4] Wasif Shadid and Sjoerd van Koningsveld, "Loyalty to a Non-Muslim Government: An Analysis of Islamic Normative Discussions and the Views of Some Contemporary Islamicists," in Wasif A. R. Shadid and Sjoerd van Koningsveld (eds.), *Political Participation and Identities of Muslims in Non-Muslim States* (Kampen: Kok Pharos Publishing House, 1996), 84–114. Also, Wasif Shadid and Sjoerd van Koninsveld, "Religious Authorities of Muslims in the West: Their View on Political Participation," in Wasif Shadid and Sjoerd van Koningsveld (eds.), *Intercultural Relations and Religious Authorities: Muslims in the European Union* (Leuven: Peeters, 2002), 149–68.

[5] Including: Alexandre Caeiro, "The Social Construction of Sharī'a: Bank Interest, Home Purchase and Islamic Norms in the West," *Die Welt des Islams* 44, 3 (2004), 435–49; "The Power of European Fatwas: The Minority Fiqh Project and the Making of an Islamic Counterpublic," *International Journal of Middle East Studies* 42, 3 (2010), 435–49; Alexandre Caeiro and Mahmoud al-Saify, "Qaradawi in Europe, Europe in Qaradawi? The Global Mufti's European Politics," in Bettina Gräf and Jakob Skovgaard-Petersen (eds.), *The Global Mufti: The Phenomenon of Yūsuf al-Qaraḍāwī* (London: Hurst & Company, 2009), 109–48; "Transnational Ulama, European Fatwas and Islamic Authorities: A Case Study of the European Council for Fatwa and Research," in Martin van Bruinessen and Stefano Allievi (eds.), *Producing Islamic Knowledge: Transmission and Dissemination in Western Europe* (Abingdon and New York: Routledge, 2011), 121–41.

[6] Andrew March, *Islam and Liberal Citizenship: The Search for an Overlapping Consensus* (Oxford and New York: Oxford University Press, 2009); "Islamic Foundations for a Social Contract in Non-Muslim Liberal Democracies," *American Political Science Review* 101, 2 (May 2007), 235–52; "Are Secularism and Neutrality Attractive to Religious Minorities? Islamic Discussions of Western Secularism in the 'Jurisprudence of Muslim Minorities' (Fiqh al-Aqalliyyat) Discourse," *Cardozo Law Review* 30, 6 (2009), 2821–54.

[7] Shammai Fishman, *Fiqh al-Aqalliyyat: A Legal Theory for Muslim Minorities* (Washington: Hudson Institute, 2006).

[8] Tauseef Ahmad Parray, "The Legal Methodology of 'Fiqh al-Aqalliyyat' and its Critics: An Analytical Study," *Journal of Muslim Minority Affairs* 32, 1 (March 2012), 88–107.

gave attention to their understanding of *daʿwa*;[9] Mathias Rohe, who analyzed several of the early decisions issued by the European Council for Fatwa and Research;[10] Yusuf Talal DeLorenzo, who analyzed the operation and a number of decisions issued by the *Fiqh* Council of North America;[11] and Alan Verskin, who offered a survey (and translations) of religious decisions dealing with the permissibility of residence in non-Muslim lands from the *Reconquista* to contemporary times.[12] A number of studies pointed to the links between the past and the present. Khaled Abou El Fadl[13] and Sami A. Aldeeb Abu-Sahlieh[14] identified such links between classic and contemporary decisions on Muslim minorities, while Umar Ryad described those between early modernist and contemporary rulings.[15]

Studies on *fiqh al-aqalliyyāt al-Muslima* have either ignored or treated anecdotally *salafī fatwās* on Muslim minorities, and neglected the dialetics between the *wasaṭī* and *salafī* approaches in this field; neither did they systematically trace the links between developments in the general ideologies and methodologies of *wasaṭiyya* and *salafiyya* and the evolution of their respective approaches to *fiqh al-aqalliyyāt al-Muslima*. This book's comparative methodology, drawing on the largest (to date) database of *wasaṭī* and *salafī fatwās* and treatises on theological, social, financial, political, and cultural issues, uncovers a broader spectrum of opinions than previous studies have done, and introduces a number of

[9] Ralph Ghadban, "Fiqh al-Aqalliyyat and its Place in Islamic Law," *Orient* 51, 2 (2010), 56–63.

[10] Mathias Rohe, *Muslim Minorities and the Law in Europe* (New Delhi: Global Media Publications, 2007), 146–54.

[11] Yusuf Talal DeLorenzo, "The Fiqh Councilor in North America," in Yvonne Yazbeck Haddad and John L. Esposito (eds.), *Muslims on the Americanization Path?* (Oxford and New York: Oxford University Press, 2000), 65–86.

[12] Alan Verskin, *Oppressed in the Land? Fatwās on Muslims Living under Non-Muslim Rule from the Middle Ages to the Present* (Princeton: Markus Wiener Publishers, 2013).

[13] Khaled Abou El-Fadl, "Islamic Law and Muslim Minorities: The Juristic Discourse on Muslim Minorities from the Second/Eight to the Eleventh/Seventeenth Centuries," *Islamic Law and Society* 1, 2 (1994), 141–87.

[14] Sami A. Aldeeb Abu-Sahlieh, "The Islamic Conception of Migration," *International Migration Review* 30, 1 (March 1996), 37–57.

[15] Umar Ryad, "A Prelude to Fiqh al-Aqalliyyāt: Rashīd Riḍā's Fatwās to Muslims under Non-Muslim Rule," in Christiane Timmerman *et al.* (eds.), *In-between Spaces: Christian and Muslim Minorities in Transition in Europe and the Middle East* (Brussels: Peter Lang: 2009), 239–70.

new points to the study of *fiqh al-aqalliyyāt al-Muslima*, and to the wider study of *wasaṭī* and *salafī* jurisprudence.

The book highlights the potential of determining *maṣlaḥa* to accommodate religious laws, and the crucial role competing interpretations and applications of *maṣlaḥa* had on the development of distinct approaches to Muslim minorities' jurisprudence. It demonstrates that the pragmatic and audacious body of *fatwās* that *wasaṭī* jurists issued since the late 1990s on situations pertaining to Muslim minorities was largely enabled by developments that occurred in the general *wasaṭī* theory of *maṣlaḥa* during the mid-1990s, which were later incorporated in the *wasaṭī* doctrine of *fiqh al-aqalliyyāt al-Muslima*. These developments, staunchly rejected by *salafī* jurists, include the depiction of facilitation as the essence of Islam, which encouraged *wasaṭīs* to search for lenient decisions that accommodate the challenges Muslim minorities face, as well as the elevation of individual needs to the rank of necessities and the broadening of the list of primary objectives of the *sharīʿa*, which made it possible for *wasaṭīs* to formulate lenient decisions within a *sharʿī* framework. The broadening of the Lawgiver's objectives led to the most intriguing move on the part of the *wasaṭīs*, as its jurists transformed an idea strongly rooted in Muslim jurisprudence—that Muslim presence in the West is permissible if it can promote *daʿwa*—to a principal objective that legitimizes the suspension of prohibitions. The vehement *salafī* opposition to this interpretation of *maṣlaḥa* reveals how similar guiding ideological objectives can lead to radically different religio-juristic results. While both approaches legitimize Muslim residence in the West by considering migrants as missionaries, one type of triumphalism legitimizes lenient adjustments of religious laws to the unique challenges Muslim minorities confront while the other, invoking a far narrower approach to *maṣlaḥa*, insists on the importance of the universal application of the laws as a way to promote proselytizing.

The sensitivity of the issue is obvious, and, as will be demonstrated in this book, jurists are very conscious of it: any type of justification based on a plan to Islamize the West can be utilized by those who claim that the acceptance of liberal political and judicial systems by devout Muslims is merely tactical, masking their true intentions. March suggested that the

Islamizing of the West is not "required or necessarily implied by the interest in *daʿwa*."[16] From a *wasaṭī* or *salafī* point of view (and March's discussion is broader) this argument is hardly convincing in terms of the ultimate goal envisioned, considering that *wasaṭīs* and *salafīs* are equally confident that Islam is the alternative system that can save the West from its moral decline. But this book identifies an ironic twist advanced through the *wasaṭī* focus on *daʿwa*, which was largely neglected in previous studies, and equally defends the claim that there is more to proselytizing than an openly declared desire to Islamize the West. Systematically, and on a number of important issues, the elevation of *daʿwa* to a *maṣlaḥa* served (albeit never exclusively) *wasaṭī* jurisprudence as a means to legitimize facilitations and make the lives of Muslim minorities easier. This is not to suggest that proselytizing is merely a pretext invoked by *wasaṭīs*. Nor is it to imply that the concept of Muslims as proselytizers is devoid of challenging normative aspects. Nevertheless, *fatwā*-analyses in this book demonstrate that in the *wasaṭī* case, theological rhetoric and jurisprudence should be evaluated separately, because the triumphant promise of Islamic ascendance introduced in the former has become inseparable from an effort to promote coexistence and integration facilitated by the latter.

Another concept debated within the discourse on *fiqh al-aqalliyyāt al-Muslima* that is highlighted in this book is *al-walāʾ wal-barāʾ*. Academic literature on "loyalty and disavowal" focuses on the evolution of this term in Saudi Arabian political and social discourse and on its contemporary usages by *jihādi-salafī* groups that seek to undermine the House of Saʿūd.[17] This study suggests that the centrality of *al-walāʾ wal-barāʾ* in the *salafī* mainstream discourse, and its implications for Muslim minorities, encouraged *wasaṭīs* to formulate narrower counter-conceptualizations of this

[16] March, *Islam and Liberal Citizenship: The Search for an Overlapping Consensus*, 179.
[17] Joas Wagemakers, "Framing the 'Threat to Islam': *al-Wala' wal-Bara'* in Salafi Discourse," *Arab Studies Quarterly* 30, 4 (Fall 2008), 7–14; "The Enduring Legacy of the Second Saudi State: Quietist and Radical Wahhabi Contestations of *al-Walāʾ wal-Barāʾ*," *International Journal of Middle Eastern Studies* 44, 1 (February 2012), 93–110; "The Transformation of a Radical Concept: *al-wala' wal-bara'* in the Ideology of Abu Muhammad al-Maqdisi," in Roel Meijer's edited volume on *salafī* movements, *Global Salafism: Islam's New Religious Movement* (London: Hurst & Company, 2009), 81–106.

concept that legitimize integration, goodwill, and constructive participation in non-Muslim societies. Those counter-conceptualizations encouraged *salafīs*, in turn, to reassert and publicize their positions. On several specific issues, ranging from Christmas celebrations to inheritance, the debate on what "loyalty and disavowal" means largely affected the formulation of contradictory religio-juristic decisions. Though a signature of the discourse of *fiqh al-aqalliyyāt al-Muslima*, *wasaṭī*, and *salafī* opinions on *al-walā' wal-barā'* are rooted, respectively, in their conflicting approaches to the relation between the Quran and the Prophetic traditions and to the discretion jurists have in reading the latter in light of the former.

The book critically approaches the academic discourse on justifications offered by jurists for the participation of Muslim minorities in non-Muslim state institutions. *Wasaṭīs*, and to a lesser extent *salafīs*, argued that while such participation is impermissible in itself, it can be legitimized based on determinations that overlaps exist between the norms non-Muslim institutions apply and Islamic norms, or, at the very least, based on determinations that participation in non-Muslim state institutions is crucial for the promotion of Islamic norms and interests (i.e., safeguards *maṣlaḥas*). Some of the academic literature on *fiqh al-aqalliyyāt al-Muslima*, particularly the works of Andrew March and his interpretation of John Rawls's political philosophy, examines the compatibility of these types of justifications with liberal political theories. There is a certain caveat to this approach, as it contextualizes religio-juristic texts with texts that draw, at least in part, on very different methods of reasoning; this approach also runs the risk of reducing analyses of *fiqh al-aqalliyyāt al-Muslima* to the question of whether Islamic norms and liberalism can live side by side, a theme which often reveals more about the orientation of those engaging with it than about what theologians and jurists actually say. Notwithstanding these reservations, this study argues that from a theoretical point of view, *any* religio-juristic legitimization of cooperation with state institutions, regardless of its content, *potentially* challenges liberal systems and is conditional and temporary rather than substantive, because the reasoning and mechanisms it applies prioritize the authority of religious jurists over elected parliaments and civil judiciaries. This type of challenge is not unique, of course, to Islam; there comes to mind the example of ultra and national Orthodox Jews in Israel, who abide by religious law and state law, with the former theoretically superseding the latter. In the context of the religious law of Muslim minorities, obviously, a decision that legitimizes participation as a means to promote certain Islamic interests can be revoked by a jurist at any given time, if it is determined that circumstances have changed; yet even legitimizations based on abstract conceptions of "overlaps" between Islamic and liberal norms are susceptible to change in cases where the jurist decides that a certain "man-made" liberal system denies the virtuous, Islamic values it previously supported. The book analyzes how in one case—*wasaṭī* decisions on military service in the United States—*fatwās* shifted from accommodating the demands of the state to challenging those demands based on the jurists' evaluation that the "overlaps" and *maṣlaḥas* that once existed no longer do. But it also highlights that direct challenges of this kind have been the exception.

The depiction by some European Muslims, including Tariq Ramadan, of *fiqh al-aqalliyyāt al-Muslima* as an essentially imported concept, and thus one that should only be considered a temporary phase, is also challenged. The book demonstrates that, particularly in the *wasaṭī* case but to a certain extent in the *salafī* as well, the religious law of Muslim minorities is the cumulative result of transnational contacts, in which individuals and communities living in the West have been active and influential participants. Muslims in the West contributed as *mustaftīs* who present queries, call attention to their unique situations, and hint to possible solutions; as activists, who determine whether decisions are disseminated or rejected, accepted or adjusted; and as jurists, who take part in decision-making.

Finally, the comparison between two conflicting corpuses of religious law dispels some illusions as to the path Muslim jurisprudence in the West is currently on. Calls for unity and cohesion have been a common theme in Islamic writing on the future of Muslim minorities, and echoed beyond them. In 2002, John Walbridge, a scholar of Islamic studies, predicted "Muslims living in the West are likely to play a key role in the renewal of the Islamic consensus," suggesting that, "as a minority of very diverse origins, they do not have the luxury of preserving the divisions of the societies they came from."[18] The sharp debates presented in this book prove this prediction wrong even in the case of the minority of Western Muslims who aim to live their lives in accordance with religious law. Islamic jurisprudence in the West is a highly polarized field, and grows increasingly so.

However, disagreements between jurists tell more than of diasporas inheriting conflicts from their homelands, imagined or real, and exacerbating them: they reveal contemporary Islamic law as a vibrant, evolving, and contested field. *Sharīʿa*, as explored in this book, is neither a coherent nor a dogmatic body, as some in the West believe it to be; it provides for a breadth of juristic discretion and accommodation, making differences an unavoidable constant. The evolution of *fiqh al-aqalliyyāt al-Muslima* demonstrates that Islamic law has the potential for accommodation and adjustment as much as civil law has. Shifting from the comparison between the approaches to Islamic law to debates within *wasaṭiyya* and *salafiyya*, respectively, the limitations of each's self-declared claims of applying juristic formalism[19] are exposed. Both *wasaṭīs* and *salafīs* struggle to present their rulings as the inevitable result of horizontal categorizations and vertical ground rules that express the intent of the Lawgiver rather than the whimsical, albeit ethically based, discretion of an individual jurist. Yet, as the *fatwās* analyzed will demonstrate, in addressing the concerns of Muslim minorities, *wasaṭīs* abandoned prohibitions in favor of legitimizations even when the realities faced by Muslim minorities did not change; what *did* change was jurists' understanding of those realities and, more importantly, the jurists' theory on the breadth of discretion they are allowed to exercise. Similarly, the *salafī* conviction that the literalism and limited discretion allowed by their methodology guarantees uniformity in the understanding of the Quran and the traditions is

[18] John Walbridge, "The Islamic Art of Asking Questions: ʿIlm al-Ikhtilāf and the Institutionalization of Disagreement," *Islamic Studies*, 41, 1 (2002), 86.

[19] By formalism I refer to the theory that the law provides a sufficient basis for deciding any case that arises, that no gaps exist in the law, and that there is but one sound decision for each case: David Lyons, "Legal Formalism and Instrumentalism: A Pathological Study," *Cornell Law Review* 66, 949 (June 1981), 950. While the *salafī* juristic approach is undoubtedly more formalist than the *wasaṭī* in the limited space it allows for rational interpretations, *wasaṭīs* struggle to attribute formalist qualities to their approach in ways and for reasons underscored in Chapter 1.

undermined by significant differences among *salafīs* on a number of important issues, naturalization being the primary example.

The *fatwās* and juristic studies examined in this book were collected between 2005 and 2014 from three main platforms:

(a) Libraries and archives, including the library of the European Council for Fatwa and Research at the Dublin Mosque and Islamic Centre, the library of the Edinburgh Central Mosque, and Abdul Hameed Shoman Foundation's library in Amman.

(b) Online databases. On the *wasaṭī* spectrum, these included systematic searches of the websites of the European Council for Fatwa and Research, al-Qaraḍāwī's personal website, and the most visited *wasaṭī* portals, supervised by al-Qaraḍāwī, islamonline.net and its successor after al-Qaraḍāwī's dismissal from its board, onislam.net. On the *salafī* spectrum, the website of the Saudi Permanent Committee for Scientific Research and the Issuance of Fatwas, the personal websites of ʿAbd al-ʿAzīz b. ʿAbdallāh b. Bāz, Muḥammad b. Ṣāliḥ al-ʿUthaymīn and ʿAbdallāh b. Ṣāliḥ al-Fawzān, and three popular *salafī* portals, Islamway.com, Islamweb.net, and Islam Question and Answer.

(c) Dozens of bookshelves in mosques, as well as bookstores attached to mosques, and Islamic-interest bookstores, in Austria, Belgium, Egypt, England, France, Germany, Iceland, Jordan, Norway, Qatar, Scotland, and the United States. Among these the following were of the greatest utility: The Salafi Bookstore, Bradford and The Salafi Bookstore, Birmingham; IPCI—Islamic Vision, Birmingham; the bookstore of the Ibnu Taymeeyah Brixton Mosque, London; the bookstore of the London Central Mosque and Islamic Cultural Centre; the bookstore of the Islamic Cultural Center of New York; the bookstore of al-Nūr mosque, Berlin; the bookstore of al-Ṣaḥāba mosque, Berlin; the bookstore of al-Raḥman mosque, Leipzig; the bookstore of al-Muḥsinīn mosque, Bonn; the bookstore of the Islamische Informations und Serviceleistungen (IIS), Frankfurt am Main; the bookstore of the Ṭāriq Ibn Ziyād Mosque, Frankfurt am Main; the bookstore Orient et Vous, Brussels; and the Parisian bookstores Librairie de l'Orient, Librairie al Bustan and Librairie-Boutique de l'Institut du Monde Arabe.

Interviews and conversations with several dozen imāms and attendees of mosques, as well as an extended visit to the offices of the European Council for Fatwa and Research, provided an opportunity to observe the processes through which *fatwās* are circulated, disseminated, accepted, rejected, or negotiated. While this study does not aim for a quantitative evaluation of these issues, it provides some reflections on the impact both *wasaṭī* and *salafī* corpuses have had, and on how these corpuses are perceived by influential individuals involved in producing and disseminating them.

The book is divided into four chapters. Chapter 1 analyzes the general ideologies and methodologies of *wasaṭiyya* and *salafiyya*, explores the historical legacies from which they draw, and comparatively analyzes their main points of consent and conflict. Chapter 2 examines the evolution of distinct *wasaṭī* and *salafī* approaches to *fiqh al-aqalliyyāt al-Muslima* and their institutionalization and popularization. Chapter 3 comparatively examines contesting *wasaṭī* and *salafī fatwās* on a variety of issues regarding interpersonal relationships and contractual interactions between Muslim minorities and non-Muslim societies: interest-based transactions (mortgages and student loans); relationships with non-Muslim families (the maintaining of marriage between converts and their non-Muslim husbands and inheriting non-Muslims); non-Muslim festive occasions, specifically Christmas; and employment in workplaces where norms that are prohibited in Islam are practiced. Chapter 4 comparatively examines contesting *wasaṭī* and *salafī fatwās* on a variety of issues pertaining to the relations between Muslim minorities and non-Muslim states: naturalization, electoral participation, service in military and police forces, and the banning of headscarves in French public schools.

1

Wasaṭiyya and *Salafiyya*

A Conflict of Ideologies and Methodologies

INTRODUCTION

This study offers a comparative analysis of two contemporary approaches to Islamic jurisprudence: *wasaṭiyya* and *salafiyya*. While comparative analyses risk reducing the understanding of the phenomena studied to a sum of similarities and dissimilarities between them, the risk is worth taking in the present case. The reason is that *wasaṭiyya* and *salafiyya* are to some degree the other's antithesis, developed dialectically. While the majority of each approach's texts carefully avoid personalizing debates, the reader of some treatises and *fatwās* easily identifies *salafīs* as the leaders of the dogmatism and the reclusiveness that *wasaṭīs* speak against, and *wasaṭīs* as the leaders of the pragmatism and the laxity that *salafīs* caution against.

Wasaṭiyya and *salafiyya* share a number of fundamental assumptions about the crisis of religion and the modern world: Islam has been attacked by external and internal forces and, as a result, much of the Muslim world has diverted from following Allah's final revelation; Islam must be reformed and reestablished as a comprehensive system governing all aspects of life; in order to reform Islam, false understandings of Islam must be rejected and Muslims must return to the Quran, the Prophetic traditions, and the example set by the first three righteous generations, the *salaf*. It is at this point that the two approaches sharply diverge. While for *salafīs* the latter contention serves to promote an agenda that largely rejects an accommodation of religious norms to the challenges of modernity, for *wasaṭīs* it serves as grounds to promote such accommodations. Accordingly, for *salafīs* the invocation of the example of the *salaf* serves to promote a strict, uncompromising image of Islam on a number of social issues, from gender to leisure activities, while for *wasaṭīs* it serves to present Islam as a pleasant, "user-friendly" religion. While the *wasaṭī* call for a return to a glorious past encourages the involvement of jurists in political affairs, the *salafī* call emphasizes obedience to the political leadership as a religious duty and urges jurists to refrain from political participation. These theoretical differences are rooted in the intellectual legacies on which jurists were educated and the political circumstances with which they engage, but also reflect personal inclinations towards flexibility and rigidity, activism and passivity.

In their quest to convince others that their approach to *fiqh* is the only legitimate one, *wasaṭīs* and *salafīs* ironically demonstrate that a coherent, essentialist, and universal "truth" cannot be derived from the revelations. Their efforts put a claim for "authenticity" at the core of revivalist projects, but expose the reflexive quality of this term. While *wasaṭīs* and *salafīs* alike consider themselves fundamentalists who return to religion in its "true" manifestations, their approaches lead to conflicting results. To paraphrase Talal Asad on frictions within contemporary Saudi religious discourse,[1] *wasaṭīs* and *salafīs* disagree profoundly over what authentic Islam is, but *as Muslims* their differences are challenged on the grounds of that very concept of what constitutes authentic Islam.

This chapter aims to analyze the respective general ideologies and methodologies of *wasaṭiyya* and *salafiyya*, explore the historical legacies from which they draw, and comparatively analyze their main points of agreement and friction.

WASAṬIYYA

In contemporary religious Arab discourses, various groups and associations champion the idea of Islam as a *wasaṭī* religion. As will be explored

[1] Talal Asad, *Genealogies of Religion: Discipline and Reasons of Power in Christianity and Islam* (Baltimore: John Hopkins University Press, 1993), 210.

below, Saudi *salafī* religious scholars also share this view. One reason is that Islam is described as *wasaṭī* in the Quran. Another is the universal preference of ideologists to present their views as centrist and mainstream rather than extremist. However, only one complete set of modern ideas about Islam has been labeled by its formulators with the title *wasaṭiyya* and gained wide recognition as such. Thus, this study's definition of *wasaṭiyya* is empirical rather than normative. It does not aim to judge which ideas best represent the *wasaṭī* ideal in Islam.

Wasaṭiyya is not a political party. Neither is it a social movement. There exists no foundational canonical text that represents it. Rather, it is an approach to Islamic law and, more broadly, a call to reform Muslim societies. This approach has been led, systemized, institutionalized, and popularized by the Egyptian-born Yūsuf al-Qaraḍāwī (b. 1926), a graduate of al-Azhar and a former member of the Muslim Brothers, who since 1961 has found intellectual shelter in Qatar and severed his official ties with the movement. Its central themes have been endorsed by other contemporary jurists and scholars of formidable stature, including one of al-Qaraḍāwī's main sources of inspiration, Muḥammad al-Ghazālī (1917–96). Yet when viewed in historical perspective, *wasaṭiyya* is a continuation of the modernist-apologetic school established by Jamāl al-Dīn al-Afghānī (1839–97), Muḥammad 'Abduh (1849–1905), and Muḥammad Rashīd Riḍā (1865–1935), particularly in its quest to provide an Islamic context to modern concepts and institutions and allow their conditional, mitigated integration into Muslim societies, as well as in its firm belief that a revived Islam is the ideal solution to the problems of humanity in modern times.[2] It is also a continuation of the Islamist project led by Ḥasan al-Bannā, himself an expounder of the

[2] Riḍā used the term *wasaṭiyya* to describe balanced reformism that is an alternative to blind *taqlīd*, which is not capable of absorbing modernity, and to Muslims who reject *sharī'a* as incapable of accommodating modernity. However, the term was not common to his writings: "Kitāb Yusr al-Islām wa-Uṣūl al-Tashrī' al-'āmm," *al-Manār* 29, 1 (March 22, 1928), 63–70. Al-Qaraḍāwī considered Riḍā as one of the intellectual fathers of *wasaṭiyya*: Yūsuf al-Qaraḍāwī, *Fiqh al-Wasaṭiyya al-Islāmiyya wal-Tajdīd: Ma'ālim wa-Manārāt* (Cairo: Dār al-Shurūq, 2010), 106–108. On al-Ghazālī's account of Riḍā's importance as a proponent of Muḥammad 'Abduh's reformism: Muḥammad al-Ghazālī, *al-Ghazw al-Thaqāfī Yamtaddu fī Farāghinā* (Cairo: Dār al-Shurūq, second printing, 1998, the writing of the book dates to the mid-1980s), 37.

modernist-apologetic legacy, in its emphasis on intense yet cautious and gradual grassroots political and social activism as a means to transform Islam into a system that governs all aspects of life. However, al-Qaraḍāwī's scholarship is characterized by an attempt to cross the factionalism of the Brothers and appeal to wider audiences.

The *wasaṭiyya* approach calls for adapting religious laws to changing times and circumstances in a way that would make the lives of Muslims easier and Islam more attractive. It promotes the objective of *al-taysīr fī al-fatwā wal-tabshīr fī al-daʻwa*—facilitation in issuing religious laws and proselytizing by gentle means and in a gradualist manner. Application of this objective emphasizes the supremacy of the Quran to all other sources and the need for a contextual reading of its verses, promotes cross-*madhhab* search, and broadly and flexibly utilizes the mechanism of determining *maṣlaḥa*. *Wasaṭī* literature endorses four main social positions as prerequisites for an Islamic revival: advancing science and technology, expanding the role of women in the public sphere, democratizing Muslim societies, and opening those societies to the constructive contributions of other civilizations, all within the limitations of Islamic law and the norms and priorities of the Muslim nation, as *wasaṭīs* interpret them.

The association of this particular set of legacies and thoughts with the term *wasaṭiyya*—and the association of *wasaṭiyya* with the teachings and leadership of al-Qaraḍāwī—is a recent development. Al-Qaraḍāwī argued that the concept of *wasaṭiyya* was already present in his first book, *The Lawful and the Prohibited in Islam* (*al-Ḥalāl wal-Ḥarām fī al-Islām*), published in August 1960.[3] The book expressed a number of ideas that would later become signatures of *wasaṭī* thought, such as the need to oppose the neglect of religion and exaggerations in its application, facilitation in issuing *fatwās*, and *maṣlaḥa* and cross-*madhhab* search as juristic

[3] Al-Qaraḍāwī, *Fiqh al-Wasaṭiyya al-Islāmiyya wal-Tajdīd Maʻālim wa-Manārāt*, 26–32; Bettina Gräf, "The Concept of Wasaṭiyya in the Work of Yūsuf al-Qaraḍāwī," in Bettina Gräf and Jakob Skovgaard-Petersen (eds.), *The Global Mufti: The Phenomenon of Yūsuf al-Qaraḍāwī* (London: Hurst & Company, 2009), 218.

mechanisms that promote facilitation.[4] However, it did not ascribe these ideas to a particular self-defined and systemized *wasaṭī* agenda.

During the 1970s and 1980s, al-Qaraḍāwī described Islam as a *wasaṭī* religion but did so without systemizing *wasaṭiyya* as a distinct approach. An effort to this end was undertaken in a book he published in 1988, in which he elaborated on the reasons for the "Islamic awakening" experienced in the Arab world and its characteristics. He described the trend of Islamic *wasaṭiyya* (*tayyār al-wasaṭiyya al-Islāmiyya*) as the most significant, the strongest and the deepest-rooted among the various trends of the "awakening" and the one that best reflects the essence of Islam. In systemizing *wasaṭiyya*, al-Qaraḍāwī stressed the balance between renewal and the ways of the *salaf*, and between the eternal and the temporary. He also pointed to the potential of Islamic law to be adapted to the times and different locales in matters on which no specific and unequivocal evidence exists.[5]

Along with al-Qaraḍāwī, a number of Egyptian Islamist authors became associated during the late 1980s and 1990s with the "*wasaṭiyya* trend." They shared a belief in the need to reassert Muslim cultural and political independence from the West and reinstate Islam as the reference for all social activities within a framework of a renewed, revitalized approach to religion that is tolerant, pluralistic, moderate, and is able to accommodate the challenges of modernity. Their writings reflected a concern that contemporary Islamic thought and jurisprudence are increasingly influenced by rigid, literalist interpretations that limit the ability of Muslim societies to accommodate challenges, and benefit their enemies. While the agenda of the *wasaṭīs*, who were also labeled the "new Islamists"[6] and

[4] Yūsuf al-Qaraḍāwī, *al-Ḥalāl wal-Ḥarām fī al-Islām* (Cairo: Maktabat Wahaba, 2004, first published August 1960), 9–38.

[5] Yūsuf al-Qaraḍāwī, *al-Ṣaḥwa al-Islāmiyya wa-Humūm al-Waṭan al-'Arabī wal-Islāmī* (Cairo: Dār al-Shurūq, second printing 2006), 33–60. The first edition of the book was published in January 1988 in Cairo by Dār al-Ṣaḥwa wal-Nashr. The 2006 edition, which is the one available in bookstores today, is identical in its content to the 1988 edition.

[6] Baker offers this definition in his elaborate discussion on this group: Raymond William Baker, *Islam without Fear: Egypt and the New Islamists* (Cambridge, MA: Harvard University Press, 2003), 1–14.

"independent Islamists,"[7] resembled that of the Egyptian Muslim Brothers in its quest to reform Islam and Islamize society, none were officially affiliated with the movement at the time. Furthermore, their writings and actions suggested a lack of confidence in the Brothers' potential to obtain power, a concern that the Brothers' had become stagnated, and a conscious effort to expand the traditional foundation of Islamism. The *wasaṭīs* included al-Ghazālī, who was dismissed from the Muslim Brothers' leadership in 1953 following an internal power-struggle but became one of the leading Islamist apologists of the second half of the twentieth century; Kamāl abū al-Majd (b. 1930), a professor of constitutional law at Cairo University and Islamic apologist; Fahmī Huwaydī (b. 1936), an Islamist journalist; Muḥammad 'Imāra (b. 1931), an Islamist apologist and prolific scholar of the works of the "al-Manār" school; Muḥammad Salīm al-'Awā (b. 1942), an Islamist author; and Ṭāriq al-Bishrī (b. 1933), a historian and a high-ranking official in Egypt's judiciary.[8]

In May 1991, al-Majd published a detailed pamphlet, "A Contemporary Islamic View: Declaration of Principles." According to the pamphlet, in 1981 al-Majd led 150 other intellectuals in efforts to crystallize an ideological alternative under the heading "Towards a New Islamic Trend," but it did not bear fruit at the time.[9] The 1991 pamphlet presented *wasaṭiyya* as a reformist approach that aimed to reassert Islam as an all-encompassing system. It gave special consideration to the advancement of the sciences, the education of women, and political liberties. As al-Qaraḍāwī did three years earlier, al-Majd described *wasaṭiyya* as the rising force in the Arab and Muslim worlds.[10] Also, like al-Qaraḍāwī,

[7] Nabīl 'Abd al-Fattāḥ, *Taqrīr al-Ḥāla al-Dīniyya fī Miṣr*, vol. 2 (Cairo: Markaz al-Dirāsāt al-Siyāsiyya wal-Istrātījiyya bil-Ahrām, 1998), 353.

[8] Raymond William Baker, "Invidious Comparisons: Realism, Postmodern Globalism, and Centrist Islamic Movements in Egypt," in John L. Esposito (ed.), *Political Islam: Revolution, Radicalism or Reform?* (Boulder, London: Lynne Rienner Publishers, 1997), 125; Baker, *Islam without Fear*; 'Abd al-Fattāḥ, *Taqrīr al-Ḥāla al-Dīniyya fī Miṣr*, vol. 2, 353–56; Sagi Polka, "The Centrist Stream in Egypt and its Role in the Public Discourse Surrounding the Shaping of the Country's Cultural Identity," *Middle Eastern Studies* 39, 3 (July 2003), 41. Intriguingly, in both of Baker's studies, as well as in al-Fattāḥ's, 'Imāra is not identified as one of the main *wasaṭī* authors.

[9] Aḥmad Kamāl Abū al-Majd, *Ru'ya Islāmiyya Mu'āṣira: I'lān mabādi'* (Cairo: Dār al-Shurūq, 1991, originally written, though then unpublished, in 1981), 5.

[10] *Ibid.*, 9.

al-Majd stressed the need for religious jurisprudence to balance between the guiding principles of Islam and issues that are subject to change. He suggested that just as the Muslim world needs the *wasaṭī* essence of Islam, so too does the non-Muslim world, which he believed has progressed materially but has declined in morals and become more violent and more anxious.[11]

Though identified as a group and primarily based in Egypt, *wasaṭī* intellectuals of the early 1990s did not cooperate to establish an institution, a journal, or any other organ to present their ideas collectively. Neither did they self-identify as a *wasaṭī* group. Rather, they authored, to use Baker's description, "texts whose cross-references provide an effective web that binds them together and creates an intellectual and cultural space within which their adherents move."[12] In January 1996, an association dominated by Egyptian activists who broke from the Muslim Brothers, together with a number of Christians, including the prolific Copt political theorist Rafīq Ḥabīb, applied to the Political Parties Committee to register a new party, Ḥizb al-Wasaṭ.[13] The application was denied. While the Egyptian regime opposed the new movement, fearing it represented Islamism in disguise, the Brothers' leadership was concerned about the new challenge. It accused its former affiliates of breaching their sacred allegiance (*bay'a*) to the movement, threatened them with excommunication, and managed to secure the return of the majority to the Brothers' ranks.[14]

Ḥizb al-Wasaṭ's platform, which was inspired by the central themes addressed by *wasaṭī* authors, emphasized cultural independence as well as Islam's moderate, tolerant essence and ability to accommodate the challenges of modernity. However, it did not commit itself to Islam as an exclusive reference.[15] A number of leading *wasaṭī* authors, including

[11] *Ibid.*, 21.

[12] Baker, "Invidious Comparisons: Realism, Postmodern Globalism, and Centrist Islamic Movements in Egypt," 125.

[13] Richard Norton, "Thwarted Politics: The Case of Egypt's Hizb al-Wasat," in Robert W. Hefner (ed.), *Remaking Muslim Politics* (Princeton and Oxford: Princeton University Press, 2004), 141; Meir Hatina, "The 'Other Islam': The Egyptian Wasat Party," *Critique: Critical Middle Eastern Studies* 14, 2 (Summer 2005), 173.

[14] Hatina, "The 'Other Islam': The Egyptian Wasat Party," 175–76.

[15] Norton, "Thwarted Politics: The Case of Egypt's Hizb al-Wasat," 143–44; Hatina, "The 'Other Islam': The Egyptian Wasat Party," 176–80; Baker, *Islam without Fear*, 195–97.

al-Qaraḍāwī and al-ʿAwā, endorsed the initiative, but none participated in its formation or was recognized officially by al-Wasaṭ's leadership as a binding authority.[16] Ultimately, al-Wasaṭ did not become a force to be reckoned with in Egyptian politics.

Since the mid-1990s, al-Qaraḍāwī has systemized, popularized, and institutionalized *wasaṭiyya*, consciously striving to be recognized as the leader of a distinct socio-juristic approach yet one that is inseparable from his public persona and stretches outside the Egyptian context to all Muslims. His theorizing on jurisprudence grew more audacious as he introduced the concepts of *taysīr* and *tabshīr* as the primary objectives of a *wasaṭī* renewal of Islamic law and broadened the mechanisms that facilitate the promotion of these objectives. He presented detailed opinions on *wasaṭiyya* in media appearances, articles, and books,[17] and friends and foes alike acknowledged him as the leader of this approach. For example, in a collection of essays written in 1996 in honor of his seventieth birthday, some of the participants introduced the concept of *wasaṭiyya* as a summation of his worldview and life efforts,[18] while a treatise critical of *wasaṭiyya* published in 1998 by a Kuwaiti liberal, Khalīl ʿAlī Ḥaydar, considered him the preeminent *wasaṭī* influence.[19] In addition, his views were diffused through the extensive use of satellite television (the call-in program *al-Sharīʿa wal-Ḥayāt*, or "Sharīʿa and

[16] Baker, *Islam without Fear*, 194, 199.

[17] For example, in a lengthy interview for al-Jazeera al-Qaraḍāwī defined *wasaṭiyya* as the trend that reflects the truths of Islam: "al-Wasaṭiyya fī al-Islām," televised interview with Yūsuf al-Qaraḍāwī moderated by Aḥmad Manṣūr, October 26, 1997, accessed September 10, 2012: http://www.aljazeera.net/home/print/0353e88a-286d-4266-82c6-6094179ea26d/f4478517-8a76-4242-9c2f-38ff3d21fece. A book he published in 2010 constitutes a detailed elaboration on the *wasaṭī* characteristics of Islam: Yūsuf al-Qaraḍāwī, *Fiqh al-Wasaṭiyya al-Islāmiyya wal-Tajdīd Maʿālim wa-Manārāt* (Cairo: Dār al-Shurūq, 2010).

[18] Rāshid al-Ghannūshī, "al-Wasaṭiyya fī al-Fikr al-Siyāsī lil-Qarāḍawī," in *Yūsuf al-Qaraḍāwī: Kalimāt fī Takrīmihi wa-Buḥūth fī Fikrihi wa-Fiqhihi* (Cairo: Dār al-Salām, 2004; the text was first published in 1996, in honor of al-Qaraḍāwī's seventieth birthday), 294–345; ʿādil Ḥusayn, "Faqīh al-Wasaṭiyya al-Islāmiyya fī ʿAṣrinā," in *Yūsuf al-Qaraḍāwī: Kalimāt fī Takrīmihi wa-Buḥūth fī Fikrihi wa-Fiqhihi* (Cairo: Dār al-Salām, 2004), 376–88; Hānī Muḥammad Ṭāyiʿ, "al-Shaykh al-Qaraḍāwī wa-Minhaj al-Wasaṭiyya al-Islāmiyya," in *Yūsuf al-Qaraḍāwī: Kalimāt fī Takrīmihi wa-Buḥūth fī Fikrihi wa-Fiqhihi* (Cairo: Dār al-Salām, 2004), 877–912.

[19] Khalīl ʿAlī Ḥaydar, *Iʿtidāl am Taṭarruf? Taʿamulāt Naqdiyya fī Tayyār al-Wasaṭiyya al-Islāmiyya* (Kuwait: Qurtas-Publishing, 1998), 28–32, 44.

Life," on Al-Jazeera) and a popular Internet portal (Islamonline.net, which he supervised until his dismissal in 2010). His personal website has featured since 2001 the Quranic verse on the *wasaṭī* essence of the umma next to his picture, epitomizing his status as the embodiment of *wasaṭiyya*.[20]

Two organizations which he has headed from their establishment, the European Council for Fatwa and Research (established 1997) and the International Union of Muslim Scholars (established 2004), provided him with an organizational platform and accorded his understanding of *wasaṭiyya* an aura of broad legitimization. The International Union considers itself a representative of the *wasaṭī* message.[21] A number of leading *wasaṭīs* joined its ranks under the leadership of al-Qaraḍāwī, including Huwaydī and al-'Awā. Despite its somewhat pretentious name, it has served less as a theological or juristic panel and more as a platform to promote al-Qaraḍāwī's status as a leader of Muslims at large, independent from his former association with the Brothers. The European Council elevated al-Qaraḍāwī's status as an authority (*marja'iyya*) on jurisprudence and, though specifically tasked with addressing issues concerning Muslims in Europe, it became a hub for theoretical discussions on jurisprudence from a *wasaṭī* perspective.

As part of promoting his standing as the leader of *wasaṭiyya*, al-Qaraḍāwī declared his lack of commitment to the teachings and instructions of others, including Ḥasan al-Bannā,[22] as well as the lack of any organizational affiliations with the Brothers or any other movement for that matter.[23] In 2002, he rejected a second invitation to become the general guide of the Egyptian Brothers. In doing so, he did not seek to

[20] Gräf, "The Concept of Wasaṭiyya in the Work of Yūsuf al-Qaraḍāwī," 224; www.qaradawi.net.

[21] In describing its missions it adopts "the centermost approach of the centermost *umma*, an approach of mediation and moderation": International Union of Muslim Scholars Project, "About Us," n.d., accessed September 10, 2012: http://www.iumsonline.net/en/default.asp?MenuID=41.

[22] Yūsuf al-Qaraḍāwī, *Naḥnu wal-Gharb: As'ila Shā'ika wa-Ajwiba Ḥāsima* (Cairo: Dār al-Tawzī' wal-Nashr al-Islāmiyya, 2006), 124. On his admiration for al-Bannā, for example: *al-Ṣaḥwa al-Islāmiyya wa-Humūm al-Waṭan al-'Arabī wal-Islāmī* (Cairo: Dār al-Shurūq, 2006; originally published, 1988), 29.

[23] Ḥasan 'Abdallāh, "al-Ṣalāt fī al-Masjid al-Aqṣā . . . Ḥarām," first section in a series of interviews with Yūsuf al-Qaraḍāwī, *Niṣf al-Dunyā* (August 16, 1998), 48.

disassociate *wasaṭiyya* from the Brothers. On the contrary, he described al-Bannā as a *wasaṭī*-leaning thinker[24] and the Brothers as the first group in the Muslim world with a *wasaṭī* orientation.[25] Indeed, since the mid-1990s, the more moderate, pragmatic, and gradualist wing of the Brothers in Egypt, known as the "wasaṭ and shabāb," has become dominant.[26] By declaring his independence from the Brothers while simultaneously giving expression to an approach that was adopted by the Brothers, al-Qaraḍāwī consciously presented himself as a true leader of Islamic reform and renewal at large and his approach as being above national and political affiliations.[27]

Wasaṭiyya, as formulated by al-Qaraḍāwī, is based on Q. 2:143: "We have made you a temperate people that you act as witnesses over man, and the Prophet as witness over you."[28] Along with temperate, median, and middle-way, *wasaṭ* can mean balanced, just and good. These words have different connotations, but *wasaṭī* thought suggests they are synonymous in the sense that the middle-way is the best way and the just way. Al-Qaraḍāwī produced a long list of Quran verses to support this notion, including Q. 2:68, 201; 17:29, 110; 25:67; 28:77; 55:7–9, as well as a number of Prophetic traditions that call to act in a just and moderate manner.[29]

Al-Qaraḍāwī and other *wasaṭīs* describe *wasaṭiyya* as reflecting the essence of Islam. Islam provides a harmonic balance between a number of contrasts, including the permanent and the temporary, revelation and rationality, liberties and duties, permissiveness and rigidness, materialism and spiritualism, individualism and communalism.[30] I choose to

[24] *Ibid.*

[25] "Al-Wasaṭiyya fī al-Islām," televised interview with Yūsuf al-Qaraḍāwī moderated by Aḥmad Manṣūr, October 26, 1997.

[26] Nabīl ʿAbd al-Fatāḥ (ed.), *Taqrīr al-Ḥala al-Dīniyya fī Miṣr* (Cairo: Markaz al-Dirāsāt al-Siyāsiyya wal-Istrātījiyya bil-Ahrām, 1995), 170–76.

[27] In al-Qaraḍāwī's own words, he considers himself a "possession" of all Muslims; just as Islam is universal, so too is he universal: Ḥasan ʿAbdallāh, "al-Ṣalāt fī al-Masjid al-Aqṣā... Ḥarām," first section in a series of interviews with Yūsuf al-Qaraḍāwī, *Niṣf al-Dunyā*, 48.

[28] Al-Qur'an, a Contemporary Translation by Ahmed Ali (Princeton: Princeton University Press, 1993).

[29] Al-Qaraḍāwī, *Fiqh al-Wasaṭiyya al-Islāmiyya wal-Tajdīd Maʿālim wa-Manārāt*, 61–99.

[30] *Ibid.*, 38; *Min Ajl Ṣaḥwa Rāshida* (Cairo: Dār al-Shurūq, 1988, accessed September 10, 2012: http://www.mlazna.com), 138; Ṭayiʿ, "al-Shaykh al-Qaraḍāwī wa-Minhaj al-Wasaṭiyya al-Islāmiyya," 881, 905; Muḥammad al-Fāḍil al-Lāfī, "al-Khiṭāb al-Dīnī al-Islāmī," *al-Majalla*

translate *wasaṭiyya* as "the harmonizing middle ground" approach, rather than the "middle-ground approach" or the "centrist school," to emphasize a point that the latter, literal translations risk blurring. *Wasaṭīs* do not call for an understanding of Allah's religion as being the middle ground between conflicting views. Instead, they argue that Allah, who knows His creation best, provided mankind with guidance that harmonizes views that in other civilizations are in conflict.[31] *Wasaṭīs* believe that Islam takes what is good and essential in differences and creates the "Islamic personality" that combines the merits of both.[32] For example, they argue that while other religions and ideologies—from Greek philosophy to Judaism and Christianity to capitalism and socialism—have failed to strike a balance between the rights of the individual and those of society, focusing on one and neglecting the other, Islam does not allow either to abrogate the other. It neither coddles individuals by providing excessive rights nor demands individuals to do more than they are able to do.[33] According to *wasaṭīs* themselves, being a *wasaṭī* does not imply one is a member of a centrist political party that advances weak compromises between ideological forces. Rather, it implies adherence to a divine system that strikes a perfect, just balance.

An obvious conclusion to be drawn from describing the essence of Islam as being a harmonizing middle ground is that other approaches to Allah's final revelation, specifically those that fail to capture this essence, are misguided. In its articulations since the 1970s, *wasaṭiyya* has been presented as an alternative to two kinds of ideological extremes. One extreme is Muslims who blindly embrace Western "imported," "man-made" ideologies and reject Islam, and Muslims who have not fallen into that trap but have nevertheless erred in adopting innovations. The other is Muslims who champion Islamic approaches that are not *wasaṭī* and in doing so injure the potential of Islam to be renewed and prevail

al-'Ilmiyya lil-Majlis al-'Ūrūbbī lil-Iftā' wal-Buḥūth, no. 6 (January 2005), 250; Federation of Islamic Organizations in Europe, "European Muslim Charter," January 2008, 4.

31 Muḥammad 'Imāra, *al-Istiqlāl al-Ḥaḍārī* (6th October City: Nahḍat Miṣr lil-Ṭibā'a wal-Nashr wal-Tawzī', 2007), 19–21.

32 *Ibid.*, 178–79.

33 Al-Qaraḍāwī, *Fiqh al-Wasaṭiyya al-Islāmiyya wal-Tajdīd Ma'ālim wa-Manārāt*, 56–60.

against its rivals. The latter groups comprise *jihādis* who reject al-Bannā's legacy of massive, grassroots peaceful mobilization as a means to promote an Islamic revolution, adhere to the later preaching of Sayyid Quṭb, excommunicate Muslims who do not apply Islam as they understand it, and act violently against them;[34] as well as Muslims who adhere to rigid interpretations of Islam and fail to understand the necessity of facing the challenges of our times.[35] *Wasaṭīs* emphasize that both approaches are equally dangerous to the future of Islam[36] and hold that *salafīs* (of all factions) must relinquish their frozen, literalist understanding of Islam and should pay attention to the spirit and objectives of Islamic law rather

[34] In a book entitled *The Islamic Awakening between Stagnation and Extremism*, published in 1982, following the assassination of Egyptian President al-Sadat, al-Qaraḍāwī used the term *wasaṭiyya* to refute Quṭbist groups. He described *wasaṭiyya* as the soul of Islam and the contrast of secular tendencies and the extremism of Islamic youth groups and political parties—extremism in hastening to excommunicate devout Muslims for thinking differently, as well as extremism in forbidding the permissible. For an overview: Gräf, "The Concept of Wasaṭiyya in the Work of Yūsuf al-Qaraḍāwī," 221. Versions of this book were printed by a number of publishing houses, including: *al-Ṣaḥwa al-Islāmiyya bayna al-Jumūd wal-Taṭarruf* (Cairo: Dār al-Shurūq, second printing, 2005); for the above described ideas, 23–101. The distinction of *wasaṭiyya* as a contrast to both secularism and Quṭbist extremism appeared also in other sources that defined the *wasaṭī* approach, especially but not only in writings by al-Qaraḍāwī or about him. Al-Qaraḍāwī described *wasaṭiyya* as deeply rooted in the movement for Islamic revival, as opposed to newly established Quṭbist-inspired groups, which are bound to be short-lived because of their extremism. His description of *wasaṭiyya* emphasized its balance between constancy and change and the rejection of stagnant groups: al-Qaraḍāwī, *al-Ṣaḥwa al-Islāmiyya wa-Humūm al-Waṭan al-'Arabī wal-Islāmī*, 33–34; al-Ghannūshī, "al-Wasaṭiyya fī al-Fikr al-Siyāsī lil-Qaraḍāwī," 297. Aḥmad Kamāl Abū al-Majd wrote against religious hardliner reactionaries who risk destroying Islam and, in the same breath, cautioned against destroying the foundations of religion under the banners of rationalism and empiricism: *Ru'ya Islāmiyya Mu'āṣira: I'lān Mabādi'*, 7–8.

[35] Already in 1976, in an article on contemporary *iftā'*, al-Qaraḍāwī suggested the middle way as the path jurists should follow as an alternative to jurists who emulate the "old ways" and those who accept the "new ways," Gräf, "The Concept of Wasaṭiyya in the Work of Yūsuf al-Qaraḍāwī," 220–21. The concept of *wasaṭiyya* as an alternative to Westernization and rigid conservatism, to eliminating Islam as well as to allowing it to stagnate, has been presented ever since in a number of his works: al-Qaraḍāwī, *Min Ajl Ṣaḥwa Rāshida* (Cairo: Dār al-Shurūq, 1988, accessed September 10, 2012: http://www.mlazna.com), 51–52, 62; "al-Wasaṭiyya fī al-Islām," televised interview with Yūsuf al-Qaraḍāwī moderated by Aḥmad Manṣūr, October 26, 1997.

[36] For example, one of al-Qaraḍāwī's discussions presents *wasaṭiyya* as an alternative to those who imitate the West as well as to Muslims who adhere to extremists and rigid ideas. Among these he includes both those who present a rigid opinion where Allah calls for facilitation as well as those who fight against everyone who disagrees with them, whether non-Muslim or Muslim. According to al-Qaraḍāwī, each of these trends is more dangerous than the other: *Khiṭābunā al-Islāmī fī 'Aṣr al-'Awlama* (Cairo: Dār al-Shurūq, 2009, first published 2004), 15.

than focus on its form and partialities. They also demand that *salafīs* stop being so arrogant and dismissive of Muslims who do not share their misled opinions.[37]

For the *wasaṭī* alternative to prevail, that is, for Islam to regain its *wasaṭī* essence, a process of *tajdīd*, or renewal of Islam, must take place. *Tajdīd* involves *ijtihād*, or the practice of interpreting and contextualizing the revelation in a way that does not blindly imitate previous explanations. *Wasaṭī* rejection of *taqlīd* (blind acceptance of previous juristic opinions) relates to the two connotations this concept has, as elaborated by Hallaq: accepting another juristic authority without doubt or evaluation of the evidence, as well as strict adherence to a school of law.[38] *Tajdīd* promotes the foundational *wasaṭī* objective of addressing religio-legal issues in a way that allows Muslim societies to meet the challenges of modern times without succumbing to the pressures of non-Muslim ideologies. In line with the modernist-apologetic tradition that they continue, *wasaṭīs* emphasize that the renewal they seek does not constitute a neglect of religion in any way but rather represents its true self. This approach—so essential for the *wasaṭī* struggle to fend off attacks against its juristic principles—is supported by four arguments. One is that the Quran and the Prophetic traditions call for renewal. Al-Qaraḍāwī noted that while the word "renewal" itself does not appear in the Quran, the idea of continually improving conditions, which is the essence of *tajdīd*, appears in a number of Quranic verses, including 16:125, 41:34, 6:152, 17:34.[39] Another is that renewal is commensurate with the Prophetic promise that once every hundred years Islam will be renewed.[40] Yet another is that the renewal sought by *wasaṭīs* is in direct opposition to that which the secularists promote and constitutes an alternative to their anti-Islamic views because, rather than using foreign concepts for the

[37] Yūsuf al-Qaraḍāwī, *al-Ṣaḥwa al-Islāmiyya min al-Murāhaqa ilā al-Rushd* (Cairo: Dār al-Shurūq, 2008, first published 2002), 201–5.

[38] Wael B. Hallaq, *Authority, Continuity and Change in Islamic Law* (New York: Cambridge University Press, 2001), 86–120.

[39] Al-Qaraḍāwī, *Fiqh al-Wasaṭiyya al-Islāmiyya wal-Tajdīd Maʿālim wa-Manārāt*, 186–87.

[40] *Ibid.*, 188; al-Qaraḍāwī, *Min Ajl Ṣaḥwa Rāshida*, 25; *al-Ṣaḥwa al-Islāmiyya wa-Humūm al-Waṭan al-ʿArabī wal-Islāmi*, 38.

sake of foreign powers, it is built on the foundations, the origins, and the traditions of Islam, adding to them and taking what is best in them.[41]

A final argument, perhaps the most audacious, is that the *wasaṭī* call for renewal in fact constitutes a call for a return to the ways of the *salaf* because their understanding and implementation of Islamic law was similar to the one endorsed by *wasaṭīs*. ʻImāra argued that *wasaṭī tajdīd* represents a *salafī* approach that is better than literalist *salafī* approaches because it reads the Quran and the Prophetic traditions in an enlightened way, one that allows Muslims to adapt to the times and be open to other civilizations, as they were in their most glorious days.[42] Al-Qaraḍāwī commented that *salafiyya* is renewal, and vice versa, and suggested that his approach to law is similar to that advocated by the Prophet's Companions and those who followed them.[43] He argued that "renewal" is synonymous with *salafiyya* because it implies a return to what Islam was upon its ascendance.[44]

The depiction of *wasaṭiyya* as *salafī* in essence is crucial to its legitimization. According to a tradition narrated by ʻAbdallāh b. ʻUmar, the Prophet said: "The best people are those living in my generation, and then those who will follow them, and then those who will follow the latter. Then there will come some people who will bear witness before taking oaths, and take oaths before bearing witness." The tradition implies that the closer Muslims were to the days of the Prophet, the better their conduct was. It is a basis for the consensus among Sunni jurists that the first three generations of Islam—the Prophet's Companions (*ṣaḥāba*), the following generation (*al-tābiʻīn*), and the generation after that (*tābiʻ al-tābiʻīn*), known collectively as the pious ancestors (*salaf*)—provide the example which Muslims should follow and thus are the ultimate reference. The genius of the modernist-apologists was their association of modernity with a claim for authenticity (However, as

[41] Al-Qaraḍāwī, *al-Ṣaḥwa al-Islāmiyya wa-Humūm al-Waṭan al-ʻArabī wal-Islāmi*, 55–56; *Fiqh al-Wasaṭiyya al-Islāmiyya wal-Tajdīd Maʻālim wa-Manārāt*, 184–86.

[42] ʻImāra, *al-Istiqlāl al-Ḥaḍārī*, 133–42.

[43] "al-Wasaṭiyya fī al-Islām," televised interview with Yūsuf al-Qaraḍāwī moderated by Aḥmad Manṣūr, October 26, 1997; *Fiqh al-Wasaṭiyya al-Islāmiyya wal-Tajdīd Maʻālim wa-Manārāt*, 199.

[44] Al-Qaraḍāwī, *al-Ṣaḥwa al-Islāmiyya wa-Humūm al-Waṭan al-ʻArabī wal-Islāmi*, 39–42.

demonstrated by Henri Lauzière, Western academics were the first to associate al-Afghānī's and 'Abduh's approach with the term *salafiyya,* and it was not coined by the two).[45] Ḥasan al-Bannā continued the legacy of associating modernism with the pious ancestors by expressly describing his movement as *salafī.*[46] In presenting his approach as *salafī,* al-Qaraḍāwī seeks similar legitimization through authentication.

The process of *tajdīd* that *wasaṭīs* call for involves the promotion of two ideological objectives: *taysīr,* or facilitation, and *tabshīr,* or the spread of Islam through pleasant and gradualist means. The two are identified with a slogan that since the late 1990s has reflected the essence of *wasaṭī* jurisprudence as systemized by al-Qaraḍāwī: *al-taysīr fī al-fatwā wal-tabshīr fī al-da'wa.*[47]

The objective of *taysīr* was dominant in al-Qaraḍāwī's writings already in *The Prohibited and the Permissible in Islam*[48] but was clarified and dealt with systematically only in a book he struggled to write over a number of years[49] and finally completed in 1996, when his ascendance as the leader of *wasaṭiyya* began to take shape. Al-Qaraḍāwī opened *Taysīr al-Fiqh* by arguing, in an apologetic tone typical of *wasaṭiyya,* that facilitation in

[45] Henri Lauzière, "The Constuction of *Salafiyya*: Reconsidering Salafism from the Perspective of Conceptual History," *International Journal of Middle Eastern Studies*, 42, 3 (2010), 373–76.

[46] Ḥasan al-Bannā, "Risālat al-Mu'tamar al-Khāmis," February 1939, in *Majmū'at Rasā'īl al-Imām al-Shahīd Ḥasan al-Bannā* (Cairo: Dār al-Tawzī' wal-Nashr al-Islāmiyya, 2006), 337.

[47] "al-Wasaṭiyya fī al-Islām," televised interview with Yūsuf al-Qaraḍāwī moderated by Aḥmad Manṣūr, October 26, 1997; Ḥasan 'Abdallāh, "al-Ṣalāt fī al-Masjid al-Aqṣā ... Ḥarām," first section in a series of interviews with Yūsuf al-Qaraḍāwī, *Niṣf al-Dunyā*, 48; al-Qaraḍāwī, *Khitābunā al-Islāmī fī 'Aṣr al-'Awlama*, 28, 59; *Fiqh al-Wasaṭiyya al-Islāmiyya wal-Tajdīd Ma'ālim wa-Manārāt*, 209. The slogan is introduced in this text as the twenty-fifth of thirty characteristics of *wasaṭiyya*; "al-Wasaṭiyya wa-Dawr al-I'lām fī Ibrāzihā," October 15, 2006, accessed September 10, 2012: http://www.qaradawi.net/2010-02-01-08-43-29/4576.html. The slogan is introduced by al-Qaraḍāwī in this text as the ninth out of twenty characteristics of *wasaṭiyya*; al-Qaraḍāwī's explanation of what distinguishes *wasaṭīs* from other approaches: "al-Bayān al-Khitāmi lil-Dawra al-'ādiyya al-Thāniyya 'Asahara," *al-Majalla al-'Ilmiyya lil-Majlis al-'Ūrūbbī lil-Iftā' wal-Buḥūth*, no. 4–5 (June 2004), 457.

[48] Al-Qaraḍāwī, *al-Ḥalāl wal-Ḥarām fī al-Islām*, 13.

[49] Already in 1990, in the introduction to a book dedicated exclusively to *taysīr* in the religious laws of fasting, he wrote on the time constraints he faces in his efforts to produce his "great project," a comprehensive work on *taysīr al-fiqh*: Yūsuf al-Qaraḍāwī, *Taysīr al-Fiqh lil-Muslim al-Mu'āṣir fī Ḍaw' al-Qur'ān wal-Sunna—Fiqh al-Ṣiyyām* (Beirut: Mu'as-sasāt al-Risāla, third printing, 1993), 5.

decisions is not a response to the pressures of modern times or to the spirit of the time but that it is a religious duty because Islam is fundamentally a religion that makes things easier rather than harder, one that spreads through pleasant and gradualist means (*tabshīr*) rather than by generating animosity and rejection (*tanfīr*).[50] Al-Qaraḍāwī supported this statement with Q. 5:6, 2:185, 4:28, which, he argued, testify that the basis of Allah's laws is making things easier; Q. 22:78 and Q. 21:107, which testify that Allah's laws aim to relieve believers of hardship (*ḥaraj*); and a number of Prophetic traditions in which Muḥammad commanded that the easier of two or more paths of action be taken.

Al-Qaraḍāwī understands *taysīr* as tasking jurists with two missions. One is to issue decisions in clear, simple language that takes into consideration how busy people are and uses modern terminology.[51] Another is to issue rulings that make it easier for them to abide by religious law and be committed to it both in *ʻibādāt* (rituals) and *muʻāmalāt* (human transactions). Al-Qaraḍāwī cautioned that *taysīr* does not mean that a new *sharīʻa* should be invented, that the impermissible can be made permissible, or that one can endorse *tajdīd* of a kind that Allah forbids.[52] Rather, it means that (a) when more than one decision is permissible, the easy option should be preferred to a difficult one;[53] (b) necessity permits the prohibited but only to the extent needed to address it (see below, *maṣlaḥa*);[54] (c) prohibitions must be tied to Quranic verses, credible Prophetic traditions, and sound analogies;[55] (d) juristic decisions must accommodate different individual hardships: the law for the strong is not similar to that for the weak, and for the young is not similar to that for the old;[56] and (e) change of places, times, habits, and circumstances must be given consideration in issuing decisions, especially in testing times.

[50] Yūsuf al-Qaraḍāwī, *Taysīr al-Fiqh lil-Muslim al-Muʻāṣir fī Ḍawʼ al-Qurʼān wal-Sunna-* (Beirut: Muʼassasāt al-Risāla, 2000), 15–35. See also his statement in *Fiqh al-Wasaṭiyya al-Islāmiyya wal-Tajdīd Maʻālim wa-Manārāt*, 124–33. Also, *Khitābunā al-Islāmī fī ʻAṣr al-ʻAwlama*, 145–48. On the centrality of *taysīr* in al-Qaraḍāwī's thought see: Akram Kassab, *al-Manhaj al-Daʻwī ʻind al-Qaraḍāwī* (Cairo: Maktabat Wahaba, 2006), 237–43. On the need for *taysīr* and specifically lifting *ḥaraj* as a *wasaṭī* fundamental see also Abū al-Majd, *Ruʼya Islāmiyya Muʻāṣira: Iʻlān mabādiʼ*, 28.

[51] Al-Qaraḍāwī, *Taysīr al-Fiqh lil-Muslim al-Muʻāṣir fī Ḍawʼ al-Qurʼān wal-Sunna*, 18–20.

[52] *Ibid.*, 28. [53] *Ibid.*, 32. [54] *Ibid.*, 29.

[55] *Ibid.*, 33. [56] *Ibid.*, 28–29.

(Al-Qaraḍāwī provided the example of Ibn Taymiyya's words, quoted by Ibn al-Qayyim al-Jawziyya: Sheikh al-Islām asked that a group of Mongols who drank alcohol not be condemned. He explained that Allah forbade drinking because it injured *dhikr*, or the recitation of Allah's names, and prayer, but in the case of the Mongols drinking prevents them from shedding blood and stealing. While not described as such, Ibn Taymiyya's action demonstrates application of *fiqh al-muwāzanāt*, see below).[57]

While *taysīr* is required at all times, al-Qaraḍāwī believes that in modern, corrupted times it is all the more necessary because people's faith has weakened.[58] *Tabshīr fī al-da'wa*—the spread of Allah's word through pleasant means and in a gradualist manner—follows from it and complements it; where people are not overburdened (that is, subject to *ta'sīr*) they do not find Islam objectionable (that is, they do not experience *tanfīr*). *Tabshīr fī al-da'wa* demands that Islam be presented to Muslims who are weak in faith, or are still learning about it, as well as to non-Muslims in a way that is compassionate and loving rather than threatening, that teaches them about Allah's mercifulness rather than about His punishments, that allows them to abide by His laws in a gradualist manner, and that ultimately brings them closer to pleasing their Creator. According to al-Qaraḍāwī, a Muslim world that engages in *taysīr* and *tabshīr* will take *Ṣīrāṭ al-Mustaqīm*, the straight path of Allah that bestows favor upon those who follow it.[59]

Al-Qaraḍāwī's writings, like those of al-Ghazālī, communicate a firm conviction in the vitality of peaceful, gentle *da'wa*. This conviction reflects the modernist-apologetic as well as the Islamist influence on their writings. Three main assumptions are inherent to their understanding of the spread of Islam. First, the Muslim world has been exposed to a Western "cultural attack" that has undermined, through a web of sophisticated methods—from missionary schools to man-made ideologies, to fashion

[57] *Ibid.*, 113–14; see also this example in al-Qaraḍāwī, *Min Ajl Shawa Rāshida*, 46.

[58] Al-Qaraḍāwī, *Taysīr al-Fiqh lil-Muslim al-Mu'āṣir fī Ḍaw' al-Qur'ān wal-Sunna*, 31.

[59] Al-Qaraḍāwī, *Khitābunā al-Islāmī fī 'Aṣr al-'Awlama*, 149–51; *Fiqh al-Wasaṭiyya al-Islāmiyya wal-Tajdīd Ma'ālim wa-Manārāt*, 235. On the centricity of *tabshir* in al-Qaraḍāwī's teachings see Akram Kassab, *al-Manhaj al-Da'wī 'ind al-Qaraḍāwī*, 244–48. On the importance of gradualism in the application of Islamic law by governments see Abū al-Majd, *Ru'ya Islāmiyya Mu'āṣira: I'lān mabādi'*, 28.

models and sporting activities—the religious identity of Muslim societies, thereby weakening them and subjecting them to foreign interests. Second, religion is not the problem within Muslim societies but rather their only path to gaining true independence from Western powers and achieving social and economic progress. While the West has dominated the world for several hundred years, its "godlessness" makes it a tree without roots in which immorality and despair spread; it is on the verge of collapse and is eager for spiritual salvation. Both deviant Muslims and the West will embrace Islam, if only it is presented to them in its true *wasaṭī* form.[60] Third, to spread Islam is the duty of all Muslims, not only religious scholars. One can fulfill this duty by writing books and by giving lectures and sermons, and also by saying a good word, being a good friend, setting an example, or donating money to proselytizing activities.[61] In advancing *daʻwa* all lawful and useful tools should be employed, and the masses should be approached in any accessible venue, not only in mosques.

The method of *tajdīd* through *ijtihād*, which promotes *taysīr* and *tabshīr*, demands that jurists exercise great discretion and produce creative solutions. Without these, the *wasaṭī* agenda will not be realized. Herein lies the central challenge *wasaṭiyya* faces: How can jurists issue groundbreaking religious decisions while avoiding the appearance of innovation? How can the credibility of their claim to follow in the footsteps of the *salaf* of the seventh century be maintained if their religious pronouncements accommodate the particular challenges of modern times? To reconcile these apparent contradictions, the *wasaṭī* approach as developed by al-Qaraḍāwī bases its *ijtihād* on mechanisms that have firm roots in Islamic jurisprudence, while applying them in a broad, flexible, and dynamic manner.

Foundational to the *wasaṭī* juristic approach as constructed by al-Qaraḍāwī is its contextual treatment of the Quran and the understanding of *maṣlaḥa* that is derived from this approach. Drawing from a legacy established by the deliberations on *maṣlaḥa* over the course of ten

[60] On the centrality of these ideas in the works of al-Ghazālī, al-Qaraḍāwī and ʻImāra: Uriya Shavit, *Islamism and the West: From 'Cultural Attack' to 'Missionary Migrant'* (London: Routledge, 2014).

[61] Al-Qaraḍāwī, *Khitābunā al-Islāmī fī ʻAṣr al-ʻAwlama*, 33.

centuries, *wasaṭīs* define the issuance of *fatwās* as a process guided by jurists' extraction from the Quran of Allah's primary intentions in revealing His laws. *Wasaṭīs* emphasize that (a) in interpreting Quranic injunctions, attention must be given to the reasons for their revelation and to the weight of their appearance and (b) the Quran comprises generalities, or universals (*kulliyyāt*) and partialities (*juz'iyyāt*). The generalities, which are constants (*thawābit*) and thus are never subject to change, should dominate decision-making; they can limit the use of partialities; (c) all sources of law, including the Prophetic traditions, must be read in light of the Quran, which is the supreme and ultimate guide; the role of traditions is to elaborate on the Quran and demonstrate its relevance. When a Prophetic tradition contradicts universals extracted from the Quran, it cannot serve as the basis for a decision; (d) because the *sharī'a* was meant to safeguard particular aims, *fatwās* can and in fact should change in correspondence with various times, places, customs, and conditions so as to enable their safeguarding.[62]

These notions legitimize the use of the mechanism of determining *maṣlaḥa* (safeguarding a fundamental goal of the *sharī'a*) as a means to affect jurisprudence. *Wasaṭī* jurisprudence has adopted a broad approach to the determination of *maṣlaḥa*, which, though rooted in medieval Islamic jurisprudence, is controversial, and is a product of a gradual transformation within *wasaṭī* jurisprudence itself.

The first to offer a systematic approach to *maṣlaḥa* was the *Shāfi'ī* jurist Abū Ḥāmid al-Ghazālī (d. 1111). He suggested that Allah's purpose in revealing His law was the preservation of religion (*dīn*), life (*nafs*), intellect (*'aql*), progeny (*nasl*) and property (*māl*). Al-Ghazālī justified this overarching argument with reference to injunctions from the revealed texts themselves. For example, the ruling to kill an infidel who leads Muslims astray preserves the fundamental value of religion and the

[62] Al-Qaraḍāwī, *Taysīr al-Fiqh lil-Muslim al-Mu'āṣir fī Ḍaw' al-Qur'ān wal-Sunna* 43, 50–52, 57–58, 70–71, 102–7, 114–25; *al-Ijtihād fī al-Sharī'a al-Islāmiyya* (Kuwait: Dār al-Qalam, 1996), 43–48; Ṭaha Jābir al-'Alwānī, *Fī Fiqh al-Aqalliyyāt al-Muslima* (6th October City: Nahḍat Miṣr lil-Ṭibā'a wal-Nashr wal-Tawzī', 2000), 53–56, 70; on the supremacy of the Quran over the Prophetic traditions, Muḥammad al-Ghazālī, *al-Sunna al-Nabawiyya bayna Ahl al-Fiqh wa-Ahl al-Ḥadīth* (Cairo: Dār al-Shurūq, third publication March 1989, first published January 1989), 101–2.

institution of retaliation preserves life. According to his theory, some *maṣlaḥas* are not validated by a specific, relevant text. These are unattested *maṣlaḥas* (*maṣāliḥ mursala*), which are divided into three ranks: necessities (*ḍarūrāt*), needs (*ḥājāt*), and, third, improvements (*taḥsīnāt*) and embellishments (*tazyīnāt*). The rank of "necessities" is the strongest of the three. Al-Ghazālī argued that a necessity (*ḍarūra*) that is both certain and communal legitimizes the accommodation of religious laws even without direct textual evidence. He illustrated his opinion with an example that, in time, became a classic case: an army of unbelievers shield themselves with a group of Muslim prisoners, compelling a Muslim armed force to choose between not shooting at their fellow Muslims, which would possibly lead to their defeat, the occupation of Islamic lands, and the killing of all Muslims, or shoot and possibly kill the innocent Muslims captives, which the *sharīʻa* expressly prohibits. While there is no specific evidence that justifies a suspension of the prohibition to kill innocent Muslims in such a situation, according to al-Ghazālī, it is justified to do so because there is no doubt that shooting at the hostages preserves life universally for all Muslims.[63]

A number of al-Ghazālī's successors relaxed the conditions for determining unattested *maṣlaḥas*. The *Shāfiʻī* jurist Fakhr al-Dīn al-Rāzī (d. 1209) argued that a ruling that entails *maṣlaḥa* and is devoid of *mafsada* (corruption or harm) inevitably has to be instituted.[64] The *Mālikī* jurist Shihāb al-Dīn Aḥmad b. Idrīs al-Qarāfī (d. 1285) also placed the promotion of *maṣlaḥa* at the core of the juristic process. He argued that a religious decision should not be instituted if it brings more harm than *maṣlaḥa* and suggested that, based on consideration of *maṣlaḥa*, analogy

[63] Felicitas Opwis, *Maṣlaḥa and the Purpose of the Law: Islamic Discourses and Legal Change from the 4th/10th to 8th/14th Century* (Leiden, Boston: Brill, 2010), 67–78; Imran Ahsan Khan Nyazee, *Theories of Islamic Law: The Methodology of Ijtihād* (Islamabad: Islamic Research Institute, 1994), 195–230. For a critical deliberation on whether the Muslim prisoners' situation is a fine example of unattested *maṣlaḥa*: Muḥammad Saʻīd Ramaḍān al-Būṭī, *Ḍawābiṭ al-Maṣlaḥa fī al-Sharīʻa al-Islāmiyya* (Beirut: Mu'assasat al-Risāla, 1977), 329–33; for short analyses on the origins of *maṣlaḥa* in Islamic jurisprudence: Wael B. Hallaq, *A History of Islamic Legal Theories* (Cambridge: Cambridge University Press, 1997), 89–90; *The Origins and Evolution of Islamic Law* (Cambridge: Cambridge University Press, 2005), 144–46; EI^2, s.v. Maṣlaḥa (Madjid Khadduri), 739.

[64] Opwis, *Maṣlaḥa and the Purpose of the Law: Islamic Discourses and Legal Change from the 4th/10th to 8th/14th Century*, 124–25.

should be given priority over a singular tradition (a *ḥadīth* whose line of transmission is traced through only one transmitter per generation). He added honor (*'irḍ*) to al-Ghazālī's list of *maqāṣid.*[65] The *Ḥanbalī* jurist Najm al-Dīn Sulaymān b. 'Abd al-Qawī al-Ṭūfī (d. 1316) went even further in transforming the determination of *maṣlaḥa* to the principal source of jurisprudence on *mu'āmalāt*, suggesting that it should be given precedence even when it contradicts a textual injunction and consensus. In doing so, he overlooked al-Ghazālī's ranks of necessities, needs, and improvements, and instead spoke of *maṣlaḥa* in general. In his view, giving precedence to *maṣlaḥa* draws on textual evidence and therefore does not constitute the denial of the supremacy of textual evidence. His application of *maṣlaḥa* relied heavily on Q. 10:57–58 and on the tradition according to which the Prophet said, "*lā ḍarar wa-lā ḍirār*" (There should not be harming or reciprocating harm).[66] Another broad approach to *maṣlaḥa* was formulated by the *Mālikī* jurist Abū Isḥāq Ibrāhīm b. Mūsā al-Shāṭibī (d. 1388), who argued that because all rulings express the Lawmaker's intention, which is to serve *maṣlaḥa*, they must accord with attaining *maṣlaḥa* for the believer. According to al-Shāṭibī, the protection not only of necessities, but also of what constitutes the needs and improvement of religion, life, progeny, property, and intellect, serves as a valid justification in the decision-making process even when such protection is not supported by textual evidence.[67]

The potential of the rich tradition on *maṣlaḥa* to allow the accommodation of religious laws to the challenges of modernity without the

[65] Shihāb al-Dīn Aḥmad b. Idrīs al-Qarāfī, *al-Dhakhīra*, vol. 1 (place of publication not mentioned: Dār al-Gharb al-Islāmī, 1994), 126–161; Opwis, *Maṣlaḥa and the Purpose of the Law: Islamic Discourses and Legal Change from the 4th/10th to 8th/14th Century*, 136, 146–48, 157.

[66] Muṣṭafā Zayd, *al-Maṣlaḥa fī al-Tashrī' al-Islāmī* (Master's dissertation submitted to Dār al-'Ulūm at the University of Cairo on May 1954, and published by Dār al-Yusr lil-Ṭibā'a wal-Nashr, n.d.), 71–113; Opwis, *Maṣlaḥa and the Purpose of the Law: Islamic Discourses and Legal Change from the 4th/10th to 8th/14th Century*, 202–5, 245.

[67] For al-Shāṭibī's most comprehensive text on his broad understanding of *maṣlaḥa*: Abū Isḥāq Ibrāhīm b. Mūsā b. Muḥammad al-Shāṭibī, *al-Muwāfaqāt*, vol. 2 (al-Khubar, Saudi Arabia: Dār Ibn 'Affān, 1997); also Wael B. Hallaq, "The Primacy of the Quran in Shatibi's Legal Theory," in Wael B. Hallaq and Donald P. Little (eds.), *Islamic Studies Presented to Charles J. Adams* (Leiden: Brill, 1991), 85–90; Opwis, *Maṣlaḥa and the Purpose of the Law*, 259–61.

introduction of radical new concepts was evident to the modernist-apologetics of the late nineteenth and early twentieth century. Rashīd Riḍā's primary goal was to demonstrate that Islamic law was intended to be a comprehensive legal structure for Muslim society. Central to this approach was his differentiation between *ʿibādāt* (ritual devotion) and *muʿāmalāt* (social transactions and interactions). He argued that the latter are only of a general character, allowing for considerable adaptation by successive generations of Muslims in light of the demands of their worldly welfare.[68]

Wasaṭīs have continued this legacy, and al-Qaraḍāwī's (as well as others') foundational *wasaṭī* writings stressed the utility of *maṣlaḥa* in promoting the accommodation of religious law to the challenges of modern times. In the late 1990s and the 2000s al-Qaraḍāwī embraced some of the more far-reaching interpretations of *maṣlaḥa* that surfaced between the twelfth and fourteenth centuries and further developed them. His positions, expressed at the time he emerged as a world-renowned media personality, signify the pinnacle of his juristic audacity and provided *wasaṭī* jurists with a greater ability to accommodate decisions. Yet, as is at times the case with juristic revolutions, these positions were stated in an unsystematic and almost casual way, and thus went almost unnoticed in academic literature.

First, in opposition to Abū Ḥāmid al-Ghazālī, al-Qaraḍāwī suggested that *maṣlaḥa mursala* does not have to rank as a necessity and apply to all Muslims in order to effect decisions. Accommodating his original view from the 1960s,[69] he pointed to al-Shāṭibī and argued that the lifting of *ḥaraj* suffices for the determination of *maṣlaḥa* and that needs can qualify as necessities in determining *fatwās* (*al-ḥāja allatī tanzilu manzalat al-ḍarūra*). He consented with al-Shāṭibī's (and Riḍā's) opinion that though

[68] "Bāb Uṣūl al-Fiqh: Adalat al-Sharʿ wa-Taqdīm al-Maṣlaḥa fī al-Muʿāmalāt ʿalā al-Naṣṣ," *al-Manār* 9, 10 (October 19, 1906), 745–70; Malcolm H. Kerr, *Islamic Reform: The Political and Legal Theories of Muḥammad ʿAbduh and Rashīd Riḍā* (Berkeley and Los Angeles: University of California Press, 1966), 187–90, 197–98; *EI*[2], Khadduri, 739; Albert Hourani, *Arabic Thought in the Liberal Age 1798–1939* (London, New York, Toronto: Oxford University Press, 1962), 232–38; Muhammad Qasim Zaman, "The ʿUlama of Contemporary Islam and their Conception of the Common Good," in Armando Salvatore and Dale F. Eickelman (eds.), *Public Islam and the Common Good* (Leiden, Boston: Brill, 2006), 133.

[69] Al-Qaraḍāwī, *al-Ḥalāl wal-Ḥarām fī al-Islām*, 38.

injunctions that deal with *'ibādāt* should be obeyed without considering their objectives, when addressing those relating to *mu'āmalāt* the objectives and the prospects for their accomplishment must be considered.[70] Second, expanding on al-Ghazālī, al-Qaraḍāwī added to the list of objectives that the *sharī'a* aims to safeguard honor, security, justice, solidarity, personal rights and liberties, and the creation of a *wasaṭī* nation.[71] Rāshid al-Ghannūshī (b. 1941, the founder and leader of the Tunisian Islamist party al-Nahḍa, and a strong supporter of al-Qaraḍāwī's *wasaṭī* views), accepted this view. Referencing al-Shāṭibī's interpretation of *maṣlaḥa*, he suggested including human rights in the list of objectives.[72] (As will be explored in the next chapter, the *wasaṭī* approach to *fiqh al-aqalliyyāt al-Muslima* elevated proselytizing to a *maṣlaḥa* while not theorizing on doing so). Al-Qaraḍāwī defended his opinion by arguing, in an indirect reference to *salafī* jurists, that it is regrettable that some jurists apply a literalist approach, failing to consider the purposes of the *sharī'a* and focusing on petty issues.[73]

Drawing from *maṣlaḥa*, al-Qaraḍāwī's *wasaṭiyya* promotes *fiqh al-muwāzanāt* (jurisprudence of balances) and *fiqh al-awlawiyyāt* (jurisprudence of priorities). The two have been a focus of al-Qaraḍāwī's discourse from the early 1990s. The jurisprudence of balances weighs the benefits and harms of decisions. It calls for jurists to consider, in cases in which a *fatwā* involves both *mafsada* and *maṣlaḥa*, which is greater and decide accordingly. An important *maṣlaḥa* should not be rejected because it involves *mafsada* that carries lesser weight. Also, when the safeguarding of a permanent *maṣlaḥa* conflicts with the safeguarding of a temporary one, the former should be preferred. *Fiqh al-muwāzanāt* gives jurists the discretion to legitimize otherwise prohibited actions if they have reason

[70] Al-Qaraḍāwī, *Taysīr al-Fiqh lil-Muslim al-Mu'āṣir fī Ḍaw' al-Qur'ān wal-Sunna*, 96–101; *al-Siyāsa al-Shar'iyya fī Ḍaw' Nuṣūṣ al-Sharī'a wa-Maqāṣiduhā* (Beirut: Mu'assasat al-Risāla, 2001), 84, 90–92; *Fiqh al-Wasaṭiyya al-Islāmiyya wal-Tajdīd Ma'ālim wa-Manārāt*, 235.

[71] Al-Qaraḍāwī, *al-Siyāsa al-Shar'iyya fī Ḍaw' Nuṣūṣ al-Sharī'a wa-Maqāṣiduhā*, 84.

[72] Rāshid al-Ghannūshī, "Ḥuqūq al-Insān fī al-Islām wa-Athariha 'alā al-Sulūk al-Iqtiṣādī lil-Muslim," *al-Majalla al-'Ilmiyya lil-Majlis al-'Ūrūbbī lil-Iftā' wal-Buḥūth*, no. 14–15 (July 2009), 228–29.

[73] Ḥasan 'Abdallāh, "al-Ṣalāt fī al-Masjid al-Aqṣā...Ḥarām," first section in a series of interviews with Yūsuf al-Qaraḍāwī, *Niṣf al-Dunyā*, 47–48.

to believe that doing so would result in a lesser *mafsada* or greater *maṣlaḥa*. It suggests that relying on specific evidence does not suffice in issuing decisions. Rather, the broader consequences of each decision in terms of safeguarding the purposes of the law must be assessed.[74] One example given by al-Qaraḍāwī for the authority of this mechanism is the Prophet's signing of the contract of Ḥudaybiyya (628), in which he consented to not being referred to as a Messenger of Allah by the people of Mecca in order to serve the greater objectives of the nation.[75] *Fiqh al-awlawiyyāt* is best understood as a category of *fiqh al-muwāzanāt* and engages in prioritizing permissible actions based on assessing the *maṣlaḥas* procured.[76] It implies that the faithful need to give precedence to specific religious duties over other duties, such as those which constitute a necessity over those which constitute a need, those which constitute a necessity that relates to religion over those which constitute a necessity that relates to other purposes of the law, those which relate to the community over those which relate to individuals, and those which affect the many over those which affect the few. For example, based on this concept, al-Qaraḍāwī approved the opinion of his "well known author and friend," Fahmī Huwaydī, who in 1992 prioritized participation in the *jihād* in Bosnia over going on pilgrimage. Al-Qaraḍāwī explained that the fight to save the Muslims there (as well as other forms of contemporary *jihād*) takes precedence because it cannot be deferred.[77] Both the concept of balancing and the concept of prioritizing serve to legitimize the *wasaṭī* call for pragmatism and moderation in political activism and against rigidness and indulgence in petty religio-legal issues that, according to *wasaṭīs*, disrupt Muslims from facing up to their main duties.

[74] Yūsuf al-Qaraḍāwī, *Awlawiyyāt al-Ḥaraka al-Islāmiyya* (unnumbered Word file), written on April 1990, accessed September 10, 2012: http://www.torathIkhwān.com/library/92443554.doc; *Fī Fiqh al-Awlawiyyāt: Dirāsa Jadīda fī Ḍaw' al-Qur'ān wal-Sunna* (September 1994, accessed November 6, 2014: http://www.al-mostafa.com), 11. Also Ḥasan ʻAbdallāh, "al-Ṣalāt fī al-Masjid al-Aqṣā . . . Ḥarām," 47.

[75] Al-Qaraḍāwī, *Fī Fiqh al-Awlawiyyāt: Dirāsa Jadīda fī Ḍaw' al-Qur'ān wal-Sunna*, 12. On the contract of Ḥudaybiyya as an example of applying *fiqh al-muwāzanāt* see also Yūsuf al-Qaraḍāwī, "Fiqh al-Muwāzanāt," *al-Rā'id*, no. 191 (August 8–10, 1997), 26–27.

[76] Ḥasan ʻAbdallāh, "al-Ṣalāt fī al-Masjid al-Aqṣā . . . Ḥarām," first section in a series of interviews with Yūsuf al-Qaraḍāwī, *Niṣf al-Dunyā*, 47.

[77] Al-Qaraḍāwī, *Fī Fiqh al-Awlawiyyāt: Dirāsa Jadīda fī Ḍaw' al-Qur'ān wal-Sunna*, 1–15.

The breadth of the *wasaṭī* approach to *maṣlaḥa* provides jurists with vast discretion in accommodating religious laws. It extends the purposes of the law to almost any aspect of human activity, grants that not only cases of necessity should affect *fatwās*, and demands that jurists engage in constant evaluations of the repercussions of applying specific religious laws. Yet it is not devoid of challenges. The notion that Islam's divine origin provides it with an all-encompassing perfection and balance that "man-made" decisions can never attain is central to *wasaṭī* apologias. To maintain the integrity of this conviction *wasaṭīs* are encouraged to clarify (just as were earlier formulators of *maṣlaḥa*) that in expanding the potential for *ijtihād* they do not write their own laws but rather extract them based on revelations. Thus, *wasaṭīs* emphasize that the duty to protect the aims of the *sharīʿa* is grounded in the Quran itself[78] and that the Prophet's companions applied *maṣlaḥa* in a similarly flexible manner by, for example, accepting *ḥāja* and not only *ḍarūra* as justification for affecting laws.[79] They also stress that the application of *maṣlaḥa* as a means to affect *fatwās* is limited to the extent needed for the protection of *maṣlaḥa* (*tuqaddiru bi-qadrihā*).[80] Another argument employed in legitimizing the broad application of *maṣlaḥa*, which is typical of the general positioning of the *wasaṭī* approach, is that *wasaṭī* methodology represents a middle ground between approaches that are too literalist and rigid and approaches that are too liberal. Thus, al-Qaraḍāwī condemns the Ṭūfīst school (alluding to the abovementioned 'Abd al-Qawī al-Ṭūfī) for giving *maṣlaḥa* precedence over specific textual evidence and presents a list of issues on which such evidence exists and there is no room for *ijtihād*.[81] As will be explored in the third chapter, in implementing the *wasaṭī* doctrine for *fiqh al-aqalliyyāt al-Muslima*, al-Qaraḍāwī eventually diverts from that statement.

Along with broadly determining *maṣlaḥas*, central to *wasaṭī* pragmatic juristic decision-making is cross-*madhhab* search. In al-Qaraḍāwī's

[78] 'Imāra, *al-Istiqlāl al-Ḥaḍārī*, 140–41.
[79] Al-Qaraḍāwī, *al-Siyāsa al-Sharʿiyya fī Ḍaw' Nuṣūṣ al-Sharīʿa wa-Maqāṣiduhā, 92*; see also his reference to al-Qarāfī on this point, *al-Ijtihād fī al-Sharīʿa al-Islāmiyya*, 157–58.
[80] Al-Qaraḍāwī, *al-Siyāsa al-Sharʿiyya fī Ḍaw' Nuṣūṣ al-Sharīʿa wa-Maqāṣiduhā*, 100.
[81] Al-Qaraḍāwī, *al-Ijtihād fī al-Sharīʿa al-Islāmiyya*, 175–79.

opinion, cross-*madhhab* search is a fundamental prerequisite in order to realize Allah's promise for a universal Islamic triumph,[82] and jurists who refuse to search for juristic solutions outside their *madhhab* represent one type of the deconstructive rigidity for which *wasaṭiyya* is an alternative.[83] The idea that jurists should not be confined to the specific *madhhab* they adhere to is not unique to *wasaṭīs*. Rather, what is exceptional is their utilization of cross-*madhhab* search as a means to promote the ideological interrelated objectives of *taysīr* and *tabshīr*. Al-Qaraḍāwī offered two reasons why cross-*madhhab* search is essential. One, which jurists of other orientations accept as well, is that it is a jurist's duty to detect and accept the juristic view that rests on the strongest evidence that the revelations provide, even if it belongs to a *madhhab* other than his. The other is that reliance on one *madhhab* exclusively may unnecessarily over-burden the believers; the *sharī'a* in its entirety is vast and rich enough to provide remedy for any problem or hardship, but the four schools of law are not.[84] This opinion can be interpreted as an encouragement to "fish" for the most lenient solution in the schools of law and beyond them, but the *wasaṭī* emphasis on *taysīr* as being an essence of Islam suggests not only that there is nothing wrong with an effort directed to that end but that it is, in fact, required.

Al-Qaraḍāwī, citing Ibn Taymiyya, emphasized that he does not object to the existence of *madhhab*s and does not call to forsake them. Instead, his call is to recognize that there is nothing in the *sharī'a* that demands obedience to one particular *madhhab* and that the founders of the four principal *madhhabs* themselves cautioned against blind imitations of their decisions.[85] He suggested that given that several centuries have passed since the formulation of the *madhhabs*, blind imitations would obstruct the need to adjust *fatwās* to changing times and circumstances.[86]

Wasaṭī authors promote—either in general theorizations or, in the case of those qualified, in particular *fatwās*—a number of social and cultural

[82] Al-Qaraḍāwī, *al-Mubashshirāt bi-Intiṣār al-Islām* (Beirut: Mu'assasāt al-Risāla, 2000), 105–6.
[83] *Ibid.*; al-Qaraḍāwī, *al-Ijtihād fī al-Sharī'a al-Islāmiyya*, 175.
[84] Al-Qaraḍāwī, *Taysīr al-Fiqh lil-Muslim al-Mu'āṣir fī Ḍaw' al-Qur'ān wal-Sunna*, 35.
[85] *Ibid.*, 37–38.
[86] Al-Qaraḍāwī, *al-Ijtihād fī al-Sharī'a al-Islāmiyya*, 181.

reforms that they believe Muslim societies are in dire need of. Common themes in their discussion are the assertion of Islam as an exclusive reference and the call for independence from any form of Western dominance, along with the need to accommodate the challenges of contemporary times, to be open to other cultures, and to integrate aspects of modernity that do not conflict with Islamic norms. Some of their views directly conflict with views espoused by *salafīs*.

One priority for *wasaṭī* jurists is advancing empirical sciences and technologies in Muslim societies. Scientific progress is first on the list of collective duties (*farḍ kifāya*) which the nation neglected in its years of decline and which it must now prioritize.[87] *Wasaṭīs* understand that in order to present an honorable face of Islam, and achieve meaningful political independence, Muslim societies must drastically improve in these fields, a mission that necessitates educational reforms and the introduction of liberties necessary for encouraging genius and innovation.[88] This mission also requires acquiring knowledge from the far more advanced West.[89] The *wasaṭī* focus on this point rests on the ideas, drawn from the modernist-apologists and early Islamist heritage,[90] that early Islam was, in contrast to Christianity, a friend of scientific pursuit of knowledge and that Western empiricism and rationality are rooted in interactions with Muslim societies in Andalusia and during the Crusades. Thus, while the process of developing modern sciences and technology calls for learning from the West, it does not constitute a neglect of Muslim tradition but rather retrieval of past glory.[91] Learning

[87] Al-Qaraḍāwī, *Fī Fiqh al-Awlawiyyāt*, 8–9.

[88] Maḥmūd Faraj, "al-Qaraḍāwī fī Riwāq al-Ghazālī: al-Islām Dīn al-Taqaddum al-'Ilmī wal-Ḥaḍārī, Niẓāmunā al-Ta'līmī lā Yu'ṭī al-Furṣa li-Takhrīj al-Nawābigh wal-Mubtakirīn," *al-Wafd* (September 13, 1996), 9. Al-Qaraḍāwī presented these ideas with 'Imāra on his side.

[89] Al-Ghazālī, *al-Ghazw al-Thaqāfī Yamtaddu fī Farāghinā*, 34–37, 95, 99–101; Abū al-Majd, *Ru'ya Islāmiyya Mu'āṣira*, 27–28; al-Qaraḍāwī, *Min Ajl Ṣaḥwa Rāshida*, 33; *Fiqh al-Wasaṭiyya al-Islāmiyya wal-Tajdīd Ma'ālim wa-Manārāt*, 202.

[90] 'Abd al-Raḥman al-Jūzū (ed.), *al-Islām Dīn al-'Ilm wal-Madaniyya*, a collection of works by Muḥammad 'Abduh (Beirut: Manshūrāt Dār Maktabat al-Hayāt, 1989), 64, 90, 140–42; "Shabha wa-Jawābuhā," *Al-Manār* 1, 37 (December 3, 1898), 733; Ḥasan al-Bannā echoed this idea in his article "Bayna al-Ams wal-Yawm," in *Majmū'at Rasā'īl al-Imām al-Shahīd Ḥasan al-Bannā* (Cairo: Dār al-Tawzī' wal-Nashr al-Islāmiyya, 2006), 520–22.

[91] Al-Ghazālī, *al-Ghazw al-Thaqāfī Yamtaddu fī Farāghinā*, 103; Muḥammad 'Imāra, *al-Ghazw al-Thaqāfī Wahm am Ḥaqīqa?* (Beirut and Cairo: Dār al-Shurūq, 1997, first

from the West does not imply that it should be blindly imitated. Since Western societies are godless, not all they have to offer is legitimate. However, Muslims should not reject advancements of a technical nature that do not contradict Islamic values and that may benefit them simply because they were developed in the West at a time when the true spirit of Islam was frozen and neglected.[92] This ensures that the process of Islamizing societies will be one of progression rather than of going backwards. To use al-Qaraḍāwī's words, calling people to Islam does not mean calling them to replace electricity with oil lamps and airplanes with camels.[93]

Another aspect of modernity emphasized by *wasaṭīs* is the democratization of Muslim societies. *Wasaṭīs* maintain that the Islamic concept of *shūrā* (consultation), as articulated in the Quran and a number of traditions, requires rather than simply allows Muslims to live under elected, transparent regimes that respect human rights, and that any form of political tyranny breaches Allah's command.[94] They preach that *shūrā* is the Islamic equivalent of Western democracy[95] and that *shūrā* has in fact preceded it.[96] These arguments, drawn from early modernist-apologetic

printed 1989), 249–69; ʿImāra, *al-Istiqlāl al-Ḥaḍārī*, 26, 153–54; al-Qaraḍāwī, *al-Ḥulūl al-Mustawrada wa-Kayfa Jannat ʿalā Ummatinā* (Mu'assasāt al-Risāla, second printing 1974, first published 1971), 44–45; *Min Ajl Ṣaḥwa Rāshida*, 58–59, 119–20; *Ta'rīkhuna al-Muftarā ʿalayhi* (Cairo: Dār al-Shurūq, 2008, fourth printing, first published 2005), 108; *Naḥnu wal-Gharb: As'ila Shā'ika wa-Ajwiba Ḥāsima*.

92 Al-Ghazālī, *al-Ghazw al-Thaqāfī Yamtaddu fī Farāghinā*, 102–4; ʿImāra, *al-Istiqlāl al-Ḥaḍārī*, 15–17, 81–124, 140–44.

93 Al-Qaraḍāwī, *Min Ajl Ṣaḥwa Rāshida*, 119.

94 Yūsuf al-Qaraḍāwī, *Min Fiqh al-Dawla fī al-Islām* (Cairo and Beirut: Dār al-Shurūq, 2001), 36, 144–46; Muḥammad ʿImāra, *al-Islām wa-Ḥuqūq al-Insān Ḍarūrāt Lā Ḥuqūq* (Damascus, Cairo: Markaz al-Rāya, Dār al-Islām, 2004–5), 60–61. The book was first published in 1985; Abū al-Majd, *Ru'ya Islāmiyya Muʿāṣira: I'lān mabādi'*, 30–31; Fahmī Huwaydī, *al-Qur'ān wal-Sulṭān* (Cairo: Dār al-Shurūq, fourth printing, 1999), 20–26.

95 Muḥammad ʿImāra wrote that *shūrā* is "Islam's and Muslims' democracy": *al-Islām wa-Ḥuqūq al-Insān Ḍarūrāt Lā Ḥuqūq*, 61. Al-Qaraḍāwī noted that the Muslim state is based on the best principals that democracies have: *Min Fiqh al-Dawla fī al-Islām*, 36. Muḥammad al-Ghazālī described democracy in the West as "the *shūrā* there": *Azmat al-Shūrā fī al-Mujtamaʿāt al-ʿArabiyya wal-Islāmiyya* (Place of publication and name of publisher not mentioned, October 1990), 69.

96 Al-Ghazālī recalled reading an interview with President Kennedy where he was asked by American journalists if his wife's trip to Europe was financed by her or by the government. This example of free-speech and accountability reminded him instantaneously of a conversation between the second Khalīfa ʿUmar and Salmān al-Fārisī, one of the Prophet's companions. Al-Fārisī questioned the Khalīfa's long clothing, noting that all

and Islamist writings,[97] are audacious, given that there is, in fact, very little if anything in the Quran and the traditions to suggest that Allah ordained electoral democracy; they are opposed as far-fetched by *salafī* literalists. Departing from the teachings of al-Bannā, who opposed factionalism,[98] *wasaṭīs* endorse multi-party political systems as expressions of the diversity that Islam allows in issues that are not pertinent to its foundations. Further, *wasaṭīs* consider multi-party politics to be no different from the plurality of juristic schools.[99] As with their approach to the sciences, *wasaṭīs* are careful to emphasize that while Western societies have been doing a far better job at maintaining Islamic political values than Muslim societies do, they do so in a godless and therefore distorted and corrupted way. The *shūrā* regime that *wasaṭīs* promote

other members of the *umma* could afford only short ones. In response, 'Umar asked his son 'Abdallāh to speak to the people. 'Abdallāh confessed to giving his father, being the tall man that he was, some of his own fabric. Al-Ghazālī concluded, that the West reached its level of freedom through bloodshed, while the Muslims were given this freedom as a present from heaven: *Azmat al-Shūrā fī al-Mujtama'at al-'Arabiyya wal-Islāmiyya*, 35–36.

[97] On al-Afghānī's advocacy of representative government: *al-A'māl al-Kāmila li-Jamāl al-Dīn al-Afghānī* (Cairo, n.d), 473–79. 'Abduh emphasized that implementing *shūrā* is an Islamic obligation rather than imitation of foreigners. He noted that Islamic law does not stipulate exactly how *shūrā* should be implemented, but his writing hinted at dissatisfaction with the limited consultative roles reserved to the assemblies of his time. He articulated these ideas in three articles he published on December 12, 24, and 25, 1881: "Fī al-Shūrā wal-Istibdād," "al-Shūrā" and "al-Shūrā wal-Qānūn": Muḥammad 'Imāra (ed.), *al-A'māl al-Kāmila lil-Imām Muḥammad 'Abduh* (Beirut: al-Mu'assasa al-'Arabiyya lil-Dirāsāt wal-Nashr, 1972), 350–66. One of his students, 'Abd al-Raḥman al-Kawākibī (1855–1902), the Syrian-born pioneer of Arab nationalism, declared in his book on the nature of despotism that Islam is based on the foundations of democratic government, and if Muslims only returned to its true nature—that of equality, fraternity and consultation—tyranny will have no place among them. He offered in this context an apologia against "European commentators" who claim the reason for tyranny in Muslim societies was their religious devoutness: 'Abd al-Raḥman al-Kawākibī, "Ṭabā'i' al-Istibdād wa-Maṣāri' al-Isti'bād," in Muḥammad 'Imāra (ed.), *al-A'māl al-Kāmila li-'Abd al-Raḥman al-Kawākibī* (Cairo: al-Hay'a al-Misriyya al-'āmma lil-Ta'līf wal-Nashr, 1970), pp. 342–55. On Ḥasan al-Bannā's advocacy of representative government that is responsible before its people, within a system of separation of powers, as compatible with the teachings of Islam: al-Bannā, "Risālat al-Mu'tamar al-Khāmis" (February 1939), in *Majmū'at Rasā'īl al-Imām al-Shahīd Ḥasan al-Bannā* (Cairo: Dār al-Tawzī' wal-Nashr al-Islāmiyya, 2006), 357.

[98] Al-Bannā, "Risālat al-Mu'tamar al-Khāmis," 370; "Risālat Mu'tamar Ṭalbāt al-Ikhwān" (February 1938), in *Majmū'at Rasā'īl al-Imām al-Shahīd Ḥasan al-Bannā* (Cairo: Dār al-Ṭawzī' wal-Nashr al-Islāmiyya, 2006), 244; "Risālat naḥwa al-Nūr," *ibid.*, 175.

[99] Al-Qaraḍāwī, *Min Fiqh al-Dawla*, 151–60. Endorsement of political pluralism is also the main theme of Fahmī Huwaydī's book *al-Islām wal-Dimūqrāṭiyya* (Cairo: Markaz al-Ahrām lil-Tarjama wal-Nashr, 1993). For his comment about al-Bannā, 73. He references the *wasaṭis* al-Ghazālī, al-Qaraḍāwī, 'Imāra, al-Majd, and al-'Awā as scholars who endorse political pluralism, 76–85.

differs from liberal democracies in a number of ways. It comprehends all aspects of life, not just the political;[100] it is grounded in divine injunctions and therefore cannot be undermined by human whims or changing circumstances;[101] and, most importantly, the authorities of its legislative organs are restricted to areas in which Allah and His Prophet have not already legislated.[102] Thus, the political transformation advocated by *wasaṭīs* is one that combines liberal and theocratic concepts, with the latter prevailing over the former.

Wasaṭīs believe that religious scholars should detest the political passivity that in their view characterizes other schools of religious thought. In a continuation of al-Bannā's legacy, they hold that the establishment of a government that abides by Islamic standards should be led by mobilizing consenting masses that demonstrate their free choice of Islam. They go so far as to argue that in cases where the establishment of an Islamic regime is impossible, it is the duty of Muslims to participate in the creation of a secular democratic regime, provided that a measure of overlap exists between Islamic objectives—for example, the promotion of justice and personal freedom—and secular ones.[103] Al-Qaraḍāwī's rejection of the violent aspect of Quṭbist radicalism is, however, more pragmatic than ethical. He does not reject violence as political means in principle. Rather, in line with al-Bannā's legacy[104] and his personal conviction of the need to apply *fiqh al-muwāzanāt*, he suggests that violence should only be applied as a last resort and cautions that it becomes impermissible if there is reason to believe that it would result in more harm than benefit.[105] The idea that actively promoting political change is a religious duty, and that such activism should be weighed in accordance with its potential impact at any given time, has provided

[100] ʿImāra, *al-Islām wa-Ḥuqūq al-Insān Ḍarūrāt Lā Ḥuqūq*, 61.

[101] Yūsuf al-Qaraḍāwī, *al-Khasā'is al-ʿāma lil-Islām* (Cairo: Maktabat Wahaba, August 1977), 87.

[102] Al-Ghazālī, *Azmat al-Shūrā fī al-Mujtamaʿāt al-ʿArabiyya wal-Islāmiyya*, 42–46; ʿImāra, *al-Islām wa-Ḥuqūq al-Insān Ḍarūrāt Lā Ḥuqūq*, 61; al-Qaraḍāwī, *Min Fiqh al-Dawla fī al-Islām*, 14; Huwaydī, *al-Islām wal-Dimūqrāṭiyya*, 8–9, 113.

[103] Rāshid Al-Ghannūshī, "Ḥukm Mushārakat al-Islāmiyyīn fī Niẓām Ghayr Islāmī," in ʿAbdallāh al-Tamīmī (ed.), *Mushārakat al-Islāmiyyīn fī al-Sulṭa* (London: Liberty for the Muslim World, 1994), 16–17.

[104] Al-Bannā, "Risālat al-Mu'tamar al-Khāmis," 352–54.

[105] Al-Qaraḍāwī, *Min Fiqh al-Dawla fī al-Islām*, 124–28.

wasaṭīs with substantial flexibility in determining social and political alliances, including cooperation with regimes that were deemed irreligious.

Another fraught socio-political issue treated by *wasaṭiyya* is gender roles and relations. *Wasaṭīs*' general attitude toward the role of women, both within the family and within society, is traditionalist. They believe that the husband is the leader of the household, that the wife must obey him (and that he may beat her lightly as a last resort if she does not), and that a woman's primary duty is to attend to her husband's needs and take care of the children.[106] They also believe that women who freely intermingle with men other then their husbands or immediate family and who do not dress modestly are a potential source of *fitna* (temptation) that risks fornication and undermines an objective of Islamic law—preservation of lineage.[107] They argue that Western feminism leads to the breakdown of the traditional family and demonstrates the faithlessness of those societies.[108] However, *wasaṭī* writings suggest that it is women's right, and in some cases even a necessity, to be granted access to higher education and to the job market in order, for example, to work as medical doctors and teachers. They believe women can serve as members of parliament[109] and even as heads of state.[110] While according to *wasaṭīs*

[106] Al-Qaraḍāwī, *al-Ḥalāl wal-Ḥarām fī al-Islām*, 181–82; Abū al-Majd, *Ru'ya Islāmiyya Mu'āṣira: I'lān mabādi'*, 44; Muḥammad al-Hawārī, "Usus al-Binā' al-Usarī fī al-Islām," *al-Majalla al-'Ilmiyya lil-Majlis al-'Ūrūbbī lil-Iftā' wal-Buḥūth*, no. 7 (July 2005), 164.

[107] Al-Qaraḍāwī, *al-Ḥalāl wal-Ḥarām fī al-Islām*, 134–38; *Qarārāt wa-Fatāwā al-Majlis al-'Ūrūbbī lil-Iftā' wal-Buḥūth—al-Majmū'atani al-'ūlā wal-Thāniyya, Fatwā* 2 (Cairo: Dār al-Tawzī' wal-Nashr al-Islāmiyya), 88.

[108] Rāshid al-Ghannūshī, "Makānat al-Usra bayna al-Binā' al-Islāmī wal-Binā' al-Gharbī," al-*Majalla al-'Ilmiyya lil-Majlis al-'Ūrūbbī lil-Iftā' wal-Buḥūth*, no. 8–9 (June 2006), 23–30.

[109] On the *wasaṭīs*' and particularly al-Ghazālī's view regarding equal rights in education and the job market, Baker, *Islam without Fear*, 49–50, 93–100. On al-Qaraḍāwī's views regarding women, higher education and the job market: Ḥasan 'Abdallāh, "Fasaḥtu Khiṭbat Ibnati Liana Khalibha Rafaḍa an Ta'malu," the second of a series of interviews with al-Qaraḍāwī, *Niṣf al-Dunyā*, August 23, 1998, 109–10. In the interview, he took pride in his daughter's academic achievements in the exact sciences. On al-Qaraḍāwī's views regarding the political participation of women: Brabara Freyer-Stowasser, "Yūsuf al-Qaraḍāwī on Women," in Bettina Gräf and Jakob Skovgaard-Petersen (eds.), *The Global Mufti: The Phenomenon of Yūsuf al-Qaraḍāwī* (London: Hurst & Company, 2009), 203–8. Also: Ṭāyi', "al-Shaykh al-Qaraḍāwī wa-Minhaj al-Wasaṭiyya al-Islāmiyya," 913, 921. See also *Qarārāt wa-Fatāwā al-Majlis al-'Ūrūbbī lil-Iftā' wal-Buḥūth—al-Majmū'atan al-'ūlā wal-Thāniyya, Fatwā* 2, 103–4; "Does Islam Oppress Women," Islamic Cultural Centre of Ireland (leaflet), 7.

[110] Al-Ghazālī, *al-Sunna al-Nabawiyya*, 44–58. He did not encourage their election as such but argued that the fittest of the nation, whether male or female, should be elected. He noted the examples of the successful reigns of the Queen of Sheba, Queen Victoria, Margaret Thatcher, Golda Meir, and Indira Gandhi. See also on Benazir Bhutto in *Qaḍāyā*

women must dress modestly and cover their body (except their hands) and hair, they are not obliged to wear a *niqāb*, or a garment that covers their faces.[111] While women must tread carefully when beyond the protection of their husbands, they are allowed a measure of independence, such as the freedom to drive cars, ride bicycles,[112] and open personal bank accounts.[113] As will be demonstrated below, in encouraging these liberties the *wasaṭī* view sharply contradicts the *salafī* one. In some *wasaṭī* writings, *salafī* strictness on gender issues is deemed as dangerous to the future of Muslim societies as the penetration of Western norms. Al-Ghazālī, who in the 1970s resided in Saudi Arabia and grew suspicious of its gender-regulations, vehemently objected to *niqābs*. He lamented that some religious scholars who possess false religious knowledge "get high fever" whenever women's rights are mentioned. Those conservative scholars, he wrote, issue the strictest of *fatwās* and articulate the worst ideas. Among these horrible ideas are that a woman should not see any man or be seen by any man other than her husband, that a man can take a woman for a wife without her consent and that the *niqāb* is the sixth pillar of Islam. They hold these positions despite the fact that Islam acknowledged women's cultural potential and mobility from its early days. These kinds of conservative opinions, al-Ghazālī concluded, turn Islam into a peculiar religion and open the gates to a Western "cultural attack."[114]

al-Mar'a bayna al-Taqālīd al-Rākida wal-Wāfida (Cairo: Dār al-Shurūq, 1994), 16. On al-Qaraḍāwī's opinion: Barbara Freyer Stowasser, "Yūsuf al-Qaraḍāwī on Women," in *The Global Mufti: The Phenomenon of Yūsuf al-Qaraḍāwī* (London: Hurst & Company, 2009), 206. Fahmī al-Huwaydī called for full participation of women in public life based on the example of the early Muslims: "Risāla fī Taḥrīr al-Mar'a," *Al-Ahrām* (May 14, 1991), 7.

[111] Al-Qaraḍāwī, *al-Ḥalāl wal-Ḥarām fī al-Islām*, 143; Aḥmad Kamāl Abū al-Majd, "Qaḍiyyat al-Ḥijāb wal-Niqāb," *al-Wafd* (January 28, 1994), 9.

[112] Muhmammad al-Ghazālī specifically attacked the Saudi *salafī* ban on women driving, noting that cars are the modern incarnation of traditional modes of transportation like camels, which women were allowed to ride, and thus there is no religio-legal justification for this prohibition: "Hadhā Dīnunā," *al-Sha'b*, November 20, 1990, 14; also *Qarārāt wa-Fatāwā al-Majlis al-'Ūrūbbī lil-Iftā' wal-Buḥūth—al-Majmū'atan al-'ūlā wal-Thāniyya*, Fatwā 38, 91–92.

[113] *Qarārāt wa-Fatāwā al-Majlis al-'Ūrūbbī lil-Iftā' wal-Buḥūth—al-Majmū'atan al-'ūlā wal-Thāniyya*, Fatwā 27, 72–74.

[114] Al-Ghazālī, *al-Ghazw al-Thaqāfī Yamtaddu fī Farāghinā*, 44, 104; on his opposition to the description of *niqābs* as a religious duty, *al-Sunna al-Nabawiyya*, 36–43.

Wasaṭī pragmatism and moderation are also evident in the realm of leisure activities. *Wasaṭīs* believe that it is permissible and in fact ordained by the Prophet for Muslims to seek out pleasure so long as religious norms are maintained. In their view, striking a balance between duties and pleasures is part of Islam's harmonizing, middle ground nature. For example, *wasaṭīs* take a permissive stance on singing and music, hotly debated issues in Islamic jurisprudence. Al-Qaraḍāwī ruled that there is no harm in singing and music, so long as they do not involve excessive indulgence, their contents are not contradictory to Islam, and they are not part of impermissible behavior such as drinking.[115] Another example is sports. While *wasaṭīs* caution against excessive indulgence and loss of modesty, they legitimize watching and practicing sports for the purpose of maintaining a healthy body as well as for the purpose of pure enjoyment. The Prophet, as *wasaṭī* jurists point out when addressing the permissibility of watching and playing football [soccer] professionally, commanded the believers to make time for leisure, "for hearts become blind when they are tired."[116] Another evidence is that when 'Umar b. al-Khaṭṭāb wanted to scold the Companions for watching Abyssinians playing with shields and spears, the Prophet said, "Leave them in order that the Jews of Medina know that our religion is spacious (and has room for relaxation) and that I have been sent with an easy and straightforward religion."[117] One *wasaṭī* jurist went so far as to deem the delay of a congregational prayer on account of a football match a *maṣlaḥa* at the rank of *ḍarūra*: "[While] it is an obvious sin to delay [the] Friday prayer or Congregational prayer from its due time," for the sake "of making matters easy for people and for the sake of preserving the unity among the Muslims, it is allowed [viz., permissible] for the Imām of a mosque

[115] Al-Qaraḍāwī, *al-Ḥalāl wal-Ḥarām fī al-Islām*, 261–65.

[116] Fayṣal Mawlawī and Jamāl al-Dīn 'Aṭiyya, "Watching Football and Playing Professionally," June 1, 2006, accessed November 6, 2013: http://www.onislam.net/english/ask-the-scholar/sports-and-games/172792-watching-football-and-playing-professionally.html?Games=.

[117] Quoted by 'Abdul-Fattah Idrees and 'Isa Zaki 'Isa: "Watching Sport Competitions," June 4, 2006, accessed September 10, 2012: http://www.onislam.net/english/ask-the-scholar/sports-and-games/172794.html?Games.

(only in case of an extreme necessity) to delay performing Friday prayer for about one or two hours (within its stipulated time) in a way that does not imply neglecting the prayer completely or performing it after its due time."[118]

Another issue emphasized by *wasaṭiyya* is the importance of good relations with non-Muslims. *Wasaṭīs* stress the duty to treat non-Muslim minorities in Muslim societies as equals. They argue that terminologies which cause non-Muslims to misunderstand Islam, particularly *dhimma* (the status of protection, under restrictions, of Jews and Christians in a Muslim state), must be expressed differently to clarify Islam's real intention.[119] They reject the *salafī* understanding of the concept of *al-walā' wal-barā'*, commonly translated as loyalty and disavowal (i.e., loyalty to Islam and to Muslims, and disavowal of other religions and non-Muslims), which, as will be explored below, prohibits friendship between Muslims and non-Muslims. While *wasaṭīs* hold and further develop the modernist-apologetic and early Islamist view of the West as a corrupt, materialistic, hedonistic, godless civilization that is bound to disintegrate and can be salvaged only through embracing Islam and its balanced way, they also hold that Muslims must interact with non-Muslims in a tolerant, just, and kind manner. Thus, interfaith dialogue should be encouraged, provided that it does not undermine Islam, and a "clash of civilizations" can be averted through tolerant, mutually respectful engagement. The importance of maintaining good relations between Muslims and non-Muslim was championed by al-Qaraḍāwī already in his first book in 1960 and reiterated in later publications. He suggested that Muslim relations with

118 'Abd al-Sattār Fatḥallāh Sa'īd and 'Abd al-Khāliq Ḥasan Al-Sharīf, "Can Imam Delay a Prayer for Watching a Soccer Match," June 2, 2002, accessed September 10, 2012: http://www.onislam.net/english/ask-the-scholar/acts-of-worship/prayer/congregational-prayer/175398-can-Imām-delay-a-prayer-for-watching-a-soccer-match.html.

119 Abū al-Majd emphasized the equality of all citizens of Egypt regardless of their religion and urged that the term *dhimma* be rethought: *Ru'ya Islāmiyya Mu'āṣira*, 38. Al-Qaraḍāwī suggested replacing *dhimma* with the term "citizens," arguing that this term does not contradict Islamic law in any way: *Khitābunā al-Islāmī fī 'Aṣr al-'Awlama*, 50–51. On *wasatis* and minorities in non-Muslim societies see: Baker, *Islam without Fear*, 106–10. On the *wasaṭī* approach to Egyptian Copts: 'Abd al-Fattāḥ, *Taqrīr al-Ḥāla al-Dīniyya fī Miṣr*, vol. 2, 365–66.

non-Muslims should be governed by Q. 60:8–9: "God does not forbid you from being kind and acting justly towards those who did not fight over faith with you, nor expelled you from your homes. God indeed loves those who are just. He only forbids you from making friends with those who fought over faith with you and banished you from your homes, and aided in your exile. Whoever makes friends with them is a transgressor."[120] His interpretation of Q. 60:8 emphasized that Allah not only commanded the believers to be just to non-Muslims who do not attack them, but also to be kind to them and do them good. Al-Qaraḍāwī stressed that this command, while also applicable to idol-worshipers, is all the more valid in the case of Jews and Christians, or "the people of the book," whether in *dār al-Islām* (the abode of Islam) or outside its realms. Because the "people of the book" are monotheists, they should be treated with even greater kindness. It is permissible to eat their meat and to marry their women, the latter entailing being affectionate and compassionate towards them.[121] Al-Qaraḍāwī did not ignore the fact that a number of verses, such as Q. 5:51–52, prohibit extending friendship to non-Muslims. He explained that these verses should *not* be understood as applying to all non-Muslims because such an interpretation would contradict the command in Q. 60:8, as well as Q. 30:21, which tell of the love and compassion between husband and wife (who may be Christian or Jewish), and Q. 5:82, which tells of the love of Christians for Muslims. Thus, drawing on the *wasaṭī* principle that verses must be contextualized to accord with the universals of the Quran, the command to disavow infidels should be interpreted as applying exclusively to those who are hostile to Islam and who fight against Muslims. Those enemies, as opposed to infidels in general, are not to be assisted or taken as confidants.[122]

[120] Al-Qur'an, A Contemporary Translation by Ahmed Ali (Princeton: Princeton University Press, 1993).

[121] Al-Qaraḍāwī, *al-Ḥalāl wal-Ḥarām fī al-Islām*, 290–92.

[122] *Ibid.*, 295–96. On the importance of religious tolerance, good relations with non-Muslims and interfaith dialogue also: al-Qaraḍāwī, *Khitābunā al-Islāmī fī* 'Aṣr *al-'Awlama*, 104–11; *Ta'rīkhuna al-Muftarā 'alayhi*, 81–96; *Nahnu wal-Gharb*, 132–33, 173–82; *Fiqh al-Wasaṭiyya al-Islāmiyya wal-Tajdīd Ma'ālim wa-Manārāt*, 226–27.

SALAFIYYA

King ʿAbd al-ʿAzīz ʿAbd al-Raḥman b. Saʿūd (1876–1953), the founder of the third Saudi Kingdom, rejected the definition of his state as *wahhābī* and declared himself a *salafī*.[123] During his reign, however, the association of the religious views endorsed by the religious and political establishments of Saudi Arabia with the term *salafiyya* was not prevalent. Rather, as b. Saʿūd himself noted, the Saudis of his time were commonly described as *wahhābīs*, that is, followers of the Najdī revivalist theologian Muḥammad b. ʿAbd al-Wahhāb (d. 1792), who played a vital role in the formation of the first Saudi state. It is not clear exactly when the term *salafiyya* became almost monopolized in popular as well as in academic discourses by an approach to Islam that fiercely rivals some aspects of the modernist-apologetic tradition and its *wasaṭī* reincarnation. Though a fairly recent development, it has had nevertheless a profoundly overwhelming effect, to the extent that in contemporary Arabic *salafiyya* is synonymous with both the teachings of the mainstream of the Saudi religious establishment and movements and individuals that identify with some crucial aspects of those teachings while challenging others. To be a *salafī* today means to reject the juristic rationalism and pragmatism represented by the modernist-apologetic school formerly known as *salafī*. *Salafī* writings and *fatwās* reflect a concern that *wasaṭīs* who claim to revive Islam inadvertently promote views that undermine and politicize it.

Saudi and affiliated jurists promoted the labeling of their teachings as *salafī* (and of *salafīs* as *Ahl al-Sunna wal-Jamāʿa*, "the people who follow the Prophet's example and are united") rather than as *wahhābī* for a reason. The latter name depicts them as followers of a religious reformer who was controversial even in his own homeland, while the former depicts them as the standard-bearers of the one and only true and legitimate understanding of Islam. *Salafī* texts hold that *wahhābiyya* is a pejorative term applied by people as a means of belittling *salafīs*.[124]

[123] For a reference of the king's speech in November 1946: AbdusSalām as-Sihaymī, *To Be a Serious Salafī* (London: Jamiah Media, 2011), 23.

[124] See an "important note" in an article entitled "Wahhābism Unveiled" in the Bradford, England-based *salafī* journal *The Ark* 21, special edition (August 2007), 1.

Salafīs consider Muḥammad b. 'Abd al-Wahhāb a "revivalist of the salafī call" and a paramount inspiration for adhering to the truths of Islam, but caution against glorifying him or any other scholar.[125] They emphasize that the word *wahhābiyya* is "not a legitimate title," neither for describing b. 'Abd al-Wahhāb's project nor for describing those "following in his steps" because b. 'Abd al-Wahhāb was merely a reviver of the call to follow the footsteps of the *salaf*.[126] They suggest that those who prefer the name *wahhābīs* to *salafīs* do so "either out of ignorance, blind imitation of others, jealousy, stubbornness or following their own whims and desires, or adherence to traditions, *bid'a* (innovation) and evil actions that go against the evidence (of *sharī'a*)."[127] *Salafīs* are a minority in the Sunni Arab world. Their ability to gain possession of the cherished banner of *salafiyya* in both popular and academic discourses is the result of two factors: first, they are the only contemporary trend in the Arab world that seeks recognition primarily as *salafī* and, second, they invest massive funds in state-of-the-art internet websites, satellite channels, books, and pamphlets that promote their agenda.

In its contemporary Saudi manifestation, *salafiyya* is an approach to Islamic law and to Islam at large that was articulated by the kingdom's highest religious authority since the early 1970s (and its grand muftī since 1993), 'Abd al-'Azīz b. 'Abdallāh b. Bāz (1910–99) and by his

[125] This evaluation of Muḥammad b. 'Abd al-Wahhāb appeared in a decision of the Permanent Committee from April 1992. The Committee addressed the decision of the Directorate of Antiques and Museums to restore the home of 'Abd al-Wahhāb. It declared it an impermissible act, explaining, "it is a means to exceeding the proper limits in shaykh Muḥammad (may Allāh be merciful to him) and similar scholars of truth [viz., glorifying them in a prohibited manner]. Furthermore, it involves seeking the blessings in their traces and consequently falling into shirk." The Committee called for the immediate destruction of the house: "It is impermissible to glorify the traces of scholars in a manner that leads to exceeding the proper limits and committing shirk," n.d., accessed September 10, 2012: http://www.alifta.com; On the parmount impact of 'Abd al-Wahhāb on contemporary *salafiyya* see also: Ṣāliḥ b. Fawzān al-Fawzān, *Mas'ūliyyat al-'Ulamā' wal-Du'āt* (Riyadh: Dār Kunūz Ishbilya lil-Nashr wal-Tawzī', 2009), 18.

[126] Abul-Hasan Maalik al-Akhdar, *In Defense of Islam in Light of the Events of September 11th* (Toronto: T.R.O.I.D Publications, 2002), 25.

[127] 'Abdallāh Ibn Jibrin, "Advise to Those Who Do Not Recognize the Salafī Scholars and Call Them Wahhābis," in Muhammad Saed Abdul-Rahman (ed.), *Islam: Questions and Answers—Inviting Others to Islam*, vol. 19 (London: MSA Publication Limited, 2007), 200–202. On the Saudi rejection of the term *Wahhābiyya*: Febe Armanios, "The Islamic Traditions of Wahhabism and Salafiyya," *Congressional Research Service Reports* (December 2003), 1–3.

second-in-command, Muḥammad b. Ṣāliḥ al-ʻUthaymīn (1928–2001). It is presented in individual works and in the studies and *fatwās* issued by Saudi Arabia's two main juristic institutions: its highest religious authority, the Council of Senior Scholars (*Hay'at Kibār al-ʻUlamā'*), established in 1971 and responsible for advising the king, and its subsidiary, the Permanent [or Standing] Committee for Scientific Research and the Issuance of Fatwas (*al-Lajna al-Dā'ima lil-Buḥūth al-ʻIlmiyya wal-Iftā'*), responsible for answering personal queries on issues relating to *ʻaqīda* (faith), *ʻibādāt* (worship), and *muʻāmalāt* (transactions). Most, but not all, prominent contemporary *salafīs* are Saudi-born. The Albanian-born Muḥammad Nāṣir al-Dīn al-Albānī (d. 1999), who taught for three years in the Islamic University of al-Madīna, is considered by some to be the only non-Saudi equal to b. Bāz and al-ʻUthaymīn in his contribution to the contemporary *salafī* approach.[128]

Historically, *salafiyya* is a continuation of the legacies of Aḥmad b. Ḥanbal (d. 855), Taqī al-Dīn Ibn Taymiyya (d. 1328), his student Ibn al-Qayyim al-Jawziyya (d. 1350), and the abovementioned b. ʻAbd al-Wahhāb. *Salafīs* consider themselves to be committed only to the teachings of the Quran and the Prophetic traditions and thus the emissaries of the beliefs and practices of the *salaf*. Central to their teachings are *tawḥīd* (the oneness of Allah) as the guiding Islamic principle, the rejection of *shirk* (associating partners with Allah) and of *bidʻa*, and the duty to engage with Muslims and non-Muslims based on the principle of *al-walā' wal-barā'* (loyalty and disavowal). The *salafī* juristic approach is literalist, heavily drawing on the authority of the Prophetic traditions and restricting (while not rejecting altogether) the accommodation of religious laws to changing circumstances. *Salafīs* demonstrate a distaste of modernity. While they favor the integration of technologies that do not contradict Islam, the need for Muslim scientific progress is marginal in their writings, which stress the importance of pure, unconditioned faith and total religious devotion. Socially, they preach for rigid gender segregation and strictly limit the roles of women in public spheres. They also

[128] ʻAlī al-Khaḍar, *al-Saʻūdiyya Ṣirat Dawla wa-Mujtamaʻ* (Beirut: Arab Network for Research and Publishing, 2010), 224–28.

discourage leisure activities. Politically they consider electoral democracy contrary to Islam, call for obedience to the ruler under almost all circumstances, and oppose open involvement of religious scholars in political processes.

Salafiyya is not a cohesive movement. In Saudi Arabia and outside the kingdom, individuals and movements which reject one or more of the core principles represented by the contemporary mainstream of Saudi Arabia's religious establishment also present themselves and are identified as *salafī*. The term "mainstream *salafiyya*" is not used in this study quantitatively. It recognizes the fact that challenges to the agenda promoted by b. Bāz, al-'Uthaymīn, and their students under the banner of *salafiyya* constitute both deviations from that agenda and, at times, conform to it. It also recognizes that the authority of Saudi *'Ulamā'* is widely recognized in *salafī* circles outside Saudi Arabia (this is especially true for Muslim *salafī* communities in the West).

Wiktorowicz's anatomy of the *salafī* movement points to two offspring of the Saudi mainstream *salafiyya*: the *jihādis* and the politicos.[129] Meijer stressed the *jihādi-salafīs*' focus on analyzing politics and devising strategies to change the political reality.[130] Hegghammer, who characterized *jihādi-salafism* as an extremist blending of the *wahhābī* religious tradition and the Quṭbist Islamist trend and pointed to its internationalist orientation, traced the earliest origins of the term to an interview given in 1994 to the London-based *jihādi* magazine *al-Anṣār* by Ayman al-Ẓawāhirī, al-Qaeda's current leader and formerly a member of the Egyptian Quṭbist Islamic Jihād.[131] While *salafīs* and *jihādi-salafīs* agree on some doctrinal issues, the fundamental difference in their respective approaches to violent dissent against Muslim regimes that do not apply Allah's laws to the letter makes the two sworn enemies. A less pronounced dispute is between the mainstream *salafiyya*, represented by

[129] Quintan Wiktorowicz, "Anatomy of the Salafi Movement," *Studies in Conflict and Terrorism* 29, 3 (April–May 2006), 208.

[130] Roel Meijer, "Introduction," in Roel Meijer (ed.), *Global Salafism: Islam's New Religious Movement* (London: Hurst & Company, 2009), 24.

[131] Thomas Hegghammer, "Jihadi-Salafis or Revolutionaries? On Religion and Politics in the Study of Militant Islamism," in Roel Meijer (ed.), *Global Salafism: Islam's New Religious Movement* (London: Hurst & Company, 2009), 251–55.

the contemporary Saudi religious leadership, and what Wiktorowicz terms "politico-*salafīs*" in Saudi Arabia and outside the kingdom. According to Wiktorowicz, the latter engage with the political reality and some reluctantly and conditionally participate in electoral processes as a means of changing it. Not withstanding the utility of this definition, mainstream Saudi *salafīs* abstention from engaging with political realities and their rejection of electoral politics has been undermined since the 1980s. Thus, the two trends do not represent categorically conflicting agendas. The surprising result of Egypt's post-Mubarak parliamentary elections in 2011, in which the candidates of the *salafī* al-Nūr party won a quarter of the seats, demonstrated the broad appeal of *salafism* outside Saudi Arabia and the influential and accomodationist nature of the concept of *salafiyya*. In deciding to compete, al-Nūr candidates broke from their past policy of refraining from political engagement as well as from their principled rejection of democracy. Their campaign platform and policies have ever since been a mixture of traditional *salafī* views focusing on the establishment of a more pious society along with support for personal and minority freedoms in which traditional *salafī* agendas could hardly be traced. As a result, a struggle between pragmatists and hardliners within the party ensued.[132]

At the heart of the *salafī* approach, as articulated by b. Bāz, al-ʿUthaymīn, and their followers is the affirmation of *tawḥīd* and the rejection of *shirk*. *Salafī* writings on *tawḥīd* continue the legacies of Ibn Taymiyya, Ibn al-Qayyim and, in particular, Muḥammad b. ʿAbd al-Wahhāb, who centered his call for reform on the conviction that the Muslims of his time had betrayed true monotheism and associated others with Allah. In particular, the betrayals al-Wahhāb pointed to included believing that particularly righteous people might intercede with Allah on behalf of believers, wearing talismans, making pictures of living creatures, asking the advice of fortune tellers, prohibiting what Allah has permitted or

[132] For the platform of al-Nūr, see their website, accessed September 10, 2012: http://www.alnourparty.org; on the history of Egyptian *salafiyya* (in the contemporary sense of the word), its political reincarnation, and internal disagreements: Stéphane Lacroix, *Sheikhs and Politicians: Inside the New Egyptian Salafism* (Brookings Doha Center, June 2012).

permitting what Allah has prohibited, and mocking Allah, His book or His Prophet.[133] *Salafīs* stress that *tawḥīd* is the essence of Islam. Ibn Bāz explained the centrality of *tawḥīd* as follows: "[Islam's] reality is recognizing the oneness of Allah in His ownership, His control of affairs, and His actions. It is also signaling Him out for worship and recognizing His uniqueness in His names and attributes. It is complying with His commands and accepting His law."[134] He asked for *da'wa* activities to focus on teaching "the elite and the general public" about *tawḥīd*, noting that the Prophet taught the people of Mecca about it before teaching them about anything else.[135] 'Abdallāh b. Ṣāliḥ al-Fawzān (b. 1935), a member of the Saudi Council of Senior Scholars and the Permanent Committee and one of the more prolific contemporary *salafī* theologians and jurists, relied on Ibn al-Qayyim when he explained that the entire Quran is about *tawḥīd* and the rejection of *shirk*, and that Islam's religious obligations were not revealed (in the Madinian *sūras*) until *tawḥīd* was presented and established within the souls of the people.[136] Breaching *tawḥīd* involves two types of *shirk*: major, such as ascribing to other than Allah something that belongs only to Him (like the belief that there is someone else who gives life), and minor, constituting anything that may lead to major *shirk* (like venerating people or objects without attributing to them attributes of Allah).[137]

[133] 'Abd al-Wahhāb presented his concept of monotheism and the rejection of *shirk* in a manifesto, *Kitāb al-Tawḥīd* (Riyadh: Imām Muḥammad b. Sa'ūd University, n.d.). A number of English translations are available online, for example: http://www.islamicweb.com/beliefs/creed/abdulwahab/. For an overview of his concept of *tawḥīd* and its reception: David Commins, *The Wahhabi Mission and Saudi Arabia* (London: I. B. Tauris, 2006), 7–70.

[134] Al-Imaam 'Abdul 'Azeez Ibn 'Abdullah Ibn Baaz, *The Legislation of Islam*, trans. Abū Sumayya 'Aqīl Walker (Grand Prairie, Canada: Ibnul Qayyim Publications, 2006), 12.

[135] 'Abdul 'Azeez Ibn 'Abdullah Ibn Baaz, *Words of Advice Regarding Da'wah* (Birmingham: al-Hidaayah Publishing and Distribution, 1998), 31–32.

[136] Saleh al-Fawzaan, "Why Do the 'Wahhabis' Always Talk about Tawheed?" *The Ark* 21 (August 2007), 4. On the essentiality of establishing *tawḥīd* and the risk of engaging in *shirk* by, for example, supplicating to the Prophet, see also: 'Abdul 'Azeez Bin Yahyaa Al Bur'ee, *A Concise Manual for the New Muslim* (USA: Salafi Ink Publications, 2012), 8.

[137] Islam Question and Answer, "What Is the True Meaning of Shirk and What Are its Types?" in Muhammad Saed Abdul-Rahman (ed.), *Islam: Question and Answers—Polytheism and its Different Forms* (London: MSA Publication Ltd, 2003), 22–32; Muḥammad b. Ṣāliḥ al-'Uthaymīn, "Anwā' al-Shirk," in Muḥammad Muḥammad Tāmir (ed.), *Fiqh al-'Ibādāt lil-Shaykh Muḥammad b. Ṣāliḥ al-'Utahymīn* (Cairo: Dār al-Risāla, 2003), 56–57.

The *salafī* emphasis on the oneness of Allah as the core of Islam is not unique, as testifying that there's no God but Allah is the first pillar of faith for all Muslims. The singularity of *tawḥīd* in *salafī* writings lies in its utilization as a means to describe *salafī* interpretations of Islam as the only ones that are truly loyal to monotheism, while chastising other interpretations as either *shirk* or sins that risk leading to *shirk*. Thus, as was the case for early *wahhābism*, *tawḥīd* enhances the quest of contemporary *salafīs* to monopolize *salafī* truths. The centrality of the concept also supports the mainstream *salafī* reluctance to participate in politics. *Salafīs* argue that because *tawḥīd* is so crucial, there is no point in attending to topical issues unless the oneness of Allah is established in the minds of Muslims. Al-Fawzān answered his rhetorical question about why *salafīs* "always talk about *tawḥīd*" instead of discussing the plights of contemporary Muslims by insisting that in order to solve the problems Muslims face, it is essential "to seek out the reasons that have led to the punishments afflicting the Muslims." These reasons are the absence of *tawḥīd* from the lives of most Muslims, manifested in behaviors such as praying to religious figures as intercessors with Allah, clinging to graves and tombs, as well as not praying, fasting, and giving charity as required. Only when *tawḥīd* is established will Muslims be triumphant once more.[138]

Another concept emphasized by *salafīs* is *bid'a* and the duty to refrain from committing it. The negative connotation of *bid'a* was first expressed in a number of Prophetic traditions, which defined it as a deviation from the straight path set by Allah's book, the example of the Prophet, and his four righteous successors. It was accorded a second, positive connotation by the second Khalīfa, 'Umar, (d. 644), who said in regard to the prayer of Ramaḍān (*ṣalāt al-tarāwīḥ*) that it is a blessed innovation. The division between welcomed and prohibited innovations was accepted by some jurists, especially *shāfi'īs* and *mālikīs*, and rejected by others, especially *ḥanbalīs*, including Ibn Taymiyya. Ibn 'Abd al-Wahhāb accepted Ibn Taymiyya's interpretation and so do contemporary *salafīs*.[139] The *salafī*

[138] Al-Fawzaan, "Why Do the 'Wahhabis' Always Talk about Tawheed?" 4.

[139] Muhammad Al-Atawneh, *Wahhābī Islam Facing the Challenges of Modernity: Dār Al-Iftā in the Modern Saudi State* (Leiden: Brill, 2010), 86–90; on Ibn Taymiyya's concept of

insistence on *bid'a* as a clear-cut concept embodying all that is prohibited in Islam rests on their loyalty to the authority of the Prophetic traditions; because the Prophet defined innovation pejoratively, no other interpretation of the concept is acceptable.[140] However, *salafīs* do not oppose any innovation as such. Their concept of *bid'a* does not include innovations that are worldly in essence, such as new types of food or technologies that do not contradict the teaching of Islam. Rather, it applies to any denial of Islam's creed and laws. Thus, denial of the attributes of Allah and the notion that the Quran was created constitute innovation. When one innovates in a matter on which there is consensus and of which any Muslim should be aware, one commits *kufr*, or infidelity.[141] As is the case with its theory on *tawḥīd*, the *salafī* theory of *bid'a* is not unique. The idea that it is unlawful to innovate in worship or to legislate against Allah is universal, but *salafī* utilization of *bid'a* is broad and supports their literalist-purist interpretations of the permissible and the impermissible. They hold that a wide range of practices constitute *bid'a* because they are not grounded in the Quran, the traditions, and the norms set by the *salaf,* as they understand them. Moreover, they dedicate considerable efforts to encourage the removal of these practices from Muslims' lives. Some of these efforts date to the time of Ibn Taymiyya, like the celebration of the Prophet's birthday, and some are modern, like the celebration of birthdays and national holidays.[142] Thus, *bid'a* constitutes another means by *salafīs* to delegitimize other opinions.

bid'a see also: Muḥammad Rawās, *Mawsū'at Fiqh Ibn Taymiyya*, vol. 1 (Beirut: Dār al-Nafā'is, 1998), 32–36.

[140] Muḥammad Ṣāliḥ al-Munajjid, "There Is No Such Thing as Bid'ah Ḥasanah in Islam," in Muhammad Saed Abdul-Rahman (ed.), *Islam: Questions and Answers—Basis for Jurisprudence and Islamic Rulings* (London: MSA Publication limited, 2007), 357–59.

[141] Muḥammad b. Ṣāliḥ Ibn al-'Uthaymīn, "Mā Ma'nā al-Bid'a wa-ma Ḍābiṭuhā" in *Fatāwā al-Balad al-Ḥarām* (Cairo: al-Maktaba al-Tawfīqiyya, n.d.), 1024–25; "Detailed Discussion of bid'ah and Shirk," in Muhammad Saed Abdul-Rahman (ed.), *Islam: Questions and Answers—Basis for Jurisprudence and Islamic Rulings* (London: MSA Publication limited, 2007), 265–72; Al-Atawneh, *Wahhābī Islam Facing the Challenges of Modernity*, 91–92.

[142] Al-Atawneh, *Wahhābī Islam Facing the Challenges of Modernity*, 94–99; al-Lajna al-Dā'ima, "Celebrating Innovated Festivals," in Muhammad Saed Abdul-Rahman (ed.), *Islam: Questions and Answers—Basis for Jurisprudence and Islamic Rulings* (London: MSA Publication limited, 2007), 124–25.

Also central to *salafī* writings is their conception of *al-walā' wal-barā'*, which conflicts with the *wasaṭī* view, and, as will be demonstrated in Chapter 2, particularly impacts on their jurisprudence for Muslim minorities. This concept finds its roots in diverse Islamic traditions. Already in the seventh century, the Khārijites, who refused to accept mediation as a resolution to the contest of power between the fourth Khalīfa, 'Alī b. Abī Ṭālib (d. 661), and his opponent, Mu'āwiyya b. Abī Sufyān (d. 680), called to preserve loyalty to their group while disavowing their opponents. A similar approach developed in the Shī'ī creed, which demanded *walā'* (loyalty) toward 'Alī and his descendants and *barā'* (disavowal) of the first three Khulafā' and their descendants. From the tenth to twelfth centuries, a number of *Ḥanbalī* jurists refuted the concept of "loyalty and disavowal," arguing that it is an innovation (*bid'a*); Wagemakers notes that it is not clear whether they did so based on doctrinal grounds or because the term was associated with the Shī'īs.[143] After several decades of relative silence in *Ḥanbalī* writings, Ibn Taymiyya treated notions of "loyalty and disavowal" extensively. While he never specifically invoked the phrase *al-walā' wal-barā'*, his condemnation of non-Muslims as enemies of Allah and his strong opposition to imitating them were major influences on the evolution of the expression. His writings demonstrated deep concern over the potential negative impact Jews and Christians could have on the purity of Muslim faith and practice, and cautioned against following their ways and befriending them.[144] He preached for a clear distinction between the friends, or loyalists, of Allah (*awliyā'*) and the loyalists of the devil (*shayṭān*). The "loyalists of Allah" are those who believe in Him and the message of His Prophet, in its entirety, and who love what Allah loves and hate what He hates; the "loyalists of the devil" are the disbelievers, the enemies of Allah. Whoever displays enmity towards a loyalist of Allah declares war against Allah.[145] According to

[143] Joas Wagemakers, "The Transformation of a Radical Concept: *al-wala' wal-bara'* in the Ideology of Abu Muhammad al-Maqdisi," in Roel Meijer's edited volume on *salafī* movements, *Global Salafism: Islam's New Religious Movement* (London: Hurst & Company, 2009), 84–85.

[144] *Ibid.*, 85–86.

[145] Shaykhul-Islam Ibn Taymiyyah, *The Friends of Allah and the Friends of Shaytan*, trans. Abū Rumaysah (Birmingham: Daar us-Sunnah Publishers, 2005), 39–84.

Ibn Taymiyya, only complete faith in and devotion to the final revelation qualify one as a loyalist to Allah. While monotheistic Jews and Christians claim to be *awliyā'* of Allah, they are in fact the enemies of Allah, and so are hypocrites who claim to be believers but do not sincerely recognize Muḥammad as the Messenger of Allah.[146]

Nineteenth century *wahhābī* scholars further addressed *walā'* and *barā'* as concepts that were foundational to their doctrine, though they did not use the terms themselves. The terms became instrumental in efforts to support Saudi rule in the Arabian Peninsula. Sulaymān b. 'Abdallāh Āl al-Shaykh (d. 1818), a grandson of b. 'Abd al-Wahhāb, argued in one treatise that to love and hate in the name of Allah are pillars of faith; he stressed that Allah commanded Muslims to avoid loyalty to His enemies and to show them enmity, and that one cannot love Allah if one loves His enemies.[147] In another treatise he argued that those who show loyalty to polytheists and acceptance of their belief, for whatever reason, become like them and thus turn into infidels.[148] According to Wagemakers, the purpose of the treatise was excommunication: al-Shaykh considered the Ottomans to be infidels, and the aim of this treatise was to delegitimize Arabians who supported the Ottoman efforts to destroy the first Saudi Kingdom.[149] During the days of the second Saudi state, the terms *walā' and barā'* were instrumental in a conflict that emerged within the House of Sa'ūd between two contenders for power, 'Abdallāh and his brother, Sa'ūd. The *wahhābī* scholar Ḥamad b. 'Alī b. 'Atīq (d. 1883), who supported Sa'ūd, took al-Shaykh's ideas further. He argued that demonstrating enmity towards non-Muslims and avoiding imitation of them or allying with them are secondary only to *tawḥīd* in terms of importance, and that anyone who does not disavow from infidels is an infidel himself.

[146] *Ibid.*, 60, 63–64.

[147] Sulaymān b. 'Abdallāh Āl al-Shaykh, *Awthaq 'Urā al-'īmān*, n.d., accessed October 28, 2013: http://www.tawhed.ws/r1?i=2351&x=vhymy7hu. Also Wagemakers, "The Transformation of a Radical Concept: *al-wala' wal-bara'* in the Ideology of Abu Muhammad al-Maqdisi," 87.

[148] Sulaymān b. 'Abdallāh Āl al-Shaykh, *al-Dalā'il fī Ḥukm Muwālāt Ahl al-Ishrāk*, n.d., accessed October 28, 2013: http://www.tawhed.ws/r?i=bm4wz4za.

[149] Joas Wagemakers, "The Enduring Legacy of the Second Saudi State: Quietist and Radical Wahhabi Contestations of *al-Walā' wal-Barā'*," *International Journal of Middle Eastern Studies* 44, 1 (February 2012), 95.

Ibn ʿAtīq emphasized that the command to refrain from demonstrating loyalty, love, or respect to Jews and Christians is even stronger than in regard to other infidels.[150] Wagemakers suggests that b. ʿAtīq's treatise was motivated primarily by his opposition to ʿAbdallāh's decision to invite the "infidel" Ottoman forces to assist him in his struggle against Saʿūd.[151]

Expanding this rich tradition in dozens of *fatwās*, treatises, and dissertations, contemporary *salafīs* have integrated "loyalty" and "disavowal" into one coherent concept that divides humanity into two profoundly hostile camps: Muslims who accept Allah's truth and non-Muslims who reject it. The proliferation of deliberations on the subject in recent decades has elevated the concept to a signature of the *salafī* doctrine and was instrumental in the efforts of *salafī* jurists to limit the interactions of Saudi society with other societies and to minimize its integration of modern practices. *Salafīs* have invoked "loyalty and disavowal" to argue that friendly personal relations between Muslims and non-Muslims are prohibited and that Muslims should not resemble infidels or imitate them. Their writings suggest that the principle of "loyalty" demands only those actions which please Allah, including the reservation of love exclusively for Allah, His Prophet, and the believers, and the reservation of friendship (or alliances) exclusively for the believers. The principle of "disavowal," on the other hand, demands despising and spurning the infidels and their religion.[152] *Salafīs* also emphasize that the unitary

[150] Ḥamad b. ʿAlī Ibn ʿAtīq, *Sabīl al-Najā' wal-Fikāk min Muwālāt al-Murtaddīn wal-Atrāk*, n.d., accessed September 10, 2012: http://www.tawhed.sw; also Wagemakers, "The Transformation of a Radical Concept: *al-wala' wal-bara'* in the Ideology of Abu Muhammad al-Maqdisi," 87–88.

[151] Wagemakers, "The Enduring Legacy of the Second Saudi State: Quietist and Radical Wahhābi Contestations of *al-Wala' wal-Bara*'," 96.

[152] ʿAbd al-ʿAzīz b. ʿAbdallāh b. Bāz explained that "loyalty and disavowal" means loving the believers and being their friend (or ally), while despising the infidels, spurning them and their religion: "al-wala' wal-bara' wa-Aḥkām al-Kuffār," in *Fatāwā al-Balad al-Ḥarām* (Cairo: Dār al-Tawfīqiyya, n.d.), 174. See also Abd el-Aziz bin Abdullah bin Baz, *The Correct Belief and its Opposite and What Negates al-Islam*, trans. Muḥammad ʿAbd al-Raḥman Abū Ḥamza Maghribī (London: al-Firdous, 1996), 24–25. The Permanent Committee for Academic Research and Issuing Fatwas argued that infidels, including Jews and Christians, are the enemies of Allāh and His Prophet and are doomed to hellfire: al-Lajna al-Dā'ima lil-Buḥūth wal-Iftā', "Ḥukm al-Da'wa ilā Waḥdat al-Adyān," in *Fatāwā al-Balad al-Ḥarām* (Cairo: al-Maktaba al-Tawfīqiyya, n.d.), 16–20. The glossary of a master's dissertation on the meaning of *al-Walā' wal-Barā'*, written by Muḥammad Saʿīd al-Qaḥānī and approved in June 1981 at Umm al-Qurā University in Mecca, defined *walā'* as "loyalty, holding fast to all

nature of Islam (i.e., Allah's demand for total submission) requires the believers to be uncompromising in their enmity toward those who reject their creator and His true religion. "Disavowal" is as important as "loyalty," and the two are parts of a whole, without which devotion cannot be complete.[153]

Along with objection to friendly relations with non-Muslims, another main limitation that the *salafī* interpretation of "loyalty and disavowal" places concerns the strong prohibition of perceived imitations of and resemblance to infidels. *Salafīs* stress the need to differ from the infidels, citing Q. 3:100, 45:18, 9:69, 59:19; the Prophet's warning, narrated by Abū Dāwud, that "whoever imitates a people is one of them"; and a number of other traditions. They identify three categories in which it is impermissible to imitate infidels: worship, customs, and the conduct of worldly affairs. First, imitating the infidels in their beliefs, rituals, or holidays is prohibited. According to al-Fawzān, this type of imitation when intentional constitutes *kufr*,[154] while according to b. ʿUthaymīn,

that is pleasing to Allāh" and *barā'* as "withdrawing from and opposing all that is displeasing to Allāh and His messenger." See: Muhammad Saeed al-Qahtani, *al-Wala' wal-Bara' According to the 'Aqeedah of the Salaf* (London: Al-Firdous Ltd, 1993), 118, 129–30. (The dissertation was supervised by Muḥammad Quṭb, a former member of the Muslim Brothers and the brother of Sayyid Quṭb, who escaped execution, was released from Egyptian prison in 1972, and found academic shelter in Saudi Arabia. A member of the dissertation's examining committee, who also endorsed the book version, was ʿAbd al-Rāziq ʿAfīfī, Deputy President of the Departments for Guidance, Iftā', Daʿwa and Scholarly Research. In referencing Sayyid Quṭb and *salafī* sources, the dissertation demonstrates the blending of Islamist and *salafī* ideas among a generation of Saudi university graduates.) Also, an introduction by an England-based president of a *salafī* organization to a treatise on *al-Walā' wal-Barā'*, first published in 1997, explained that "in the context of Islam, *al-wala'* is loyalty to Allāh and whatever He is pleased with as well as friendship and closeness to the believers, whereas *al-bara'* is freeing oneself from that which is displeasing to Allāh and disowning the disbelievers": Abū Muntaṣir ibn Mohar ʿAlī (president of Jamʿiyyat Ihya' Minhaj al-Sunna), "Introduction," in Saalih bin Fouzan al-Fouzan, *al-Walaa' wal-Baraa': Allegiance and Association with the People of Islaam and Eeman and Disassociation and Enmity with the People of Falsehood and Disbelief in Islaam*, trans. Abū ʿAbd al-Raḥmān Bansfield (Ipswich: Jamʿiyyat Ihyā' Minhaj al-Sunna, 1997), 4–5.

[153] Muhammad al-Qahtani, *al-Wala' wal-Bara' According to the 'Aqeedah of the Salaf*, 42–43, 115; see also: ʿAbd al-Raḥman Ibn ʿAbd al-Khāliq, *al-Walā' wal-Barā'* (September 1986, accessed September 10, 2012: http://www.al-mostafa.com/), 22; Murshid al-Arshānī, *al-Walā' wal-Barā'* (Ṣanʿā': Maktabat Khālid b. al-Walīd, 2004) (the author is a Yemenite Qāḍī and Justice Minister).

[154] ʿAbdallāh b. Ṣāliḥ al-Fawzān, *Aḥkām al-Tashābuh bil-Kuffār*, 4, n.d., accessed November 10, 2013: http://alfuzan.islamlight.net/index.php?option=com_remository&id=&Itemid=0&limit=50&limitstart=0.

whoever imitates the infidels in their acts of worship "puts himself at great risk and that may lead to him becoming an infidel who is beyond the pale of Islam."[155] Imitation of infidel customs also prohibits, for example, shaving or dressing in a way similar to that of the infidels. Al-Fawzān quoted the Prophet: "These are the garments of the infidels; do not wear them." This type of imitation, if intentional, constitutes infidelity because it signifies breaching one of the foundations of faith, loving of Allah, which demands despising infidelity and its manifestations.[156] Al-Fawzān cautioned against differentiating between "important" and "unimportant" in imitating the social patterns of infidels. Possibly influenced by Ibn Taymiyya's understanding of the issue,[157] he explained that garments should not be considered as purely external because they reflect a person's consciousness and tendencies, and thus, in wearing European clothes, a Muslim subconsciously fuses his tendencies and those of the European, an act that will eventually lead to a fusion of his views with those of the European.[158]

A third category of imitation, comprising worldly affairs such as sciences and technology, is less conclusive. If *maṣlaḥa* is served by learning from the infidels in these fields, then there is no harm in doing so, as long as what is learned does not exist in Muslim societies, does not breach the teachings of the *sharīʿa*, and does not humiliate Muslims in the process. Evidence for the permissibility of learning from the technical achievements of the infidels is the Prophet's adaptation of Persian trench techniques in the battle of the confederates (*Ghazwat al-Aḥzāb*, 627 AD).[159] This approach, in principle, does not differ from the *wasaṭī* approach. Like *wasaṭīs*, *salafīs* also hold that religion is not the reason for Muslims'

[155] Muḥammad b. Ṣāliḥ al-ʿUthaymīn, "Benefiting from What the Kaafirs Have," in Muhmmad Saed Abdul-Rahman (ed.) *Islam: Questions and Answers—Alliance and Amity, Disavowal and Enmity* (London: MSA Publication Ltd, 2003), 39.

[156] Fawzān, *Aḥkām al-Tashābuh bil-Kuffār*, 5.

[157] In warning against imitating Jews and Christians, Ibn Taymiyya explained that customs—clothes, food, housing etc.—affect beliefs and wishes, and vice versa; a person who wears the clothes of a certain group identifies with that group: *al-Ṣirāṭ al-Mustaqīm* (Cairo: Dār al-Futūḥ al-Islāmiyya, 1995), 56–58.

[158] Fawzān, *Aḥkām al-Tashābuh bil-Kuffār*, 6–8.

[159] *Ibid.*, 5; *al-wala' wal-bara'*, 15, "Mawqifunā min al-Ḥaḍāra al-Gharbiyya," in *Fatāwā al-Balad al-Ḥarām* (Cairo: al-Maktaba al-Tawfīqiyya, n.d.), 1072–73; al-ʿUthaymin, "Benefiting from What the Kafirs Have," 39.

scientific and technological backwardness, and there is nothing in Islam to hinder advancement in these fields.[160] However, while proving the compatibility of Islam and modern sciences and promoting scientific progression are central ideological objectives for *wasaṭīs*, these are marginal issues for *salafīs*. The latter's occasional engagement with these issues emphasizes the importance of returning to the fundamentals of faith as a means for Muslim revival and the hellfire that awaits the infidels despite their worldly advances; they are less concerned about the alleged indispensability of advancing sciences and technology.

In commenting on *walā' and barā'*, contemporary members of the Saudi religious establishment and their followers outside the Kingdom shifted the focus back to the field of social relations. This, however, does not imply that the term became "apolitical and strictly social," as Wagemakers suggested.[161] One can argue the contrary: in refraining from applying the concept to sensitive issues such as American–Saudi relations, Saudi and other *salafī* scholars sought to refute the main *jihādi-salafī* contention that military and political alliances between Muslims and non-Muslims breach the religious duty to reserve loyalty to Muslims alone.[162] Furthermore, the concept has been applied by contemporary *salafīs* not only in a social context but also in a political, as a means to distance their followers from Muslims who potentially endanger Saudi interests. In discrediting the Muslim Brothers as a deviant group (an opinion that is derived from the Brothers' *wasaṭī* orientation but also serves the Saudi regime well; as a result of the regime's concern about the Brothers' subversive potential, the organization was banned in the Kingdom[163]), *salafīs* have argued that

160 Muḥammad b. Ṣāliḥ Ibn 'Uthaymin, "Ḥukm Man Yadd'ā Anna Sabab Takhalluf al-Muslimīn Huwa Tamassukuhum bi-Dīnhim," in *Fatāwā al-Balad al-Ḥarām* (Cairo: al-Maktaba al-Tawfīqiyya, n.d.), 1069–71.

161 Wagemakers, "The Enduring Legacy of the Second Saudi State: Quietist and Radical Wahhabi Contestations of *al-Wala' wal-Bara*," 97.

162 Joas Wagemakers, "Framing the 'Threat to Islam': *al-Wala' wal-Bara'* in Salafī Discourse," *Arab Studies Quarterly* 30, 4 (Fall 2008), 7–14.

163 For detailed analyses and biographies of Islamist personalities who have been active in Saudi Arabia since the 1950s, see: 'Abd al-'Azīz al-Khaḍar, *al-Sa'ūdiyya Sīrat Dawla wa-Mujtama'* (Beirut: Arab Network for Research and Publishing, 2010), 208–40. For analysis of the early relations between Ḥasan al-Bannā and the Saudi regime, Saudi refusal to allow the establishment of a branch of the Muslim Brothers in the Kingdom, and a list of prominent Islamists who worked in the kingdom: Hāshim 'Abd al-Razzāq Ṣāliḥ al-Ṭā'ī,

the followers of Ḥasan al-Bannā have neglected "loyalty and disavowal" by calling for Shīʿī-Sunni reconciliation and agreeing to cooperate with Muslims who do not follow the ways of the *salaf*.[164] Conversely, *salafīs* have also argued that the Brothers err in extending loyalty exclusively to those who join their ranks and disavowing anyone who does not.[165]

Cook described the defining moment in Muḥammad b. ʿAbd al-Wahhāb's life as "something like a conversion." At some point towards the middle of the eighteenth century, al-Wahhāb considered most of the professed Muslims of his day polytheists that should be fought until they accepted Islam.[166] Contemporary *salafīs* share this elitist element of his mindset. They believe that other approaches to Islam reflect not simply errors of judgment but rather complete deviations for which the punishment will be hellfire. This warning is based on the tradition—narrated by ʿAbdallāh b. ʿUmar, invoked by ʿAbd al-Wahhāb and referenced by contemporary *salafīs*—according to which the Prophet said: "This *umma* will divide into seventy-three sects. All of them will be in the fire except for one." When the Companions asked the Prophet which is the one group to be saved, he answered that it would be the group that is based upon the values and traditions that he and his companions hold dear. *Salafīs* believe that they are the group that follows the example of the Prophet and the Companions and thus will be saved.[167] This elitist belief is coupled with *salafīs*'

al-Tayyār al-Islāmī fī al-Khalīj al-ʿArabī, Dirāsa Taʾrīkhiyya 1945–1991 (Beirut: Muʾassasāt al-Intishār al-ʿArabī, 2010), 133–37. For analyses of the impact of the Islamist presence in the kingdom: Gilles Kepel, *The War for the Muslim Mind: Islam and the West* (Cambridge, MA and London: The Belknap Press of Harvard University Press, 2004), 171–75; David Commins, "Contestation and Authority in Wahhābi Polemics," in Mohammad Ayoob and Hasan Kosebalaban (eds.), *Religion and Politics in Saudi Arabia* (Boulder, CO and London: Lynne Rienner Publishers, 2009), 48; Toby Craig Jones, "Religious Revivalism and its Challenge to the Saudi Regime," in Mohammad Ayoob and Hasan Kosebalaban (eds.), *Religion and Politics in Saudi Arabia* (Boulder, CO and London: Lynne Rienner Publishers, 2009), 111–12.

[164] Abū al-Ḥasan Mālik Ibn Ādam (ed.), *The Crime of Hizbiyyah against the Salafi Daʿwah* (Grand Rapids, MI: Sunnah Publishing, 2009), 46–47.

[165] In a collection of Fatwās on politics by leading salafī jurists, ʿAbd al-Muḥsin b. Ḥamad al-ʿIbād, "Fatwā," in Abū Farīḥān Jamāl b. Farīḥān al-Ḥarīthī (ed.), *al-Fatāwā al-Muhimma fī Tabṣīr al-Umma* (Cairo: Maktabat al-Hady al-Muḥammadī, 2009), 178.

[166] Michael Cook, "On the Origins of Wahhābism," *Journal of the Royal Asiatic Society* 2, 2 (July 1992), 191.

[167] See the words of ʿAbd al-Wahhāb and al-Fawzān's contemporary elaboration on them: Muhammad Ibn ʿAbdul Wahhab, *The Best Religion for Mankind, Explained by Saalih*

demand for total devotion, which draws from another division within the *umma*, one that Ibn Taymiyya emphasized. He declared that the *awliyā'* of Allah are divided into two categories: the forerunners (*sābiqūn muqarribūn*) and the Companions of the Right (*aṣḥāb al-yamīn al-muqtaṣidūn*). The Companions of the Right do what Allah has ordered and refrain from doing what He prohibited, but do not perform the recommended acts of worship and do not refrain from unnecessary permissible actions. The forerunners perform optional acts of worship after having performed the obligations. They draw closer to Allah by doing all that is within their capability. Therefore, they are beloved by Him and will drink directly from the fountain of heaven (*tasnīm*), as opposed to the Companions of the Right who will not.[168] Combined, the "saved sect" and the "forerunners" concepts establish *salafism* as a call for the most devout and able only. One common explanation for the favor *salafiyya* finds among some Muslims is the appeal of its claim for authenticity.[169] This, however, is only a partial explanation considering that, as described above, *wasaṭiyya* (and the apologetic-modernism formerly identified as *salafī*) make a similar claim. What gives *salafiyya* its unique appeal is its association of a myth of authenticity with particularly harsh standards, its encouragement of individuals to judge themselves by their ability to meet those standards, and its promise that those who do will become part of an exclusive, committed group to be redeemed.

Salafīs are aware that they are condemned as reactionaries and fanatics. Their defense against these allegations is simple: Allah has given to humanity through His Prophet a set of perfected, comprehensive, clear, and beneficial rules. Happiness, salvation, strength, honor, and security await those who follow those rules.[170] Whatever is in accordance with

Ibn Fawzaan Ibn 'Abdullah al-Fawzaan (New York: Daarul Isnaad, May 2010), 79–82. Also 'Abdul-'Azīz Ibn Bāz, *The Correct Islamic Aqīdah* (Birmingham: Daar us-Sunnah Publishers, 2008), 43–54; Abū al-Ḥasan Mālik Ibn Ādam (ed.), *The Crime of Hizbiyyah against the Salafi Da'wah*, 4–5, 24–25, 57–60.

[168] Ibn Taymiyya, *The Friends of Allāh & The Friends of Shaytan*, 92–107.

[169] Bernard Haykel, "On the Nature of Salafī Thought and Action," in Roel Meijer (ed.), *Global Salafism: Islam's New Religious Movement* (London: Hurst & Company, 2009), 37.

[170] Ibn Baaz, *The Legislation of Islam*, 18–28.

His laws is moderate; whatever contradicts them is extreme.[171] Ibn Taymiyya depicted his approach to Islam as *wasaṭī*, a middle ground between the deviations of groups that do not follow the ways of the Prophet.[172] While not central to their teachings, *salafīs* also maintain that their version of Islam is *wasaṭī*. Unlike *wasaṭīs*, they hold that *taysīr* is not the essence of Islam's *wasaṭī* nature and argue that to deliberately choose the easier juristic opinion on a controversial issue may lead to infidelity.[173] Instead, they suggest that to be a *wasaṭī* is to adhere strictly to the Prophet's example without exaggeration or negligence.[174] Al-Fawzān emphasized in a clear, albeit indirect, reference to *wasaṭīs* that violating the *sharīʿa* in the name of *wasaṭiyya* is not the essence of *wasaṭiyya* at all. Rather, *wasaṭiyya* is to follow Allah's laws and abide by His book and the Prophetic example without exaggeration but also without negligence.[175] *Salafīs* caution that though there are issues of greater and lesser importance in Islamic law, nothing that Allah and His Prophet commanded should be taken lightly. The *sharīʿa* should be obeyed in all aspects of life, and neglect of any part of the *sharīʿa* is equal to neglect of all of it.[176] For example, the Prophet ordered the believers to let their beards grow and trim their mustaches. Ibn Bāz, in his answer to a query on whether this is a trivial matter, cautioned that there are no trivial matters in Islam because, based on Q. 9: 65–66, "there is the fear that the

[171] Muḥammad b. Ṣāliḥ al-ʿUthaymīn, "Don't be Such a Fanatic!" in Muḥammad Saed Abdul-Rahman (ed.), *Islam: Questions and Answers—Islamic Politics* (London: MSA Publication Limited, 2003), 3.

[172] Takī al-Dīn Aḥmad Ibn Taymiyya, "al-ʿAqīda al-Wasaṭiyya," an Arabic text included in *The Creed of al-Wasaṭiyyah*, trans. Abū Rumaysah (Birmingham: Dār al-Sunnah Publishers, 2009), 139. See also his depiction of Islam's *wasaṭī* way as an alternative to corruption as well as gratuitous rightouesness: Takī al-Dīn Ibn Taymiyya, *al-Siyāsa al-Sharʿiyya fī Iṣlaḥ al-Rāʿi wal-Raʿiyya* (Dār al-Kitāb al-ʿArabī bi-Miṣr, 1969), 58–60.

[173] ʿAbd al-Karīm al-Khuḍayr, "Is it Permissible for a Muslim to Choose the Easiest Scholarly Opinion," in Muḥammad Saed Abdul-Rahman (ed.), *Islam: Questions and Answers—Basis for Jurisprudence and Islamic Rulings* (London: MSA Publication limited, 2007), 93.

[174] Muḥammad b. Ṣāliḥ Ibn al-ʿUthaymīn, "Mā Huwa al-Wasaṭ fī al-Dīn?" in *Fatāwā al-Balad al-Ḥarām* (Cairo: al-Maktaba al-Tawfīqiyya, n.d.), 1051–52.

[175] Ṣāliḥ b. Fawzān al-Fawzān, *al-Wasaṭiyya fī al-Islām* (Riyadh: Dār Kunūz Ishbīlya lil-Nashr wal-Tawzīʿ, 2010), 27, 32.

[176] Ṣāliḥ b. Fawzān b. Abdallāh al-Fawzān, *Wujūb al-Taḥākum ilā mā Anzala Allāh wa-Taḥrīm al-Taḥākum ilā Ghayrihi* (Riyadh: Dār al-ʿāṣima, 1993), 10–11.

person who says such a thing by way of belittling or mocking may be apostatizing from his religion thereby."[177]

The Quran and the Prophetic traditions are considered by *salafīs* to be a body of directives that address all human conditions; the traditions both develop the directives of the Quran and serve as an equally valid independent source. The essence of the *salafī* juristic methodology is that the Quran and the traditions, as they were understood by the *salaf*, should guide Muslims, and that nothing revealed should be rejected by the intellect.[178] This does not mean, however, that *salafī* jurisprudence is a simple process of referencing the appropriate verse or tradition, leaving no room for *ijtihād*, but that the discretion allowed for jurists is narrower, as indicated by the *salafī* approach to *maṣlaḥa*. *Salafī* jurists accept the general premises of *maṣlaḥa*: the idea that the *sharī'a* is intended to safeguard particular objectives, that religious decisions can change in order to facilitate the safeguarding of these objectives, and that jurists should consider the results of decisions under given conditions and accommodate them accordingly.[179] Yet they apply *maṣlaḥa* with far greater restraint than *wasaṭīs*. Ibn Taymiyya never systemized a coherent theory of *maṣlaḥa*. He refuted al-Ghazālī's approach to *maṣlaḥa mursala*, insisting on the need for textual evidence and arguing that if the *maṣlaḥa* of a particular divine directive is not clear to the jurist, then the only possible reason is failure to recognize it.[180] His concern was that the use of *maṣlaḥa mursala* frequently resulted in decisions that contradict Allah's laws and served, for jurists, as a central justification for unlawful innovations.[181]

[177] 'Abd al-'Azīz b. 'Abdallāh Ibn Bāz, "There Are No Trivial Issues in Islam," in Muḥammad Saed Abdul-Rahman (ed.), *Islam: Questions and Answers—Basis for Jurisprudence and Islamic Rulings* (London: MSA Publication limited, 2007), 194–96.

[178] AbdusSalām as-Sihaymī, *To Be a Serious Salafī*, 60; Rabee Bin Haadi al-Madkhali, *The Necessity of Conforming to the Understanding of the Salaf* (Jedda: Miraath Publications, 2012), 24–25; 'Ukāsha 'abd al-Manān al-Ṭībī, *Fatāwā al-Shaykh al-Albānī wa-Muqāranatuhā bi-Fatāwā al-'Ulamā'* (Beirut: Dār al-Jīl, 1995), 135–48.

[179] Without referencing Ibn Taymiyya specifically, Ibn Bāz demonstrates the *fiqh* of balances through the example of a man who will start murdering people if he stops drinking. He argues that in this case it is better to refrain from denying the potential murderer his drink: Ibn Bāz, *The Legislation of Islam*, 52–53.

[180] Opwis, *Maṣlaḥa and the Purpose of the Law: Islamic Discourses and Legal Change from the 4th/10th to 8th/14th Century*, 176–97.

[181] Abdul Hakim I. al-Matroudi, *The Hanbali School of Law and Ibn Taymiyyah* (London and New York: Routledge, 2006), 78–80.

Contemporary *salafī* jurisprudence applies *maṣlaḥa* more broadly, yet still more narrowly and reluctantly than *wasaṭī* jurisprudence. Like Ibn Taymiyya, contemporary *salafī* jurisprudence does not offer a systemized theory of *maṣlaḥa*. Though it accepts in practice unattested *maṣlaḥa* as grounds for suspending otherwise prohibited actions, it does so only in cases of necessity. *Salafī* jurisprudence is more inclined to permit the impermissible based on *maṣlaḥa* involving either strategic state interests or an individual's need to obey state organs, reflecting the influence of the *salafī* theory of political authority.[182] When legitimizing the accommodation of decisions based on changing circumstances, *salafī* jurisprudence emphasizes the responsibility to toughen regulations or penalties in order to hinder deviations, and does not consider making life easier as grounds for accommodation.[183]

[182] An example is b. Bāz's approval of the invitation of American soldiers following Saddam Hussein's occupation of Kuwait on August 2, 1990, which provided religio-juristic legitimization for the House of Saud at a critical historical juncture. Based on Q. 6:119, he argued that necessities permit the otherwise impermissible, including the assistance of an infidel army in defending against a corrupt regime ("Ḥukm al-Tashkīk bi-Sha'n al-Isti'āna bi-Ghayr al-Muslimīn fī Qitāl Ṭāghiyat al-'Irāq," n.d., accessed November 6, 2013: http://www.binbaz.org.sa/mat/254. Also, the discussion in Al-Atawneh, *Wahhābī Islam Facing the Challenges of Modernity*, 43–44). Another example is his approval of signing agreements with the infidel Israeli enemy based on *maṣlaḥa*. Two of his *fatwās* on the matter emphasized that it is for the leader, or *walī al-amr*, to decide what constitutes *maṣlaḥa*: "Mā Taqtaḍīhi al-Maṣlaḥa Ya'mal bihi min al-Ṣulḥ wa-'Adamihi," first published in *al-Muslimūn* 520 (January 21, 1995), accessed November 6, 2013: http://www.binbaz.org.sa/mat/1950; "Jawāz al-Hudna ma'a al-A'dā' Muṭlaqa wa-Mu'aqqita Idhā Ra'ā Walī al-Amr al-Maṣlaḥa fī Dhalika," first published in *al-Muslimūn* 516 (December 24, 1994), n.d., accessed November 6, 2013: http://www.binbaz.org.sa/mat/1943. Another *fatwā* stated that a *maṣlaḥa* or *ḍarūra*—without distinguishing between the terms—legitimizes such agreements: "al-Sulḥ ma'a al-Yahūd aw Ghayrihim min al-Kafara Lā Yalzam minhu Mawaddatahum aw Muwālātahum," first published by *al-Muslimūn* 520 ((January 21, 1995), n.d., accessed November 6, 2013: http://www.binbaz.org.sa/mat/1948. Another example is that while *salafī* jurists in principle prohibit photography, they consider being photographed for the purpose of state-issued identity cards, passports, and other official documents a necessity and thus allow it: al-Lajna al-Dā'ima lil-Buḥūth wal-Iftā', "al-Ṣuwar lil-Ḍarūra," in *Fatāwā al-Balad al-Ḥarām* (Cairo: al-Maktaba al-Tawfīqiyya, n.d.), 707; The Permanent Committee, "The Keeping of Photos of Young Children," in *Islamic Fataawa Regarding the Muslim Child*, trans. Abū Ziyād ibn Maḥmūd Ibn 'Abd al-Ghafūr (London: Invitation to Islam Publishers, 2007), 37; The Standing Committee, "Pictures of any Living Creatures Are Forbidden Except Due to Necessity," in Muhammad bin Abdul-Aziz Al-Musnad (ed.), *Islamic Fatawa Regarding Women* (Riyadh: Darussalam Pubslihers & Distributers, 1996), 336–37.

[183] Ibn 'Uthaymīn argues that *fatwās* do not change with the changing of time, place or population. However, they can be accommodated to promote their purpose and thus jurists can prohibit something that is *ḥalāl* if they find that it leads people to act

The *salafī* approach to cross-*madhhab* search draws on its foundational principle of strictly adhering to the Quran and the Prophetic traditions. Jurists must not accept an opinion simply because it was stated by one of the four *imāms*; rather, they should accept the opinion with the strongest evidence on any given matter.[184] In the words of al-Fawzān: "It is not permissible to blindly follow anyone of them [the four *imāms*]. We only take from them if they bring evidence."[185] This opinion is in accordance with the teachings of Ibn Taymiyya, who prohibited accepting decisions based on *madhhabī* affiliation and ruled that it is impermissible for a ruler to ask *qāḍīs* to decide based on a specific *madhhab*.[186] Today, the *salafī* approach to cross-*madhhab* search is firmly entrenched in the Saudi judicial system. When establishing the *sharī'a* court system in 1927, Ibn Sa'ūd declared that it is "not restricted by any particular *madhhab*; rather, it decides according to what appears to be [applicable] from any of the *madhhab*s, and there is no difference between one and the other." In 1934, Ibn Sa'ūd reemphasized, "we obey neither Ibn 'Abd al-Wahhāb nor any other person, unless what they say is clearly endorsed by Allah's Book and the Prophet's Sunna... [Wherever] we find strong evidence in any of the four *madhhabs*, we refer and hold to it." However, he also added that where strong evidence is lacking, the opinion of the *Ḥanbalī* school should be adopted. Saudi jurists continue this norm today. Their preference for the *Ḥanbalī* school, as interpreted

impermissibly. He provided two examples from the time of the second khalīfa 'Umar: his prohibition of men from returning to their divorcees, having found that men began taking divorces too lightly, and his decision, having found that the phenomenon of drinking intensified, to increase the penalty for drinking to eighty lashes instead of the forty lashes that were the norm during the days of the Prophet and his first successor Abū Bakr: "Ta'thīr al-Zamān 'alā al-Fatāwā," in *Fatāwā al-Balad al-Ḥarām* (Cairo: al-Maktaba al-Tawfīqiyya, n.d.), 937.

[184] 'Abd al-'Azīz b. 'Abdallāh Ibn Bāz, "Mawqif al-Muslim min al-Khilāfat al-Madhhabiyya al-Muntashira," in *Fatāwā al-Balad al-Ḥarām* (Cairo: al-Maktaba al-Tawfīqiyya, n.d.), 941; Al-Lajna al-Dā'ima, "Ikhtilāf al-A'imma," in *Fatāwā al-Balad al-Ḥarām* (Cairo: al-Maktaba al-Tawfīqiyya, n.d.), 943; Ṣāliḥ b. Fawzān al-Fawzān, *al-Ijtihād*, 16–17, n.d., accessed September 10, 2012: http://www.islamcountry.com; 'Abd al-Karīm al-Khuḍayr, "Is it Permissible for a Muslim to Choose the Easiest Scholarly Opinion," in Muḥammad Saed Abdul-Rahman (ed.), *Islam: Questions and Answers—Basis for Jurisprudence and Islamic Rulings*, 93.

[185] Muhammad Ibn 'Abdul Wahhab, *The Best Religion for Mankind*, Explained by Saalih Ibn Fawzaan Ibn 'Abdullah Al-Fawzaan, 72.

[186] Muḥammad Rawās, *Mawsū'at Fiqh Ibn Taymiyya*, vol. 1, 22, 467.

by Ibn Taymiyya and his disciples, is explained by its greater reliance on the Quran and the Prophetic traditions in comparison to other schools. Nevertheless, jurists are advised to study the different methods of argumentation of the four schools and benefit from their principles and guidelines.[187] In one respect, the *salafī* approach to cross-*madhhab* search is similar to the *wasaṭī*: both reject blind imitation and task jurists with basing their decisions on the strongest evidence. In another respect, they radically differ: *wasaṭiyya* calls for a cross-*madhhab* search in order to identify the most pragmatic solution from within a number of sensible options. This concept is completely rejected by *salafī* jurisprudence, which is only concerned with the strength of the evidence.

Salafīs enact their harshest decisions when addressing the status of women. Based on a literalist interpretation of verses and traditions, they emphasize the physical, mental, and intellectual inferiority of a woman in comparison to a man; a woman's duty to obey her husband or her guardians; and the need for her complete separation from the company of men in order to avoid *fitna* (temptation). *Salafī* writings are riddled with contempt for women based on a strong conviction that Allah created them inferior to men. Ibn ʿUthaymīn considered apologetics about Islam as a religion of equality to be a lie; Islam, he argued, believes in justice, not equality, and justice is based on treating equally those who are equal and differentiating between those who are different. Women are different than men, who are stronger, tougher, and have a better capacity for understanding matters. Therefore different laws are applied to them. For example, the testimony of one man is equivalent to the testimonies of two women because, while there are some women who are wiser than a man, "such women are not in the majority" and Islamic law is based on what is most common. Women's "reason is often overtaken by their emotions, and this happens to women more often than it happens to man."[188] Ibn Bāz demonstrated a similar lack of confidence in women's

[187] Al-Atawneh, *Wahhābī Islam Facing the Challenges of Modernity*, 70–77.

[188] Quoted by Muḥammad Ṣāliḥ al-Munajjid in his response to the query, "Does Islam Regard Men and Women as Equal?" in Muḥammad Saed Abdul-Rahman (ed.), *Islam: Questions and Answers—Basis for Jurisprudence and Islamic Rulings* (London: MSA Publication Ltd, 2007), 57–67.

abilities in his prohibition on women serving as heads of state (which *wasaṭī* jurists legitimize). He based this opinion on the Prophet's words, "No people will ever prosper who appoint a woman in charge of them," which *wasaṭīs* contextualize narrowly. He added that "rationally speaking, women should not be given positions of public office, because what is required of one who is chosen for such a position is that he should [be] a man of great resolve, determination, smartness, will power and good management skills. These characteristics are lacking in women because they have been created with weakness in their intellect and thinking."[189]

Salafīs describe the sexual desires of men as being so strong that any glimpse of a woman's body risks leading to the gravest of sins: adultery and fornication. Thus, it is the duty of women to seclude themselves from the presence of men outside their family circle and, in those cases that necessitate their presence in the public sphere, to totally cover themselves. This fear of fornication provided the rationale for decisions which established patterns that became signatures of Saudi society and of *salafī* communities elsewhere. *Salafīs* argue (as did Ibn Taymiyya)[190] that women must wear a veil, *niqāb*, covering their entire face and not just the hair, not only because adherence to the Prophetic traditions calls on women to do so, but also because the face is where a woman's beauty concentrates and is the main source of temptation. To even ridicule this opinion is, they believe, tantamount to an act of infidelity.[191] The *salafī* objection to the participation of women in the job market is also based on the fear that men would be tempted. Al-Fawzān, for example, suggested that efforts to "remove" women from their homes, where they belong, and place them into professions that serve men, such as nursing or teaching in mixed classrooms, are led by "Muslims who have sickness in their hearts" and "wish to transform the woman into a cheap commodity in the

[189] As quoted in "Is it Permissible in Islamic Sharee'ah for a Women to Be a Ruler?" in Muhammad Saed Abdul-Rahman (ed.), *Islam: Questions and Answers—Islamic Politics* (London: MSA Publication Ltd, 2003), 12–18.

[190] Rawās, *Mawsū'at Fiqh Ibn Taymiyya*, vol. 1, 582.

[191] Al-Lajna al-Dā'ima, "Ruling on Making Fun of the Hijab," in Muhammad Saed Abdul-Rahman (ed.), *Islam: Questions and Answers—Polytheism (Shirq) and its Different Forms* (London: MSA Publication Ltd, 2003), 75–76. The "correct *hijab*" is defined in the *fatwā* as one that covers the face and hands.

marketplace of the desirous and satanic temptations." He ruled that women should only join the job market if no man can do their job, if working remains secondary to their primary duties at home, and if they are segregated from men.[192] The *salafī* objection to women driving is motivated by the concern that driving would make wives too independent of their husbands, as well as overcrowd the streets and deprive young men, "who are more deserving," the opportunity to drive their cars. Moreover, *salafīs* object to women driving out of a fear that driving would encourage or force women to unveil themselves in public (for example, when stopping at gas stations or at police checkpoints).[193] The *salafī* objection to the participation of women in physical activities outside the home, even when segregated from men, also raises the fear of promiscuity. Ibn 'Uthaymīn advised against allowing wives to attend swimming pools and fitness gyms, invoking Q. 33:33 and the Prophet's urging that women should stay in their homes. He wrote:

> If a woman gets used to that [viz., going to sports clubs] she will form a strong attachment to it because her emotions are so strong. Then it will distract her from her religious and worldly duties, and it will become all that she thinks and talks about. If a woman does something like this [viz., practicing sports], it will be a means of taking away her modesty, and if a woman's modesty is taken away from her, do not even ask about the evil consequences that may follow.[194]

Salafīs apply similarly rigid logic when considering the issue of leisure. Their decisions profess aversion for and distrust of many forms of amusement that *wasaṭīs* conditionally legitimize. This position is based on the conviction that most forms of entertainment are vanities that involve deviation from religious norms, as well as from the insistence

[192] Al-Fauzan, *Rulings Pertaining to Muslim Women*, 15–17.

[193] "Qiyādat al-Mar'a lil-Sayyāra"—*fatwās* on women driving by 'Abd al-'Azīz b. 'Abdallāh b. Bāz, Ṣāliḥ Fawzān and the Permanent Committee, in *Fatāwā al-Mar'a al-Muslima* (Cairo: Dār Ibn Ḥazm, 2007), 528–30; Islam Question and Answer, "Does The Ruling on Driving a Car Vary from One Country to Another?" analysis of opinions by Ibn Bāz and Muḥammad b. Ṣāliḥ al-'Uthaymīn, in Muhammad Saed Abdul-Rahman (ed.), *Islam: Questions and Answers—Basis for Jurisprudence and Islamic Rulings* (London: MSA Publication Ltd, 2007), 3–13.

[194] Muḥammad b. Ṣāliḥ al-'Uthaymīn , "Ruling on Women Going to Women's Clubs," n.d., accessed September 10, 2012: http://www.islam-qa.com/en/ref/9460.

that the truly devout must dedicate each and every moment of their lives for the sake of Allah. Music is one example: while permitted by *wasaṭīs*, it is strongly prohibited by *salafīs*, who draw from Ibn Taymiyya's depiction of it as strengthening satanic states.[195] *Salafīs* hold that decisions that legitimize music deviate from the ways of the *salaf*, and those who promote them have no knowledge of Islam.[196] The prohibition on music is strict. For example, b. Bāz ruled that it is only permissible to listen to radio programs that contain music if one turns down the volume when music is played.[197] There are no exceptions: music is forbidden for children as it is for adults, and patriotic and religious songs accompanied by music are equally prohibited.[198] Restrictions on playing sports are another example of the *salafī* approach to leisure. While *wasaṭīs* accept Muslims' having fun for the sake of having fun, *salafīs* encourage physical exercise as a means to enhance one's health and readiness for *jihād* and emphasize that in Islam, sports are never a goal in and of themselves.[199] Playing sports for the purpose of winning a trophy is legitimate only if is serves the fight against the infidels, and thus professional football (soccer), for example, is impermissible.[200] Cheering for teams and following professional competitions is also impermissible. When asked about subscribing to sports channels by a man who said he does not want to be "one of those who frequent cafés," the editors of the Saudi-based *salafī* website Islam Question and Answer—operated by Ṣāliḥ al-Munajjid (b. 1960), a devotee to the legacy of b. Bāz and 'Uthaymīn—wondered

[195] Shaykhul-Islam Ibn Taymiyyah, *The Friends of Allāh and the Friends of Shaytan*, 341.

[196] Al-Lajna al-Dā'ima, "al-Ishtighāl bil-Mūsīqā wal-'Ilāj bihā," in Aḥmad b. 'Abdallāh al-Shafi'ī (ed.), *500 Jawāb fī al-Buyū' wal-Mu'āmalāt* (Cairo: Dār Ibn Ḥazm, 2010), 277.

[197] 'Abd al-'Azīz b. 'Abdallāh Ibn Bāz, "Ruling Concerning Listening to Radio Programs that Contain Music," in Muhammad bin Abdul-Aziz Al-Musnad (ed.), *Islamic Fatawa Regarding Women* (Riyadh: Darussalam Publishers & Distributers, 1996), 324.

[198] The Permanent Council, "The Ruling on Children's Songs," in *Islamic Fataawa Regarding the Muslim Child*, 220–21. On the impermissibility of music, see also: Muḥammad Ṣāliḥ al-Munajjid, *Muḥarramāt Istahāna bihā Kathīr min al-Nās Yajibu al-Ḥadhar Minhā* (al-Madina: al-Maktab al-Ta'āwunī lil-Da'wa wal-Irshād bil-Madīna al-Munawwara, 1994), 67–70.

[199] Islam Question and Answer, "Bodybuilding," n.d., accessed November 10, 2013: http://islamqa.info/en/ref/40527.

[200] Al-Lajna al-Dā'ima, "Ḥukm Lu'bat Kurat al-Qadam wa-Musābaqāt al-Mulākama wal-Muṣāra'a al-Mawjūda al-Āna," in Aḥmad b. 'Abdallāh al-Shafi'ī (ed.), *500 jawāb fī al-Buyū' wal-Mu'āmalāt* (Cairo: Dār Ibn Ḥazm, 2010), 222.

why the idea of not watching the matches at all did not occur to the inquirer. They expressed sadness that the "young men of the *umma* are distracted by watching sports matches, following sports teams, and venerating the people of leisure and idleness, which only makes the *umma* more backward in all fields." They continued: "What is the benefit in watching these games for years on end? Enjoyment, learning to play well, killing time, hanging out with one's friends, then what? Are these aims that a wise Muslim should be striving to attain?... We advise you to fear Allah and to remain steadfast in obedience to Him, and beware of disobeying Him."[201]

The *salafī* theory of politics rests on two foundations. One is the rejection of democracy as an infidel, man-made system. This view corresponds with the general *salafī* antagonism to Western concepts and, specifically, with the political interests of the House of Sa'ūd to quell external and internal calls for political liberalization. *Salafīs* utterly deny any compatibility between democracy and Islam or that the former is rooted in the latter. They believe democracy constitutes a form of *shirk*, and that its essence denies the sovereignty of the Creator and His absolute right to issue laws. Therefore, in their view parliaments are unlawful. This view is supported by some Saudi-based Islamists who caution that *wasaṭīs*, who consider themselves to be the first line of defense against the Westernization of Muslim societies, have unintentionally become instrumental in that process. As opposed to the implication of Wiktorowicz's analysis, the mainstream *salafī* prohibition on being elected to parliaments that govern by laws other than Allah's is not categorical; it is lawful to run for office and to vote, if the purpose is to change the system into one that abides exclusively by Allah's laws.[202]

Another foundation of *salafī* political theory is the duty to obey the political leader, or *walī al-amr*, and avoid oppositionist or subversive

[201] Islam Question and Answer, "Ruling on Subscribing to Sports Channels," n.d., accessed November 6, 2013: http://islamqa.info/en/ref/82718.

[202] Islam Question and Answer, "Ruling on Democracy and Elections and Participation in that System" (based on *fatwās* by al-'Uthaymīn and the Saudi Permanent Committee for Academic Studies and Issuing Fatwās), n.d., accessed November 6, 2013: http://islamqa.info/en/ref/107166; Uriya Shavit, "Is Shura a Muslim Form of Democracy?" *Middle Eastern Studies*, 46, 3 (2010), 358–60, 366–68.

actions in almost all circumstances. This foundation rests on three historical legacies. One is the *ḥanbalī*, particularly Ibn Taymiyya's, concept of authority. Ibn Taymiyya believed that to rule a people is one of the most important religious duties, without which religion cannot exist.[203] The ruler, tasked with maintaining law and order and enabling the believers to perform their duties towards Allah, was to be entrusted with absolute powers, regardless of his character, the title he assumes, or how he came to power.[204] A second legacy is the eighteenth century alliance of b. 'Abd al-Wahhāb with Muḥammad b. Sa'ūd, which created a system in which political decisions were monopolized by the Sa'ūds and legitimized by religious scholars. Yet another legacy is the breakdown of the first and second Saudi Kingdoms during the nineteenth century, which demonstrated the great danger of internal strife. The latter legacy was reinforced by the trauma of the very short-lived support granted by b. Bāz to the religious movement opposed to the Saudi invitation of American military forces, which gathered momentum during 1991 and called to transfer the monopoly on strategic decisions from the House of Sa'ūd to a council of religious scholars. The Saudi religious establishment retracted its support for the dissenters within two months and has been unequivocal ever since in publicizing its resentment of religious scholars' and the general public's involvement in politics. That includes describing demonstrations, petitions, strikes, open criticism, and meddling in strategic affairs as impermissible, and stressing that so long as a regime acknowledges Allah's laws as binding, it is a legitimate regime (even if a sinning one) and rebelling against it is impermissible.[205] *Salafī* political thought

[203] Ibn Taymiyya, *al-Siyāsa al-Shar'iyya fī Iṣlāḥ al-Rā'ī wal-Ra'iyya*, 161.

[204] Askar H. al-Enazy, *The Creation of Saudi Arabia* (London and New York: Routledge, 2010), 14–19; Muḥammad Rawās, *Mawsū'at Fiqh Ibn Taymiyya*, vol. 1, 285–300.

[205] Abū Farīḥān Jamāl b. Farīḥān al-Ḥarīthī (ed.), *al-Fatāwā al-Muhimma fī Tabṣīr al-Umma*, 15–40, 97, 102, 106 (*fatwās* by Ibn B. al-'Uthaymīn, Fawzān and other leading salafī jurists); *The Crime of Hizbiyyah against the Salafi Da'wah*, 54; Muḥammad b. Ṣaliḥ Ibn 'Uthaymīn, "Ḥukm Tā'at al-Ḥākim alladhī Lā Yaḥkumu bi-kitāb Allāh wa-Sunnat Rasūlihi," in *Fatāwā al-Balad al-Ḥarām* (Cairo: al-Maktaba al-Tawfīqiyya, n.d.), 172–73; 'Abdallāh al-Ghunaymān, "The Kufr of Those Who Rule by Man-made Laws," in Muḥammad Saed Abdul-Rahman (ed.), *Islam: Questions and Answers—Polytheism and its Different Forms* (London: MSA Publication Ltd, 2003), 131. A *fatwā* by Muḥammad b. Ṣaliḥ al-'Uthaymīn quoted in Muḥammad b. Ḥusayn al-Qaḥṭānī (ed.), *Masā'il al-A'imā' fī Nawāzil al-Mudlahimma* (Riyadh: Dār al-Awkhiyyā' lil-Ṭibā'a wal-Nashr, 2003), 175–76; AbdusSalām

stresses that obedience to the leader is a foundation of the *salafī* creed, noting that religion can only exist if a community exists, a community can only exist if leadership exists, and leadership can only exist if it is obeyed.[206]

According to *salafī* political theory, even in cases where the ruler is identified as commiting acts of infidelity, it is not self-evident that Muslims should rebel against him. In such cases, Ibn Bāz argued for applying *fiqh al-muwāzanāt*, stating, "[it is] not permitted to remove an evil by means of greater evil"; rebelling against a ruler is only permissible if the rebels "can bring in a good and righteous leader without that leading to a greater trouble for the Muslims or a greater evil than the evil of this ruler."[207] The latter statement was intended to delegitimize *jihādi-salafī* theorizing.

as-Sihaymī, *To Be a Serious Salafī*, 84; "The Punishment against One Who Rebels against a Muslim Ruler," in Alee bin Yahyah al-Haddaadee (ed.), *The Book of Forty Hadeeth Regarding the Madhab of the Salaf* (Birmingham: Minhaj al-Sunnah Publications, 2005), 32. According to the *hadith* quoted, narrated by the Companion 'Arfaja b. Harthama al-Bāriqī, the Prophet said: "Whoever comes to you while you are united under a single Ruler, wishing to split and divide your united body, then slay him." For analysis of *salafi* concepts of political conformity: 'Abd al-Ḥākim Abū al-Lawz, "al-Salafiyya al-Taqlīdiyya wal-Salafiyya al-Jihādiyya," *Majallat al-Dīmqrāṭiyya*, no. 38, April 2010, 40–41.

[206] Fahd b. Mubārak Muḥammad al-Dusārī, *al-Ghuluww fī al-Dīn wa-Wasaṭiyyat al-Islām* (Riyadh: Madār al-Waṭan lil-Nashr, 2005), 106–7.

[207] 'Abd al-'Azīz b. 'Abdallāh Ibn Bāz, "Is it Permissible to Rebel against the Ruler," in Muḥammad Saed Abdul-Rahman (ed.), *Islam: Questions and Answers—Islamic Politics* (London: MSA Publication Limited, 2003), 89–90.

2

The *Wasaṭī* and *Salafī* Approaches to the Religious Law of Muslim Minorities

INTRODUCTION

According to Yūsuf al-Qaraḍāwī, *fiqh al-aqalliyyāt al-Muslima* is the field in Islamic jurisprudence that deals with issues pertaining to Muslim minorities. He states that it is essential that this field be developed because massive waves of migration have created challenges unfamiliar to jurists in the past. As a particular category of *fiqh*, it can be compared to the jurisprudence of medicine (*al-fiqh al-ṭibbī*), the jurisprudence of economics (*al-fiqh al-iqtiṣādī*), and the jurisprudence of politics (*al-fiqh al-siyāsī*), all areas in which recent innovations and complications present new challenges that jurists must address.[1] Al-Qaraḍāwī's definition, which this study applies, suggests that *fiqh al-aqalliyyāt al-Muslima* is not necessarily identical to his systematic efforts in the field, but can instead define any comprehensive treatment of juristic issues faced by Muslim minorities.

In recent decades, particularly since the 1990s, *wasaṭīs* and *salafīs* based in both the Arab world and the West developed, individually and as part of juristic panels, approaches to *fiqh al-aqalliyyāt al-Muslima* that drew from their competing ideologies and methodologies. *Wasaṭī* jurisprudence on Muslim minorities made use of theoretical developments in the general *wasaṭī* discourse to produce a number of groundbreaking, audacious decisions, which *salafīs* vehemently rejected, resulting in the creation of

[1] Yūsuf al-Qaraḍāwī, *Fī Fiqh al-Aqalliyyāt al-Muslima* (Cairo: Dār al-Shurūq, 2007, first published 2001), 32.

two corpuses of religious laws that differ in the general visions they delineate and on several specific and important practical issues.

As will be demonstrated in this chapter and the ones that follow, the respective evolutions of these corpuses were, in part, dialectic: foundational *wasaṭī* codifications on the desirability of Muslim presence in the West and the nature of relations with non-Muslim majorities are, to some extent, responses to *salafī* texts on "loyalty and disavowal," while some *salafī fatwās* that reject facilitations (concessions) for Muslim minorities constitute refutations of previous *wasaṭī fatwās* that contradicted *salafī* rulings. Where dialectics surface they are mostly devoid of direct or personal criticisms, as are *wasaṭī-salafī* controversies at large. One possible reason is the desire to avoid the impression of defaming other Muslims. Another is the converse desire to avoid giving publicity and dignifying opponents by directly addressing their opinions. While the evolution of the *wasaṭī* and *salafī* approaches to *fiqh al-aqalliyyāt al-Muslima* cannot be understood apart from their conflicting agendas, other actors are also important. For example, *wasaṭī* theories on "integration" read as efforts to provide acceptable alternatives to demands made by Western governments and mainstream Western media, while strong condemnations of terror activities by *salafīs* read primarily as a direct attack on *jihādi-salafī* groups and an attempt to distance *salafiyya* from these groups.

Wasaṭīs, applying their general understanding of *taysīr* as an essence of Islam and of *tabshīr* as an important objective that is tied to *taysīr*, stress that Muslim minorities are entitled to special juristic facilitations and encourage Muslims to reside in the West because of their potential to spread Islam while residing there. To promote these objectives they engage in cross-*madhhab* search, broadly apply *maṣlaḥa*, including elevating proselytizing to a *maṣlaḥa* that justifies their accommodating religious rulings, and introduce a narrow contextualization of the principle of "loyalty and disavowal." Their approach, institutionalized in the form of the European Council for Fatwa and Research, emphasizes the importance of promoting good relations with non-Muslims and being law-abiding and constructive participants in Western societies while protecting and enhancing Islamic identity. *Salafīs*, in contrast, consider residence in non-Muslim lands to be at best tolerable and justifiable almost exclusively as a means for proselytization. They stress the universality of Islamic laws and thus reject, in principle though not always in practice, the accommodation of decisions to the unique conditions of Muslim minorities or the issuance of concessions as a means to enhance proselytization. Their decisions reject the *wasaṭī* approach to *maṣlaḥa* and emphasize the impermissibility of friendly relations with non-Muslims based on a broad understanding of "loyalty and disavowal." Nevertheless, they demand that Muslim minorities abide by the laws of the infidel states in which they reside.

This chapter examines the evolution, institutionalization, and popularization of the *wasaṭī* and *salafī* approaches to *fiqh al-aqalliyyāt al-Muslima*, and comparatively analyzes their historical background, ideological objectives, and juristic methodologies.

A STRUGGLE FOR HEGEMONY

The religious law of Muslim minorities is a discourse involving jurists and juristic panels who champion specific approaches as to how Allah's laws should be interpreted and implemented in non-Muslim lands. Participants have no official status; while formal actors (governments, local governments, state judiciaries) may occasionally consult with them or consider their opinions, their authority is only moral. The challenges *wasaṭī* and *salafī* jurists and panels confront in their quest to dominate the discourse—that is, to delineate boundaries of religio-juristic legitimacy and illegitimacy in accordance with their respective ideologies—is formidable. First, they are forced to recognize the coercive powers of state actors and the limitations these powers place on their efforts while concurrently considering popular discourses in which the future of Islam in the West is debated, often in critical terms. Second, each campaigns for its interpretation of the *sharī'a* to predominate over other public actors, including against the other.

Common critiques of *fiqh al-aqalliyyāt al-Muslima* argue that as an intellectual construct it is external to the experiences of Muslim minorities, establishes center–periphery relations, and asserts the hegemony of Arab jurists over Western Muslims. These criticisms are not baseless, considering that a Qatar-based jurist dominates *wasaṭī* jurisprudence on Muslim minorities and Saudi-based jurists dominate the *salafī*. Tariq Ramadan argued that because *wasaṭī fiqh al-aqalliyyāt al-Muslima* is an external project it must constitute a transitional phase only. Moreover, according to Ramadan, Muslim minorities must, with time, develop independently and "think for themselves, develop theses appropriate for their situation, and put forward new and concrete ideas. They must refuse to remain dependent either on the intellectual level or, more damagingly, on the political and financial levels."[2]

But the reality of the evolution of *fiqh al-aqalliyyāt al-Muslima*, particularly in its *wasaṭī* form, is more complicated than Ramadan allows. It was constructed *by* Muslims in the West no less than it was constructed *for* them. Masud, Messick, and Powers observed that in Islamic law, the *mustaftī*, or the person who presents a query, largely determines the field of response by the formulation of the question.[3] The case of *fiqh al-aqalliyyāt al-Muslima* proves this observation correct in a number of ways that will be elaborated in this chapter and the following ones. The initial interest of jurists based in the Arab world in different aspects of life in non-Muslim lands developed in direct response to queries presented by individuals and communities in the West. Most Muslims who migrated to the West were not motivated by religious ambitions, and it is unlikely that lack of juristic legitimization would have terminated their stay. The legitimization offered by jurists for their continued stay, which serves as the basis for both *wasaṭī* and *salafī fiqh al-aqalliyyāt al-Muslima*, was thus a retroactive rationalization of a reality which jurists realized they could not reverse. The quantity of queries by individual Muslim *mustaftīs* on specific issues, the levels of distress conveyed in them, and the *maṣlaḥas* they pointed to, focused jurists' efforts and established the

[2] Tariq Ramadan, *Western Muslims and the Future of Islam* (Oxford and New York: Oxford University Press, 2004), 6.

[3] Muhammad Khalid Masud, Brinkley Messick, and David S. Powers, "Muftis, Fatwas and Islamic Legal Interpretation," in Muhammad Khalid Masud, Brinkley Messick, and David S. Powers (eds.), *Islamic Legal Interpretation: Muftis and their Fatwas* (Cambridge, MA: Harvard University Press, 1996), 20–22.

main polemics of the discourse. *Mustaftīs* often masked their queries in concern for the welfare of the Muslim nation or Muslim communities in order to encourage the application of *maṣlaḥa*, but their requests originated, quite naturally, in experiences of personal hardships.

Moreover, in both the *wasaṭī* and the *salafī* cases, the dissemination of decisions required the voluntary will and cooperation of activists living in the West. As will be demonstrated in this chapter and the next, imāms and activists who affiliate with a certain approach make a point of emphasizing their lack of commitment to any panel or jurist, and some decisions are adjusted to the pressures of reality on local levels, even when the authority of jurists based in the Arab world who issued them is not directly challenged. In both approaches (but far more profoundly so in the *wasaṭī*) jurists based in the West played a leading role in the composition and approval of theological theses and juristic decisions pertaining to their situation as a minority. And because *fiqh al-aqalliyyāt al-Muslima* became a "testing-ground" for audacious *wasaṭī* decisions that were rooted in the general *wasaṭī* theory of jurisprudence, it reflected also on the larger *wasaṭī* project and on the *wasaṭī–salafī* polemic, and thus on the status and prestige of the jurists involved in its formulation in the Arab world.

The *wasaṭī* and *salafī* approaches to *fiqh al-aqalliyyāt al-Muslima* constitute objectives and methodologies that draw respectively from each's general approach to *fiqh*. These approaches have guided specific decisions issued by juristic panels and individual jurists that have accumulated over time, yielding rich corpuses of *fatwās* on life in the West. Religious activists, cultural centers, and media organs that identify with these respective approaches constantly popularize these corpuses.

As noted by Fishman, al-Qaraḍāwī and Ṭaha Jābir al-'Alwānī are the founders of what this study terms *wasaṭī fiqh al-aqalliyyāt al-Muslima.*[4] Al-'Alwānī (b. 1935 in Iraq) received his PhD in Islamic jurisprudence from al-Azhar in 1973 and, from 1974, taught at Imām Muḥammad b. Sa'ūd University in Riyadh. In 1984, he resigned and moved to the United

[4] Shammai Fishman, *Fiqh al-Aqalliyyāt: A Legal Theory for Muslim Minorities* (Washington: Hudson Institute, 2006), 2.

States. Two years later, while in the United States, he established and headed the Fiqh Council of North America, a panel affiliated with the Islamic Society of North America that originated from the Islamist-oriented Muslim Student Association of North America. Al-ʻAlwānī testified that he began work on constructing a doctrine for Muslim minorities in the mid-1970s after he visited the United States and met with American Muslims. His efforts to convince prestigious jurists to join him failed and so, in the early 1990s, he began to issue independent religious edicts that dealt with the challenges faced by Muslims in the United States based on his understanding of what the foundations of *fiqh al-aqalliyyāt* should be.[5] Al-Qaraḍāwī's journey to recognizing the need for a specific doctrine for minorities was even longer. His first major work on Islamic law, *al-Ḥalāl wal-Ḥarām fī al-Islām*, published in 1960, was written at the request of Muḥammad al-Bahī, a Muslim Brother who served as the director of al-Azhar's Institute of Islamic Culture. Though it became a textbook and a bestseller in the Arab world, its aim was to bring Muslims in the West back into the fold of Islamic practices in harmony with al-Qaraḍāwī's *wasaṭī* views.[6] The book dealt with dozens of everyday issues faced by Muslims, but the idea that the challenges faced by Muslim minorities require the formulation of a special approach was absent from the work. Al-Qaraḍāwī only concluded that a special approach was needed in the late 1990s, following three decades of visiting communities of Muslim minorities in the West and gaining first-hand knowledge of their unique situation.[7]

A number of milestones signified the emergence of a *wasaṭī* approach to the jurisprudence of Muslim minorities. One is al-ʻAlwānī's *fatwā* obligating Muslims to participate in American politics. According to Masud, it was the first time the term *fiqh al-aqalliyyāt* was used to signify

[5] Ṭaha Jābir al-ʻAlwānī, "Madkhal ilā Fiqh al-Aqalliyyāt," *al-Majalla al-ʻIlmiyya lil-Majlis al-ʻŪrūbbī lil-Iftā' wal-Buḥūth*, no. 4–5 (June 2004), 39–40.

[6] Yūsuf al-Qaraḍāwī, *al-Ḥalāl wal-Ḥarām fī al-Islām* (Cairo: Matkabat Wahaba, 2004, first published 1960), 9–11.

[7] Al-Qaraḍāwī, *Fī Fiqh al-Aqalliyyāt al-Muslima*, 24–30; Alexandre Caeiro and Mahmoud al-Saify, "Qaradawi in Europe, Europe in Qaradawi? The Global Mufti's European Politics," in Bettina Gräf and Jakob Skovgaard-Petersen (eds.), *The Global Mufti: The Phenomenon of Yūsuf al-Qaraḍāwī* (London: Hurst & Company, 2009), 112.

Muslim minorities' jurisprudence[8] (but not *fiqh al-aqalliyyāt al-Muslima*, which would only later come to distinguish this field of jurisprudence from the jurisprudence of non-Muslim minorities in Muslim countries). The *fatwā* was largely an apologia against those who call upon Muslims to migrate to Muslim countries or demand that Muslim minorities refrain from contributing to infidel societies. Masud dates its origin to 1994. It only gained attention, however, after it was introduced before the fourth session of the European Council for Fatwa and Research, held October 27–31, 1999, in Dublin, and subsequently published in *al-Sharq al-Awsaṭ*, introducing al-ʻAlwānī's ideas to a wider audience beyond his immediate American circles.[9] At that fourth session, the European Council conditionally legitimized mortgages for Muslims in Europe. The dramatic decision, discussed in depth in Chapter 3, masterfully demonstrated the main *wasaṭī* objectives for Muslim minorities and applied a new and broad approach to the mechanism of safeguarding *maṣlaḥas*. It echoed across mosques in Europe and the Arab world. In 2001, at a time when a body of *fatwās* issued by the European Council and representing the foundations of his approach already existed, al-Qaraḍāwī published a book commissioned by the Saudi-based Muslim World League, *Fī Fiqh al-Aqalliyyāt al-Muslima*, or *On the Religious Law of Muslim Minorities*—a systematic presentation of his approach to Muslim minorities' jurisprudence.[10] A year earlier, in 2000, al-ʻAlwānī published a short book on his doctrine for *fiqh al-aqalliyyāt al-Muslima* in a *wasaṭī*-oriented series on "Islamic enlightenment";[11] an English-language version of the book, including a reference to false representations of Islam in post 9/11 America, was published in 2003.[12] In 2004, the European Council's journal published an extended revised version of these works. This

[8] Muhammad Khalid Masud, "Islamic Law and Muslim Minorities," *ISIM Newsletter* 11 (2002), 17.

[9] Imām Muḥammad Imām, "al-Ḥukm al-Sharʻī fī Mushārakat al-Muslimīn fī al-Ḥayāt al-Siyāsiyya al-Amrīkiyya," *al-Sharq al-Awsaṭ* (November 13, 1999), 26.

[10] The approach was presented in al-Qaraḍāwī, *Fī Fiqh al-Aqalliyyāt al-Muslima*, 5–60. The rest of the book comprises discussion of *fatwās* that demonstrate the approach.

[11] Ṭaha Jābir al-ʻAlwānī, *Fī Fiqh al-Aqalliyyāt al-Muslima* (6th October City: Nahḍat Miṣr lil-Ṭibāʻa wal-Nashr wal-Tawzīʻ, June 2000).

[12] Taha Jabir al-Alwani, *Towards a Fiqh for Minorities*, trans. Ashur A. Shamis (London and Washington: The International Institute of Islamic Thought, 2003).

version presented a more expansive list of foundations for *fiqh al-aqalliyyāt al-Muslima*, as well as a positive assessment of the American attitude towards Muslims in the aftermath of 9/11.[13]

The exact influence al-ʿAlwānī and al-Qaraḍāwī had on the evolution of the other's approach to Muslim minorities' jurisprudence is hard to establish. While they each almost simultaneously formulated doctrines that presented essentially similar foundations and encouraged similar results in issuing decisions, their works did not acknowledge the other's contributions to the field. Al-ʿAlwānī did not join al-Qaraḍāwī's European Council but served on the advisory board of its journal. While al-ʿAlwānī preceded al-Qaraḍāwī in identifying the need for a specific jurisprudence for Muslim minorities and publishing a systemized version of his approach, he recognized the latter's seniority as a juristic authority, as al-ʿAlwānī indicated in 2001 when he approached al-Qaraḍāwī while he was struggling with the permissibility of service in a non-Muslim military fighting in Afghanistan (discussed in Chapter 4).

Since its establishment in March 29–30, 1997 on the initiative of an umbrella-organization, the Federation of Islamic Organizations in Europe, The European Council for Fatwa and Research (*al-Majlis al-'Ūrūbbī lil-Iftā' wal-Buḥūth*, ECFR) has served as the institutional hub for studies and *fatwās* that reflect *wasaṭī fiqh al-aqalliyyāt al-Muslima*. Its efforts were complemented, and in some areas independently preceded, by those of the Fiqh Council of North America, which reaches out to a far smaller Muslim population and lacks the prestige granted to its European counterpart by al-Qaraḍāwī's leadership. The European Council never declared adherence to *wasaṭī* views a condition for membership, and some publications it disseminated were critical of various aspects of al-Qaraḍāwī's agenda, including the broad utilization of *maṣlaḥa*. However, the majority of its theoretical output echoed, defended, and expanded the main points presented by al-Qaraḍāwī and al-ʿAlwānī in their foundational works, and the *fatwās* it issued have been consistently in line with their theory of Muslim minorities' jurisprudence. The Council was initiated in London but transferred its operations to the Islamic Cultural

[13] Ṭaha Jābir Al-ʿAlwānī, "Madkhal ilā Fiqh al-Aqalliyyāt," 17–92.

Centre (and mosque) of Dublin after the nomination of the Dublin-based Ḥusayn Ḥalāwa as its secretary general. It does not employ any paid staff and does not operate an archive, but it does publish a biannual journal in Arabic, *al-Majalla al-ʿIlmiyya*. Lifelong membership is contingent on the recommendation of a Council member and approval by the other members. Convening every year in June (until 2008 it convened twice every year), it discusses the most challenging queries that arrive at its offices or at the offices of the committees for *fatwā* issuance in France, Germany, and England, as well as queries directed from governmental bodies. The head subcommittee for the issuance of *fatwās* initially deliberates all queries, and some deliberations are based on studies commissioned by the Council. Its structure both establishes and challenges center–periphery relations. The Qatar-based al-Qaraḍāwī has served as its president from its inception, and a Lebanese Islamist, Fayṣal al-Mawlawī (b. 1941), was nominated as its vice president, a position he held until his death in 2011. Al-Mawlawī was succeeded by two jurists: the England-based ʿAbdallāh b. Yūsuf al-Judayʿ and the Kurdish-Iraqi Qatar-based Muḥyī al-Dīn al-Qara Dāghī (b. 1949). An absolute majority authorizes juristic rulings, and al-Qaraḍāwī does not possess the right to veto a decision. When it was established, two-thirds of the Council's members were based in Europe.[14] This proportion of representation is based on a cornerstone of the *wasaṭī* approach: a jurist must be intimately acquainted with the situations on which he decides. It also corresponds with the conception of the Council by the Federation of Islamic Organizations as a temporary solution until a generation of European-based jurists well acquainted with the European reality emerges.[15] Thus, the

[14] The information in this paragraph comes from the author's visit to the Council's offices in February 2012, and from its constitution (*al-Niẓām al-Asāsī*) as retrieved from its website: http://www.e-cfr.org/ar/index.php?cat_id=006. It is also based on a summary of its constitution, Ḥusayn Ḥalāwa, "About the European Council for Fatwa and Research," in *Fatwās of European Council for Fatwa and Research,* trans. Anas Usāma al-Tikritī and Shākir Nāṣif al-ʿUbaydī (Cairo: Islamic INC, 2002), 1–7. For the Arabic version: Ḥusayn Ḥalāwa, "Taʿrīf al-Majlis al-'Ūrūbbī lil-Iftā' wal-Buḥūth," in *Qarārāt wa-Fatāwā al-Majlis al-'Ūrūbbī lil-Iftā' wal-Buḥūth,* first and second compilations (Cairo: Dār al-Tawzīʿ wal-Nashr al-Islāmiyya, 2002), 11–16.

[15] Alexandre Caeiro, "Transnational Ulama, European Fatwas and Islamic Authority: A Case Study of the European Council for Fatwa and Research," in Martin van Bruinessen

Council was not only initiated by European-based Muslims, but is also structurally controlled by them. However, the appeal by European-based Muslim organizations to al-Qaraḍāwī to head the Council, as well as al-Qaraḍāwī's continued and unchallenged direction of its agenda, established a measure of dependency of *wasaṭī* European jurists on an authority that is external to European realities. Without the Qatar-based jurist, it is unlikely that the Council would have become a juristic panel of any import or influence. The Council, in turn, promoted al-Qaraḍāwī's status as one of the leading Sunni jurists of our time, in both the Arab world and the Western media.

The Secretary General of the Council, Ḥusayn Ḥalāwa, told the author he believes that most Muslims in Europe, including those of Turkish origin, embrace the Council's approach as well as its decisions. Asked specifically to compare the influence of *wasaṭīs* and *salafīs* on Muslims in Europe, he said that only the *wasaṭīs* have formulated a methodology for Muslim minorities and that the Council's views in particular have gained wide acceptance, while *salafīs* constitute a small minority among Muslims in Europe.[16] Indeed, it is fair to argue that far more Muslims in the West who deem religious law important are more inclined, in their general approach and daily practice, to the kind of pragmatism and integration-minded decisions that are endorsed by the Council than to *salafī* methodologies and norms. However, visits to dozens of mosques across Europe suggest that the Secretary General's assessment of the diffusion of the Council's approach and decisions is possibly too generous. More often than not, the leaders and attendees of mosques with whom the author spoke were either ignorant of the existence of the Council, critical of some of its decisions, or inclined to accept it as only one of several possible references. There are, to the best of my knowledge, no mosque or community leaders in Europe who declared their full commitment to the Council's *fatwās*.

and Stefano Allievi (eds.), *Producing Islamic Knowledge: Transmission and Dissemination in Western Europe* (Abingdon and New York: Routledge, 2011), 123.

[16] Interview with Ḥusayn Ḥalāwa, Dublin, February 13, 2012.

Moreover, even jurists and religious leaders who are members of the Council are not necessarily committed to its decisions. Maḥbūb al-Raḥman, a Pakistani-Norwegian and head of the Islamic Cultural Center Norway, the largest mosque in Oslo, has been a member of the Council from the day of its establishment and a supporter of al-Qaraḍāwī. Asked in his Oslo-office by the author what the Council's greatest achievement is, he mentioned uniformity in the issuance of *fatwās* through a cross-European network of jurists. But he also said that he accepts or rejects each of the Council's decisions based on its merit, and that just as his being a disciple of Abū al-A'lā al-Mawdūdī (d. 1979), the founder of Pakistani Islamism, does not imply that he accepts all of al-Mawdūdī's teachings, so too is he also not wholly committed to al-Qaraḍāwī's teachings.[17] On the one hand, this absence of strict commitmment is consistent with the *wasaṭī* demand that Muslims reject adherence to a specific *madhhab* or jurist. On the other hand, it further highlights al-Qaraḍāwī's failure to achieve his declared goal for the Council, which was "to promote a uniform Fatwa in Europe and to prevent controversy and intellectual conflicts regarding the respective issues wherever possible."[18]

Since the Council is a voluntary organization with limited funding, its capacity to print and circulate its decisions is limited. My impression, somewhat contrary to Caeiro's,[19] is that its publications are hard to find in Islamic bookstores and cultural centers around Europe. Thus, the dissemination of its concepts and *fatwās* is highly dependent on media, in particular websites and satellite television. Indeed, some voices in the Council argue that greater efforts must be exerted to circulate and disseminate its views in Europe.[20] *Wasaṭī* religious law of Muslim minorities took shape precisely at the time when Yūsuf al-Qaraḍāwī and other jurists recognized and seized upon the potential of mass media to reach

[17] Interview with Maḥbūb al-Raḥman, Imām of the Islamic Cultural Center Norway, at the offices of the Center, Oslo, March 22, 2014.

[18] Al-Qaraḍāwī, "Introduction," in *Fatwās of European Council for Fatwa and Research*, trans. Anas Usāma al-Tikritī and Shākir Nāṣif al-'Ubaydī, (Cairo: Islamic INC, 2002), ix.

[19] Alexandre Caeiro, "The Power of European Fatwas: The Minority Fiqh Project and the Making of an Islamic Counterpublic," *International Journal of Middle East Studies* 42, 3 (2010), 440–41.

[20] 'Abd al-Majīd al-Najjār, *Fiqh al-Muwāṭana lil-Muslimīn fī 'Ūrūbbā* (Beirut: al-Majlis al-'Ūrūbbī lil-Iftā' wal-Buḥūth, 2009), 69–70.

Muslims globally. These media allow jurists and individual Muslims to transcend geographical locations; a *fatwā* issued in Doha can be read simultaneously in Paris, and queries that originate in Detroit or Copenhagen can be addressed in Doha without any delay or costs. The two most effective organs at *wasaṭīs'* disposal have been al-Qaraḍāwī's weekly television show on al-Jazeera and the internet portals he inspired and supervised. On the show, *al-Sharīʿa wal-Ḥayāt,* he discusses questions relating to diverse aspects of Islamic law. According to al-Qaraḍāwī himself, it is broadcast on Sundays at 19:05 GMT because that is the most convenient time for Muslims living in Western countries.[21] The website Islamonline.net, which was established under his supervision in June 1997, included a state-of-the-art, *wasaṭī*-oriented *fatwā* archive. After a managerial dispute led to al-Qaraḍāwī's dismissal from its board of directors in 2010, al-Qaraḍāwī's supporters launched a spin-off site, onislam.net, which became the new platform for *wasaṭī* jurisprudence. (Egypt-based workers argued that the Qatari management of Islamonline.net was seeking to transform the portal from *wasaṭiyya* to *salafiyya* and to curb its strong anti-Israel agenda.)[22] The European Council also operates a website, but it has a poor design and fails to provide the entirety of the Council's publications.

The *salafī* approach to the jurisprudence of minorities was constructed and has been institutionalized differently. Since the 1970s, *salafī* jurist and juristic panels have discussed the realities of Muslim residence in non-Muslim lands. Their efforts corresponded with the investments of the Saudi regime in *daʿwa* activities outside the kingdom. (Ironically, as noted above, Saudi funding also sponsored the evolution of the *wasaṭī* approach on Muslim minorities.) *Salafīs* never endeavored to devise a specific juristic approach to Muslim minorities. On the contrary, one of their underlying objectives in writing about Muslim minorities was to clarify that Islamic law applies universally. Nevertheless, if one accepts

[21] Ehab Galal, "Yūsuf al-Qaraḍāwī and the New Islamic TV," in Bettina Gräf and Jakob Skovgaard-Petersen (eds.), *The Global Mufti: The Phenomenon of Yūsuf al-Qaraḍāwī* (London: Hurst & Company, 2009), 158.

[22] Mona Abdel-Fadil, "The Islam-Online Crisis: A Battle of Wasatiyya vs. Salafi Ideologies?" *CyberOrient* 5, 1 (2011), accessed June 27, 2013: http://www.cyberorient.net/article.do?articleId=6239.

the abovementioned definition that the juristic treatment of issues pertaining to Muslim minorities—rather than the method and objective of that treatment—constitutes the field of *fiqh al-aqalliyyāt al-Muslima*, then by the turn of the century (the time of b. Bāz's and al-'Uthaymīn's death), a rich and distinct corpus of theoretical *salafī* deliberations and *fatwās* in that field already existed. These addressed conditions for residence in non-Muslim countries, the relations between Muslim minorities and non-Muslim majorities, how Muslim minorities should apply the *sharī'a*, and specific issues from the Ramaḍān fast to Christian holidays. During the 2000s, the corpus was expanded further by a number of jurists, both in Saudi Arabia and outside the kingdom. Little from the *salafī* treatment of *fiqh al-aqalliyyāt al-Muslima* has been published and canonized in a way that indicates its specific relevance to Muslim minorities. The two primary examples are "Muslim Minorities," a compilation of English translations of lectures given by 'Abd al-'Azīz b. 'Abdallāh b. Bāz and Muḥammad b. Ṣaliḥ al-'Uthaymīn to Muslims in the West, as well as collections of their *fatwās* addressing queries on challenges that are unique to minorities, published in London in 1998,[23] and an Arabic-language compilation of *fatwās* by the senior Saudi jurists and the Permanent Committee, published in Cairo in 2004 as part of a series of *salafī fatwā* compilations regarding different fields.[24] Other examples are *An Advice to the Salafīs Living in the West*, a book published in 2012 in Birmingham, England by Rabī' b. Hādī al-Madkhalī, a former head of the Department of Sunna at the Islamic University of al-Madīna and a staunch critic of *jihādi-salafism*;[25] and *The Beautiful Advice to the Noble Salafīs of the West*, a short pamphlet published by the *salafī* mosque of Brixton, London, based on the lecture of Saudi scholar 'Abd al-'Azīz al-Rayyis to the "*salafīs* of France."[26] Most other *salafī* texts that address Muslim minorities are scattered in platforms and

[23] Shaykh Ibn Baz and Sheykh Uthaymeen, *Muslim Minorities* (Hounslow, United Kingdom: Message of Islam, 1998).

[24] Ṣalāḥ al-Dīn Maḥmūd al-Sa'īd (ed.), *Fatāwā al-'Ulamā' ḥawla al-Aqalliyyāt al-Muslima fī al-'ālam* (Alexandria: Dār al-'Īmān, 2004).

[25] Rabī b. Hādī al-Madkhalī, *An Advice to the Salafis Living in the West*, trans. Khadīja 'Abd al-Waḥīd bin-Ṣāliḥ (Birmingham, United Kingdom: Salafi Publications, 2012).

[26] 'Abdul-Aziz Ar-Rayyis, *The Beautiful Advice to the Noble Salafis of the West*, trans. 'Abd al-Ḥaqq Al-Ashantī (London: Jamiah Media, 2010).

sources whose scope is broader, such as *fatwā* compilations on commerce, child-raising, women, or prisons. When compiled, these texts amount to a comprehensive and distinct view on Muslim conduct in non-Muslim countries that draws from and applies general *salafī* norms.

There exist no pan-continental or even national-level *salafī* panels or organizations in the United States or Europe. *Salafī fiqh* finds its institutional home in independently initiated mosques, associations, Islamic centers, and publishers that function on a local level. These *salafī* organizations accept *salafī* Saudi-based jurists and panels as a reference (*marjaʿiyya*). They endorse, publicize, and sell books, pamphlets, and sermons given by *salafī* scholars. Some mosques affiliate with *salafiyya* in their title or by bearing the name of one of *salafiyya*'s main protagonists, while others do not. In England several communities expressly declare themselves as *salafī* and make a point of their strong association with Saudi teachings, while in Germany, *salafī*-oriented communities struggle to distance themselves from this banner. The reason is that the *Verfassungsschutz*, the organ tasked with protecting German democracy, supervises organizations it defines as *salafī*, and the media associates *salafiyya* with terror. In the words of one of the leaders of al-Muḥsinīn Mosque in Bonn, Germany, who asked not to be identified, "In this country, if we call ourselves *salafīs* then we have already lost."[27] In line with *salafī* teachings, even communities that declare their loyalty to Saudi jurists and panels do not consider themselves as strictly committed to any specific decision. While expressing great regard for the contemporary authorities of *salafiyya*, members emphasize that they are not adherents of a specific *madhhab*, panel, or jurist, but rather only adherents to the teachings of the Quran and the Sunna, and thus they accept or reject any decision based on its correctness.

Some *salafīs* in Europe make an ideological point of their lack of structural unity. Asked why no continental-level or national-level *salafī* organization resembling the *wasaṭī* European Council for Fatwa and Research ever developed, two of the leaders of the Salafī Mosque and Islamic Centre of Birmingham, England—Abū Khadīja and Bilāl Davis

[27] Interview at the al-Muḥsinīn Mosque bookstore, Bonn, July 27, 2013.

(Abū Ḥakīm)—suggested that, first, the correctness of the decisions issued by the Saudi Council of Senior Scholars and the Permanent Committee render the establishment of such a panel unnecessary; and second, that unlike the Muslim Brothers-oriented, Dublin-based European Council (as they put it), *salafīs* possess no political aspirations in Europe and thus do not require a European council.[28] Yet there is another reason for the lack of *salafī* cohesion. Organizations that preach doctrinal and ideological purity are often more inclined to divide than to unite. *Salafīs* in Europe split, at times, because of differences that seem negligible to an outsider. For example, at the Salafī Mosque and Islamic Centre of Birmingham, I was told that a nearby mosque called Green Lane that is also considered *salafī* is not really so because it "holds magic acts" to be lawful. At Green Lane, I was told that the opinion that permitted magic was only articulated once in the mosque and immediately refuted. The imām at the Ibnu Taymeeyah Brixton Mosque, London, 'Umar Jāmāykī, suggested that the Salafī Mosque and Islamic Centre of Birmingham is itself not what it claims to be: while its members claim to abide by the rulings of the Permanent Committee, in reality they do so only when they feel like doing so. He suggested that the lack of cooperation between *salafīs* in Europe is largely based on personal differences, as well as on differences of opinion.[29] Thus, there is little wonder that al-Rayyis' "beautiful advice" to *salafīs* in Europe centered on lamenting that "many of the *salafī* centers in Europe—after being places of knowledge, learning and study—change into places of differing, problems and argumentation among the *salafīs* themselves."[30] Al-Rayyis called on European *salafīs* to change course and to realize that there are issues on which there can be differences of opinion,[31] as well to appreciate that not every person with ties to Saudi Arabia is necessarily correct in what he says.[32]

Salafī mosques and associations are led by imāms who studied in Saudi religious universities or were inspired by imāms who graduated from

[28] Interviews at the Salafi Mosque and Islamic Centre, Birmingham, England, July 19, 2013.
[29] Interview at Ibnu Taymeeyah Brixton Mosque, London, July 20, 2013.
[30] 'Abdul-Aziz Ar-Rayyis, *The Beautiful Advice to The Noble Salafis of the West*, 3.
[31] *Ibid.*, 5–6. [32] *Ibid.*, 20–21.

Saudi universities. The imāms were taught at these institutions that *salafī* ideology and methodology are the only true representations of Islam, a conviction that, as is the case with *salafīs* in the Arab world, translates to an elitist mentality that belittles or rejects those who follow other approaches. As noted by Adraoui in his study of *salafīs* in France, *salafīs* are Muslims who consider Saudi Arabia "the most perfect political and religious system in the world" and the one that comes closest to emulating the model of the first three generations of Islam. Furthermore, they appreciate the hostility Saudi Arabia demonstrates toward other religions and consider the oil wealth of the Kingdom and the Kingdom's ability to promote its form of Islam around the world to be a heavenly reward for Saudi Arabia's strict adherence to true Islamic values.[33] Some *salafīs* explain their preference for decisions that originated in Saudi Arabia in essentialist terms. At the Bradford, England, al-Sunnah mosque, established in July 2011 by the al-Baseerah Association, attendants told me that "it is logical" to follow contemporary Saudi Arabian jurists because "Islam was born in Saudi Arabia, not in England or in Germany."[34]

Observers agree that the small minority of devout Muslims in the West, particularly young people, who find *salafiyya* appealing, are attracted to the sense of rigidity, elitism and universalism, which *salafī* mosques offer. In his study of British *salafiyya*, Sadeq Hamid argued that the motivation of some Muslims in the West to accept *salafiyya* is their perception of its understanding of Islam as rigorous and evidence-based, as opposed to cultural, folkloristic, localized manifestations, which they reject.[35] Tariq Ramadan argued that *salafīs* attract "young people looking for clarity or going through crises and to whom their approach gives a sense

[33] Mohamed-Ali Adraoui, "Salafism in France: Ideology, Practices and Contradictions," in Roel Meijer (ed.), *Global Salafism: Islam's New Religious Movement* (London: Hurst & Company, 2009), 369–71. On the Saudi links of a number of the fathers of *salafiyya* in Germany: Nina Wiedl, *The Making of a German Salafiyya* (Aarhus, Denmark: Aarhus University, Centre for Studies in Islamism and Radicalisation, October 2012), 17–18. On the Saudi contribution and impact on the rise of *salafiyya* in England in the 1990s: Sadek Hamid, "The Attraction of 'Authentic Islam': Salafism and British Muslim Youth," in Roel Meijer (ed.), *Global Salafism: Islam's New Religious Movement* (London: Hurst & Company, 2009), 387–89.

[34] Visit by the author, February 17, 2012, al-Sunnah mosque, Bradford.

[35] Sadek Hamid, "The Attraction of 'Authentic Islam': Salafism and British Muslim Youth," 390.

of security."[36] Natalie Doyle argued, "*salafism* has fed the dream of marginalized second- or third-generation of European Muslims to leave their countries where they were born and return to the land of Islam, which assumes the mythical dimension."[37] Considering that in any large community of migrants one can find some disaffected individuals who feel marginalized and search for a reassuring identity and an ultimate truth, these observations still do not explain why *salafīs* developed a strong presence in some cities in the West but not in others. In my visit to the Ibnu Taymeeyah Brixton mosque I was offered a *salafī* point of view on this matter, which made sense: *Salafiyya* spreads only where a *salafī* presence has been established. Thus, the spread of *salafiyya* in the West is restricted to the cities where *salafī*-oriented activists have, possibly by accident, decided to settle.[38]

Salafī leaders and community members in the West reject the general *wasaṭī* approach to Muslim minorities' jurisprudence as well as specific *wasaṭī* decisions. I was not given the impression that refuting the European Council is central to the *salafī* agenda. Neither did I meet a single *salafī* who read the Council's more controversial decisions in depth, rather than simply having heard about them. However, once the issue of *wasaṭiyya* was broached, it always generated a lively discussion. Levels of opposition to the *wasaṭīs* differ. At the Salafī Mosque and Islamic Centre of Birmingham, I was told by Abū Khadīja and Abū Ḥakīm that the European Council promotes the politicization of religion instead of focusing on an individual's duty to practice *tawḥīd*, and that al-Qaraḍāwī's decisions deviate from Islam. (They would not sell any of his books in their bookstore.)[39] The imām of the *salafī* al-Raḥman mosque in Leipzig, Germany, the Syrian-born Ḥasan Dabbāgh, told me that the European Council misinterprets the mechanism of *maṣlaḥa*. When I protested that al-Qaraḍāwī also considers himself an adherent of the

[36] Tariq Ramadan, *What I Believe* (Oxford and New York: Oxford University Press, 2010), 49.

[37] Natalie J. Doyle, "Lessons from France: Popularist Anxiety and Veiled Fears of Islam," *Islam and Christian-Muslim Relations*, 22, 4 (2011), 484–85.

[38] Interviews at the Ibnu Taymeeyah Brixton Mosque, London, July 21, 2013.

[39] Interviews at the Salafī Mosque and Islamic Centre, Birmingham, England, July 19, 2013.

salaf, he replied: "Anyone can call himself a *salafī* just like anyone, including Netanyahu [Israel's prime minister] can say he wants peace."[40] Youth at the al-Iṣlāḥ mosque, in the Parisian suburb of Sur Marne, grimaced when I mentioned al-Qaraḍāwī's name. They said Muslims should abide by the Quran and the Sunna rather than by pragmatic, modernist decisions.[41] In the bookstore of al-Nūr mosque in Berlin, as well as in that of al-Muḥsinīn in Bonn, books by al-Qaraḍāwī are offered for sale on the *salafī*-oriented bookshelves. In both mosques, the presence of these books was explained as part of a broader policy of pluralism and tolerance. Nāṣir al-'Īsā, the Palestinian-German imām of al-Nūr, one of Europe's largest *salafī* mosques, told me that while al-Qaraḍāwī made mistakes, he regards him as a great *mujtahid* and *mujaddid*. Nevertheless, al-'Īsā does not consider al-Qaraḍāwī's European Council as a reference because he thinks its members are not prominent scholars and because, in his opinion, al-Qaraḍāwī does not really have the time to read the Council's *fatwās*.[42] One young Egyptian-German attendant of the mosque suggested that the Council is not respected because it serves "the interests of European governments instead of ruling in accordance with Islam."[43]

While only a small minority of Muslims in the West are *salafīs*, the *salafī* approach enjoys considerable marketing reach, one that is massively disproportionate to the number of its loyalists. The amount of Arabic and translated *salafī* titles on sale is one aspect of this reach. Time and again, I was surprised to notice the quantity of *salafī* works in mosques and Islamic-interest bookstores in Europe that have no particular sympathy to this approach. The other aspect of *salafī* marketing is state-of-the-art websites, which include general guidance and vast *fatwā* archives and allow Muslims all across the world to submit queries. Along with the websites of the Saudi Permanent Committee and individual jurists, the most popular among these platforms are the Riyadh-based ar.Islamway.net (formerly Islamway.com, launched August 1998, and its English version en.Islamway.net; it was ranked in 2007–8 by alexa.com as

[40] Conversation at al-Raḥman Mosque, Leipzig, July 29, 2013.
[41] Interviews at al-Iṣlaḥ mosque, Sur Marne, October 12, 2012.
[42] Interview at al-Nūr mosque, Berlin, August 1, 2013.
[43] Interview at al-Nūr mosque, July 31, 2013.

the most visited Islam-interest portal in the world; it has since lost its top status, but remains popular); the multilingual Islamweb.net, sponsored by the Qatari ministry for Endowments and Religious Affairs; and Muḥammad Ṣāliḥ al-Munajjid's multilingual Islam Question and Answer. Blind-queries on Islamic jurisprudence (pejoratively known in European mosques as "sheikh Google") demonstrate the effectiveness of *salafī* online operations. In my classes on Islamic law, I ask the students—including some native Arabic speakers and some who read only English—to select a subject of interest that relates to Muslims in the West and use Google's search engine to find, in English or Arabic, one decision issued by a *wasaṭī* jurist and one by a *salafī* jurist. For seven years now, every semester students have reported that it was much easier to find *salafī*-oriented *fatwās*.

THE *WASAṬĪ* OBJECTIVES AND METHODOLOGY FOR MUSLIM MINORITIES

The *wasaṭī* approach to *fiqh al-aqalliyyāt al-Muslima* is an extension of *wasaṭī* ideology and methodology, particularly in their more delineated and audacious articulations by al-Qaraḍāwī from the late 1990s. It promotes the two interconnected ideological objectives of general *wasaṭī fiqh—al-taysīr fī al-fatwā wal-tabshīr fī al-da'wa*[44]—and, relying on a broad approach to *maṣlaḥa* and cross-*madhhab* search, applies them to situations that are unique to Muslim minorities, formulating a unique dependency between them. According to this approach, *taysīr* requires jurists to consider the special hardships faced by Muslims living as a minority and accommodate their decisions accordingly. *Tabshīr* appears in two contexts: bringing deviant Muslims in the West back to religion by presenting Islam in a pleasant and gradualist way, and bringing

[44] In his introduction to the first and second collections of the European Council's *fatwās*, al-Qaraḍāwī presented *taysīr fī al-fatwā and tabshīr fī al-da'wa* as the "message" of the Council: Yūsuf al-Qaraḍāwī, "*Taqdīm*," in *Qarārāt wa-Fatāwā al-Majlis al-'Ūrūbbī lil-Iftā' wal-Buḥūth*, 8. The Council accepted this slogan in its eleventh session as one of the defining characteristics of the "Islamic speech in the age of globalization": *Qarārāt wa-Fatāwā al-Majlis min al-Dawra al-Thāmina ilā al-Khāmisa 'Ashara* (PDF file), 25–26.

non-Muslims to Islam. The latter prospect serves *wasaṭīs* as a central (albeit not exclusive) legitimization of Muslim presence in non-Muslim lands, as well as a vital justification for permitting practices that are otherwise impermissible. Thus, *tabshīr* in the context of Muslims in non-Muslim lands is more than a complementary dimension of *taysīr* that encourages appealing presentations of Islam; it is elevated to the rank of a principle *sharʿī* objective and expands the ability of *wasaṭī* jurists to provide Muslims in the West with lenient decisions applying only to them.

The European Council for Fatwa and Research characterizes *taysīr* as its main objective. When I asked the Secretary General of the Council, Ḥusayn Ḥalāwa, what he believes to be the panel's greatest achievement, he replied succinctly and without hesitation: "That Muslims in Europe live without *ḥaraj* [hardship]." In a separate interview, he defined *taysīr* as the essence of Islam and the objective of the *sharīʿa*.[45] While *taysīr fī al-fatwā* for Muslim minorities was presented as a foundation of the Council's juristic methodology in its constitution[46] and was described as such already in 1999 by one of its members,[47] the concept was only systematically presented in al-Qaraḍāwī's 2001 book *Fī Fiqh al-Aqalliyyāt al-Muslima*. Al-Qaraḍāwī's deliberation was divided into two parts. First, he summarized his theory on facilitation presented in his book *Taysīr al-Fiqh*, which he had completed five years earlier. He noted that the Prophet was more inclined than any other person to the easy way, and that the Companions and those who followed them shared this inclination, understanding it to be the way ordained by the Quran and practiced by the Prophet; unfortunately, *taysīr* was gradually forsaken by future generations.[48] After asserting that *taysīr* constitutes an essence

[45] Interviews by the author with Ḥusayn Ḥalāwa at the Islamic Cultural Center of Ireland, February 13 and 14, 2012.

[46] See the constitution of the European Council section seven, clause 32, accessed September 25, 2013: http://www.e-cfr.org/ar/index.php?cat_id=006; Ḥusayn Ḥalāwa, "About the European Council for Fatwa and Research," 4. For the Arabic version: Ḥusayn Ḥalāwa, "Taʿrīf al-Majlis al-'Ūrūbbī lil-Iftā' wal-Buḥūth," 13.

[47] For a discussion on the Council's inclination to allow greater *taysīr* for Muslim minorities, see the words of ʿAbdallāh Ibn Bayyah (b. 1935), a former Mauritanian education and justice minister and a member of the European Council, in a speech he gave on July 31, 1999 in Santa Clara, California on "Muslims Living in Non-Muslim lands," accessed November 2, 2013: http://www.themodernreligion.com/world/muslims-living.html.

[48] Al-Qaraḍāwī, *Fī Fiqh al-Aqalliyyāt al-Muslima*, 48–50.

of Islam, al-Qaraḍāwī explained why one of the principles of *taysīr*—accommodating *fatwās* to different circumstances—requires that jurists allow Muslim minorities special concessions. Al-Qaraḍāwī reasoned that Muslim minorities are weaker than Muslim majorities; thus, just as a sick person is entitled to more facilitation than a healthy one, a traveler is entitled to more facilitation than a permanent resident, a person facing a necessity is entitled to more facilitation than one who does not, the poor are entitled to more facilitation than the rich, and the handicapped are entitled to more facilitation than the fit, so are Muslims living as minorities entitled to greater facilitation than those living as majorities. Al-Qaraḍāwī added that all the *madhhabs* agree that a change of geographical location may justify a change of ruling, and no such change is more fundamental than moving outside of *dār al-Islām* (land of Islam). The reason is that, despite all the shortcomings and deviations of Muslim societies, they nevertheless encourage Muslims to perform religious duties and refrain from the prohibited, while non-Muslim societies do not.[49]

Al-ʿAlwānī highlighted *taysīr* as a foundation of Islam in his second major systematic deliberation on *fiqh al-aqalliyyāt al-Muslima*, published in 2004. He had not explicitly done so in his first work, published in 2000, in which he nevertheless argued that given the unique conditions in which Muslim minorities live, some juristic decisions that are not suitable for others are suitable for them.[50] One possible explanation for this omission is technical: the second treatise is longer and allows greater detail. Yet a more likely explanation is the apologetic nature of al-ʿAlwānī's undertaking and his expressed desire that his approach not be labeled as *fiqh* for the weak. To present *taysīr* as an ideological objective in his initial introduction of *fiqh al-aqalliyyāt al-Muslima* could have exposed the developing *wasaṭī* approach to the allegation that making the lives of Muslims minorities easier was the real motivation behind its formulation. His discussion in the 2004 work pointed to Q. 2:190, 279, and 9:36, as well the Prophet's words *lā ḍarar wa-lā ḍirār*, to argue that Allah does not wish for people to accept situations in which their bodies, capital, necessities, needs, and improvements are harmed, or situations in which

[49] *Ibid.*, 50–52. [50] Al-ʿAlwānī, *Fī Fiqh al-Aqalliyyāt*, 5.

they harm others. He called upon jurists to consider this principle when deciding on issues pertaining to Muslim minorities, suggesting that by doing so jurists would allow minorities to lead good Islamic lives and develop their communities without finding themselves in conflict with majority societies.[51] Still, an apologetic tone was not absent from the discussion: al-'Alwānī clarified that making the lives of Muslim minorities easier is not an objective in and of itself but rather a means of making those minorities an elite and an example capable of representing Islam in the lands where they live.[52] Equally apologetic, al-'Arabī al-Bishrī, a French-based member of the European Council, explained that while *fiqh al-aqalliyyāt al-Muslima* considers the special conditions in which Muslim minorities live, it is not a jurisprudence of exceptions and concessions but of resolve, and it offers facilitations only when needed and in line with the foundations of the *sharī'a*.[53] Another French-based member of the European Council, 'Abd al-Majīd al-Najjār, cautioned that *taysīr* should be applied only in cases that contribute to the objective of creating a permanent, integrated presence of Muslims in Europe, enabling them to contribute to the societies in which they reside and present the message of Islam. For example, in his opinion (addressing the *Ḥanafī* legitimization of prohibited transactions in non-Muslim lands), to allow Muslims in Europe to sell alcohol and pork products is wrong because it would corrupt Western societies rather than reform them.[54]

Tabshīr fī al-da'wa appears in two contexts in *wasaṭī fiqh al-aqalliyyāt al-Muslima*. The first draws from the general *wasaṭī* theory on *tabshīr*. *Wasaṭīs* suggest that Muslims in the West who have deviated from Islam, or face considerable difficulties when practicing it, could not be brought back to Islam at once. Consideration must be given to their situation and, more specifically, to their level of alienation with the hope that over time they would commit to Allah's laws. Al-Qaraḍāwī emphasized that the

[51] Al-'Alwānī, "Madkhal ilā Fiqh al-Aqalliyyāt," 76–77.
[52] *Ibid.*, 49; and see also in al-'Alwānī's *Fī Fiqh al-Aqalliyyāt*, 5.
[53] Al-'Arabī al-Bishrī, "Munṭalaqāt li-Fiqh al-Aqalliyyāt," *al-Majalla al-'Ilmiyya lil-Majlis al-'Ūrūbbī lil-Iftā' wal-Buḥūth*, no. 4–5 (June 2004), 204–5.
[54] Al-Najjār, *Fiqh al-Muwāṭana lil-Muslimīn fī 'Ūrūbbā*, 110–11.

gradualism required when dealing with Muslim minorities is the gradualism that was applied in revealing the Quran and was the way of the *salaf*.[55] The European Council for Fatwa and Research embraced *tabshīr* as a means to bring Muslims in the West closer to Islam in its first session, when it addressed the issue of *ḥijāb*. It advised exercising gentleness rather than harshness when dealing with a new convert who refuses to wear a headscarf because, she claims, it puts her in a state of hardship. The Council explained that while the headscarf is obligatory, it is only a partiality of law; based on *fiqh al-muwāzanāt*, if imposing it may lead the woman to a state of *tanfīr* (alienation) and cause her to forsake Islam altogether, it should not be imposed.[56]

Tabshīr fī al-da'wa also enjoins Muslims in the West with spreading the word of Islam through peaceful and pleasant means. This notion results in an integration of *wasaṭī* triumphalism with its pragmatism and produces a cyclical result in which the two reinforce one another: Muslim presence in the West is regarded as a milestone in the Islamizing of humanity, and its appreciation as such serves to legitimize pragmatic decisions aimed to make proselytizing more realistic. *Wasaṭīs* present a number of assumptions. First, Islam is a universal message that must be spread to humanity at large. Second, non-Muslim territories in which Muslims can practice their religion should not be regarded *dār al-ḥarb* (abode of war). Third, the West, being morally corrupt and spiritually desolate, is in dire need of Islam's message and will embrace it if it is presented in accordance with its true essence. Fourth, it is permissible for Muslims to reside in non-Muslim countries, and they should even be encouraged to do so, as long as they are able to maintain their religious identity and practice it (which *wasaṭīs* believe is the case in Western, liberal, secular societies), as their presence can contribute to the spread of Islam and serves the interests of the Muslim nation. From these assumptions, *wasaṭī* decisions on queries dealing with situations that are unique to non-Muslim lands invoke proselytizing as a justification

[55] Al-Qaraḍāwī, *Fī Fiqh al-Aqalliyyāt al-Muslima*, 53. On the importance of gradualism in Muslim minorities' fiqh also: al-Bishrī, "Munṭalaqāt li-Fiqh al-Aqalliyyāt," 213–15.
[56] *Fatwā* no. 6, *Qarārāt wa-Fatāwā al-Majlis al-'Ūrūbbī lil-Iftā' wal-Buḥūth*, 28–30.

to support lenient decisions based on the following motivations: to provide Muslims with greater opportunities to spread Islam, to present a respectable and friendly face of Muslims and of Islam that would encourage conversion, and to remove obstacles that could hinder non-Muslims from accepting Islam.

The idea that serving as missionaries in non-Muslim lands legitimizes Muslim residence outside *dār al-Islām* is at the core of al-ʿAlwānī's and al-Qaraḍāwī's systematizations of *fiqh al-aqalliyyāt al-Muslima*. This is not a novel idea. It draws from decisions issued by jurists since the eleventh century, modernist-apologetic writings on the West from early twentieth century, and an abundance of writings published during the 1980s and 1990s by jurists, including leading Islamists, on the future of Muslim migration in the West.

The four *madhhabs* struggled with the question of residence in non-Muslim lands since their inception. Abū Ḥanīfa (d. 768) disapproved of Muslims residing in non-Muslim territory, while Mālik (d. 796) strongly opposed even traveling to the lands of unbelievers for purposes of trade because Muslims might become subject to the laws of unbelievers. Al-Shāfiʿī (d. 820) offered a different approach. He argued that residing among non-Muslims is permissible, noting that even after the establishment of an Islamic state in al-Madīna, the Prophet allowed some Muslims to reside in non-Muslim territories.[57] The *Shāfiʿī* Abū al-Ḥasan b. Ḥabīb al-Māwardī (d. 1058) introduced proselytizing as another justification. He argued that if a Muslim is able to manifest his religion in one of the unbelievers' countries, this country becomes part of *dār al-Islām* and, hence, it is better to reside there than migrating because the Muslim living as a minority would potentially convert non-Muslims to Islam.[58] Since the twelfth century, the four schools of law formulated distinctive perceptions of residence in non-Muslim territories, an issue that became

[57] Khaled Abou El-Fadl, "Islamic Law and Muslim Minorities: The Juristic Discourse on Muslim Minorities from the Second/Eight to the Eleventh/Seventeenth Centuries," *Islamic Law and Society* 1, 2 (1994), 146–47. On al-Shāfiʿī see also: Sami A. Aldeeb Abu-Sahlieh, "The Islamic Conception of Migration," *International Migration Review* 30, 1 (March 1996), 43.

[58] Khaled Abou El-Fadl, "Islamic Law and Muslim Minorities: The Juristic Discourse on Muslim Minorities from the Second/Eight to the Eleventh/Seventeenth Centuries," 150.

more acute following the *Reconquista*. The *Shāfiʿī* opinion continued to be the most lenient and to invoke proselytizing as justification. Shams al-Dīn al-Ramlī (d. 1596), the grand muftī of Egypt, cited the example of the group of Muslims the Prophet allowed to remain in non-Muslim Mecca to argue that Muslims who live in Aragon and are able to manifest their religion are not required to migrate to Muslim lands. Instead, they are required to remain because their residence among infidels might help to propagate Islam. He asserted that the area in which these Muslims reside is part of *dār al-Islām* and if they would leave, it would become *dār al-kufr* (abode of unbelief).[59] *Ḥanafī* jurists also ruled that territories in which Muslims can apply the laws of Islam are part of *dār al-Islām*.[60] The *Mālikī* opinion, articulated by jurists who faced the threat of Christian occupations from the closest distance, was generally the strictest: Muslims should not reside in a non-Muslim territory, primarily because they would be subjected to non-Muslim laws. However, if a person cannot leave due to physical or economic circumstances, then residence is permissible as long as the impediment persists.[61] *Ḥanbalīs* argued that if Muslims are able to practice their religion in a non-Muslim territory, are secure from harm, and do not fear the loss of their religion, then they may stay. However, even if all these conditions are maintained, it is recommended that they emigrate to a Muslim land.[62]

[59] *Ibid.*, 159–60; Alan Verskin, *Opressed in the Land? Fatwās on Muslims Living under Non-Muslim Rule from the Middle Ages to the Present* (Princeton: Markus Wiener Publishers, 2013), 31–33.

[60] Khaled Abou El-Fadl, "Islamic Law and Muslim Minorities: The Juristic Discourse on Muslim Minorities from the Second/Eight to the Eleventh/Seventeenth Centuries," 161.

[61] *Ibid.*, 153–57; Sami A. Aldeeb Abu-Sahlieh, "The Islamic Conception of Migration," 47–49; Verskin, *Opressed in the Land? Fatwās on Muslims Living under Non-Muslim Rule from the Middle Ages to the Present*, 21–30; Sarah Davis-Secord, "Muslims in Noram Sicily: The Evidence of Imām al-Māzārī' *Fatwās*," *Mediterranean Studies*, vol. 16 (2007), 51–59; Jocelyn N. Hendrickson, *The Islamic Obligation to Emigrate: Al-Wansharīsī's Asnā al-matājir Reconsidered* (PhD dissertation, Emory University, 2009), 56–70, 136–76.

[62] Khaled Abou El-Fadl, "Islamic Law and Muslim Minorities: The Juristic Discourse on Muslim Minorities from the Second/Eight to the Eleventh/Seventeenth Centuries," 157; Sālim b. ʿAbd al-Ghānī al-Rāfiʿī, *Aḥkām al-Aḥwāl al-Shakhṣiyya lil-Muslimīn fī al-Gharb* (Beirut: Dār Ibn Ḥazm, 2002), 58–60. On Ibn Taymiyya's opinion on the matter: Khālid bin ʿAli bin Muḥammad al-ʿAnbari, *The Impact of Man-made Laws in Determining the Judgment of an Abode as Being One of Disbelief or Islam* (Amman: Jamiah Media, 2007, originally published in Arabic in 2004), 64–66.

The modernist-apologetic legacy, particularly the writings of Rashīd Riḍā, also significantly impacted the *wasaṭī* treatment of proselytizing. Riḍā shared the opinion that Muslims are not required to migrate from a non-Muslim land if they are able to practice their religion. He cited al-Māwardī's opinion on the potential of proselytizing as encouragement for remaining in a non-Muslim land.[63] The Islamizing of the West was not a detached theoretical prospect for him; his writings were infused with its consideration as a plausible objective. While serving as the editor of *al-Manār* (1898–1935), the potential for a massive Western conversion to Islam was one of his primary focuses. During the first two decades of the twentieth century, *al-Manār* expressed the hope that the West would convert to Islam. In one essay, Riḍā claimed that if the English nation had only learned what Islam truly is, it would have Islamized; this would have allowed the English to control the East and possibly also the West, relying on the assistance of 100,000 Muslim soldiers who would have joined the English ranks.[64] Riḍā's final substantial work, published in 1933, was a manifesto in which he argued that Islam is the only savior for the deteriorating West. He wondered why European countries had not yet embraced Islam[65] and suggested that a persistent, truly Islamic proselytization effort by Muslims could demolish the wall separating Westerners from salvation.[66] *Al-Manār* also frequently reported on the conversion of European Christians to Islam. The narratives published presented several motivations for embracing Islam, including its compatibility with science and respect for Christianity, as well as Muslims' devotion.[67] Riḍā tried to promote proselytization efforts not only through his words but his deeds. In Cairo in March of 1912, he established a

[63] Umar Ryad, "A Prelude to Fiqh al-Aqalliyyāt: Rashīd Ridā's *Fatwās* to Muslims under Non-Muslim Rule," in Christiane Timmerman *et al.* (eds.), *In-between Spaces: Christian and Muslim Minorities in Transition in Europe and the Middle East* (Brussels: Peter Lang, 2009), 241–44.

[64] "Al-Wifāq al-Islāmī al-Inklīzī," *al-Manār* 5, 14 (October 18, 1902), 545–50.

[65] Muḥammad Rashīd Riḍā, *al-Waḥī al-Muḥammadī* (Cairo: Maṭba'at al-Manār, 1955), 18.

[66] *Ibid.*, 20–25.

[67] For example, Riḍā publicized the story of English convert 'Abdallāh Browne, who converted after reading a Quranic verse (Q. 10:22) that stressed the divine power to traverse land and sea. After reading it, Browne started to read other relevant Quranic descriptions of the sea, sea life, and ship building. After learning that the Prophet had never

college dedicated to the education of a young generation of proselytizers among Muslims and non-Muslims: *Dār al-Daʿwa wal-Irshād* (the College for Proselytizing and Instruction). Graduates were to be sent to countries of idolaters and monotheists that allow for freedom of religion, or to Muslim countries where the risk of conversion from Islam exists.[68] A three-year track entitled students to a diploma permitting them to engage in *daʿwa* in Muslim countries; completion of a six-year track was required to engage in *daʿwa* among non-Muslims.[69] The scheme never materialized, however, reminding Riḍā that financial support is as necessary for proselytizing as religious passion.[70]

During the 1940s and 1950s, leading Islamists discussed Islam as the future of the West,[71] but the potential of Muslims living there to facilitate its propagation was not. As mass migration to the West began, literature in the 1960s and 1970s discussing Muslim minorities—including al-Qaraḍāwī's *al-Ḥalāl wal-Ḥarām fī al-Islām*—focused on the need to protect their religious identity; there was no mention of a missionary role prescribed for them.[72] It was only in the early 1980s that a concept of

traveled by sea, Browne was persuaded to become a Muslim and wrote a book on the evidence for the truth of Islam: Ryad, "A Prelude to Fiqh al-Aqalliyyāt," 276–77.

[68] "Jamāʿat al-Daʿwa wal-Irshād," *al-Manār* 14, 2 (March 1, 1911), 114–20.

[69] Charles C. Adams, *Islam and Modernism in Egypt: A Study of the Modern Reform Movement Inaugurated by Muḥammad ʿAbduh* (New York: Russel & Russel, 1968, first printed 1933), 196–98.

[70] "Al-Islām fī Inkaltra," *al-Manār* 18, 1 (February 14, 1915), 73–79.

[71] Consider Ḥasan al-Bannā's "Towards the Light" and "Peace in Islam": "Risālat naḥwa al-Nūr" (October 1936), in *Majmūʿat Rasāʾil al-Imām al-Shahīd Ḥasan al-Bannā* (Cairo: Dār al-Tawzīʿ wal-Nashr al-Islāmiyya, 2006), 159; *al-Salām fī al-Islām* (Manshūrāt al-ʿAsr al-Ḥadīth, 2nd edn. June 1971), 7–18, first published in *al-Shihāb* 2 (December 13, 1947); as well as a number of Sayyid Quṭb's apologias against Western ideologies, including those based on his negative impressions of American society during his sojourning there in 1948–50: *al-ʿAdāla al-Ijtimāʿiyya fī al-Islām* (Cairo: Dār al-Shurūq, 16th printing 2006, first published in the late 1940s); "Amrīkā allatī Raʾaytu: fī Mizān al-Qiyam al-Insāniyya" (second part), *al-Risāla* 19, 959 (November 19, 1951), 1301–6; *al-Salām al-ʿālamī wal-Islām* (Cairo: Dār al-Shurūq, 1974, first published 1951).

[72] One seminal example is ʿAlī b. al-Muntaṣir al-Kittānī's report on the state of Muslims in Europe and the Americas, published in 1975. Al-Kittānī (1941–2001) was a Moroccan-born specialist in nuclear and plasma engineering and the son of King Fayṣal's personal envoy to North African heads of states in the 1960s. Between October 1973 and January 1974, al-Kittānī led a Muslim World League delegation that surveyed Muslim communities in twenty-eight countries in the Western hemisphere, from the United States to France and Lichtenstein to Trinidad and Tobago. His surveys detailed the number of Muslims in each of the countries visited and the origins of communities; described the mosques, cultural centers, and organizations they had established; analyzed which forces seek to limit them;

"the migrant as a missionary" began to surface. Two separate, though not mutually exclusive, developments encouraged this outcome. On the one hand, it became clear that the Western sojourning of some Muslims was of a permanent nature. The millions of Muslims who had already migrated after the Second World War were joined by new arrivals, including those reuniting with their families and refugees escaping the Middle Eastern political turmoil of the late 1970s. It also became clear that some Muslims in the West were in the process of assimilating into their receiving societies and were losing whatever connection they had with their religion. On the other hand, three encouraging developments were recognized: the renaissance of religious sentiments among other Muslim migrants, the gradual development of Islamic communal institutions in the West, and conversions of Western Christians to Islam. One of the first to suggest that Muslims in the West should act as missionaries was Muḥammad al-Ghazālī. In 1984, he concluded several years of Saudi-sponsored visits to Western countries with the publication of *Islam Outside Its Boundaries*, the first book by a major *wasaṭī* scholar dedicated exclusively to the issue of migration and a first attempt, albeit a spontaneous rather than a systematic one, to design a framework of identity for migrants. While al-Ghazālī's main concern remained protecting Muslim minorities' religious identity, he also conveyed confidence that Muslim migrants, provided with suitable education and funding, would not only grow stronger in their religiosity but also become useful for the global propagation of Islam. The book opened with an analysis of French newspaper reports on the conversion of tens of thousands of French to Islam;[73] it concluded by arguing that if the Muslim nation works for that to happen, then the masses of Muslim migrants will not only remain Muslim but will also become the vanguard in the advancement of Islam.[74]

and proposed plans to protect and enhance Muslim minorities' religious identity. However, he did not consider minorities a force for proselytizing: 'Alī b. al-Muntaṣir al-Kittānī, *al-Muslimūn fī 'Ūrūbbā wa-Amricā* (Beirut: Dār al-Kutub al-'Ilmiyya, 2005).

[73] Muḥammad al-Ghazālī, *Mustaqbal al-Islām Khārij Arḍihi: Kayfa Nufakkiru fīhi?* (Cairo: Dār al-Shurūq, 1997, first published 1984), 5–11.

[74] *Ibid.*, 78.

In 1989, the journal of the Fiqh council of the Muslim World League published an essay by one of its members, the muftī of Tunisia, Muḥammad al-Shādhilī al-Nayfar, who defended the permissibility of Muslim residence in non-Muslim countries. Addressing the traditional *Mālikī* hostility to such residence, he emphasized the difference between historical conditions. During the *Reconquista*, Spain waged war against Islam and tried to convert Muslims. Today, Muslims living in non-Muslim lands enjoy freedom of religion and some are able to engage in Islamic activity. Furthermore, their residence may be of merit, for if they manifest Islam's ideals and values, non-Muslims will embrace it.[75]

In the mid-1990s, contemporary migration entered *fiqh* departments as a topic worthy of dissertations, and the concept of the "missionary migrant" was formulated in more systematic fashion as a religious-legal legitimization of Muslim residence in the West. In his 1996 master's dissertation, submitted to the University of Jordan, the Bosnian-born Sulaymān Muḥammad Tūbūlyāk relied on the *Ḥanafī*, *Shāfiʿī*, and *Ḥanbalī* traditions to refute the *Mālikī* position and suggest that so long as Muslims maintain their religiosity, they are permitted to reside among the infidels. He based this decision on two main justifications. One was that the example of the Prophet, who allowed believers to remain in Mecca before it was Islamized, indicates that living in a non-Muslim territory is permissible even if one can migrate. In any case, according to Tūbūlyāk, a true Muslim state does not exist in our times; the distinction between Muslim and non-Muslim lands is not clear as it was in the past. Another justification is proselytizing: residing among the infidels is permissible because it is the only way to fulfill the duty to bring non-Muslims the message of Islam. In this context, Tūbūlyāk invoked the universality of Islam's message, the *hijra* to Ethiopia and settlement there under the Prophet's orders, and the civil rights that Muslim minorities enjoy today in many countries, including the freedom to practice their religion and build mosques and religious centers.[76] Another young

[75] Muḥammad al-Shādhilī al-Nayfar, "al-Tajannus bi-Jinsiyya Ghayr Islāmiyya," *Majallat al-Majmaʿ al-Fiqhī al-Islāmī* 2, 4 (1989), 177–252.

[76] Sulaymān Muḥammad Tūbūlyāk, *al-Aḥkām al-Siyāsiyya lil-Aqalliyyāt al-Muslima fī al-Fiqh al-Islāmī* (Amman and Beirut: Dār al-Nafāʾis, Dār al-Bayāriq, 1998), 49–55. The book is

jurist, a specialist on Ibn Taymiyya's works, the Lebanese Khālid Muḥammad 'Abd al-Qādir (b. 1961), who studied *sharī'a* at the undergraduate level in al-Qaraḍāwī's department at the University of Qatar, expressed grave concern for the religious identity of Muslim minorities in his book *Min Fiqh al-Aqalliyyāt al-Muslima*, published in 1998 by Qatar's Ministry for Endowments and Religious Affairs. However, 'Abd al-Qādir argued that it is permissible for Muslims to reside among the polytheists if they are able to practice their religion and be active in *da'wa*, or if their presence serves another communal *maṣlaḥa* that benefits Muslims, such as gaining knowledge in a scientific field.[77] The editor of the book series in which 'Abd al-Qādir's work was published, the Syrian-born (1935) and Qatari-based author and journalist 'Umar 'Ubayd Ḥasana, declared in his introduction that Muslim presence in the lands of the infidels is a necessity for the spread Islam and noted that, historically speaking, Islam had spread through migration.[78]

It follows from this review that a rich variety of classic, modern and contemporary sources on *da'wa* as justification for residence in infidel lands existed before al-'Alwānī and al-Qaraḍāwī formulated their respective approaches to *fiqh al-aqalliyyāt al-Muslima*. The original contribution of al-'Alwānī and al-Qaraḍāwī lies in the intensity of their engagement with the concept of the "missionary migrant" as a means to legitimize migration, and in their integration of that concept as part of a larger effort to develop a new *ijtihād* for the unique challenges faced by Muslim minorities that enhances their integration to their societies.

Al-'Alwānī invoked four main points in his formative discussion, published in 2000. (He previously broached the topic in his *fatwā* on the permissibility of political participation in the United States and revisited it in his 2004 treatise.) All four points supported a conclusion that Muslim presence in contemporary Western societies is permissible and,

based on a master's dissertation approved in 1996 by the religious law faculty at the University of Jordan.

[77] Khālid Muḥammad 'Abd al-Qādir, *Min Fiqh al-Aqalliyyāt al-Muslima* (Doha: The Ministry for Endowments and Religious Affairs, January 1998), 69–70.

[78] 'Umar 'Ubayd Ḥasana, "Taqdīm," in Khālid Muḥammad 'Abd al-Qādir, *Min Fiqh al-Aqalliyyāt al-Muslima* (Doha: The Ministry for Endowments and Religious Affairs, January 1998), 36.

in fact, essential in order for Islam to fulfill its call. First, Islam is a universal message. The Quran is intended for humanity at large and is the only solution to its contemporary situation. The Muslim nation, the best of the nations, raised up for the benefit of men (Q. 3:110), is tasked with presenting Islam to the non-believers and transforming humanity from worshipping people to worshipping Allah.[79] Second, given that the earth in its entirety is Allah's possession, and Islam is His religion, all lands should be regarded as present or future *dār al-Islām*. Relying on the Persian Sunni jurist Fakhr al-Dīn al-Rāzī (d. 1209), al-'Alwānī suggested the term *dār al-ḥarb* to be invalid; humanity at large is the "Muslim nation," and therefore it is divided between *ummat milla* (the religious nation), or *dār al-ijāba* (the land of those who accepted Allah's call), and *ummat da'wa* (the proselytizing nation), or *dār al-da'wa* (land of proselytizing). Muslims should penetrate the latter so that they can propagate Allah's religion.[80] Third, any land in which a Muslim can practice his religion becomes *dār al-Islām*; in this context, al-'Alwānī referenced the abovementioned argument of al-Māwardī, that in cases where a Muslim can practice his religion in *dār al-kufr*, it not only becomes *dār al-Islām* but a land in which he should remain in order to bring non-Muslims to Islam.[81] Fourth, much has changed in international relations between the past and present; today, minorities' rights are protected by international law, the relations between states are not governed by force, and the world has been transformed, almost in its entirety, into a global village. The culture of conflict, which was the context in which the works of past jurists like Ibn Taymiyya were written, no longer exists.[82] Al-'Alwānī

[79] Al-'Alwānī, *Fī Fiqh al-Aqalliyyāt al-Muslima*, 32, 41; "Madkhal ilā Fiqh al-Aqalliyyāt," 73, 83–84; he is referenced and similar ideas are presented by Ṣalāḥ al-Dīn Sulṭān: "al-Muwāṭana fī Gahyr Diyār al-Islām bayna al-Nāfīn wal-Muthbitīn," *al-Majalla al-'Ilmiyya lil-Majlis al-'Ūrūbbī lil-Iftā' wal-Buḥūth*, no. 12–13 (July 2008), 164–68.

[80] Al-'Alwānī, *Fī Fiqh al-Aqalliyyāt al-Muslima*, 32, 43–44; "Madkhal ilā Fiqh al-Aqalliyyāt," 21.

[81] Al-'Alwānī, *Fī Fiqh al-Aqalliyyāt al-Muslima*, 43; "Madkhal ilā Fiqh al-Aqalliyyāt," 85; see also Rāshid al-Ghannūshī, "Naḥnu fī 'ālam maftūḥ," *al-Majalla al-'Ilmiyya lil-Majlis al-'Ūrūbbī lil-Iftā' wal-Buḥūth*, no. 12–13 (2008), 379.

[82] Al-'Alwānī, *Fī Fiqh al-Aqalliyyāt al-Muslima*, 16–18; "Madkhal ilā Fiqh al-Aqalliyyāt," 57–58. In the latter work he celebrates the good treatment of Islam and Muslims in the United States and the rise of the number of new converts in America following the 9/11 attacks, 28–34.

highlighted the story of the first *hijra* to Ethiopia as the definitive demonstration of the permissibility of migration to non-Muslim lands and its potential to boost the spread of Islam. He compared the state of weakness Muslims experienced then and their state of weakness now and pointed out that Muslims found shelter in a Christian land during the time of the Prophet. He also recounted traditions[83] according to which the Ethiopian King al-Najashi refused the request of a delegation from Mecca to surrender the Muslim migrants, was impressed by their devotion, gained their support when his reign was challenged, and finally converted to Islam.[84]

Al-Qaraḍāwī's approach to proselytizing and migration is similar to al-ʻAlwānī's. Already in 1992, he gave a lecture in France at a conference on integration in which he argued that the presence of Muslims outside the Muslim world is a prerequisite for the spread of Islam.[85] However, the systematization of this view came only later, in his 2001 formative presentation of *wasaṭī fiqh al-aqalliyyāt al-Muslima*. He legitimized residence in non-Muslim lands with a broad array of justifications. These included the need to make a living, to escape political persecution, and to study.[86] The duty to propagate Islam, however, transforms migration to Western lands from a permissible act to a religious duty. Muslims, wrote al-Qaraḍāwī, possess a universal message and must recognize, not ignore, the "important truth" that the West leads the world today politically, financially, and culturally. Thus, if there were no Muslims in the West, Muslims would have been compelled to unite and create such a presence in order to protect the identity of native Muslims and new converts living there and in order to spread Islam among non-Muslims.[87] He noted that had residence among

[83] For an overview of the traditions on conversion of Ethiopians: Muḥammad Yasin Mazhar Siddiqi, *The Prophet Muḥammad: A Role Model for Muslim Minorities*, trans. ʻAbd al-Raḥman Kidawī (Markfield: The Islamic Foundation, 2006), 77–80.

[84] Al-ʻAlwānī, *Fī Fiqh al-Aqalliyyāt al-Muslima*, 46–48; "Madkhal ilā Fiqh al-Aqalliyyāt," 88–90.

[85] Wasif Shadid and Sjoerd van Koningsveld, "Loyalty to a Non-Muslim Government: An Analysis of Islamic Normative Discussions and the Views of Some Contemporary Islamists," in Wasif A. R. Shadid and Sjoerd van Koningsveld (eds.), *Political Participation and Identities of Muslims in Non-Muslim States* (Kampen: Kok Pharos Publishing House, 1996), 103.

[86] Al-Qaraḍāwī, *Fī Fiqh al-Aqalliyyāt al-Muslima*, 17.

[87] *Ibid.*, 33.

non-Muslims been impermissible, Islam would never have spread outside the Arabian Peninsula. Its expansion in Asia and Africa was the work of merchants, whose attitudes impressed the natives. Its spread elsewhere was also peaceful and pleasant in essence; force was only used to remove physical obstacles that prevented the people from deciding for themselves whether they wanted to embrace Islam.[88] In a 2008 treatise, al-Qaraḍāwī reasserted that *da'wa* was the most important justification for migration (provided that the migrant is able to practice his religion)[89] and identified several distinctive aspects of Western countries that support Muslim residence in them: they are liberal-democratic, secular, and religiously neutral, and allow freedom of religion.[90] He also noted that Islam gives special treatment to the people of the book (Christians and Jews).[91]

There is no doubt in al-Qaraḍāwī's mind that, in light of the moral collapse of the West, Westerners are ready to accept Islam should Allah's final revelation be presented to them. In a book published in 2000 on the signs for the eventual triumph of Islam, al-Qaraḍāwī quoted a tradition reported by Abū Qābīl: When the Prophet was asked which of the cities would be conquered first by Islam—Constantinople or Rome—he replied that the city of Herkel, the Byzantine Emperor, would be the first. Al-Qaraḍāwī explained that this tradition demonstrates that the Companions of the Prophet already knew that both cities would be conquered and their inhabitants would Islamize. He wrote that the first part of the Prophet's prophecy was validated with the Ottoman occupation of Constantinople in 1453, while the second part of that prophecy had yet to occur. When would that happen? Islam, explained al-Qaraḍāwī, had been rejected from Europe twice—once in Andalusia (the *Reconquista*) and once in the Balkans (the disintegration of the Ottoman Empire). The third Muslim conquest of Europe will complete the Prophet's promise by Islamizing Rome. This third Islamic conquest will be accomplished

[88] *Ibid.*, 33–34; also al-Ghānnūshī, "Naḥnu fī 'ālam Maftūḥ," 380–82.

[89] Yūsuf al-Qaraḍāwī, "al-Waṭan wal-Muwāṭana fī Ḍaw' al-Uṣūl al-'Aqdiyya wal-Maqāṣid al-Shar'iyya," *al-Majalla al-'Ilmiyya lil-Majlis al-'Ūrūbbī lil-Iftā' wal-Buḥūth*, no. 12–13 (July 2008), 75–76, 85–87.

[90] *Ibid.*, 72–73.

[91] *Ibid.*, 86.

using the pen and the tongue, rather than the sword and the lance, because the Western world, having been devastated by materialist philosophies and man-made ideologies, will embrace Islam voluntarily.[92] Al-Qaraḍāwī's confidence that Islam will be embraced if only it is presented in a palatable way led him to declare, in a concise *fatwā* issued in 2006 on the duties of Muslims living in the West, that in addition to maintaining their religious identity, uniting with other Muslims and promoting the political interests of the Muslim nation, Muslims living in the West must engage in proselytizing. He stated,

> Muslims in the West ought to be sincere callers to their religion. They should keep in mind that calling others to Islam is not restricted to scholars and Sheikhs, but it goes far to encompass every committed Muslim. As we see scholars and Sheikhs delivering *khuṭbas* (sermons) and lectures, writing books to defend Islam, it is no wonder we find lay Muslims practicing *daʿwa* while employing wisdom and fair exhortation.[93]

According to a tradition narrated by Abū Dāwud, the Prophet said that he disavows any Muslim who settles among the polytheists. Q. 4:97 tells that the angels will say to the deceased who will claim they were oppressed: "Was not God's earth large enough for you to migrate?" and will condemn the "oppressed" to hellfire. As will be demonstrated below, this tradition and verse were frequently cited by *salafīs* to demonstrate the general impermissibility of residence in non-Muslim lands. *Salafīs* challenge the *wasaṭī* treatment of migration and residence in the West as desirable and their broad legitimization of it. *Wasaṭīs* addressed this challenge by contextualizing the abovementioned tradition and verse as applying to specific situations. For example, al-Qaraḍāwī argued that the Prophet's intention was not to prohibit residence among non-Muslims in all cases but to clarify that he would not be responsible for the death of Muslims who chose to reside among the polytheists who fight Islam.[94] Thus, the

[92] Yūsuf al-Qaraḍāwī, *al-Mubashshirāt bi-Intiṣār al-Islām* (Beirut: Mu'assasat al-Risāla, 2000), 32–34.

[93] Yūsuf al-Qaraḍāwī, "Duties of Muslims Living in the West," originally posted May 7, 2006 on Islamonline.net, accessed June 14, 2013: http://www.onislam.net/english/ask-the-scholar/dawah-principles/dawah-to-non-and-new-muslims/175226.html.

[94] Al-Qaraḍāwī, "al-Waṭan wal-Muwāṭana fī Ḍaw' al-Uṣūl al-ʿAqdiyya wal-Maqāṣid al-Sharʿiyya," 79–81.

ḥadīth is not relevant to the current state of Muslim migrants. Other *wasaṭī* discussions on the permissibility of living in a non-Muslim country provided similar interpretations of this tradition.[95] Q. 4:97 was contextualized by a member of the European Council, Ḥamza b. Ḥusayn al-Faʻr al-Sharīf, as being applicable only to the situation of Muslims who cannot profess their religion and, thus, is irrelevant to the situation of most Muslims minorities today.[96] Al-Qaraḍāwī[97] and Ṣalāḥ al-Dīn Sulṭān (a lecturer of Islamic law at Cairo University, a senior member of al-Qaraḍāwī's International Union of Muslim Scholars and a member of the European Council for Fatwa and Research), contextualized the verse as calling on Muslims to migrate whenever they face oppression, regardless of whether the land is non-Muslim or Muslim; Sultan even suggested that due to the oppression of Islamic activists in some Muslim countries, the verse should be interpreted as encouraging migration to the West in some cases.[98] The impermissibility of residence in non-Muslim lands was also refuted by *wasaṭīs* who cited the examples of Muslims who were permitted to live under non-Muslim rule during the life of the Prophet. Al-Qaraḍāwī[99] and al-Bishrī[100] noted that even after a Muslim state was established in al-Madīna, the Prophet did not order the Muslims who found shelter in Ethiopia to return at all.

The synthesis of *taysīr* with *tabshīr* is manifested in the *wasaṭī* understanding of "integration," a concept that Western governments and mainstream Western media articulate to express their expectation that religious minorities, particularly Muslims, give preference to the norms

[95] Al-Bishrī, "Munṭalaqāt li-Fiqh al-Aqalliyyāt," 207; *Fatwās of European Council for Fatwa and Research*, trans. Anas Usāma al-Tikritī and Shākir Nāṣif al-'Ubaydī (Cairo: Islamic INC, 2002), *Fatwā* 1 (on the permissibility of residing permanently in non-Muslim lands), 25–26. Also: Muḥammad al-Shādhilī al-Nayfar, "al-Tajannus bi-Jinsiyya Ghayr Islāmiyya," 23–24.

[96] Ḥamza b. Ḥusayn al-Faʻr al-Sharīf, "Ḥukm Mushārakat al-Muslimīn fī Mujtamaʻāt al-Aqalliyyāt Ijtimāʻiyyan wa-Siyāsiyyan," *al-Majalla al-'Ilmiyya lil-Majlis al-'Ūrūbbī lil-Iftā' wal-Buḥūth*, no. 12–13 (July 2008) 276–80.

[97] Al-Qaraḍāwī, "al-Waṭan wal-Muwāṭana fī Ḍaw' al-Uṣūl al-'Aqdiyya wal-Maqāṣid al-Sharʻiyya," 27.

[98] Ṣalāḥ al-Dīn Sulṭān, "al-Muwāṭana fī Gahyr Diyār al-Islām bayna al-Nāfīn wal-Muthbitīn," 162–64.

[99] Al-Qaraḍāwī, "al-Waṭan wal-Muwāṭana fī Ḍaw' al-Uṣūl al-'Aqdiyya wal-Maqāṣid al-Sharʻiyya," 77.

[100] Al-Bishrī, "Munṭalaqāt li-Fiqh al-Aqalliyyāt," 206.

of the majority and restrict religious practices to private or religious domains. *Wasaṭī* texts aim to propose, in the best tradition of *wasaṭiyya*, a middle ground between adhering to these expectations and disengaging from Western societies. They envision Muslims who are active, constructive, law-abiding participants in their majority non-Muslim societies and, at the same time, foster their Islamic identity and their religiously based communal ties and proselytize through the example of their good, moral conduct. In his formative book, published in 2001, al-Qaraḍāwī defined "preserving [the identity] without introversion and integrating without assimilating" as one of the objectives of his approach, adding that *fiqh al-aqalliyyāt al-Muslima* should allow Muslims to present the West with the best that they possess (Islam) while taking the best that the West possesses.[101] Writing in 2012, he argued that "what preserved the Jewish identity throughout past history is that the Jews maintained their own small community that is distinguished for its own thoughts and rituals, that is the 'Jewish ghetto,'[102] so Muslims should work hard to establish their own 'Muslim ghetto.'" However, his historical analogy aimed to encourage not introversion and isolation from majority societies but "openness that does not lead to assimilation."[103] Muṣṭafā Mala'ughlu, a member of the European Council, called for Muslims in Europe to follow the example of the Muslims in Ethiopia, who did not consider that land *dār al-ḥarb* and assisted and contributed to the majority society.[104] In 2008, Ḥusayn Ḥalāwa, the Secretary General of the European Council, encouraged "positive integration" that would make it possible for Muslims to follow the Jewish example, as he understands it, of acclimatizing in

[101] Al-Qaraḍāwī, *Fī Fiqh al-Aqalliyyāt al-Muslima*, 34–35.

[102] Compare to Muḥammad al-Ghazālī's 1984 book in which he called on Muslim countries to provide funding to establish Muslim schools that will maintain the immigrants' "relation to their heritage, traditions, and rituals *as if all that changed in their lives is their location*" (emphasis added). He also called for the establishment of Muslim social clubs that would bring Muslims together in a Muslim atmosphere of friendship and affection, increasing the prospect that Muslim men marry Muslim women instead of infidels: al-Ghazālī, *Mustaqbal al-Islām Khārij Arḍihi*, 78–79.

[103] Yusuf al-Qaradawi, "Muslim Minorities and Politics," April 30, 2012, accessed June 23, 2013: http://www.onislam.net/english/shariah/contemporary-issues/critiques-and-thought/456871-muslim-minorities-and-politics.html?Thought.

[104] Muṣṭafā Mala'ughlu, "al-Mabādi' al-Akhlāqiyya lil-Ta'āmul al-Mālī fī 'Ūrūbbā," *al-Majalla al-'Ilmiyya lil-Majlis al-'Ūrūbbī lil-Iftā' wal-Buḥūth*, no. 14–15 (July 2009), 258.

their societies and affecting them without assimilating into them.[105] He called upon Muslims to cooperate and coexist with their non-Muslim neighbors, abide by the laws of the land, engage in dialogues and avoid introversion, as well as develop strong communal institutions, take Muslim spouses to protect the family from assimilation, and prepare for a change in the civilizational balance of power in favor of Islam.[106]

There is a distinct, even if not always obvious, difference between the *wasaṭī* concept of proselytizing and other integration-minded conceptualizations, including 'Amr Khālid's and Tariq Ramadan's. Whereas *wasaṭīs* endorse integration, to a large measure, as a means to spread Islam. Khālid, the Egyptian-born (1967) and England-based popular television preacher, who in 2003 presented a comprehensive thesis on the desired identity of Muslims in the West, considers Muslims as goodwill ambassadors whose task is to improve the image of Islam. While he leaves the door open for a European embrace of Islam, he makes a point of emphasizing that the objective of Muslim migrants is not to convert Westerners, who should be left to choose whether or not to convert. It is not a coincidence that, contrary to al-'Alwānī, his narration of the migration to Ethiopia neglected to mention the conversion of the king.[107] Ramadan argues that it is a duty for Muslims to explain the contents of their faith and the teachings of Islam, but his understanding of *da'wa* mainly highlights other issues, primarily the duty to socially engage with the larger society in all the fields where one can contribute.[108]

As is the case with the general *wasaṭī* theory, the promotion of *taysīr* and *tabshīr* as objectives in the context of *fiqh al-aqalliyyāt al-Muslima* calls for *ijtihād*, a process of interpretation that considers anew past juristic decisions and rediscovers neglected ones, as well as broadly applies juristic mechanisms to address challenges and affect decisions.

[105] Ḥusayn Ḥalāwa, "Qawā'id al-Indimāj al-'Ījābī lil-Muslimīn fī 'Ūrūbbā," *al-Majalla al-'Ilmiyya lil-Majlis al-'Ūrūbbī lil-Iftā' wal-Buḥūth*, no. 12–13 (July 2008), 306–9.

[106] *Ibid.*, 309–38.

[107] Amr Khaled, *Integration im Islam: Über die Rolle der Muslime in Europa* (Karlsruhe, Andalusia Verlag, 2005); Uriya Shavit, *Islamism and the West: From "Cultural Attack" to "Missionary Migrant"* (London and New York: Routledge, 2014), 163–65.

[108] Tariq Ramadan, *Western Muslims and the Future of Islam* (Oxford and New York: Oxford University Press, 2010), 73–75.

This *ijtihād* aims to provide minorities with solutions that accommodate the unique difficulties they face and fulfill their communal tasks without traversing the limitations set by the *sharīʿa*. Its indispensability is explained by al-ʿAlwānī, al-Qaraḍāwī, and al-Najjār, respectively, as follows: First, *ijtihād* for Muslim minorities is necessary because there is much confusion as to what is permissible and what is impermissible for them, as well as about basic concepts that define minorities' existence and their relations with majority societies.[109] Second, the challenges faced by Muslim minorities are particularly grave and, therefore, the general need of contemporary *fiqh* for *ijtihād* is of even greater urgency.[110] Third, while the situation of Muslims living as minorities is not new, the religious laws of the Muslim minorities of the past were decided at a time when *ijtihād* was weak and *taqlīd* was prevalent.[111]

In constructing a framework for *ijtihād* pertaining to *fiqh al-aqalliyyāt al-Muslima*, *wasaṭīs* reasserted that a broad approach to *maṣlaḥa* is an indispensable means to imbue religious laws with the flexibility that their approach desires. Al-Qaraḍāwī's and al-ʿAlwānī's formative texts on Muslim minorities suggested broadening *maṣlaḥa* in the context of Muslim minorities' jurisprudence in a way similar to that suggested by al-Qaraḍāwī's general theorizing on *fiqh* in the late 1990s, though their respective emphases differed. Al-Qaraḍāwī stressed that the *sharīʿa* is pragmatic rather than idealistic and asserted that both necessities, as well as some individual (and not only communal) needs permit otherwise prohibited actions.[112] Al-ʿAlwānī suggested adding new objectives to the list of *maqāṣid al-sharīʿa*.[113] *Maṣlaḥa* as a means to affect the religious law of Muslim minorities was highlighted in other deliberations. Unattested *maṣlaḥa* was mentioned in the European Council's formative document as a source of jurisprudence,[114] and the importance of adjusting decisions

[109] Al-ʿAlwānī, *Fī Fiqh al-Aqalliyyāt al-Muslima*, 10–11; "Madkhal ilā Fiqh al-Aqalliyyāt," 52–53.

[110] Al-Qaraḍāwī, *Fī Fiqh al-Aqalliyyāt al-Muslima*, 41.

[111] Al-Najjār, *Fiqh al-Muwāṭana lil-Muslimīn fī ʾŪrūbbā*, 73–75.

[112] Al-Qaraḍāwī, *Fī Fiqh al-Aqalliyyāt al-Muslima*, 55.

[113] Al-ʿAlwānī, *Fī Fiqh al-Aqalliyyāt al-Muslima*, 27–28; "Madkhal ilā Fiqh al-Aqalliyyāt," 68–69.

[114] Section Seven, clause thirty, n.d., accessed September 25, 2013: http://www.e-cfr.org/ar/index.php?cat_id=006; also "Taʿrīf bil-Majlis al-ʾŪrūbbī lil-Iftāʾ wal-Buḥūth," in

in order to meet the objectives of the Lawmaker was further discussed in a number of works published by the Council. One concept addressed at length was *ma'ālāt al-af'āl* (the results of actions), a variation of *fiqh al-muwāzanāt* that calls upon jurists to assess whether the prospective repercussions of their decisions meet the objectives of *sharī'a* and then accommodate them accordingly. Al-Najjār stressed its importance to *fiqh al-aqalliyyāt al-Muslima*, noting that the situation of Muslim minorities is complicated.[115] He argued that it is often the case that the objectives of laws intended for a majority Muslim society in which Islam's laws are applied cannot be accomplished when Muslims constitute a minority. Thus, decisions need to be accommodated so that they do not breach the Lawmaker's intention.[116]

The most innovative and audacious contribution of *wasaṭī fiqh al-aqalliyyāt al-Muslima*, based on the notion that the list of the primary objectives of the Lawgiver can be expanded, is its consideration of proselytizing as a *maṣlaḥa* that justifies the suspension of the prohibited. Remarkably, this contribution is hardly theorized by *wasaṭīs*, and perhaps that is the reason why it has been largely neglected in previous scholarly analyses of *wasaṭī* jurisprudence. As was demonstrated in the preceding paragraphs, al-Qaraḍāwī and al-'Alwānī regard proselytizing as a duty for Muslims in the West and a legitimization for their presence there. As will be detailed in the next two chapters, *wasaṭī fatwās* on Muslim minorities, particularly those suspending stronger prohibitions, invoked the need to provide greater opportunities for the spread of Islam as justification, i.e., broadened the primary objectives of the Lawgiver to include proselytizing. But while the link between facilitation and proselytizing is direct and clear, al-Qaraḍāwī and al-'Alwānī have not explicitly declared *da'wa* to be an objective of religious law that justifies accommodations. There are two possible explanations for this silence. One is the "chicken and egg" issue: declaring *da'wa* a *maṣlaḥa* could expose the *wasaṭī* approach to the

Qarārāt wa-Fatāwā al-Majlis al-'Ūrūbbī lil-Iftā' wal-Buḥūth, 13; "About the European Council for Fatwa and Research," 3.

115 'Abd al-Majīd al-Najjār, "Ma'ālāt al-Af'āl wa-Athruhā fī Fiqh al-Aqalliyyāt," *al-Majalla al-'Ilmiyya lil-Majlis al-'Ūrūbbī lil-Iftā' wal-Buḥūth*, no. 4–5 (June 2004), 149–50.

116 *Ibid.*, 187–90.

allegation that its triumphalist tone is merely a pretext for permitting the prohibited; al-ʿAlwānī revealed this concern when he expressed dismay over the principle "necessities permit prohibitions" being used to effect the religious law of Muslim minorities. (He believes it reflects negatively on the Islamic personality of Muslim minorities).[117] Yet while he insists on positive phrasings, his theory nevertheless opens the door for legitimizing, in the case of Muslim minorities, otherwise prohibited actions based on consideration of *maṣlaḥa*. Another possible concern is that elaborate discussion on the juristic implications of proselytizing may encourage dismissing *wasaṭī fiqh al-aqalliyyāt al-Muslima* as a conspiracy to take over Western lands that is merely veiled in gentle speech. Indeed, when I asked Ḥusayn Ḥalāwa about proselytizing, the Secretary General emphasized that the Council's approach does not seek the Islamization of Europe, nor does it consider *daʿwa* as an objective or a *maṣlaḥa*.[118] To support his assertion, he noted that though the Council permitted Muslims to take mortgages when no alternative exists for them to purchase a home, it did not permit doing so for the purpose of building mosques and enhancing proselytizing. The *fatwā* permitting mortgages (see discussion in Chapter 3) is unambiguous in its treatment of *daʿwa* as a *maṣlaḥa* that justifies *taysīr*. It was retrospectively interpreted as such by al-Najjār, a member of the Council, in his theorizing on *maqāṣid al-sharīʿa* and the religious law of Muslim minorities. He supported the idea that in some cases facilitation in decisions is essential in order to promote proselytizing.[119] Nevertheless, Ḥalāwa's words demonstrate the sensitivity of the issue in the European context.

Along with a broad approach to *maṣlaḥa*, *wasaṭī fiqh al-aqalliyyāt al-Muslima* draws from the general *wasaṭī* theory of jurisprudence also in

[117] Al-ʿAlwānī, *Madkhal ilā Fiqh al-Aqalliyyāt*, 52; *Fī Fiqh al-Aqalliyyāt*, 10. The 2000 book addresses only the usage of "necessities" and not that of "necessities permit the prohibited."

[118] Interview by the author with Ḥusayn Ḥalāwa at the Islamic Cultural Center of Ireland, February 14, 2012.

[119] Al-Najjār, "Maʾālāt al-Afʿāl wa-Athruhā fī Fiqh al-Aqalliyyāt," 198–99; in his 2011 treatise al-Najjār claims a "civilizational dialogue" takes places in which Muslims in the West take from it material advances and endow it with Muslim values essential to resolving the West's problems. He calls for the establishment of *daʿwa* institutions that will present Islam as the practical solution to the West's problems: "al-Dawr al-Ḥaḍārī lil-Waqf al-Islāmī bil-Gharb," *al-Majalla al-ʿIlmiyya lil-Majlis al-ʾŪrūbbī lil-Iftāʾ wal-Buḥūth*, no. 18 (July 2011), 156–57, 174.

stressing the importance of cross-*madhhab* search as a means for addressing Muslim minorities' conditions in harmony with the objectives of relieving Muslims from *ḥaraj* (hardship) and increasing the potential for non-Muslim conversion. Writing on the jurisprudence of Muslim minorities, al-Qaraḍāwī described *sharīʿa* as a vast field that, when thoroughly explored, reveals hidden treasures from the past that can resolve the difficulties of the present. He provided a long list of examples for the merit of this mechanism in making the lives of Muslim minorities easier. One is the *Mālikī* opinion that dogs are not impure; he believes that based on cross-*madhhab* search that aims for facilitation, this opinion (which only *Mālikīs* endorse) should be embraced in the case of Muslims who live in the West because pets are commonplace there.[120] Al-Najjār understood the issue similarly, emphasizing that some prior juristic decisions that had not been found suitable may prove upon rediscovery to be applicable in contemporary situations.[121] The European Council for Fatwa and Research declared cross-*madhhab* search as one of its juristic foundations in its formative document.[122] In its first session, it advised a convert that she need not choose a school of law and that her only duty is to follow the Quran and the traditions of the Prophet. The Council cautioned that confining oneself to a single *madhhab* risks limiting the potential for *taysīr* and *tabshīr*, which must be enhanced, especially in the case of new Muslims.[123]

THE *SALAFĪ* OBJECTIVES AND METHODOLOGY FOR MUSLIM MINORITIES

The *salafī* approach to the jurisprudence of Muslim minorities is similar to that of the *wasaṭīs'* in one crucial aspect. Like the *wasaṭīs*, *salafīs* regard Muslim residence in non-Muslim lands permissible for those who can

[120] Al-Qaraḍāwī, *Fī Fiqh al-Aqalliyyāt al-Muslima*, 58–60.

[121] Al-Najjār, *Fiqh al-Muwāṭana lil-Muslimīn fī 'Ūrūbbā*, 108.

[122] The constitution of the European Council, section seven, clause 31, n.d., accessed September 25, 2013: http://www.e-cfr.org/ar/index.php?cat_id=006; Ḥusayn Ḥalāwa, "Taʿrīf bil-Majlis al-'Ūrūbbī lil-Iftā' wal-Buḥūth," in *Qarārāt wa-Fatāwā al-Majlis al-'Ūrūbbī lil-Iftā' wal-Buḥūth*, 13; "About the European Council for Fatwa and Research," 3.

[123] *Qarārāt wa-Fatāwā al-Majlis al-'Ūrūbbī lil-Iftā' wal-Buḥūth, Fatwā* 6, 38–40.

practice Islam and stress proselytizing as a justification for migration. Unlike *wasaṭīs*, their legitimization is caustic. Based on Q. 4:97 and the tradition according to which the Prophet stated his disavowal of Muslims who live among polytheists, *salafīs* hold that, in general, Muslims must live in *dār al-Islām*. They consider residence in infidel lands as extremely risky and highly undesirable, conditionally tolerable at best, and characterize *daʿwa* efforts by Muslims who are strong in faith and can practice their religion as an almost exclusive justification for voluntary residence in non-Muslim lands. As opposed to *wasaṭīs*, *salafīs* do not believe that Muslim minorities are entitled to any kind of concessions based on the unique hardships they face or on their duty to proselytize. Thus, *taysīr*—a foundation of *wasaṭī fiqh al-aqalliyyāt al-Muslima* and its main practical implication—is absent from *salafī* theorizing on residence among non-Muslim majorities, and some *salafī fatwās* on Muslim minorities read as negations of *wasaṭī* facilitations.

The grudging tolerance of *salafīs* of Muslim residence in non-Muslim lands is rooted in the approach of the *Ḥanbalī* school and broadened to highlight proselytizing as a potential legitimization. As noted above, *Ḥanbalīs* chose a middle ground between the *Mālikī* approach that prohibited residence in infidel lands and the *Shāfiʿī* approach, which legitimized and even encouraged residence that could enhance proselytizing. *Ḥanbalīs* argued that if Muslims are able to practice Islam in a non-Muslim territory then they may remain, though it is recommended that they ultimately move to Muslim territory. Wahhābī jurisprudence in the nineteenth century maintained this line of thought. The Saudi jurist Ṣāliḥ b. Muḥammad al-Shithrī (d. 1889) suggested that it is permissible to live under the rule of infidels, but only if the Muslim can manifest his religion and demonstrate animosity towards non-Muslims, or disavow them. He based the latter argument on Q. 109:1–2, 10:41, 104 and 60:4; referring to the latter verse, which describes Abraham's and his followers' disassociation from and animosity towards idol worshipers, al-Shithrī explained that Muslims who follow this pattern may reside among infidels.[124]

[124] Ṣāliḥ b. Muḥammad al-Shithrī, *Ḥukm al-Lujūʾ wal-Iqāma fī Bilād al-Kuffār* (Riyadh: Dār al-Ḥabīb, 2001), 69–70.

Contemporary *salafī* jurisprudence on Muslims living as a minority addressed two situations: visits to non-Muslim lands and permanent residence. *Salafīs* strongly prohibited visits, but this prohibition is not without exceptions. The Permanent Committee, headed by b. Bāz, ruled that it is not permissible to go on vacations in Europe for fear of temptation and based its decision on the tradition according to which the Prophet said he disavowed Muslims who live among the polytheists.[125] Ibn 'Uthaymīn similarly ruled that vacations in infidel lands are impermissible, noting that there are plenty of tourist options in Muslim countries.[126] The approach to sojourns in non-Muslim lands for academic study or business has been more nuanced. *Salafīs* strongly advised against studying in Western institutions but accepted that it is permissible in cases where no Muslim institution provides a parallel program and the Muslim's faith is strong enough to avoid doubts and temptations.[127] Ibn Bāz ruled that it is impermissible to travel to a non-Muslim country for the purpose of commerce or personal visits.[128] His deputy in the Permanent Committee, 'Abd al-Rāziq 'Afīfī, offered a more lenient position (and exceptional, in the *salafī* context). He ruled that a Muslim who can find a job in a Muslim country is not permitted to sojourn for the purpose of working, but a Muslim who cannot find work is permitted if he is able to avoid imitating the infidels and can maintain his religion there.[129] In this instance, the necessity of providing for one's family was cited as a *maṣlaḥa* that legitimizes an act which is otherwise prohibited. The only case in which sojourning is not only conditionally legitimate but also potentially desirable is when intended for *da'wa* activities among Muslim minorities. Ibn 'Uthaymīn approved of knowledgeable Muslims

[125] As quoted by Muḥammad b. Nāṣir al-Shithrī in the introduction to Ṣāliḥ b. Muḥammad al-Shithrī's *Ḥukm al-Lujū' wal-Iqāma fī Bilād al-Kuffār* (Riyadh: Dār al-Ḥabīb, 2001), Fatwā 2393, 6–7.

[126] Muḥammad b. Ṣāliḥ Ibn 'Uthaymīn, "al-Safar ilā Bilād al-Kuffār," in *Fatāwā al-Balad al-Ḥarām* (Cairo: al-Maktaba al-Tawfīqiyya, n.d.), 189.

[127] *Ibid.*; al-Lajna al-Dā'ima, "Mā Ḥukm al-Safar wal-Dirāsa fī Bilād al-Kuffār" (decision 20968), in *Fatāwā al-Balad al-Ḥarām* (Cairo: al-Maktaba al-Tawfīqiyya, n.d.), 191–92.

[128] 'Abd al-'Azīz b. 'Abdallāh Ibn Bāz, "al-Safar Khārij al-Bilād al-Islāmiyya," in *Fatāwā al-Balad al-Ḥarām* (Cairo: al-Maktaba al-Tawfīqiyya, n.d.), 187–88.

[129] 'Abd al-Razāq al-'Afīfī, "Ḥukm al-Safar ilā Bilād al-Kufr lil-'Amal," in Aḥmad b. 'Abdallāh al-Shāfi'ī (ed.), *500 Jawāb fī al-Buyū' wal-Mu'āmalāt* (Cairo: Dār Ibn Ḥazm, 2010), 68.

traveling to lands of disbelief "for the sake of Muslim brothers who are living there but have insufficient knowledge to respond to specious arguments." In fact, "it might be imperative" for them to sojourn "in order to help and support them [Muslim minorities] and to show them that they have brothers elsewhere."[130]

The *salafī* approach to Muslims who are already settled in non-Muslim lands is uncompromising in tone but leaves open the possibility for interpretations that legitimize permanent settlement. *Salafīs* argue that it is strictly forbidden for a Muslim to settle in an infidel society but offer two particular exceptions: being unable to migrate to a Muslim country or being active in proselytizing. While this approval appears narrow and circumspect, *salafīs* avoid detailing what kind of hindrances legitimize continuous residence among a majority infidel society or how active a Muslim should be in *da'wa* in order for his efforts to legitimize his choice of staying. *Salafīs* do not state, for example, that the nature of the hindrance has to be such that prevents any possibility of moving to a Muslim land or that proselytizing should be the exclusive occupation of the Muslim living in a land of infidels. This vagueness, untypical of *salafī fatwās*, suggests that *salafī* jurists understand the improbability of a massive Muslim return from the West.

Thus, their *fatwās* aim to encourage Muslim minorities to consider their religious status as severely endangered, to strengthen their devotion and enthusiastically engage in proselytizing. To note a few examples, the Permanent Committee, headed by b. Bāz, answered a query by a 75-year-old Lebanese Muslim who married a non-Muslim and settled in Brazil. His two sons had neglected Islam, and he was concerned that upon his death he would not receive an Islamic burial. Based on Q. 4:97, the Committee advised him to move to a Muslim country but said that if he were unable to do so he would still be eligible for an Islamic burial, based on Q. 4:98, so long as he continued to practice his religion.[131] The decision was careful not to describe what constitutes legitimate reasons

[130] Muhammad ibn Saalih al-'Uthaymeen, Question 17, in Ibn Baz and Shaykh Uthaymeen, *Muslim Minorities* (Hounslow, United Kingdom: Message of Islam, 1998), 77.

[131] As quoted by Muḥammad b. Nāṣir al-Shithrī in the introduction to Saliḥ b. Muḥammad al-Shithrī's *Ḥukm al-Lujū' wal-Iqāma fī Bilād al-Kuffār*, *Fatwā* 19670, 11–13.

for being unable to move or, for that matter, what constitutes practicing Islam. Ibn Bāz ruled, based on Q. 4:97 and the tradition according to which the Prophet disavows Muslims living among polytheists, that "living in a land where shirk, disbelief, Christianity and other false creeds are prevalent is not permissible" whether the reason is work, business, or study. It is obligatory to migrate, "except for a man who has knowledge and insight" and toils "to call people to Allah."[132] Al-Munajjid ruled that "migrating from the land of the *kufr* to a Muslim country is obligatory upon every Muslim who is able to do it; whoever does not migrate when able to is wronging himself and is subject to Allah's warning of server torment." He based this decision on Q. 4:97, the tradition according to which the Prophet disavows Muslims living among polytheists and the *ijtihād* of the *Mālikī* jurist Abū al-Walīd Muḥammad Ibn Rushd (the grandfather, d. 1126). However, al-Munajjid also advised that so long as a Muslim is unable to migrate—if, in the specific case of the *fatwā*, she is divorced and has no male guardian in a Muslim country—she should adhere to her religion as much as she can and convey the call of Islam to others, "especially non-Muslim women and Muslim women who are negligent about their religion."[133] Ibn 'Uthaymīn ruled that residence in infidel lands poses a grave danger to one's religion, morals, and practices and is therefore permissible only if the Muslim is strong in faith and is able to practice his religion. He based the latter ruling on Q. 4:97. One's possible activities when residing among the infidels are divided, according to b. 'Uthaymīn, into only two categories: either he dedicates his time to *da'wa*, which is a religious duty and a form of *jihād*, or to the study of the moral corruption of the infidels, which is also a form of *jihād* because it helps warn against their corrupting influence.[134]

[132] 'Abd al-'Azīz b. 'Abdallāh Ibn Bāz, "It Is Not Permissible to Reside in a Country Where Disbelief Is Prevalent Except for the Call of Allah," n.d., accessed September 25, 2011: http://www.alifta.org/Fatāwā/Fatāwācoeval.aspx?View=Page&HajjEntryID=0&HajjEntryName=&NodeID=4656&PageID=1327&SectionID=14&SubjectPageTitlesID=98552&MarkIndex=5&0.

[133] Muḥammad Ṣāliḥ al-Munajjid, "Ruling on Migrating to a Muslim Country and Staying There without a Mahram," in Muhammad Saed Abdul-Rahman (ed.), *Islam: Questions and Answers—Islamic Politics* (London: MSA Publication Ltd), 18–20.

[134] Muḥammad b. Ṣāliḥ Ibn 'Uthaymīn, "al-Iqāma fī Bilād al-Kuffār," in *Fatāwā al-Balad al-Ḥarām* (Cairo: al-Maktaba al-Tawfīqiyya, n.d.), 189–91.

The *salafī* conceptualization of Muslim residence in infidel lands makes its point not only through the evidence it chooses to present but also through the sources it neglects. A particularly telling example is the *hijra* to Ethiopia. It is hardly mentioned in *salafī* texts for exactly the same reasons that made it so essential to *wasaṭī* ones: its potential to demonstrate that non-Muslim countries can serve as a safe haven for Muslims and that Muslims can establish strong, friendly ties with their non-Muslim hosts.

Contrary to *wasaṭīs, salafīs* do not hold that Muslim minorities are entitled to facilitation because of the unique hardships they encounter. This position is derived from the foundational *salafī* view that Allah's laws are universal and should be interpreted and applied literally, and that strictly adhering to these laws constitutes the essence of Islam's *wasaṭī* nature. In the eyes of *salafīs*, the grave challenges which Muslim minorities face are opportunities for demonstrating strong devotion. This point of view obviates the need to highlight specific methodologies for Muslim minorities. While *wasaṭī* foundational texts on *fiqh al-aqalliyyāt al-Muslima* focus on the potential of *maṣlaḥa* and *cross-madhhab* search to effect decisions in line with specific objectives, the *salafī* ambition when addressing Muslim minorities is to assert the authority of existing *fatwās* in non-Muslim lands. An early example of this ambition was the decision of the Saudi Council of Senior Scholars in 1978 concerning the Ramaḍān fast in countries where the sun sets late at night. The Council asserted that with the exception of medical excuses, the rules of fasting must be applied in countries where the sun sets late as in any other region because "Islamic *sharīʻa* is universal for all people in all countries."[135] This decision was challenged by a decision of Egypt's Dār al-Iftā', which permitted Norwegian Muslims and those in other countries where the days are long to fast for a similar number of hours as the people of Mecca and Medina.[136] The opinion of the Council of Senior Scholars was repeated in a number of other decisions, including by

[135] Hay'at Kibār al-'Ulamā', "Ṣiyām Man Yaṭālu Nahāruhum" (decision 61, March 22, 1978), *al-Mujtama'* 1769 (September 10, 2007), 38.
[136] 'Abd al-Qādir, *Min Fiqh al-Aqalliyyāt al-Muslima*, 126.

al-'Uthaymīn, who insisted in response to a query about Scandinavian states, where daylight may last twenty-two hours, that one must fast all day long so long as the night is separated from the day,[137] and by b. Bāz, who emphasized that this regulation also applies in the opposite scenario, if the days of Ramaḍān happen to be very short.[138] (In 2010, the European Council embraced, both in principle and in practice, the *salafī* opinion, suggesting that the pragmatic view of Dār al-Iftā' was not supported by evidence. Nevertheless, it left an opening for facilitations by permitting Muslims in countries where the days are long, who experience hardship that does not allow them to continue to work, to break their fast. Maḥbūb al-Raḥman, head of the Islamic Cultural Center Norway and a member of the Council, informed me in 2014 that the issue is still being deliberated at the Council; his assistants said that they do not find a seventeen-hour fast difficult at all, so long as "one maintains a routine." An attendee stated that some attendees choose a middle ground: they fast in accordance with Paris time (which represents the nearest-by moderate timing and the limits of Islam's conquests).[139]

Salafī emphasis on strict adherence to the divine law does not mean that jurists always approach situations that are unique to Muslim minorities by referencing the appropriate verse or tradition. Rather, as will be demonstrated in Chapters 3 and 4, they follow the general tendency of their approach and are literalist and uncompromising when considering individual hardships in the social and financial spheres. But *salafīs* apply *maṣlaḥa* and accommodate decisions in some instances when the relations between individuals and the state, as well as communal *maslaḥas*, are at stake.

137 Muḥammad b. Ṣāliḥ al-'Uthaymīn, "Ṭūl al-Layl wal-Nahār," in Muḥammad Muḥammad Tāmir (ed.), *Fiqh al-'Ibādāt lil-Shaykh Muḥammad b. Ṣāliḥ al-'Utahymīn* (Cairo: Dār al-Risāla, 2003), 223–24.

138 'Abd al-'Azīz b. 'Abdallāh Ibn Bāz, "Ṣiyām Man Yaṭālu Nahāruhum Jidan wa-Kadhā Man Yaqṣuru Nahāruhum," in Ṣalāḥ al-Dīn Maḥmūd al-Sa'īd (ed.), *Fatāwā al-'Ulamā' ḥawla al-Aqalliyyāt al-Muslima fī al-'ālam* (Alexandria: Dār al-'īmān, 2004), 95–100.

139 Al-Majlis al-'Ūrūbbī lil-Iftā' wal-Buḥūth, "Ḥawla Ikhtilāf Sā'at al-Ṣiyām fī al-Buldān dhāt Khuṭūṭ al-'Arḍ al-'āliyya," session 20, decision 7, June 28, 2010, accessed August 19, 2013: http://www.e-cfr.org/ar/index.php?ArticleID=1039; interview with Maḥbūb al-Raḥman, Oslo, March 22, 2014.

In general, *salafīs*, like *wasaṭīs*, believe all Muslims should take part in spreading the word of Allah and His Prophet.[140] They hold, like *wasaṭīs*, that Western societies are miserable and desperate for Islam's salvation[141] and that Muslims should undertake *daʿwa* activities among non-Muslims for the latter's own benefit, to endow them with happiness and success.[142] Proselytizing is considered by *salafīs* a communal duty (*farḍ kifāya*), that is, if a sufficient number of Muslims engage in it, the rest may be exempted,[143] and *salafī* texts tend to emphasize the importance of qualified individuals engaging in *daʿwa*. While proselytizing is at the heart of the *salafī* conceptualization of Muslim life in non-Muslims lands, they do not hold it to justify facilitation, but the opposite: it is essential that Muslim minorities obey Allah's laws uncompromisingly in order to convince others to convert. Ibn Bāz remarked that one of the most important matters is that Muslim minorities adhere to Allah's religion, "understand it well and cling to it whatever their situation; in times of difficulty and ease, health and sickness, travel and residence." Firm adherence to Allah's laws is particularly important for Muslim minorities because they need to "become a good model for their enemies around them and a living example of Islam in their behavior, speech, and deeds. Thus, their enemies will see them and understand from their behavior and character the greatness and virtue of Islam."[144] Echoing this opinion, al-Madkhalī, in his book *Advice to the Salafis Living in the West*, called for Muslim minorities to abide exclusively by the Quran and the Sunna in order to bring non-Muslims to Islam.[145]

While *salafīs* believe that strictly adhering to Allah's laws as they interpret them is crucial for bringing non-Muslims to Islam, some are

[140] ʿAbdul ʿAzeez Ibn ʿAbdullah Ibn Baaz, *Words of Advice Regarding Daʿwah* (Birmingham: al-Hidaayah Publishing and Distribution, 1998), 47–48.

[141] "Limādha Yuwāṣilu al-Islām Najāḥahu fī al-Duwal al-Mutaqaddima," Ṣalāḥ al-Dīn Maḥmūd al-Saʿīd (ed.), *Fatāwā al-ʿUlamāʾ ḥawla al-Aqalliyyāt al-Muslima fī al-ʿālam* (Alexandria: Dār al-ʾĪmān, 2004), 265–57.

[142] Ṣāliḥ b. Fawzān al-Fawzān, *Aḥkām al-Taʿāmul maʿa Ghayr al-Muslimīn* (Riyadh: Daār Kunūz Ishbīliya lil-Nashr wal-Tawzīʿ, 2009), 14.

[143] *Ibid.*, 15.

[144] ʿAbdul Azeez Ibn Baaz, "The Importance of Muslim Minorities Adhering to Islam," in Shaykh Ibn Baz and Shaykh Uthaymeen, *Muslim Minorities* (Hounslow, United Kingdom: Message of Islam, 1998), 15.

[145] Rabīʿ b. Hādī al-Madkhalī, *An Advice to the Salafis Living in the West*, 20–45.

aware that the most effective way to propagate Islam in the West is in a gentle and gradualist manner rather than an intimidating one. In his article "Inviting to Allah in Communities Where There Are Muslim Minorities," al-'Uthaymīn noted that *da'wa* activists must bear in mind that "each person has his own state and condition." Just as Allah revealed some of his commands in a gradualist manner, so should propagators of Islam evaluate a person's openness and ability to accept the invitation to Islam so as to avoid alienation and antipathy.[146] However, in another context, al-'Uthaymīn stressed that once a non-Muslim decided to convert, he or she cannot determine his or her own conditions (*wasaṭīs*, as noted above, endorsed a measure of leniency in such cases). A French Catholic who contemplated embracing Islam but argued that she would not be able to pray five times a day and rejected the plurality of wives was answered by al-'Uthaymīn that if she wished to escape hellfire she must abide by Allah's laws rather than make up her own. Asked whether the *maṣlaḥa* gained by one's converting to Islam is greater than the potential *mafsada* incurred by one's neglect of some rituals, he replied that such a case would constitute *maṣlaḥa* for the new Muslim but would result in *mafsada* to Islam because other Muslims would seek facilitations similar to those enjoyed by the new Muslim. Thus, new Muslims should be told that they must embrace Islam in its entirety.[147]

DEBATING LOYALTY AND DISAVOWAL

The concept of *al-walā' wal-barā'* became a focus of the *salafī–wasaṭī* polemic on the jurisprudence of Muslim minorities. The *salafī* understanding of "loyalty and disavowal" places three primary restrictions on Muslims: not to be loyal to non-Muslims, not to befriend or show affection toward non-Muslims, and not to imitate non-Muslims. While most

[146] Muhammad Ibn Saalih al-'Uthaymeen, "Inviting to Allaah in Communities Where There Are Muslim Minorities," in Shaykh Ibn Baz and Shaykh Uthaymeen, *Muslim Minorities* (Hounslow, United Kingdom: Message of Islam, 1998), 48–52.

[147] Quoted in Ṣalāḥ al-Dīn Maḥmūd al-Sa'īd (ed.), *Fatāwā al-'Ulamā' ḥawla al-Aqalliyyāt al-Muslima fī al-'ālam* (Alexandria: Dār al-'Īmān, 2004), 293–95.

contemporary *salafī* writings on *al-walāʾ wal-barāʾ* do not specifically address the condition of living in non-Muslim societies, translated treatises and *fatwās* on the subject have proliferated in the past two decades in *salafī* mosques in the West and on multilingual *salafī* websites and have become a hallmark of the distinguishable *salafī* approach to the jurisprudence of Muslim minorities. In a Saudi context, and possibly in other majority Muslim contexts, the insistence that Muslims avoid friendship with non-Muslims, as well as avoid any type of physical resemblance to them, may or may not impact daily life. In the case of Muslim minorities, however, such behavior is more likely to have an impact. Thus, when *salafī al-walāʾ wal-barāʾ* is communicated to Muslim audiences in the West, its context is more relevant and intense. Since the *salafī* concept challenges the foundations of Muslim presence in the West as conceptualized by *wasaṭīs*, the latter dedicated considerable efforts to refute it in their writing and *fatwās*.

Salafī fatwās make it clear that it is the religious duty of Muslims to resent and despise those who are not Muslim while reserving their affection for and loyalty to those who are Muslims because they are Muslims. The language used seemingly obviates discussion about interfaith dialogues, mutual respect and trust building, and cooperation between majorities and non-Muslim minorities. To note several examples, b. Bāz ruled, based on Q. 49:10 and the Prophet's words, as narrated by ʿAbdallāh b. ʿUmar, according to which "the Muslim is the brother of the Muslim," that Muslims must not take non-Muslims as friends, and must disavow and hate them.[148] Muḥammad al-Munajjid replied with amazement to a Muslim who was about to marry a Chinese woman who had agreed to convert but had been struggling with his deep love for her parents, who had refused to convert: "By Allah, it is extremely astonishing how a Muslim man that believes in Allah and [in] the last day [day of judgment] can love people who are non-believers that don't believe in Allah and [in] the last day and don't forbid what Allah forbids and don't practice the religion of truth and refuse the religion of Islam."

[148] ʿAbd al-ʿAzīz b. ʿAbdallāh Ibn Bāz, "Ḥukm Muṣāḥabat al-Kāfir," in Aḥmad b. ʿAbdallāh al-Shāfiʿī (ed.), *500 Jawāb fī al-Buyūʿ wal-Muʿāmalāt* (Cairo: Dār Ibn Ḥazm, 2010), 241.

Al-Munajjid stated that affection for non-Muslims breaches Q. 58:22, which forbids friendship with and love for infidels, and added that it is obligatory upon the future son-in-law to scorn his fiancée's parents for their disbelief.[149] Ibn 'Uthaymīn, relying on Q. 60:4 (see above) as well as Q. 58:22 (which forbids believers from socializing with infidels), cautioned that it is "impermissible for a Muslim to feel any love in his heart towards the enemies of Allah who are in fact his enemies."[150] Relying on Q. 11:45–46, he wrote that a Muslim should not address a non-Muslim as "my brother" unless the non-Muslim were his biological brother or they shared a wet nurse because, other than these two kinds of brotherly bonding, the only brotherhood is that of the believers. Relying on Q. 58:22, he argued that a Muslim must not address a non-Muslim as a "friend" or a "mate" in a way that signifies affection; it is permissible to do so only in neutral situations such as when addressing someone whose name is not known.[151] He stressed, citing Q. 60:1 and 5:51–52, that any infidel is an enemy of Allah and His Prophet and that Muslims must hate him with all their hearts.[152]

The editors at al-Munajjid's "Islam Question and Answer" relied on a tradition narrated by al-Tirmidhī and Abū-Dāwud, according to which the Prophet commanded, "Do not keep company with anyone but a believer and do not let anyone eat your food but one who is pious," to caution Muslim women against forging friendships with non-Muslim women because such friendships may lead to disobeying the principle of *al-walā' wal-barā'*.[153] Addressing the concerns of a male university student who

[149] Muḥammad Ṣāliḥ al-Munajjid, "Ruling on Loving Non-Muslims," in Muhammad Saed Abdul-Rahman (ed.), *Islam: Questions and Answers—Alliance and Amity, Disavowal and Enmity* (London: MSA Publication Ltd, 2003), 159–61.

[150] Muḥammad b. Ṣāliḥ al-'Uthaymīn, "Doesn't the Hadeeth 'Do Not Initiate the Greeting with a Jew or a Christian' Put People off Islam?" in Muhammad Saed Abdul-Rahman (ed.), *Islam: Questions and Answers—Alliance and Amity, Disavowal and Enmity* (London: MSA Publication Ltd, 2003), 34.

[151] Muḥammad b. Ṣāliḥ Ibn 'Uthaymīn, "Ḥukm Qawl Akhī aw Ṣadīqī aw al-Ḍaḥk li-Ghayr al-Muslimīn li-Ṭalb al-Mawadda," in *Fatāwā al-Balad al-Ḥarām* (Cairo: al-Maktaba al-Tawfīqiyya, n.d.), 186.

[152] Muḥammad b. Ṣāliḥ Ibn 'Uthaymīn, "Tawḍīḥ al-Walā' wal-Barā'," in *Fatāwā al-Balad al-Ḥarām* (Cairo: al-Maktaba al-Tawfīqiyya, n.d.), 175–76.

[153] "Making Friends with a Kaafir Women," in Muhammad Saed Abdul-Rahman (ed.), *Islam: Questions and Answers—Alliance and Amity, Disavowal and Enmity* (London: MSA Publication Ltd, 2003), 64.

testified to spending most days of the week with non-Muslim female friends, the editors asked the student, based on Q. 9:71, to remember that he must take Muslims as close friends, to love and respect them, while based on Q. 60:1 he must reject non-Muslims and feel no love in his heart towards them. They demanded that he remember that even infidels who possess good manners and some good qualities hold to a number of "seriously wrong things," any one of which nullifies the good deeds that they may do. Among these is the Christian belief in the concept of the Holy Trinity. On a different note, they reminded the student that he must obey the regulations concerning gender segregation, whether they are Muslim or not.[154] Answering a query about "being friends with Christians and gays," the editors, relying on Q. 5:51 and Q. 3:118, argued that it is impermissible for a Muslim to be a friend to Christians and other infidels, and encouraged him to "stop keeping company with Christians and replace them with Muslim friends."[155] Preference must also be reserved for Muslims in all types of business transactions.[156] The Saudi Permanent Committee decided that if a Muslim sells goods that are of poor quality or deceives his customers, it is then permissible to choose his non-Muslim competitor. However, if this is not the case, doing business with the non-Muslim is prohibited because it "weakens the sales of the Muslims."[157]

It is ironic that such a particularly antagonistic contextualization of "loyalty and disavowal" evolved and was canonized and promoted mainly in a kingdom so dependent on Western powers for its survival. Perhaps an even greater irony is that a concept calling for contempt and enmity toward non-Muslims is championed among *salafīs* who voluntarily chose Western lands as their homes. This irony does not escape some *salafī*

[154] "Being Friends with Non-Muslims," in Muhammad Saed Abdul-Rahman (ed.), *Islam: Questions and Answers—Alliance and Amity, Disavowal and Enmity* (London: MSA Publication Ltd, 2003), 45–55.

[155] "Being Friends with Christians and Gays," in Muhammad Saed Abdul-Rahman (ed.), *Islam: Questions and Answers—Alliance and Amity, Disavowal and Enmity* (London: MSA Publication Ltd, 2003), 57–59.

[156] Muḥammad b. Ṣāliḥ Ibn ʻUthaymīn, "al-Ḍābiṭ fī Mas'alat al-Tashābuh bil-Kuffār," in *Fatāwā al-Balad al-Ḥarām* (Cairo: al-Maktaba al-Tawfīqiyya, n.d.), 182.

[157] Fatāwā al-Lajna al-Dā'ima, "What Is the Ruling on Buying from the *Kuffar* When There Are Muslims Around?" in Muhammad Saed Abdul-Rahman (ed.), *Islam: Questions and Answers—Alliance and Amity, Disavowal and Enmity* (London: MSA Publication Ltd, 2003), 59–60.

scholars. Al-Madkhalī wrote in his book *Advice to the Salafīs Living in the West* that "many who ascribe themselves to Islam, and in particular the zealots, those who call [for] enmity towards the Jews and Christians" nevertheless "do not find ease and comfort except in the capital cities of non-Muslims... they [those Muslims] are doing a service for, and aiding the enemies of Islam."[158] This kind of condemnation, however, is not common in *salafī* writings. Indeed, even al-Madkhalī, despite his sarcasm, appears to be more concerned with amending the ways of Muslims in the West in accordance with the *salafī* approach than with convincing them that they must migrate to Muslim lands.

While *salafīs* interpret "loyalty and disavowal" in a way that promotes enmity towards non-Muslims, they are careful to emphasize that it is the duty of Muslim minorities to respect the laws of their receiving states, to avoid cheating and stealing for personal gain, to act justly towards the non-Muslims who do not attack them, and to shun terror activities. Hatefulness should be confined to the heart rather than outwardly expressed. These demands are based on four main justifications: Allah's permission for Muslims to respect and be just with infidels who do not fight against Muslims and the prohibition of harming the innocent; the concern for the wellbeing of the Muslim community and the safeguarding of its interests (that is, a communal *maṣlaḥa*); the religio-legal duty to abide by contracts, and the belief that visas or citizenship constitute forms of contracts; and the *salafī* rejection of individualistic subversive political or violent acts, which they also apply to non-Muslim states.

To note several examples, b. Bāz, while stating that Muslims must hate non-Muslims and disavow them, emphasized that the principle of "loyalty and disavowal" in no way means to mistreat them or attack them or avoid being gentle to them, unless they attack Muslims.[159] Al-Munajjid wrote, citing Q. 42:15, that "hating them in our hearts does not mean that we should oppress or mistreat them under any circumstances" and, citing

[158] Al-Madkhalī, *An Advice to the Salafis Living in the West*, 39.

[159] 'Abd al-'Azīz b. 'Abdallāh Ibn Bāz, "al-Walā' wal-Barā' wa-Aḥkām al-Kuffār," in *Fatāwā al-Balad al-Ḥarām* (Cairo: al-Maktaba al-Tawfīqiyya, n.d.), 174–75; also Shaykh 'Abdul Azeez Ibn Baaz, "The Importance of Muslim Minorities Adhering to Islam," in Shaykh Ibn Baz and Shaykh Uthaymeen, *Muslim Minorities* (Hounslow, United Kingdom: Message of Islam, 1998), 20.

Q. 60:8, that it is permissible for a Muslim to treat with kindness non-Muslims who are not hostile. Treating non-Muslims who are not hostile with kindness may involve offering financial help, feeding the hungry, giving loans, interceding with regard to permissible actions, speaking kindly to them, and returning their greetings. Muslims are not permitted to commit aggression, frighten, or terrorize a non-Muslim who "is not hostile towards Islam." They must remember that it is

> obligatory upon a Muslim to honor treaties or agreements made with a non-Muslim party. If a Muslim has agreed to their [the infidels'] conditions when seeking permission to enter their country (i.e., a visa) and has promised to adhere to that, then it is not permissible for him to commit mischief in their lands, to betray anyone, to steal, to kill or do any destructive actions and so on.[160]

According to al-Fawzān, while infidels hate, betray, and plot against Muslims, wishing that Muslims be harmed by any means, Muslims must nevertheless treat with justice and kindness those who do not fight them, hate them, or drive them out of their homes.[161]

The impermissibility of violent attacks on Western targets was highlighted by *salafī* Western-based publications after the 9/11 and 7/7 attacks. These texts discouraged Muslims, especially enthused youth, from engaging in such acts and established a clear distinction between *salafiyya* and *jihādi-salafism*. For example, a book published in Canada and containing condemnations of the 9/11 attacks by leading *salafī* jurists asserted that "none have been harder against the tide of terrorism and the ideologies that cultivate this bitter fruit than those of the salafī methodology." The author argued that to associate *salafiyya* with the acts of Bin Laden is no different than describing Fidel Castro as an ardent

[160] Muḥammad Ṣāliḥ al-Munajjid, "Principles and Guidelines for Muslims' Relations with Non-Muslims," in Muhammad Saed Abdul-Rahman (ed.), *Islam: Questions and Answers—Alliance and Amity, Disavowal and Enmity* (London: MSA Publication Ltd, 2003), 70–71.

[161] Saalih bin Fouzan al-Fouzan, *al-Walaa' wal-Baraa': Allegiance and Association with the People of Islaam and Eeman and Disassociation and Enmity with the People of Falsehood and Disbelief in Islaam* translated by Abū 'Abd al-Raḥman Bansfield (Ipswich: Jam'iyyat Ihyā' Minhaj al-Sunna, 1997, 13, 24; also *Aḥkām al-Ta'āmul ma'a Ghayr al-Muslimīn* (Riyadh: Dār Kunūz Ishbīlya lil-Nashr wal-Tawzī', 2009), 20.

supporter of democracy.[162] A similar refutation published by a *salafī* organization in London attacked the claim by *jihādi-salafīs* that they are *salafīs*, noting, among other issues, the impermissibility of suicide in Islam, as well as the duty of Muslims to respect the covenants which are represented by citizenships or visas granted to them in the West.[163] Another apologia published after the 7/7 attacks by a Bradford-based *salafī* journal cautioned that even though Muslims are subject to injustice and live in trying times, Islam "commands that the Muslims deal justly with non-Muslims."[164] The journal published the strong condemnation by 'Abd al-Muḥsin al-'Ubaykān (b. 1952 or 1953), a member of the Council of Senior Scholars and the Permanent Committee, of the 7/7 attacks in London and similar attacks. Al-'Ubaykān declared the conspirators to be worse than the *Khārijites* for having added the sins of violating their covenants and transgressing against the "people of the book" to the crime of declaring Muslims infidels and killing them. He explained that Islam prohibits the killing of the innocent and that the bombings placed Muslims in Britain in a difficult situation.[165] Similar condemnations of terror attacks by leading Saudi jurists appeared in other Western-based *salafī* platforms.[166]

The Prophetic tradition narrated by Abū Hurayra, according to which the Prophet said, "Do not initiate a greeting with a Jew or a Christian, and if you meet one of them on the road, push him to the narrowest part of it," asserts the *salafī* concept of "loyalty and disavowal" but also potentially challenges the *salafī* rejection of violent and unjust behavior. As such, the tradition is the subject of intense deliberation. On the one hand, it affirms that non-Muslims should be despised; on the other hand, if read literally, as required by *salafī* doctrine, it can be understood as inciting violence

[162] Abul-Hasan Maalik al-Akhdar, *In Defense of Islaam in Light of the Events of September 11th* (Toronto: T.R.O.I.D Publications, 2002), 10–11.

[163] AbdurRahman Mahdi, *Martyrdom in Jihad Versus Suicide Bombing* (London: Islamic Knowledge, 2010), 41–52, 58–59.

[164] "'Wahhabis' Call for the Bad Treatment of Non-Muslims," *The Ark* 21 (August 2007), 2.

[165] Abdul Muhsin al-Ubaykaan, "7/7: A Warning against the Extremists," *The Ark* 21 (August 2007), 3.

[166] For a collection of such condemnations, see in the portal of al-Baseerah al-Quran wa as-Sunnah Society of New York: "Terrorism, Suicide Bombings and Hijackers," n.d., accessed June 30, 2013: http://www.albaseerah.org/forum/showthread.php?t=3338.

against infidels without provocation, which is not the *salafī* intention. 'Abd al-'Azīz b. 'Abdallāh Āl al-Shaykh (b. 1940), b. Bāz's successor as the grand muftī of Saudi Arabia, clarified that the intention is not that a Muslim should crash his car into a non-Muslim's car but that the non-Muslim should be made to use the narrower road and that friendship should not be extended to him.[167] Ibn 'Uthaymīn also struggled to explain this tradition. He asserted that on the one hand, if one understands the words of the Prophet in a manner that does not make sense, then one should question one's understanding. On the other hand, one should not measure the traditions based on one's understanding because human minds are imperfect. Thus, "basic principles" of Islamic law should be applied to avoid confusion. Based on evidence that neither the Prophet nor his Companions pushed infidels who crossed their way "against the wall," b. 'Uthaymīn suggested that the *ḥadīth* should be interpreted as commanding that a Muslim should not initiate a greeting to infidels and should not make way for them. Rather, the Muslim should continue in the direction in which he was headed, and if the road is not wide enough, he should make sure that the infidel is the one constricted. This constitutes a manifestation of Muslim pride and shows that a Muslim does not humble himself before anyone except his Lord.[168]

While befriending non-Muslims is impermissible according to *salafīs*, socializing with them in order to convert them to Islam is legitimate, so long as great caution is exercised to ensure that interactions will not negatively influence the Muslim. Thus, *salafī* condemnation of extending friendship to infidels or imitating them does not entirely prohibit associating with non-Muslims or learning from them, provided that the sole purpose of such interactions is to benefit Islam. Ibn 'Uthaymīn explained that accepting invitations from infidels can serve as an opportunity to expose them to Islam and noted that the Prophet accepted the invitation of a Jew who gave him bread, barley, and dissolved fat. Muslims who

[167] *Fatwā* by 'Abd al-'Azīz b. 'Abdallāh Āl al-Shaykh, in Abū Farīḥān Jamāl b. Farīḥān al-Ḥarīthī (ed.), *al-Fatāwā al-Muhimma fī Tabṣīr al-Umma* (Cairo: Maktabat al-Hadī al-Muḥammadī, 2009), 66–67.

[168] Muḥammad b. Ṣāliḥ al-'Uthaymīn, "Doesn't the Hadeeth 'Do Not Initiate the Greeting with a Jew or a Christian' Put People off Islam?" 32–33.

accept such invitations with the purpose of *da'wa* must, however, remember that friendship and love for infidels is "not permitted because the need to have a sound and pure heart is extremely important for Muslims."[169] Ibn Bāz stated, relying on Q. 60:4, that for a Muslim woman to visit her non-Muslim neighbors for "worldly purposes" such as "leisure, idle talk, or eating" is not permissible because "this may lead to corruption of one's religious commitment or morals," and also because the infidels "are enemies to us, so we should not take them as close friends." However, if a visit is for the purpose *da'wa*, then it becomes a necessity and thus permissible.[170] According to b. 'Uthaymīn and other *salafīs*, paying visits to non-Muslims who fall ill is permissible only if it involves an effort to bring the sick to Islam. This statement is supported by a number of Prophetic traditions. According to one, narrated by Sa'īd b. al-Musayyab, the Prophet visited his uncle, Abū Ṭālib, on his deathbed and pleaded with him to embrace Islam. According to another, narrated by Anas, the Prophet visited a Jewish child servant and managed to convert him. Upon leaving, the Prophet said, "Praise to Allāh Who has saved him [the boy] from the fire."[171]

Refutations of the *salafī* concept of "loyalty and disavowal" and assertions of its narrower contextualization, as endorsed by al-Qaraḍāwī already in the 1960s, have been part of the construction of *wasaṭī fiqh al-aqalliyyāt al-Muslima* from its early articulations. While *wasaṭī* texts on the issue of Muslim relations with non-Muslims never directly addressed the *salafī* view, their apologetic and dialectic nature revealed that *wasaṭīs*

[169] Muhammad Ibn Saalih al-'Uthaymeen, "Inviting to Allaah in Communities Where There Are Muslim Minorities," 83.

[170] 'Abd al-'Azīz b. 'Abdallāh Ibn Bāz, "Muslim and Non-Muslim Woman Visiting One Another," in Muhammad Saed Abdul-Rahman (ed.), *Islam: Questions and Answers—Alliance and Amity, Disavowal and Enmity* (London: MSA Publication Ltd, 2003), 43–44.

[171] "Making Friends with a Kaafir Women," in Muhammad Saed Abdul-Rahman (ed.), *Islam: Questions and Answers—Alliance and Amity, Disavowal and Enmity* (London: MSA Publication Ltd, 2003), 64–65; Sulayman al-'Alwam, "Ruling on Visiting a Sick Kafir," in Muhammad Saed Abdul-Rahman (ed.), *Islam: Questions and Answers—Alliance and Amity, Disavowal and Enmity* (London: MSA Publication Ltd, 2003), 88–90; Muḥammad b. Ṣāliḥ Ibn 'Uthaymīn, "Ḥukm Ziyārat al-Naṣrānī," in Aḥmad b. 'Abdallāh al-Shafi'ī (ed.), *500 Jawāb fī al-Buyū' wal-Mu'āmalāt* (Cairo: Dār Ibn Ḥazm, 2010), 238; 'Abd al-Raḥman Ibn 'Abd al-Khāliq, *al-Walā' wal-Barā'* (September 1986, accessed September 10, 2012: http://www.al-mostafa.com/), 27.

were conscious of the proliferation of *salafī* literature on the subject in Western mosques and Islamic media. Establishing the alternative view was essential in order to legitimize the *wasaṭī* call for Muslim minorities to cultivate good, friendly relations with majorities, engage in multi-faith dialogues, and introduce Islam by the example of noble behavior and constructive contributions to society at large.

Already in his *fatwā* on the permissibility of Muslim participation in American politics (see discussion in Chapter 4), which presented the foundations for his doctrine for Muslim minorities, al-'Alwānī cautioned against transforming *walā'* into an exclusive concept that prevents Muslims from interacting with non-Muslims, serving the *maṣlaḥa* of the believers, and winning new converts to Islam. He clarified that the "loyalty" to non-Muslims against which the Quran cautioned is one that comes at the expense of the believers.[172] The Quranic verses 60:8–9 were invoked by al-'Alwānī in his systematizations of *wasaṭī fiqh al-aqalliyyāt al-Muslima* as evidence that justice and righteousness are the principles governing Muslim relations with non-Muslims.[173] In explaining the hierarchy between the different sources of jurisprudence in his 2001 book on *fiqh al-aqalliyyāt al-Muslima*, al-Qaraḍāwī deliberately chose to discuss the abovementioned tradition, according to which the Prophet said, "Do not initiate the greeting with a Jew or a Christian, and if you meet one of them on the road, push him to the narrowest part of it." Drawing on the *wasaṭī* paradigm that all sources should be contextualized in light of the supremacy of the universals of the Quran, al-Qaraḍāwī explained that while this is a confirmed (*ṣaḥīḥ*) tradition, it must be interpreted narrowly because it contrasts Q. 60:8 as well as Q. 4:86 (which commands Muslims to greet in kind those who greet them). Thus, the tradition should be applied only to those who fight against Muslims.[174]

During the 2000s, members of the European Council for Fatwa and Research expounded on Muslim–Christian relations in a number of

[172] Imām Muḥammad Imām, "al-Ḥukm al-Shar'ī fī Mushārakat al-Muslimīn fī al-Ḥayāt al-Siyāsiyya al-Amrīkiyya," 26.

[173] Al-'Alwānī, *Fī Fiqh al-Aqalliyyāt al-Muslima*, 40; "Madkhal ilā Fiqh al-Aqalliyyāt," 82–83.

[174] Al-Qaraḍāwī, *Fī Fiqh al-Aqalliyyāt al-Muslima*, 38–39.

essays published by the Council. Authors emphasized that the supremacy of the Quran over all other sources and its contextual reading discredit the notion that Muslims must disavow non-Muslims. Rather, Muslims should be kind and just to non-Muslims, reach out to them, and assist them. The Egyptian-born and Canadian-based Jamāl Badawī—a professor emeritus of business administration at St. Mary's University, Halifax, a prolific Islamic preacher, and a member of the European Council for Fatwa Research and the Fiqh Council of North America—offered one thorough contribution to the polemic in 2005. In a treatise on the importance of promoting good relations between Muslims and non-Muslims, Badawī alluded to *salafīs* in arguing that misconceptions of how Muslims should treat non-Muslims had been assisting, albeit unintentionally, those who seek to present a distorted picture of Islam, particularly after 9/11.[175]

Drawing on al-Qaraḍāwī's argument, Badawī explained that the root of those misconceptions lay in ignoring several principles of Islamic jurisprudence: the supremacy of the Quran; the necessity of interpreting the Prophetic traditions in light of the Quran; the precedence of the Quran in cases of seeming contradictions between the Quran and the Prophetic traditions; verses should be contextualized in light of the circumstances of their revelation (which, in dealing with non-Muslims, are the specific hardships which the first Muslims faced); when verses conflict, more weight should be given to what is said in many than to what is said in a few.[176] According to Badawī, when these principles are applied, the following truths are derived from the revelations: Muslims should extend their love and friendship to non-Muslims who do not fight them and are not hostile to Islam, and act justly and compassionately to them, as indicated by Q. 3:119, 60:6–8. The Quran acknowledges religious pluralism, as indicated by Q. 11:118 and Q. 10:99. Islam is not forced upon nonbelievers, as indicated by Q. 2:256. The punishment for disbelief is not exacted in this life, as indicated by Q. 42:48. While fraternity based on

[175] Jamāl Badawī, "'Alāqat al-Muslim bi-Ghayr al-Muslim: Naẓarāt fī Kitāb Allāh Ta'ālā," *al-Majalla al-'Ilmiyya lil-Majlis al-'Ūrūbbī lil-Iftā' wal-Buḥūth*, no. 6 (January 2005), 71.

[176] *Ibid.*, 72–76.

religion is the noblest of fraternities, other kinds of bonds between humans, including between Muslims and non-Muslims, are also permissible, as indicated by Q. 4:1 and Q. 49:13. All human beings are respected for being human beings, as indicated by Q. 17:70 and 5:32.[177] Following al-Qaraḍāwī, Badawī argued that the Prophetic tradition according to which a Muslim should not initiate a greeting with a Jew or a Christian and should push them to the narrowest part of the road should be interpreted along the abovementioned juristic principles and, therefore, it cannot be applied to all non-Muslims because that would contrast the Quran's commands to act justly towards non-Muslims.[178]

Another refutation of the *salafī* interpretation of *al-walā' wal-barā'* was offered in 2008 by Ṣalāḥ al-Dīn Sulṭān as part of his broader defense of al-Qaraḍāwī's *wasaṭī fiqh al-aqalliyyāt al-Muslima*. His work argued that it is permissible, even essential in light of Islam's universality and the promotion of proselytizing, that Muslims reside in the West and attain the citizenship of Western countries. In this context, Sulṭān argued against reading the verses that command loyalty and disavowal independently from verses that command dealing justly and kindly with non-Muslims who do not commit aggression against Muslims. He explained that "despite plenty of writings" that argue to the contrary, prohibited friendship with non-Muslims only applies to (a) loving them while despising Muslims, (b) following their lead in breaching Allah's laws, and (c) assisting them against Muslims.[179]

Yet another refutation of *salafī al-walā' wal-barā'*, published in 2008 by a French-based member of the Council, Aḥmad Jāballāh, focused on discrediting the *salafī* objection to extending loyalty in non-religious contexts. His article argued that even in cases when a non-Muslim country acts unjustly against others, including Muslims, Muslims in that country cannot betray or cheat its government because Islam prohibits the breaching of contracts (and citizenship or visas constitute contracts). What Muslims should do in such cases is to protest using the extensive

[177] *Ibid.*, 76–80. [178] *Ibid.*, 81.
[179] Sulṭān, "al-Muwāṭana fī Diyār al-Islām bayna al-Nāfīn wal-Muthbitīn," 150–51.

freedom of speech granted in the West. Jāballāh further argued that upholding national unity in non-Muslim countries does not breach the principle of religious fraternity because Islam does not forbid non-religious bonds. This is indicated by verses that tell of the strong bond prophets felt with their people, despite the animosity expressed by some of the latter for the former, as indicated in Q. 7:65, 73, 80, and 85. He concluded that nothing should prevent a Muslim from seeking the prosperity of the society he lives in, even if that society is not Muslim, because Islam wishes good for all, as indicated by Q. 60:8 and by the Prophet's words, according to which "None of you is a believer until he loves for his brother what he loves for himself." This statement was interpreted by al-Nawāwī (d. 1278) as applying to Muslims and non-Muslims alike. Thus, Muslims should prefer interactions with non-Muslims to segregation, even if the latter act unlawfully, because the Prophet ordered them to do so.[180]

[180] Aḥmad Jāballāh, "al-Wasaṭiyya bayna Muqtaḍayāt al-Muwāṭana fī 'Ūrūbbā wal-Ḥifāẓ 'alā al-Huwiyya al-Islāmiyya," *al-Majalla al-'Ilmiyya lil-Majlis al-'Ūrūbbī lil-Iftā' wal-Buḥūth*, no. 12–13 (July 2008), 264–68.

3

Muslim Minorities and Non-Muslim Societies

INTRODUCTION

Responding to queries by Muslims in the West and drawing on the respective ideologies and methodologies, *wasaṭī* and *salafī* panels and jurists offered a range of decisions regarding social relationships, financial transactions, and engagement in social and cultural activities with non-Muslims in the West. *Wasaṭīs* departed, not without hesitation, from a number of well-established *shar'ī* norms in order to accommodate challenges faced by Muslims living as minorities. *Salafīs* consistently and fiercely declined to offer such accommodations. The issues debated are far from theoretical; at stake is the practical ability of Muslims to secure their families' financial futures as well as to develop and maintain close interpersonal relations with non-Muslim family and friends. Analysis of conflicting decisions is indispensible to understanding the potential practical implications of different theories of *sharī'a* and seemingly technical juristic mechanisms.

Wasaṭī decisions were directed by the notion that *taysīr* and the lifting of hardship are an essence of Islam, and that being a minority in majority non-Muslim societies is a unique state of weakness that justifies unique facilitations. In justifying legitimizations, jurists invoked the narrower *wasaṭī* interpretation of *al-walā' wal-barā'*, cross-*madhhab* search as a means to locate and apply more pragmatic solutions, the principle that in evaluating *maṣlaḥas* individual needs can be regarded as necessities, and the consideration of proselytizing as a primary objective of the Lawgiver. In applying the latter interpretations, *wasaṭī fatwās* on Muslim minorities demonstrated the utility of the broad approach to *maṣlaḥa* embraced by *wasaṭīs* in the late 1990s as a means to affect decisions. In no other field of jurisprudence have *wasaṭīs* made such radical use of the theoretical possibilities opened by their theory of jurisprudence.

Salafī decisions on social issues are, in a number of important fields, the antithesis of *wasaṭī* ones, exemplifying the *salafī* conviction that Allah's laws must be literally and strictly applied and that such an application is the only path to triumph and salvation. Their decisions refute the broad *wasaṭī* approach to *maṣlaḥa*, and the application of cross-*madhhab* search as a means to find the easier solutions. They reveal the general *salafī* reluctance to consider non-life-threatening individual hardships as reasons for accommodations; their opinion that neither the condition of living as a minority, nor the prospect of enhancing the spread of Islam, justify facilitations; and their understanding of *al-walā' wal-barā'* as a concept that calls to minimize socializing with non-Muslims.

The following chapter presents and analyzes a broad array of *fatwās* in four areas in which *wasaṭīs* and *salafīs* produced contesting decisions: interest-based transactions (mortgages and student loans); relations with non-Muslim families (the maintaining of marriage between converts and their non-Muslim husbands and inheriting from non-Muslims); non-Muslim festive occasions, in particular Christmas; and employment in workplaces where activities that are prohibited in Islam are practiced.

USURIOUS TRANSACTIONS

The Quran strictly prohibits usury, or *ribā* (Q. 2:275–79, 3:130, 4:161, 30:39). Q: 2:279 warns that Allah and His Prophet will wage war against those who do not obey this command. The prohibition creates a challenge in modern economies, in which corporate and individual transactions often rely on interest-based loans. Islamic banking systems have developed several mechanisms that circumvent the prohibition on *ribā*. In real estate, the most popular one is *murābaḥa*: the bank serves as an intermediary that buys a house at the request of a customer and then sells the house at a higher price, which the customer pays in installments.[1] In some Western countries, Islamic banking systems are not available. Since most Muslims in the West are not affluent and cannot afford to buy a house without a mortgage, the issue has become highly relevant.

For most of his career, al-Qaraḍāwī highlighted the impermissibility of charging and paying interest as *naṣṣ qaṭʿī*, a decisive text that does not allow room for juristic discretion except in the most exceptional cases. In his deliberations on *ijtihād*, usury was invoked to demonstrate that there are clear boundaries to the application of *maṣlaḥa* in *wasaṭī* jurisprudence. In his first major work, *al-Ḥalāl wal-Ḥarām fī al-Islām*, he emphasized the moral and social importance of this prohibition and argued that only a "true necessity," and not a "need," could legitimize the paying of interest.[2] He noted that in Islam the prohibition on usury is universal, whereas in Judaism it applies only to transactions between Jews.[3] He articulated in his 1988 book on the need for the renewal of religion his unequivocal view that *ijtihād* on usury not only breaches a decisive text but is unnecessary.[4] He maintained the same position in the mid-1990s while formulating a broader approach to *maṣlaḥa* as a foundation of *wasaṭiyya*. He pointed to interest (along with alcohol and pork) as examples of prohibitions that are based on decisive evidence, and thus should not be subject for *ijtihād*. He rejected the opinion that in the modern economic system paying interests became a necessity that justifies the suspension of prohibitions, explaining that there is no benefit in usurious transactions and that, in any case, people should not ignore Allah's guidance when judging what their *maṣlaḥas* are.[5] In his visits to Muslim communities in the West since the 1970s, al-Qaraḍāwī personally

[1] Mervyn Lewis and Latifa M. Algaoud, *Islamic Banking* (Northampton, MA: E. Elgar Publishing, 2001), 52–55; Saeed Abdullah, *Islamic Banking and Interest: A Study of the Prohibition of Riba and its Contemporary Interpretation* (Leiden: Brill, 1996), 76–95; Maha-Hanaan Balala, *Islamic Finance and Law: Theory and Practice in a Globalized World* (London, New York: I. B. Tauris, 2011), 28–29.

[2] Yūsuf al-Qaraḍāwī, *al-Ḥalāl wal-Ḥarām fī al-Islām* (Cairo: Matkabat Wahaba, 2004, first published 1960), 230–33.

[3] *Ibid.*, 36.

[4] Yūsuf al-Qaraḍāwī, *Min Ajl Ṣaḥwa Rāshida* (Cairo: Dār al-Shurūq, 1988, accessed August 2, 2012: http://www.mlazna.com), 44–45.

[5] Yūsuf al-Qaraḍāwī, *al-Ijtihād fī al-Sharīʿa al-Islāmiyya* (Kuwait: Dār al-Qalam, 1996), 160–1, 179.

witnessed the hardships some face because of their inability to buy homes. Yet he remained steadfast in his opinion that the prohibition on interest-based loans must apply to Muslims living in non-Muslim societies as well.

However, his opinion changed two years after the establishment of the European Council for Fatwa and Research, when al-Qaraḍāwī gave his consent to a decision that conditionally permitted taking mortgages in Europe. He candidly, yet apologetically, attributed his change of heart to the tenderness and confidence that comes with age.[6] These words exposed a truth that most jurists hesitate to articulate: the issuance of rulings is never entirely formalistic or objective, and is always influenced, at least to a certain extent, by a jurist's personal inclinations, status, and prestige, as well as by the pressures exerted on him by individuals and communities.

Analyses of the *fatwā*, including by Caeiro,[7] who offered the first authoritative study of the decision, did not fully appreciate its audacity and innovation. While the obvious importance of the legitimization offered by the European Council was that it was issued by a panel led by a prominent jurist, the *fatwā* was groundbreaking not because of its result, but because of the theory of jurisprudence it introduced. Other jurists and panels had legitimized mortgages before; the European Council's *fatwā* was the first to integrate and apply within the context of *wasaṭī fiqh al-aqalliyyāt al-Muslima* the principle that individual needs can be regarded as necessities, the idea that in Europe *daʿwa* is a *maṣlaḥa* that justifies the suspension of the prohibited, and the concept of searching within the schools of law for the most pragmatic decision. These notions were inspired by al-Qaraḍāwī's general theory of jurisprudence as delineated in the late 1990s, and demonstrated in a systematic way what the *wasaṭī* approach to the jurisprudence of Muslim minorities signifies, and how it has the potential to radically impact the practices of Muslims in the West.

[6] Yūsuf al-Qaraḍāwī, *Fī Fiqh al-Aqalliyyāt al-Muslima* (Cairo: Dār al-Shurūq, 2007, first published 2001), 169–70.

[7] Alexandre Caeiro, "The Social Construction of Sharīʿa: Bank Interest, Home Purchase and Islamic Norms in the West," *Die Welt des Islams* 44, 3 (2004), 435–49.

Legitimizations of mortgages in non-Muslim lands were introduced long before the European Council was established. The *Ḥanafī* legitimization of otherwise prohibited transactions in non-Muslim countries made it possible for adherents of this *madhhab* to take interest-based loans. Rashīd Riḍā legitimized borrowing and lending money with interest based on his view that the rules of *mu'āmalāt* do not apply in non-Muslim lands, or else Muslims would become dependent and powerless.[8] A number of contemporary jurists and Councils ruled that mortgages can be legitimized in the West based on *maṣlaḥa*. For example, the Kuwaiti Public Council for Fatwa (*al-Hay'a al-'āma lil-Fatwā bil-Kuwayt*) decided on June 13, 1985, in response to a query by an American who pointed to the difficulty large families faced in finding homes for rent in the United States, that in such cases mortgages are permissible because they constitute a communal need that qualifies as necessity (*al-ḥāja allatī tanzilu manzalat al-ḍarūra*).[9]

The problem of mortgages was brought to the Council's attention in its first session, held in Sarajevo on August 28–30, 1997, by four of its French-based members: Aḥmad Jāballāh, al-'Arabī al-Bishrī, Ṭāhir Mahdī and Unīs Qurqāḥ. According to Caeiro, based on an internal source in the Council, their request to study financial transactions in the West "raised a few eyebrows," but won the support of al-Qaraḍāwī. Following the session, al-Bishrī, an economist by training, was tasked with preparing a study on the matter as a basis for a final decision.[10] A version of that study, which was not made public at the time of its authorship, was published in the Council's journal in 2005.

Al-Bishrī's work laid the foundations for the legitimization of mortgages by the Council. Yet his treatment of juristic mechanisms was in some respects more conservative than that of the ultimate *fatwā* issued by the panel, placing far less emphasis on *taysīr*, and invoking a more restrictive approach to *maṣlaḥa*, than that invoked by the Council.

[8] Khaled Abou El Fadl, "Striking a Balance: Islamic Legal Discourse on Muslim Minorities," in Yvonne Yazbeck Haddad and John L. Esposito (eds.), *Muslims on The Americanization Path?* (Oxford and New York: Oxford University Press, 2000), 54.

[9] As quoted by al-Qaraḍāwī, *Fī Fiqh al-Aqalliyyāt al-Muslima*, 164.

[10] Caeiro, "The Social Construction of Sharī'a: Bank Interest, Home Purchase and Islamic Norms in the West," 354.

At the core of al-Bishrī's analysis is his evaluation of home ownership in the European context as a *maṣlaḥa*. He suggested that in principle a house serves purposes in different ranks: it secures one's life, honor, and property, which are necessities, and provides one with peace of mind and stability, which are needs. From this evaluation it follows that having a roof over one's head qualifies as a necessity while purchasing a home only qualifies as a need. However, according to al-Bishrī, owning houses in Europe also serves the necessity of protecting religion.[11] First, it is a necessity that Muslims reside in Islamic environments and private homes so as to protect their children from bad influences such as drugs and violence. This necessity cannot be achieved in most cases without taking mortgages, and thus mortgages become a necessity, and as such are permissible. Second, it is a necessity that Muslims settle down in Europe, and renting apartments cannot facilitate this objective. It is unrealistic to expect Muslims to fulfill their duty and spread Islam if they live all their lives like tourists without permanent homes.[12] Al-Bishrī emphasized that the necessity that mortgages provide is not an individual one but a communal one—protecting religion—and thus it is of the highest rank in terms of legitimizing prohibitions.[13] To this he added that even if one does not accept his interpretation of mortgages as a necessity and considers it a need, then it is a communal need, and communal needs rank as necessities.[14]

A supplementary argument by al-Bishrī was based on cross-*madhhab* search and the *Ḥanafī* legitimization of otherwise prohibited transactions in *dār al-Ḥarb*. Al-Bishrī embraced Abū Ḥanīfa's logic that it is impermissible to suspend laws pertaining to individual practices, but it is permissible to do so for laws pertaining to social ones because the latter's objectives, as opposed to the former's, cannot be achieved unless society at large abides by them. He explained that European societies have a different concept of corruption; even if Muslims do not take mortgages, the social objective of this prohibition would not be met.[15]

[11] Al-ʿArabī al-Bishrī, "Shirāʾ al-Buyūt ʿan Ṭarīq al-Qarḍ al-Bankī," *al-Majalla al-ʿIlmiyya lil-Majlis al-Urūbbī lil-Iftāʾ wal-Buḥūth*, no. 6 (January 2005), 165.
[12] *Ibid.*, 166–68. [13] *Ibid.*, 169.
[14] *Ibid.*, 170, 178. [15] *Ibid.*, 175–78.

The *fatwā* that conditionally legitimized mortgages was based on a deliberation on al-Bishrī's study and issued by the Council in its fourth session, held in Dublin on October 27–31, 1999. The decision marked a milestone in the Council's quest for recognition and its transformation into a controversial panel. It was front-page news in the London-based *al-Sharq al-Awsaṭ*, one of the most respected Arabic newspapers, and was fiercely debated in mosques across Europe, where, as my field studies indicate, it is still well known and debated today.

The *fatwā* opened with a reaffirmation of Islam's prohibition on usury, emphasizing that there is consensus that usury constitutes one of the seven worst sins and that Allah and His Prophet will wage war against those who charge or pay it. It went on to encourage Muslims in the West to find religiously legitimate alternatives to mortgages, such as the *murābaḥa* system offered by Islamic banks. It also encouraged Islamic organizations in Europe to ask European banks to adopt Islamic systems in order to attract Muslim customers. If, however, there is no alternative, then a Muslim living in Europe who does not own a house and does not have the means to purchase one without a loan is permitted to take a mortgage.

The Council based its arguments on both promoting facilitation and proselytizing, and applied *maṣlaḥa* and cross-*madhhab* search. It cited the juristic principles that necessities permit prohibitions (*al-ḍarūrāt tubīḥu al-Maḥẓūrāt*) and that a need (*ḥāja*) can be regarded as a necessity (*ḍarūra*). The *fatwā* explained that a "necessity" is something without which a Muslim cannot live and a "need" is something without which a Muslim would be put in a state of hardship (*ḥaraj*). Q. 22:78 and 5:6 declare that Islam will not put Muslims in a state of hardship. While having a home (rented or owned) is a necessity for a Muslim family (as indicated in Q. 16:80), in the European context owning a home is a need that should be regarded as a necessity. A Muslim who does not take a mortgage may be forced to pay rent to a non-Muslim landlord for many years without getting any closer to ownership and remaining under the threat of eviction, while a Muslim who is permitted to take a mortgage will be relieved of these concerns and will be able to choose a home that is close to a mosque and to an Islamic school. Furthermore, buying a home can help bring Muslims together with other Muslims and enable them to create small Islamic enclaves within the larger society.

By embracing the broad approach to *maṣlaḥa* delineated by al-Qaraḍāwī in the late 1990s (without hinting at the controversy that surrounds it) at the beginning of the *fatwā*, the Council suggested that even if purchasing a home ranks as an individual need only, rather than a communal one, this need justifies permitting mortgages in order to lift a hardship caused by the absence of Islamic banking systems.

However, according to the *fatwā* the individual need and avoiding *ḥaraj* are not the only reasons for suspending the ban on mortgages; the "communal need" of spreading Islam was also suggested as a justification. The *fatwā* explained that mortgages advance proselytizing efforts in two ways: Muslims will present a respectable face to non-Muslims by becoming homeowners, and relief from the financial burden of renting a house will make it possible for Muslims to pursue their duty to engage in *daʿwa*. Thus, proselytizing was invoked as a *maṣlaḥa* that affects the suspension of the prohibited.

Another argument presented in the *fatwā* drew on the *wasaṭī* method of cross-*madhhab* search in order to identify the most pragmatic solution. As did al-Bishrī, the *fatwā* invoked the *Ḥanafī* opinion that prohibited contracts between Muslims and non-Muslims are permitted outside *dār al-Islām*. It emphasized two notions. First, while living among infidels a Muslim is not obligated to follow the rulings of the *sharīʿa* on civil, financial, political, and similar matters because following them is beyond his ability, and Allah does not require people to do more than they are able. Second, Islam seeks to strengthen its followers in all respects, including the elimination of financial hardships. The *fatwā* specifically criticized the argument of several *Ḥanafī* jurists that Muslims in non-Muslim societies can charge interest but not pay it because they do not benefit from paying interest. It explained that no consensus was reached on this issue and that by paying interest on a mortgage, the Muslim receives a benefit because he will eventually own a home. The Council stressed that it regarded the *Ḥanafī* legitimization of mortgages in Europe merely as a supplement to its main argument, to wit, that where the option of Islamic banking does not exist a mortgage may be considered a "need" that qualifies as a "necessity."[16]

The Council's argument that renting an apartment is dishonorable overlooked the fact that renting apartments is a common practice among all social classes across Europe and tenants' rights are firmly protected by law. The Council's argument that the purchase of houses will encourage the creation of Islamic enclaves in European cities ignored the fact that such enclaves have already been created in less privileged areas, in part due to the absence of financial resources.

The European Council's approval was not the final *wasaṭī* word on mortgages in the West, but those that followed were less audacious in terms of theory of jurisprudence. On November 19, 1999, less than a month after the Council legitimized mortgages, a group of North American jurists convened in Detroit for the "First Conference on Islamic Law and Jurisprudence," which was sponsored by the Fiqh Committee of the Sharī'a Scholars Association of North America, a body associated with the Fiqh Council of North America. Al-Qaraḍāwī participated in the conference, and the majority of jurists present supported the legitimization of mortgages. However, their justifications were more conservative than those presented by the European Council. They did not invoke proselytizing as a justification and, unlike the European Council, they also did not argue that any need, individual or communal, may constitute a necessity. They noted, as did the Kuwaiti *fatwā* from 1985, the difficulty large families face in finding appropriate apartments and stated that mortgages qualify as necessity only to the extent that they safeguard a communal need—thwarting social, economic, moral, and religious harms, and protecting religion and the Islamic identity.[17]

[16] For the full text of the *fatwā* see Imām Muḥammad Imām, "Fatwā Tujīzu Shirā' al-Manāzil bi-Qarḍ Ribāwī lil-Muslimīn fī Ghayr Bilād al-Islām," *al-Sharq al-Awsaṭ* (November 3, 1999), 25; Yūsuf al-Qaraḍāwī, "Shirā' Buyūt al-Suknā fī al-Gharb 'an Ṭarīq al-Bunūk," in *Fī Fiqh al-Aqalliyyāt al-Muslima* (Cairo: Dār al-Shurūq, 2007, first published 2001), 174–79. For an English translation, *Fatwās of European Council for Fatwa and Research*, trans. Anas Usāma al-Tikritī and Shākir Nāṣif al-'Ubaydī (Cairo: Islamic INC, 2002), 160–68.

[17] As Quoted by al-Qaraḍāwī, *Fī Fiqh al-Aqalliyyāt al-Muslima*, 183–84. See also Caeiro, "The Social Construction of Sharī'a," 363, footnote 25.

The European Council approved the legitimization of mortgages by a majority of eighteen to four and only after a heated debate. According to Caeiro, three jurists in the minority resigned in protest, but only the Syrian Muslim Brother Fu'ād al-Barāzī, based in Denmark, never returned. The debate that ensued exemplified the fluidity of the concepts and mechanisms used in *wasaṭī* jurisprudence and their vulnerability to severe criticisms.

Al-Barāzī and the England-based Pakistani Ṣuhayb Ḥasan criticized the *fatwā* on two grounds. First, they argued that the Council misinterpreted the *Ḥanafī* school because (a) *Ḥanafīs* permit usury only in *dār al-ḥarb*, a category that does not apply to contemporary European countries and (b) *Ḥanafīs* allow Muslims in non-Muslim societies to take interest but not to pay. Second, al-Barāzī and al-Ghaffār asserted that the Council wrongly applied the principle of a "need" that becomes a "necessity." They argued that usurious transactions can only be legitimized based on a clear, immediate necessity, not a speculated or anticipated one, and this is not the case for Muslims in Europe who do not own houses as there is no real danger to any of al-Ghazālī's five *maqāṣid* for those who do not own homes. Furthermore, the financial weakness experienced by Muslims in Europe is not the result of avoiding mortgages but of disunity and lack of organization. It is therefore legitimate for a Muslim to take a mortgage only if he is unable to rent a home for an appropriate price or to purchase one in a religiously lawful way.[18]

The decision continued to be a subject for debate in the pages of the Council's journal in following years. Ibn Bayyah's condemnation of the *fatwā*, albeit without specifically addressing it, focused on the rules of determining "necessities" and "needs." Citing al-Shāfiʿī, al-Ghazālī and other authorities, he rejected the notion that needs qualify as necessities in all cases[19] and emphasized that *ḥāja* only affects weak, general prohibitions.[20] This, in his opinion, is clearly not the case of usury, citing Ibn

[18] Al-Qaraḍāwī, *Fī Fiqh al-Aqalliyyāt al-Muslima*, 179–81.

[19] ʿAbdallāh Ibn Bayyah, "al-Farq bayna al-Ḍarūra wal-Ḥāja Taṭbīqan ʿalā baʿḍ Aḥwāl al-Aqalliyyāt al-Muslima," *al-Majalla al-ʿIlmiyya lil-Majlis al-ʿUrūbbī lil-Iftāʾ wal-Buḥūth*, no. 4–5 (June 2004), 107–8.

[20] *Ibid.*, 127–29.

Taymiyya's argument that the prohibition on *ribā* is even stronger than the prohibition on gambling.[21] Ḥamza b. Ḥusayn al-Sharīf suggested that because Western lands should no longer be considered *dār al-ḥarb* (a foundation of *wasaṭī fiqh al-aqalliyyāt al-Muslima*), the *Ḥanafī* legitimization for prohibited transactions no longer applies. He sarcastically noted that acting in accordance with the *sharī'a* leaves a greater mark on non-Muslims than books and sermons.[22] 'Abdallāh b. Yūsuf al-Juday', the England-based deputy of al-Qaraḍāwī, published in the Council's journal a detailed refutation of the *Ḥanafī* view on transactions outside *dār al-Islām*[23] in which he urged the Council to revise its original decision, omit its second foundation that is based on the *Ḥanafī* legitimization, and base its decision only on its first foundation that mortgages are a need that qualifies as a necessity.[24] These examples demonstrate that though the 1999 decision was approved by an overwhelming majority and never revoked, the unease it caused at the Council continued (Maḥbūb al-Raḥman, a member of the Council, who endorses the 1999 decision based on both of its foundations, told the author that he does not consider this ongoing debate a problem; if there are five things that the members of the Council agree on, and five things on which they disagree, then "we should focus on the five things on which we agree").[25]

More than a quarter of al-Qaraḍāwī's 2001 book on the religious law of Muslim minorities is dedicated to his Council's 1999 *fatwā*. It is clear from his apologetic tone that he felt the need to defend it. The *fatwā* also served as an example for the systematic approach to *fiqh al-aqalliyyāt al-Muslima* introduced in his book.

In his response to al-Barāzī and al-Ghaffār, al-Qaraḍāwī stressed the openness in which the decision was deliberated and that the *Ḥanafī* justification—the core of their attack—was only supplementary to the

[21] *Ibid.*, 108, 129.

[22] Ḥamza b. Husayn al-Fa'r al-Sharīf, "Ḥukm Mushārakat al-Muslimīn fī Mujtama'āt al-Aqalliyyāt Ijtima'iyyan wa-Siyāsiyyan," *al-Majalla al-'Ilmiyya lil-Majlis al-Urūbbī lil-Iftā' wal-Buḥūth*, no. 12–13 (July 2008), 279–80.

[23] 'Abdallāh b. Yūsuf al-Juday', "Ribā wal-'Uqūd al-Māliyya al-Fāsida fī Ghayr Bilād al-Islām," *al-Majalla al-'Ilmiyya lil-Majlis al-Urūbbī lil-Iftā' wal-Buḥūth*, no. 14–15 (July 2009), 279–336.

[24] *Ibid.*, 331.

[25] Interview with Maḥbūb al-Raḥman, Oslo, March 22, 2014.

justification that mortgages are a "need" that qualifies as a "necessity." He emphasized that to determine whether owning an apartment constitutes a "need" that qualifies as "necessity," one should consult not only jurists but also experts in other fields as well as European Muslims who rent apartments.[26] In his defense of the *fatwā* he added several elements to the Council's description of ownership as a condition for leading an Islamic life in the West and promoting Islam. He argued that Muslims who own apartments have access to better education; reside in greater proximity to local mosques, Islamic centers, and other Muslims; enjoy better public services; enable their wives to walk around the house without being watched by neighbors (as is the case in rent-based residential areas); and gain the respect of people from all walks of life, from school teachers to garbage-truck drivers. Al-Qaraḍāwī hinted that the belatedness of his juristic transformation on the matter had been harmful to the interests of the Muslim nation, noting that Muslims from the Indian subcontinent, who adhere to the *Ḥanafī* school and have taken mortgages, are some of the richest men in contemporary London.[27] The Council's decision was endorsed also by al-Qaraḍāwī's American counterpart, Muzammil H. Siddiqi (b. 1943), an American of Indian origin who succeeded al-ʿAlwānī at the Fiqh Council of North America and who earned a PhD in comparative religion from Harvard University. Siddiqi nevertheless emphasized the restrictions placed by the *fatwā* and argued that Muslims must exhaust all lawful options before relying on it.[28]

The permissibility of interest-based loans in the West based on necessity continued to engross *wasaṭī* jurists in the years that followed, with the 1999 *fatwā* serving as an inevitable reference. One issue discussed was whether mortgages could be taken to reconstruct mosques. Members of an Islamic center in an unidentified country wrote that it was housed "in an old, five-story building that does not reflect any aspect of Islamic architecture." An opportunity arose to build on the same spot a new center "in an excellent Islamic style." The estimated cost was 5 million

[26] Al-Qaraḍāwī, *Fī Fiqh al-Aqalliyyāt al-Muslima*, 182–83.
[27] *Ibid.*, 154–61.
[28] Muzammil H. Siddiqi, "Necessity that Allows Buying a House on Mortgage," October 20, 2010, accessed July 5, 2013: http://www.onislam.net/english/ask-the-scholar/principles-of-islamic-jurisprudence-usul-ul-fiqh/concepts-and-term/174462-aquotnecessityaquot-that-allows-buying-a-house-on-mortgage.html?Term=.

dollars. The money needed could not be obtained unless a mortgage was taken. Thus, they inquired whether the potential for proselytizing justifies the suspension of the prohibited based on *maṣlaḥa*:

> The European Council for Fatwa and Research issued a *fatwā* on the permissibility of taking a mortgage from the traditional banks to purchase a house when necessary. In light of this, are we allowed to take a mortgage because of necessity, taking into consideration that we have other reasons? 1. The center lies in an excellent location accessible to public transportation, and if it is rebuilt in an Islamic style it will attract people's attention and serve as a means of *da'wa*. Nonetheless, it is the oldest center in the city. 2. There are other mosques erected after this center in inhabited areas. The buildings of these mosques were financed by money earned through usury. The people in these mosques practice *bid'a* and they have no *da'wa* programs. But these mosques attract the attention of non-Muslims when they want to visit a mosque. 3. If we do not start building on the spot, the planning permission will be withdrawn and it will be very difficult to get it again. In addition, the building costs increase on a daily basis.

The European Council's response was unequivocal: taking a mortgage to reconstruct a mosque is not permissible. The *fatwā* presented three reasons, all establishing that the case does not constitute a necessity or a need that qualifies as a necessity. First, "in spite of the fact that the current building is old, it still satisfies people's needs. It can accommodate prayers, gatherings on religious occasions, and teaching children." Second, "to have such a center is essential. Nonetheless, it does not justify spending this huge amount of money to compete with other mosques financed by money earned through usury." Third, "Allah does not overburden a person. This rule, as it applies to individual Muslims, applies to the Muslim nation since it is required to establish the Islamic rites within the limits of its capacity." The Council concluded:

> We advise the officials of the center to search for alternative legal methods, such as limiting the project to be within their capacity, restoring the current building so that it appears in the Islamic style, or exerting more efforts to collect donations from other places to complete the fund for the project.[29]

[29] European Council for Fatwa and Research, "Getting a Mortgage to Build a Mosque," June 25, 2007, accessed July 7, 2013: http://www.onislam.net/english/ask-the-scholar/morals-and-=manners/173265.html?Manners. For an Arabic version see, "Qarḍ min al-Bank li-Binā' Markaz Islāmī," *al-'ūrūbbīyya* 45 (May 2006), 5.

As noted in the second chapter, this *fatwā* was cited by the Secretary General of the European Council, Ḥusayn Ḥalāwa, to emphasize that proselytizing is not an objective of *wasaṭī fiqh al-aqalliyyāt al-Muslima*. Notwithstanding his explanation, the potential to enhance *daʿwa* is mentioned explicitly as a communal need in the 1999 *fatwā*. The ban on usurious loans for the purpose of reconstructing a mosque demonstrates a different point, specifically that *wasaṭīs* are not inclined to invoke proselytizing alone as justification for permitting the prohibited. Rather, proselytizing serves as a vital supplementary justification. This hierarchy is also demonstrated in other *fatwās* analyzed in this chapter and the next. A possible explanation in the context of the mortgages *fatwā* is the following: The *taysīr* that mortgages promote meets an individual need (i.e., financial security) that is applicable to most Muslims in Europe (and thus is also communal). The *tabshīr* promoted, on the other hand, meets a communal need only. Thus, the latter carries more weight than the former.

Student loans are another issue that was discussed in light of the Council's 1999 decision. The issue demonstrated how the objectives and mechanisms used in order to legitimize mortgages can also be applied to legitimizing other interest-based loans.

Sālim al-Shaykhī (b. 1964), a Libyan-born, Saudi-educated, and England-based jurist and member of the Council, authored a study on the English context of the matter, in which he argued, based on cross-*madhhab* search and consideration of *maṣlaḥa*, that student loans that are matched to the rise in price index are legitimate. Al-Shaykhī presented the general controversy on whether interest matched to inflation constitutes usury at all. He accepted the view that it does not, based on Q. 6:152 and 26:182 that demand fairness in transactions, the tradition *lā ḍarar wa-lā ḍirār*, and the *ḥadīth* narrated by Abū Saʿīd al-Khudrī, according to which the Prophet ordered payments to be made based on the principle of "*mithlan bi-mithl*" (equal for equal).[30] To return money

[30] For a discussion on this ḥ*adīth* see, Rauf A. Azhar, *Economics of an Islamic Economy* (Brill: Leiden, 2010), 359–71.

that is worth less than what one received would be a form of exploitation and harm.[31]

Nevertheless, al-Shaykhī argued that even if one does not accept this opinion, student loans should be legitimized based on *maṣlaḥa*. Since Muslims in Britain do not have access to reliable Islamic-regulated, interest-free loans, the principle that a need can be regarded as a necessity legitimizes the taking of interest-based student loans. The need is individual as well as communal. Higher education is required for individuals to find good jobs. Since most Muslims in the United Kingdom work in low-paying occupations, they will not be able to afford higher education if student loans remain prohibited. As for the communal need, unless student loans are legitimized, the Muslim minority will be harmed, and Islamic law rejects such harm. Furthermore, to facilitate integration, Muslims are required to establish a presence in the public and private sector, and they can do so only if they have access to higher education. Al-Shaykhī concluded that considering that the Council legitimized mortgages based on the notion that a need can be regarded as necessity, the legitimization of student loans is all the more justified, especially when considering that, unlike mortgages, student loans are matched to the rise in price index (and thus are considered by some jurists as legitimate in any case).[32]

Based on al-Shaykhī's study, the European Council legitimized student loans in Europe in its eighteenth session in July 2008. The decision, however, only pointed to the fairness of the system and its being matched to the rise in price index, not to the individual and communal needs presented in al-Shaykhī's study.[33] Writing in the American context, in which some student loans carry interest that is above the rise-in-price index, Muzammil Siddiqi stressed that student loans are permitted so long as they do not involve interest. However, if a loan is essential for studies and there is no other option but an interest-based one, then for

[31] Sālim al-Shykhī, "Ḥukm al-Qurūḍ al-Ṭullābiyya fī 'ūrūbbā," *al-Majalla al-'Ilmiyya lil-Majlis al-'Ūrūbbī lil-Iftā' wal-Buḥuth*, no. 14–15 (July 2009), 432–44.

[32] *Ibid.*, 446–53.

[33] "Ḥukm al-Qurūḍ al-Ṭullābiyya fī 'ūrūbbā" (decision 18/4), published in the concluding declaration of the eighteenth session of the European Council, July 1–5, 2008, accessed July 7, 2013: http://www.e-cfr.org/ar/index.php?ArticleID=575.

reasons of necessity it is possible to take it and then pay it back as soon as possible. Nonetheless, "if it is only a matter of enhancing one's knowledge, then one should not take loans with interest."[34]

Salafī jurisprudence vehemently opposed *wasaṭī* facilitations on interest-based loans. In addressing the issue, *salafīs* rejected the broad *wasaṭī* approach to *maṣlaḥa* and applied two foundations of their approach to the jurisprudence of Muslim minorities: Allah's laws are universal and do not accommodate changing times and places, and only a *maṣlaḥa* at the rank of necessity, which is dire and unquestionable, justifies permitting the prohibited. Lifting a hardship does not qualify as justification, neither does promoting proselytizing. The unlikely situation of a family finding itself without any kind of roof over its head might qualify though. In all the *salafī* mosques I visited, I documented unreserved acceptance of this view and rejection of the European Council's opinion as a deviation from Islam.

These opinions are rooted in the general *salafī* approach to interest. *Salafīs* condemn all forms of interest and loans and all bank operations charging interest, and consider only Islamic banking systems legitimate.[35] They emphasize that profiting from interest is the most strongly prohibited form of financial gain. They reject legitimizations that are based on arguments that interest became a universal practice and, thus, there exists an imperative to legitimize it.[36] They also reject the *Ḥanafī* view that prohibited transactions become permissible outside *dār al-Islām*.[37] Thus, the special conditions of Muslims in the West are no

[34] Referenced in Group of Muftis, "Student Loans with an Interest Rate Linked to Inflation," September 18, 2002, accessed July 6, 2013: http://www.onislam.net/english/ask-the-scholar/financial-issues/usury/174613.html.

[35] Muhammad Al-Atawneh, *Wahhābī Islam Facing the Challenges of Modernity: Dār Al-Iftā in the Modern Saudi State* (Leiden: Brill, 2010), 121–34.

[36] Ṣāliḥ b. Fawzān b. ʿAbdallāh al-Fawzān, *al-Ribā wa-Baʿḍ Ṣuwariha al-Muʿāṣira* (Cairo: Dār al-Imām Aḥmad, 2005), 18, 24–25.

[37] Islam Question and Answer, "Ruling on Dealing with Mortgages in a Non-Muslim Country," n.d., accessed July 7, 2013: http://islamqa.info/en/ref/159213. Another *fatwā* suggests that even according to the *Ḥanafī* view it is permissible for a Muslim outside *Dār al-Islām* to charge interest but not to pay it. So even according to the mistaken *Ḥanafī* view Muslims in the West cannot take mortgages: Islam Question and Answer, "Ruling on Buying a House with Riba in a Kafir Country," n.d., accessed June 30, 2013: http://www.islamqa.com/en/ref/101080/mortgages.

exception, as mortgages are "not permissible in Muslim countries or in non-Muslim countries."[38]

The considerable number of queries directed in the 2000s to *salafī* jurists on the matter suggests that the European Council's decision left its mark also on *salafī*-leaning individuals. Often, *mustaftīs* pointed to *maṣlaḥas* that could be incurred if a loan is taken in the hope that it would convince the jurist or the panel to offer a lenient decision. In response, they were instructed that with regard to interest-based loans, leniency is not an option no matter what the personal or communal gains may be. The editors of Islamweb.net were asked, five years after the issuance of the controversial *fatwā*, whether a decision had been issued by al-Qaraḍāwī permitting interest-based mortgages for Muslims who were not home-owners; they replied, without repeating al-Qaraḍāwī's name, that they were not aware of such a decision, and that mortgages are prohibited based on the Prophet's words that those who charge or pay interest will be cursed.[39] It is unlikely that the editors had never heard of one of the more controversial decisions in contemporary Islamic jurisprudence, or that they could not locate it and engage with it. Their response possibly suggests a reluctance to dignify the European Council with a debate that could further publicize its decision, or a reluctance to engage in a personified quarrel with a well-known jurist who resides in their homeland.

Other queries produced similar results. The Permanent Committee was asked whether, in a case of "urgent need" (*ḥāja māssa*) and when no alternative is available, it is permissible for heads of families to take an interest-based loan for academic studies or the purchase of a car or a home. It replied that all forms of interest are forbidden for all and that those who charge it, pay it, or assist in doing so are cursed. It stressed that this prohibition applies regardless of the rate of the interest charged.[40] A man from the United Kingdom presented an interesting case: he lives in

[38] Islam Question and Answer, "Ruling on Dealing with Mortgages in a Non-Muslim Country."

[39] Islamweb.net, "Fatāwā bi-Sh'an Shirā' Manzil bi-Qarḍ Ribāwī," Islamweb.net, accessed April 8, 2013: https://mail.google.com/mail/u/0/#search/shani/142c4366b5629e0f.

[40] Al-Lajna al-Dā'ima, "Ḥukm Akhdh al-Qarḍ al-Ribāwī lil-Ḥāja al-Māssa," in Ṣalāḥ al-Dīn Maḥmūd al-Sa'īd (ed.), *Fatāwā al-'Ulamā' ḥawla al-Aqalliyyāt al-Muslima fī al-'ālam* (Alexandria: Dār al-'īmān, 2004), 133–34.

a rented apartment, but if he takes a mortgage, which is the custom in his country, he will pay less every month and in the end the house will be his. Is it then *ḥalāl*? Al-Munajjid responded that it is not, no matter how great the need, because the payment of interest is prohibited according to the Quran, Sunna, and scholarly consensus. A need is not an excuse to do something that Allah has forbidden. A Muslim must fear Allah and remember that He is always watching, and he should prefer the Hereafter to this life. If he cannot find anyone to lend him money lawfully, then he should be patient in the hope of earning eternal reward, for Allah will compensate whoever gives something up for His sake with something better.[41]

A bank employee in a country in which Islamic banks do not exist asked Islamweb.net whether he might take advantage of a preferential loan he was offered. He may well have regretted raising the question: the editors not only informed him that taking such a loan is a grave sin but instructed that he must quit his job in the usurious bank. Their *fatwā* stipulated that if a person can live in a house of a friend or a relative, or rent a house, then his circumstances do not justify taking a mortgage.[42]

A Muslim from Norway explained that he was forced to take a mortgage from a bank because he has "a large family with five children and it is almost impossible to rent a house here for such large families. What does Islam say in such circumstances?" As noted above, *wasaṭīs* cited this condition in the American context as justification. The editors of Islamweb.net were not satisfied. They explained that based on Q. 2:278–79, taking *ribā* is a declaration of war against Allah and His Prophet. It can only be justified through a "compulsion of necessity which cannot be avoided." They scolded the inquirer: "you should have tried to get a person or an institution to deal with you in a *ribā*-free transaction or

[41] Muḥammad Ṣāliḥ al-Munajjid, "Should He Go for an Interest-based Mortgage if that Is Cheaper than Renting?" Islam Question and Answer, accessed June 10, 2013: http://islamqa.info/en/ref/21914.

[42] Islamweb.net, "Bank Loan to Buy a House," July 14, 2002, accessed April 1, 2010: http://www.islamweb.net/emainpage/index.php?page=showfatwa&Option=FatwaId&Id=84495; Muḥammad b. Ṣāliḥ Ibn 'Uthaymīn also prohibited working in a usurious bank, "al-'Amal fī al-Bunūk al-Ribbāwiyya wa-Mu'āmalatihā," in *Fatāwā al-Balad al-Ḥarām* (Cairo: Dār al-Tawfīqiyya, n.d), 488.

even leave the whole issue and simply rent a house. These were possibilities open to you to avoid *ribā*." Now that the sin had been committed, the inquirer must acknowledge the severity of his situation, repent and rid himself of that loan as soon as possible.[43]

Salafī prohibitions on usury apply to additional aspects of housing contracts. For example, the editors of Islam Question and Answer advised a person interested in signing a contract to buy a flat that stipulates a fine of 2,000 pounds for any delay in payment that the contract is illegitimate because it involves usury.[44] A nephew who was a witness to an interest-based loan taken by his uncle said he felt "constantly depressed," having realized that he had done something wrong; the Permanent Committee confirmed that he was involved in a forbidden transaction and asked him to repent and seek the forgiveness of Allah.[45] The editors of Islam Question and Answer advised a Muslim who wanted to take an interest-based loan in a foreign country and then avoid paying the interest that the transaction would still be considered impermissible because it involved the signing of a prohibited agreement. The editors added that usury is a major sin, whether the transaction is between two Muslims or between a Muslim and an infidel.[46]

Despite their strict opposition to mortgages, *salafīs* do not order believers who have committed the sin to leave their homes. The Permanent Committee decided that a person who had taken a mortgage must repent, ask for forgiveness, and resolve not to repeat the sin but should not "knock the house down, but rather make use of it."[47] Wives, furthermore, are not held responsible for the sins of their husbands. A German-Muslim

[43] Islamweb.net, "Buying a House with a Bank Loan," January 30, 2000, accessed July 7, 2013: http://www.islamweb.net/emainpage/index.php?page=showfatwa&Option=FatwaId&Id=82102.

[44] Islam Question and Answer, "Buying a Flat by Installments When There Is a Clause in the Contract that Stipulates a Penalty in the Event of Late Payment," n.d., accessed April 1, 2010: http://www.islam-qa.com/en/cat/76.

[45] Standing Committee on Academic Research and Issuing Fatwas, "Ruling on Being a Witness to a Riba-based Loan," n.d., accessed July 7, 2013: http://islamqa.info/en/ref/10235.

[46] Islam Question and Answer, "Should He Take a Riba-based Loan if He Does Not Intend to Pay the Interest," n.d., accessed July 7, 2013: http://islamqa.info/en/ref/87542.

[47] Islam Question and Answer, "He Took a Loan with Riba to Buy a House under Pressure from his Father," n.d., accessed July 7, 2013: http://islamqa.info/en/ref/95005.

married to a German convert to Islam was told that she should gently advise her husband against his plan to buy a house with an interest-based loan and that she has done her duty even if he ignores her recommendation.[48]

Student loans are equally rejected so long as any interest is charged. *Salafīs* do not accept the view that paying back a loan based on the rise-in-price index does not constitute *ribā*. In their opinion, any payment that is higher than the loan constitutes unlawful interest, and this matter is not debatable. They cite the Companions ʿUbay b. Kaʿb, ʿAbdallāh b. ʿAbbās, and ʿAbdallāh b. Masʿūd, who forbade loans that bring benefit.[49] Thus, they consider the English student-loans system, approved by *wasaṭīs*, as impermissible.[50] The editors of Islam Question and Answer were presented with a more complicated situation of a Muslim student in Norway who was entitled to a loan. If he passes his midterm it will become a grant, yet if he drops out or his grades do not allow him to pursue his studies further, the loan will be valid and will carry interest. Is it a permissible loan? The editors answered that the money is only permissible if it does not carry any interest and the amount paid back is the exact amount given. If there is a potential for being charged interest, then the loan is impermissible.[51]

FAMILY RELATIONS WITH NON-MUSLIMS

Islamic law allows Muslim men to marry Jewish and Christian women but prohibits their marriage to idolaters. It forbids Muslim women from marrying non-Muslim men, including monotheists, because men have authority over their spouses, and it is not desirable that disbelievers

[48] Islamweb.net, "Reluctant to Live in an Apartment her Husband Bought with Riba," June 23, 2009, accessed July 13, 2013: http://www.islamweb.net/emainpage/index.php?page=showfatwa&Option=FatwaId&Id=124015.

[49] Islam Question and Answer, "Is it Haram to Pay Interest Based on Inflation," n.d., accessed July 7, 2013: http://islamqa.info/en/ref/12541.

[50] Islam Question and Answer, "Paying Interest because of Inflation Is Riba," n.d., accessed July 7, 2013: http://islamqa.info/en/ref/23388.

[51] Islam Question and Answer, "Ḥukm al-Qurūḍ allatī Tumnaḥu li-Ajl al-Dirāsa," n.d., accessed July 7, 2013: http://islamqa.info/ar/ref/181723.

have authority over believers. Love is, at times, blind to religious and ethnic affiliations. In Western societies, there is a greater probability that a Muslim woman and a non-Muslim man will become romantically involved. If the future male-spouse is willing to convert to Islam (as a sacrifice in the name of love, or because religion is not important to him, or because he is impressed with what he learned about Islam) the problem resolves itself from the point of view of religious law. If, however, he declines to convert, his female partner is confronted with a difficult choice, as Muslim jurists of all orientations, including *wasaṭīs*, have maintained the opinion that such marriages are prohibited, even in the West.

Another issue is the legitimacy of marriages between non-Muslim man and Muslim women who converted only *after* they married. All four schools of law oblige women who converted to Islam to leave their husbands if the latter did not convert by the end of the *'idda*, the "waiting" period after which women can remarry. This requirement, which weighs heavily on some Western women who consider converting, became a hotly debated topic of *fiqh al-aqalliyyāt al-Muslima*. *Wasaṭīs* legitimized maintaining marriages between new female converts and their non-Muslim husbands. Their deliberations highlighted their understanding of facilitation as an essence of Islamic law. They also highlighted the utility of applying cross-*madhhab* search and treating *da'wa* as a primary *maṣlaḥa* as a means to legitimize prohibitions. *Salafīs* strongly rejected this position and stressed that the marriages of female converts with husbands who refuse to convert must be terminated. Their decisions highlighted the *salafī* antipathy to allowing Muslims in the West exceptional concessions and, in particular, their refusal to consider proselytizing as a *maṣlaḥa* that justifies facilitations.

The issue attracted less scholarly attention than the legitimization of mortgages did, perhaps because it potentially affects a far smaller number of individuals. But in terms of jurisprudence theory, the audacity its legitimization required was even greater than that required to legitimize mortgages. While interest-based loans could be considered legitimate in the West according to one of the schools of law, no such plurality existed regarding the question of marriage between female converts and non-Muslim husbands. *Wasaṭī* deliberations on the matter testified to enormity of the challenge. The European Council revealed that it addressed the issue in three consecutive sessions between 1999 and 2001, and emphasized that it reached a decision only after taking into account prevailing juristic opinions as well as the purposes of the law and the "special conditions" of female converts whose husbands remain non-Muslim.[52] When I described the mortgages *fatwā* as the most audacious decision taken by the Council, the Secretary General of the Council, Ḥusayn Ḥalāwa, corrected me and said that the *fatwā* on marriages of female converts was just as revolutionary because it broke away from a well-established juristic opinion. He revealed that al-Qaraḍāwī's initial opinion was against its legitimization but that he changed his mind in the course of deliberations.[53]

Al-Qaraḍāwī himself testified that for most of his life he agreed with the consensus opinion that marriages should be terminated if the husband does not convert. He mentioned his participation in the 1970s in a conference in the United States where the Sudanese scholar Ḥasan al-Turābī (b. 1932) created a firestorm when he argued in favor of the continuation of marriages between female converts and their non-Muslim husbands. Al-Qaraḍāwī's explanation for his late embrace of a position he had rejected for most of his career was that no single person possesses all the knowledge, and that a Muslim should strive to continue to learn from the cradle to the grave.[54] Yet, as with the legitimization of mortgages, his justification of the new opinion was enabled not because al-Qaraḍāwī was faced with new realities or evidences; rather, it was a result of the broader theory of *sharʿī* objectives and mechanisms he developed in the late 1990s.

The *mustaftī* who drew al-Qaraḍāwī's attention to the problem paved the way for the application of *maṣlaḥa* by noting that women in the West

[52] Al-Majlis al-ʾŪrūbbī lil-Iftāʾ wal-Buḥūth, *Qarārāt wa-Fatāwā al-Majlis min al-Dawra al-Thāmina ilā al-Khāmisa ʿAshara*, decision 3/8 (Word file from the Council's website, accessed September 13, 2010: http://www.e-cfr.org), 4.

[53] Interview by the author with Ḥusayn Ḥalāwa at the Islamic Cultural Center of Ireland, February 13, 2012.

[54] Al-Qaraḍāwī, "Islām al-Marʾa dun Zawjiha Hal Yufarriqu Baynahimā?" *Fī Fiqh al-Aqalliyyāt al-Muslima* (Cairo: Dār al-Shurūq, 2007, first published 2001), 105–6.

are more inclined to embrace Islam than men. He argued that the demand to divorce their non-Muslim spouses imposes a burden on Western women who contemplate converting but love their husbands and families.[55]

Al-Qaraḍāwī was convinced, and declared the issue to be a demonstration of the function of cross-*madhhab* search as a means to provide *taysīr*.[56] He stressed that the insistence on breaking interfaith marriages could result in *tanfīr* and discourages women who wish to convert to Islam from doing so.[57] He justified his legitimization as an example of returning to the *salaf* and neglecting the *taqlīd* of later generations.[58]

His study of the matter noted that Ibn al-Qayyim al-Jawziyya found that it was not the opinion of all jurists that new Muslims are required to terminate their marriage with non-Muslim husbands, and the *salaf* have left Muslims with nine different opinions on the matter. The opinion favored by Ibn al-Qayyim (and Ibn Taymiyya) permitted the continuation of such marriages based on the words of 'Umar b. al-Khaṭṭāb, who was reported by 'Abdallāh b. Yazīd al-Khaṭmī to have said that women who convert should be given the option whether to divorce or not. However, Ibn al-Qayyim emphasized that wives must yearn for their husbands' conversion and that they should only resume their marital relations once the husbands embrace Islam.[59] Al-Qaraḍāwī cautiously argued that Ibn al-Qayyim's interpretation of 'Umar b. al-Khaṭṭāb words need not be accepted entirely. If the *khalīfa*'s opinion is taken literally, then new Muslims in non-Muslim countries may be allowed to continue their maritial relations with their husbands while waiting for them to convert, an opinion which accords with their needs, particularly in the case of those who have children.[60] His review suggested that Q. 60:10, which stipulates the impermissibility of marital relations between a convert and her non-Muslim husband, should be contextualized as forbidding the forced return of the convert to the *kuffār* (unbelievers) rather than disallowing the convert to wait for her husband to become a believer.[61]

Al-Qaraḍāwī's late inclination to offer facilitation for married converts should not be confused, though, as welcoming interfaith couples in the

[55] *Ibid.*, 105. [56] *Ibid.*, 59–60. [57] *Ibid.*, 116.
[58] *Ibid.*, 122–23. [59] *Ibid.*, 106–8.
[60] *Ibid.*, 120–21. [61] *Ibid.*, 112–13.

West. Throughout his career, he emphasized that it is undesirable for Muslim men in the West to choose Christian and Jewish spouses and placed strong limitations on such marriages. He first presented this opinion in his introductory book on religious law in 1960[62] and then again in his 2001 systematic theorization on the jurisprudence of Muslim minorities.[63] Writing in 1988, he pointed to the importance of cross-*madhhab* search—in this case, attempting to find the most suitable answer beyond the four schools—by demonstrating that it potentially provides evidence for *limiting,* in case the need arises, the marriages between Muslim men and non-Muslim women.[64]

Fayṣal al-Mawlawī, al-Qaraḍāwī's deputy, rejected his view on the continuation of marriages. The decision of the European Council, following a deliberation on their conflicting opinions, was approved in its eighth session, held in Valencia, Spain on July 18–22, 2001.[65] While reflecting the Council members' lack of consensus, the opinion, in the end, indirectly legitimized the continuation of marriages based on the importance of encouraging conversions. The decision stressed that Muslim women must not marry non-Muslim men, and that wives who converted before having intercourse with husbands who do not wish to convert must separate from them at once. However, a woman who converted after having intercourse with a non-Muslim husband who refuses to convert can, if she wishes, wait for her husband to convert even after the *ʿidda* is over, even if that "takes a long time." Once the husband converts, their marriage contract does not need to be renewed. The Council, succinct and cautious in its language, explained that while the four schools of law call for the termination of such marriages, "some scholars" believe it is the right of wives who converted to remain with their non-Muslim husbands, with all the martial rights and duties involved, so long as they can

[62] al-Qaraḍāwī, *al-Ḥalāl wal-Ḥarām fī al-Islām*, 9, 164.

[63] al-Qaraḍāwī, "Zawāj al-Muslim bi-Ghayr al-Muslima," in *Fī Fiqh al-Aqalliyyāt al-Muslima* (Cairo: Dār al-Shurūq, 2007, first published 2001), 97–104.

[64] Yūsuf al-Qaraḍāwī, *Min Ajl Ṣaḥwa Rāshida*, 49–50.

[65] Alexandre Caeiro, "Transnational Ulama, European Fatwas and Islamic Authority: A Case Study of the European Council for Fatwa and Research," in Martin van Bruinessen and Stefano Allievi (eds.), *Producing Islamic Knowledge: Transmission and Dissemination in Western Europe* (Abingdon and New York: Routledge, 2011), 134–35.

manifest their religion and so long as they yearn for the husbands to become Muslim. The reason for this opinion, according to the Council, is to avoid *tanfīr* of women who wish to become Muslim but are afraid to lose their husbands. The Council based its decision on the abovementioned words of 'Umar b. al-Khaṭṭāb and on the words of 'Alī b. Abī Ṭālib, who gave similar legitimization.[66]

Salafīs strongly defended the prohibition of maintaining marriage between new converts and non-Muslim husbands prior to—and even more fiercely after—the *wasaṭīs* offered their legitimization. *Salafī fatwās* made clear that prospects for bringing non-Muslims to the fold of Allah's truth constitute no justification for facilitation but, on the contrary, should motivate strict, uncompromising adherence to His laws. The issue was presented before al-'Uthaymīn in words encouraging legitimization of the prohibited: some women, wrote the questioner, wish to convert while their husbands do not; pointing to *maṣlaḥa*, the *mustaftī* noted that, alas, the fear of losing beloved husbands who also provide financial support, as well as the concern for the children, make these women hesitate. In many cases, the husbands embrace Islam after a year or so, and wives hope to promote their conversion by remaining with them. Considering that times have changed, and based on *maṣlaḥa* and the principle of choosing the lesser of two evils, is there room for *ijtihād* on the matter? Al-'Uthaymīn replied that there is not. Based on the elaborate words in Q. 60:10, the explicit law prohibiting the continuation of marriages between Muslim converts and non-Muslim husbands belongs to the category of laws on which there is no room for *ijtihād*. Even if under certain circumstances the *maṣlaḥa* of a law belonging to that category is not evident, and even if abiding by the law is difficult, one must still abide by the law. The *salaf*, he noted, did not hesitate to kill even their own fathers and sons for the sake of Allah.[67]

[66] Al-Majlis al-'Ūrūbbī lil-Iftā' wal-Buḥūth, *Qarārāt wa-Fatāwā al-Majlis min al-Dawra al-Thāmina ilā al-Khāmisa 'Ashara*, decision 3/8, 4–5.

[67] Muḥammad b. Ṣāliḥ al-'Uthaymīn, "Idhā Aslamat al-Zawja wa-Jawzuhā lam Yaslam," in Ṣalāḥ al-Dīn Maḥmūd al-Sa'īd (ed.), *Fatāwā al-'Ulamā' ḥawla al-Aqalliyyāt al-Muslima fī al-'ālam* (Alexandria: Dār al-'Īmān, 2004), 278–80.

Another query presented al-ʿUthaymīn with a different kind of dilemma and demonstrated once again his reluctance to compromise when individual hardships are at stake. The query argued that Muslim centers receive women, especially those who have children and are married to men of good character, who wish to convert but hesitate to do so because of their husbands' insistence that they will not embrace Islam. Clearly Q. 60:10 prohibits maintaining such marriages, but is it permissible not to inform women that they would have to divorce and focus first on Islamizing them? Al-ʿUthaymīn said it is not: to hinder women from knowledge about their duty to divorce may result in the much graver problem of converts renouncing Islam after embracing it. Instead, these women should be informed that love for Allah and His Prophet must be given precedence over love for anyone else, and that Allah compensates those who sacrifice for Him. If forced to divorce, these women should be matched with eligible Muslim men who would take care of their children.[68]

Ṣāliḥ al-Fawzān's decision on the matter was issued following the European Council's decision. The query addressed to al-Fawzān noted that "a body that is called the European Council for Issuing Fatwas" issued a *fatwā* that allows an infidel woman who became a Muslim to remain with her infidel husband. Is the *fatwā* correct? Al-Fawzān answered that the abovementioned *fatwā* is invalid based on Q. 60:10. If a woman converted to Islam, she must separate from her infidel husband. If the husband becomes a Muslim during the *ʿidda* period, she should return to him. If not, based on Q. 2:221, she must leave him for good.[69]

Another issue concerning family relations with non-Muslims in which *wasaṭīs* and *salafīs* differ is inheritance. The four schools of Islamic law prohibited Muslims from inheriting from infidels and infidels from inheriting from Muslims, based on the Prophet's words on the matter, narrated by Usāma b. Zayd. However, a Muslim can give up to a third of

[68] Muḥammad b. Ṣaliḥ al-ʿUthaymīn, "Turīdu al-Islām wa-lā Turīdu Tark Zawjahā al-Kāfir," in Ṣalāḥ al-Dīn Maḥmūd al-Saʿīd (ed.), *Fatāwā al-ʿUlamāʾ ḥawla al-Aqalliyyāt al-Muslima fī al-ʿālam* (Alexandria: Dār al-ʾīmān, 2004), 297–99.

[69] Al-Fawzān, *al-Ribā wa-Baʿḍ Ṣuwariha al-Muʿasira*, 59–60.

his property according to his will to individuals other than the relatives who are the rightful heirs, and non-Muslim relatives can be included in this share. As with interfaith marriages, this matter also concerns a relatively small number of Muslims (and prospective Muslims), but potentially bears heavily on their financial situation.

To legitimize facilitation, *wasaṭīs* drew on their narrow contextualization of the principle of "loyalty and disavowal" and the application of cross (and beyond) *madhhab* search. In its fifth session, the European Council decided that "Muslims must not be prohibited from inheriting [from] their non-Muslim relatives." It argued that the Prophetic tradition which forbade inheriting from non-Muslims should be understood as applying only to non-Muslims who are at state of war with Muslims. It also explained that in the "initial stages" of Islam, Muslims were not prohibited from inheriting from non-Muslim relatives.[70] This opinion is rejected by *salafīs*. Al-Munajjid ruled that a "Muslim is not permitted to inherit anything of the wealth of a non-Muslim relative," based on the Prophet's words, "The believer does not inherit from a kāfir and the kāfir does not inherit from a believer." He noted, however, that if a non-believer makes a will leaving one-third or less of his wealth to his Muslim child (whether male or female), then the Muslim is entitled to take it because this is a will as opposed to inheritance.[71]

CHRISTMAS AND OTHER CELEBRATIONS

An American Muslim medical doctor wrote in a Qatari-based publication that for "a Muslim living in the West, the Christmas holiday is one of the most stressful times."[72] Christmas festivities present Muslim minorities

[70] European Council for Fatwa and Research, "The Ruling on a Muslim Inheriting his Non-Muslim Relatives (resolution 1/5)," in *Fatwās of European Council for Fatwa and Research* (Cairo: Islamic INC, 2002), 148–49.

[71] Muḥammad Ṣāliḥ al-Munajjid, "Inheritance from a Non-Muslim," n.d., accessed November 6, 2013: islamqa.info/en/ref/428.

[72] Zeyd Ali Merenkov, "A Muslim Perspective on Christmas," part 1, December 28, 2011, accessed July 10, 2013: http://www.islamweb.net/emainpage/index.php?page=articles&id=155792.

with two challenges. One is the temptation to join in celebrations full of colorful lights, communal warmth, and gift-giving, which children and some adults find almost irresistible. The other is the central position occupied by Christmas festivities in Western educational institutions and workplaces and the commercial function of the holiday, which makes it almost impossible for Muslims living in Western countries to avoid any connection with it. Devout Muslims in the West face numerous dilemmas pertaining to the holiday, e.g., is it permissible to accept a Christmas cash bonus or to congratulate Christians on their holiday?

The issue is not unique to Muslim minorities. Similar dilemmas have been faced by generations of Jews living in majority Christian countries. The evolution of Hanukkah among European and American Jewry into its current child-oriented and commercialized character was influenced by the similar evolution of Christmas during the nineteenth century.[73] Concern about the participation of Jewish students in Christmas celebrations played a role in the German-Jewish Orthodox insistence on Jewish rather than public schooling during the late nineteenth and early twentieth centuries.[74] Some Jews who celebrate Christmas or integrate aspects of Christmas into the celebrations of Hanukkah point to the national, civil, and commercial character of the holiday. In response, even liberal rabbis have declared that it is prohibited to participate in a celebration of Christ's birth, and some place rigid restrictions on any Jewish participation in the holiday, including extending holiday greetings to Christians.[75]

[73] Gideon Reuveni, "Bourgeois Lifestyle, Jewishness, and Consumer Culture in Weimar Germany (in Hebrew)," *Chidushim: Studies in the History of German and Central European Jewry* 14 (Jerusalem: Leo Baeck Institute, 2010), 80.

[74] Mordechai Breuer, *Jüdische Orthodoxie im Deutschen Reich 1871–1918* (Jerusalem: Zalman Shazar Center for Jewish History, 1990, in Hebrew), 95.

[75] For example, Rabbi Jacob Walter of the traditional wing of the Reform movement in America wrote that a Jew may not join in Christmas celebrations, but he permitted congratulating Christians on the occasion: Walter Jacob, *Contemporary American Reform Responsa* (Pennsylvania: Central Conference of American Rabbis, 1987), 257–62. Rabbi Yuval Sharlo of the Jewish-Israeli national orthodox establishment holds that a Jew may not congratulate Christians or give them presents on their religious holidays: "Ḥag Ha-Molad," December 11, 2009, accessed July 11, 2013: http://www.kipa.co.il/ask/show/168472-%D7%97%D7%92-%D7%94%D7%9E%D7%95%D7%9C%D7%93. Conversely, he argued that congratulating should be avoided unless there is no way around it and avoidance may result in hostility: "Levarech Notzri le-Ḥag Ha-Molad," December 11, 2006, accessed July 11, 2013: http://www.moreshet.co.il/web/shut/shut2.asp?id=65351. Responding to a query by an Israeli employee in an Israeli-owned shop in New York,

Dilemmas relating to Christmas are one of the most hotly debated issues between *wasaṭī* and *salafī* jurists. Both approaches prohibit the celebration of Christmas, but they disagree over participation in certain aspects of the holiday. The disagreements constitute another demonstration of the practical implications conflicting *wasaṭī* and *salafī* interpretations of *maṣlaḥa* and "loyalty and disavowal" have in social Western spheres. *Wasaṭī* jurists allow some participation in Christmas-related events and extending congratulatory greetings to Christians on the occasion. Crucial to their argument is the *wasaṭī* emphasis on the importance of maintaining friendly relations with non-Muslims and their elevation of *da'wa* to a central religio-legal duty that justifies concessions. In contrast, *salafī* jurists strictly prohibit any participation by Muslims in Christmas celebrations, and they also prohibit Muslims from congratulating Christians on their holiday. Central to their argument is their objection to innovations, their belief that effective proselytizing calls for rigid application of the law rather than for concessions, and their interpretation of *al-walā' wal-barā'* as strongly prohibiting imitation or acknowledgment of infidel holidays as well as forging friendly relations with non-Muslims.

Probably more than any other issue, *salafī* decisions on Christmas and other holidays celebrated in the West expose their aversion to any prospect of Muslim integration to non-Muslim societies. The *salafī* campaign on the matter is intense, and affects non-*salafīs* as well. In the words of one 23-year-old English-Muslim professional, who related that he had been repeatedly advised by one of his devout friends that it is not permissible to congratulate non-Muslims: "personally I think he [my friend] is wrong, but it is difficult to argue against him because all the information he gets is taken from the internet and it makes him sound very knowledgeable."[76]

In contrast to *salafī* jurists, *wasaṭī* jurists distinguish between actively taking part in non-Muslim religious rituals and festivities, which they

Rabbi Sharlo wrote that a Jew may not place a Christmas tree near the Hanukkah menorah: "Etz Ḥag Ha-Molad Bemekom 'Avoda," December 4, 2007, accessed July 11, 2013: http://www.moreshet.co.il/web/shut/shut2.asp?id=81513.

[76] Jerome Taylor, "Can a Muslim Say Happy Christmas to his Friends?" *The Independent* (November 26, 2009).

prohibit, and engaging with those events in ways that are technical or merely courteous, which they legitimize. In one query, an American Muslim identified as K. described the stresses experienced by his family during the holiday season. At Christmas time, he explained, Christians illuminate their houses with lights, put up Christmas trees and exchange gifts, the television is full of holiday-related programs, and all the stores are decorated for the holiday. Some Muslims, wrote K., cannot resist the temptation: they put up Christmas trees and lights to keep their children happy, justifying their actions by claiming that Christmas commemorates the birth of Jesus, who, according to Islam, is a prophet. K. asked whether these Muslims act permissibly. In his *fatwā*, Muzammil Siddiqi explained that while Christmas has become a national, commercial holiday, it is still a Christian holiday, in which Christians celebrate the "day of the birth of God's son." From the Islamic point of view, the belief that God had a son is blasphemous and, by participating in Christmas, it is possible that Muslims would slowly lose their awareness of this basic point. Siddiqi recognized that "the festivities and glitter of this holiday" affect children deeply but emphasized that this does not legitimize the placement of Christmas trees and lights inside or outside the house. Instead, parents should tell their children that "we are Muslims, and Christmas is not our holiday" and try to take them to Islamic camps and conferences at that time of year. Parents should also give special attention to Muslim holidays, so that "our children will be attracted to our own celebrations rather than looking at others." Siddiqi repudiated the suggestion that Muslims can celebrate Christmas because Islam recognizes Jesus as a prophet. He explained that Jesus was one of twenty-four prophets and messengers, so it is illogical for Muslims to celebrate his birthday and neglect those of other prophets.[77]

Answering a query from Ṣābir, "a convert for about five years" from the United Kingdom, the editors of onislam.net explained that he must not permit his children to celebrate Christmas, which he described as merely

[77] Muzammil Siddiqi and Ahmad Kutty, "Can Muslims Celebrate Christmas?" December 23, 2012, accessed July 9, 2013: http://www.onislam.net/english/ask-the-scholar/morals-and-manners/customs-and-traditions/174414-can-muslims-celebrate-christmas.html?Traditions=.

a "folk tradition." The "most important" reason is that, according to a tradition, the Prophet Muḥammad once saw people celebrating non-Muslim holidays and disapproved of the act, explaining to them that Allah has given Muslims two better holidays, *'īd al-fiṭr* and *'īd al-aḍḥā*. An additional reason "to this already sufficient" one is that celebrating Christmas, even as a non-religious holiday, would set the wrong example for Ṣābir's children and create a crisis from which they will suffer in the future. The editors advised Ṣābir to try to distract his children from the holiday spirit by spending quality time with them, by traveling with them, and by avoiding television and shopping malls in order to decrease their exposure to the holiday.[78]

According to *wasaṭī* jurists, one may not participate in Christmas plays. Manāl Sa'd from Belgium asked whether it is legitimate for her child to play the role of an angel in a narration of Jesus' birth. Jamāl Badawī answered that it is not, because the play is based on religious beliefs that contradict Islam.[79]

Participation in other holidays that have religious roots is also prohibited. Valentine's Day[80] and Halloween are rejected because of their Christian and pagan roots. Muzammil Siddiqi described Halloween as a "repugnant" holiday in which pumpkins are wasted in vain and reasonable people act bizarrely and engage in dangerous acts.[81] However, *wasaṭī* jurists permit participation in secular non-Islamic holidays. Answering a query from Ziyād, a Muslim-American teacher, Badawī wrote that celebrating Thanksgiving is legitimate because it is a cultural

[78] Onislam.net, "As a New Muslim, Can My Kids Celebrate Christmas?" December 18, 2012, accessed July 11, 2013: http://www.onislam.net/english/ask-the-scholar/dawah-principles/dawah-to-non-and-new-muslims/169126-as-a-new-muslim-can-my-kids-celebrate-christmas.html?New_Muslims=.

[79] Jamāl Badawī, "Our Kids & Non-Islamic Feasts" (Live Dialogue with a Jurist in IslamOnline.net), December 24, 2003, accessed July 11, 2013: http://mcadams.posc.mu.edu/blog/moslems_christmas.htm.

[80] Su'ād Ṣāliḥ, "Valentine's Day from an Islamic Perspective," February 13, 2013, accessed July 11, 2013; http://www.onislam.net/english/ask-the-scholar/morals-and-manners/customs-and-traditions/175209-valentines-day-from-an-islamic-perspective.html?Traditions=.

[81] Muzammil Siddiqi, "Celebrating Halloween," accessed January 30, 2010 (link no longer valid): http://www.islamonline.net/servlet/Satellite?pagename=IslamOnline-English-Ask_Scholar/FatwaE/FatwaE&cid=1119503543074.

and social event with no religious basis.[82] The European Council for Fatwa and Research ruled that there is "no objection whatsoever" to Muslim participation in Independence Day, Union Day, Mother's Day, and Childhood Day in their receiving states, so long as Islamic manners are observed at all times.[83]

While unequivocal about the impermissibility of Muslim participation in Christmas celebrations, *wasaṭī* jurists hold that it is permissible for Muslims to congratulate non-Muslims on that occasion, an opinion that has strong roots in modernist jurisprudence. In 1904, Riḍā replied to a query by a Muslim "living under a Christian government" who noted that Christians pay Muslims visits on Muslim holidays and expect a similar courtesy on their own holidays. Riḍā replied that Muslims should indeed do so based on two justifications. First, Muslims should be kind to non-Muslims, as established by the tradition according to which the Prophet visited his sick Jewish servant child. Second, it is in the interest of a Muslim minority and constitutes a *maṣlaḥa* in the rank of necessity to show kindness to the majority that rules it. Riḍā emphasized that even if a *maṣlaḥa* was not involved, the Muslims of that country were obliged to show kindness to Christians because the latter were kind to them, and the Islamic norm is that Muslims must be kinder than others.[84]

Wasaṭī jurists adopted Riḍā's line of thinking in their decisions on the matter. The decision issued by the European Council for Fatwa and Research demonstrates the importance *wasaṭīs* attribute to promoting good relations with non-Muslims and their elevation of proselytizing to a principal religio-juristic objective. To a great extent, it reads as a refutation of the *salafī* understanding of "loyalty and disavowal" and previous *salafī* decisions on Christmas greetings (see below) although, in a manner typical to these dialectics, the contesting party is not mentioned by name.

[82] *Ibid.*

[83] European Council for Fatwa and Research, "Ruling on Offering Congratulations to Non-Muslims on their Festive Occasions" (decision 3\6), in *Fatwās of European Council for Fatwa and Research*, 184. See also European Council for Fatwa and Research, "Congratulating Non-Muslims on their Festive Occasions," May 2, 2013, accessed July 11, 2013: http://www.onislam.net/english/ask-the-scholar/dawah-principles/dawah-to-non-and-new-muslims/169282-congratulating-non-muslims-on-their-festive-occasions.html?New_Muslims=.

[84] "Ziyārat al-Muslim li-Ghayr al-Muslimīn," *al-Manār* 7, 1 (March 18, 1904), 26–27.

The Council noted that it had received numerous queries on this issue from Muslims living in the West. One may congratulate non-Muslims "either verbally or by sending a card that contains no symbols or icons of religious implications that may contradict Islamic faith and principles, such as a cross." The decision is based on Q. 60:8–9 and additional evidence according to which Allah commanded Muslims to differentiate between non-Muslims who fight against Muslims and non-Muslims who interact with Muslims in peace. The latter must be treated in a kind manner. Furthermore, a Muslim must never be less charitable or pleasant than a non-Muslim and should return good treatment with similar treatment. "Indeed, the permissibility of congratulating non-Muslims on their festive days becomes more of an obligation if they were to offer their greetings on Islamic festive occasions, as we are commanded to return good treatment with similar treatment, and to return the greeting with a better one, or at least with the same greeting (Q. 4:86)."[85] Invoking proselytizing as a religio-legal objective, the Council argued that the significance of congratulating non-Muslims on their festive occasions "increases dramatically if we are interested in inviting them to Islam and to liken Muslims to them, which is an obligation upon us all." It is impossible to achieve the goal of converting non-Muslims by treating them roughly, sternly, and violently. Instead, they should be treated in a way that builds trust, as was the way of the Prophet with the polytheists in Mecca despite the animosity directed against him and his companions.[86]

Al-Qaraḍāwī also elaborated on the matter. In response to a query from a Muslim PhD candidate from Germany, he held that it is not permitted to celebrate Christian and Jewish holidays, "as they have their holidays and we have ours." However, it is permissible to congratulate Christians and Jews on those holidays. As in the case of his Council's *fatwā*, his decision is largely based on the permissibility of treating non-Muslims who do not fight against Muslims kindly, citing Q. 60:8–9 and other evidence central

[85] European Council for Fatwa and Research, "Ruling on Offering Congratulations to Non-Muslims on their Festive Occasions," 177–82.
[86] *Ibid.*, 182.

to the *wasaṭī* refutation of *salafī* "loyalty and disavowal," as well as on the objective of converting non-Muslims. In reference to *salafī fatwās* on non-Muslim holidays, which invoke Ibn Taymiyya's (d. 1328) strong opposition to any form of participation in or endorsement of a non-Muslim holiday (see below), al-Qaraḍāwī argued that had Ibn Taymiyya lived today, he would have adapted his ideas to changing circumstances, which necessitate congratulations. Among the circumstances he cited are: (a) the world has become a global village, and Muslims need to interact with non-Muslims who, regrettably, have become their mentors in many sciences and industries; (b) Muslims need to be gentle in order to proselytize, engaging in *tabshīr* rather than *tanfīr*; and (c) Christian holidays today are most commonly celebrated as national traditions. Therefore, if Muslims congratulate Christians, there is no risk that their false religious ideas will be reaffirmed.[87]

Other than prohibiting non-Islamic religious symbols, neither al-Qaraḍāwī nor his Council specified what the limitations on the contents of seasonal greetings are. Al-Qaraḍāwī noted that the "customary greetings" for festive occasions do not involve recognition of Christianity and are nothing but a courtesy,[88] but he did not provide examples. This possibly intentional vagueness leaves the door open to using greetings without religious connotations, e.g., "have a nice holiday" and "enjoy your vacation," but also to greetings with religious connotations, e.g., "merry Christmas" and "a happy new year."

Other *fatwās* by *wasaṭī* jurists legitimized passive participation in a range of events related to Christmas so long as they do not signify recognition of beliefs that contradict Islam and do not involve impermissible activities. For example, the Fiqh Council of North America decided in 1992 that it is permissible for a new Muslim to spend Christmas with his family because "one's maintaining the best relations with one's family, in addition to being part of a Muslim's duty to treat all people in the very best manner, may be considered a subtle form of *da'wa* as well." However,

[87] Yūsuf al-Qaraḍāwī, "Tahni'at Ahl al-Kitāb bi-A'yādihim," in *Fī Fiqh al-Aqalliyyāt al-Muslima* (Cairo: Dār al-Shurūq, 2007, first published 2001), 145–50.
[88] *Ibid.*, 149.

the Muslim should not join religious services except when necessary as an observer.[89] Hind, a Muslim from Canada, was advised by Ahmad Kutty (b. 1945)—a Canadian of Indian origin who pursued his doctoral studies on Islamic law at McGill University, served on the Fiqh Council of North America, and is a senior lecturer at the Islamic Institute of Toronto—that it is permissible to accept her Catholic mother's invitation to Christmas dinner because, as a Muslim, it is her duty to treat her parents in a kind and gentle manner even if they are infidels (Q. 31:15).[90] A Muslim identified as Ḥasan asked whether it is permissible to attend a Christmas dinner to which friends invited him. Badawī responded that it is not *ḥarām* to eat with non-Muslims even on their holiday, but it is undesirable to sing religious songs along with them. He encouraged Ḥasan to organize alternative Muslim events, such as Quran competitions with awards followed by pizza parties.[91] Badawī told 'Īmān from Australia that there is nothing wrong with her children learning in school about the festivities of other cultures.[92] Tato from Singapore was advised that it is legitimate to receive a Christmas bonus because bonuses are usually given to employees without regard for their religious affiliation. The decision was supported with a *fatwā* of Sano Koutoub Moustapha, professor of *fiqh* at the International Islamic University in Malaysia, who condoned accepting a Christmas bonus based on the fact that Jesus was a Messenger of Allah.[93] His justification contradicts several of the abovementioned *fatwās*, which emphasize that Christianity distorted the truth about Christ and his birth and that Muslims, therefore, cannot join Christians in their celebrations of his birth.

[89] Quoted in Yusuf Talal DeLorenzo, "The Fiqh Councilor in North America," in Yvonne Yazbeck Haddad and John L. Esposito (eds.), *Muslims on the Americanization Path?* (Oxford and New York: Oxford University Press, 2000), 81–82.

[90] Ahmad Kutty, "May I Celebrate Christmas with My Christian Mother?" December 24, 2012, accessed July 11, 2013: http://www.onislam.net/english/ask-the-scholar/morals-and-manners/customs-and-traditions/169105-may-i-celebrate-christmas-with-my-christian-mother.html?Traditions=.

[91] Jamāl Badawī, "Our Kids and Non-Islamic Feasts," live dialogue, December 24, 2003, accessed March 11, 2015: http://mcadams.posc.mu.edu/blog/moslems_christmas.htm.

[92] *Ibid.*

[93] Sano Koutoub Moustapha, "Can Muslims Accept Christmas Cash Bonus," December 25, 2011, accessed July 11, 2013: http://www.onislam.net/english/ask-the-scholar/ideologies-movements-and-religions/170681-can-muslims-accept-christmas-cash-bonus.html?Religions=.

Like *wasaṭīs*, *salafī* jurists prohibit the celebration of Christmas. Based on their conceptualization of "loyalty and disavowal," and drawing on Ibn Taymiyya's particularly firm position on the issue, *salafīs* emphasize the totality of this prohibition. "It is not permissible," wrote the Permanent Committee, "to join infidels in their holidays as well as to express joy and happiness in this or to take a day off work because this would constitute an imitation of the enemies of Allah."[94] Unlike *wasaṭīs*, there are no exceptions to this rule, including the potential for proselytizing, the duty to respect parents, or a combination of both. Al-Munajjid emphasized that Muslims are not permitted to take part in non-Muslim celebrations even if the sole purpose is to encourage the infidels to take part in Muslim celebrations. He invoked the tradition according to which the Prophet said, "Whoever imitates a people is one them," and the saying of the Khalīfa 'Umar, "avoid the enemies of Allah during their festivals."[95] A woman who wanted to convert but feared she might not be able to attend Christmas celebrations with her family was instructed by al-'Uthaymīn that it is not permissible to join her family for their holiday because the first thing she should do after being blessed with Islam is to distance herself from her former religion and its festivities.[96] The editors of Islamweb.net advised a man who had been a Muslim for three years that he can still visit his non-Muslim family but may not join them in their festivities. The editors emphasized that calling his parents or anyone else to Islam is "one of the greatest forms of kindness that you do to them."[97]

[94] The Permanent Committee, "Prohibition on Celebrating the Festivals of the Kuffar," in Muhammad Saed Abdul-Rahman (ed.), *Islam: Questions and Answers—Alliance and Amity, Disavowal and Enmity* (London: MSA Publication Ltd, 2003), 79; Islam Question and Answer, "Ruling on Joining in the Kaafir Festivals," in Muhammad Saed Abdul-Rahman (ed.), *Islam: Questions and Answers—Alliance and Amity, Disavowal and Enmity* (London: MSA Publication Ltd, 2003), 80–81.

[95] Muḥammad Ṣāliḥ al-Munajjid, "Taking Part in Non-Muslim Celebrations in Order to Encourage Them to Take Part in Our Celebrations," n.d., accessed July 11, 2013: http://islamqa.com/en/3325.

[96] Muḥammad b. Ṣāliḥ al-'Uthaymīn, "Can She Attend Christmas Celebrations in Order to Greet her Relatives?" n.d., accessed July 11, 2013: http://islamqa.com/en/11650.

[97] Islamweb.net, "A New Muslim Attending a Christmas Family Gathering," December 24, 2009, accessed July 11, 2013: http://www.islamweb.net/emainpage/index.php?page=articles&id=155840.

Salafīs exhort believers to not allow any Christian celebration at home, even in the case of a mixed marriage. The editors of Islam Question and Answer hold that a Muslim husband can prohibit his non-Muslim wife from participating in Christmas celebrations. They explained that the obligation to obey a husband does not distinguish between a Muslim and a non-Muslim wife, and that non-Muslim women should accept the principle of obedience before marrying a Muslim. While the Muslim husband does not have a right to compel his Christian or Jewish wife to become a Muslim, he does have the right to forbid her from going to church and from openly committing evil in the house, e.g., by displaying statues of Jesus or ringing bells. This right should be exercised according to his obligation to his family, as stipulated in Q. 66:6: "O You who believe, save yourselves and your families from the Fire whose fuel is men and rocks."[98]

Contrary to the *wasaṭī* view, the celebration of any non-Islamic holiday, including a civil one, is prohibited by *salafīs*, who consider civilian holidays as innovations and participation in Western ones an imitation of infidels and therefore a breach of the duty to disavow them. A Muslim from Minnesota asked whether it is permissible to hold a Thanksgiving dinner; he emphasized that Thanksgiving is one of the rare occasions on which his entire family gets together. The editors of Islamweb.net stated that it is forbidden because this is an imitation of non-Muslims. They based their decision on the Prophet's statement that a person who imitates a people is one of them.[99] Responding to a son who feared that his mother would be angry with him if he stops celebrating Mother's Day, al-'Uthaymīn wrote that this celebration is forbidden for two reasons: it is an innovation because it was not celebrated by the Prophet and his Companions, and it is an imitation of the infidels, with respect to whom "we have been commanded to differ." To explain why ignoring Mother's

[98] Islam Question and Answer, "Muslim Forbidding his Non-Muslim Wife to Celebrate her Religious Festivals," n.d., accessed April 1, 2009: http://islamqa.com/en/cat/2021#3019. Translation of the verse: al-Qur'an, A Contemporary Translation by Ahmed Ali (Princeton: Princeton University Press, 1993).

[99] Islamweb.net, "Muslims Preparing a Turkey Dinner on Thanksgiving Day," December 24, 2009, accessed July 12, 2013: http://www.islamweb.net/emainpage/index.php?page=articles&id=155839.

Day is not a breach of the duty to respect and obey one's parents, he drew on a tradition narrated by al-Bukhārī according to which the Prophet said, "There is no obedience if it involves sin; obedience is only in that which is right and proper." Muslims, he stated, are commanded to respect their mothers at all times, "so what is the point of singling out a particular day to honor her." Ironically, he added, Mother's Day was invented by societies in which "disobedience toward parents is widespread, in which mothers and fathers can find no refuge except [in] old people's homes, where they are left alone and no one visit[s] them."[100] Ibn Bāz prohibited the celebration of birthdays on the grounds that they constitute an unlawful innovation and imitation of Jews and Christians.[101] The Saudi jurist ʻAbdallāh b. ʻAbd al-Raḥman al-Jibrīn (d. 2009) wrote that one may not celebrate the year 2000 even as an act of courtesy to Christians because the celebration of an infidel holiday is tantamount to recognition of an innovation and it strengthens the innovators.[102]

The *salafī* aversion to practices that originated in Western societies led jurists to oppose some gestures that are not related to festivities, religious or otherwise. For example, al-Jibrīn rejected the custom of bringing flowers to hospitals as blind imitation of a Western practice and a waste of money, as the flowers do not help cure patients and are thrown away after an hour or a day.[103]

Unlike *wasaṭī* jurists, *salafī* jurists allow almost no exception to the prohibition of engaging with a non-Muslim holiday, even if it results in substantial financial losses. According to *salafīs*, a Muslim may not accept a Christmas cash bonus "because it is a kind of honoring their festivals and approving of them, and helping them in their falsehood."[104] Neither

[100] Islam Question and Answer, "His Mother Will Be Angry if He Does Not Celebrate Mother's Day," n.d., accessed September 25, 2013: http://www.islam-qa.com/en/59905.

[101] ʻAbd al-ʻAzīz b. ʻAbdallāh Ibn Bāz, "Mā Ḥukm al-Iḥtifāl bi-ʻĪd al-Mīlād," in *Fatāwā al-Balad al-Ḥarām* (Cairo: Matktabat al-Tawfīqiyya, n.d), 1031–32.

[102] ʻAbdallāh b. ʻAbd al-Raḥman al-Jibrīn, "Ḥukm al-Iḥtifāl bi-ʻām Alfayn," in *Fatāwā al-Balad al-Ḥarām* (Cairo: Matktabat al-Tawfīqiyya, n.d), 23.

[103] ʻAbdallāh b. ʻAbd al-Raḥman al-Jibrīn, "al-Taqlīd al-Aʻmā lil-Gharb," in *Fatāwā al-Balad al-Ḥarām* (Cairo: Matktabat al-Tawfīqiyya, n.d), 201.

[104] Islam Question and Answer, "His Company Gives its Employees a Christmas Bonus," n.d., accessed July 11, 2013: http://islamqa.info/en/ref/146328.

may he eat food prepared by infidels for their holidays;[105] exchange gifts related directly to an infidel holiday;[106] distribute candies on those holidays;[107] hold parties that imitate an infidel celebration;[108] sell the infidels items that they use to celebrate their holidays, such as clothes, perfumes, decorations, and greeting cards;[109] or collect donations for poor families on the occasion of Christmas.[110] *Salafī* jurists base these *fatwās* on what they call the illegitimacy of Muslim participation in acts of blasphemy and Muslim imitation of infidel innovative practices. They invoke Ibn Taymiyya's strong prohibition of any form of Muslim participation in or imitation of non-Muslim holidays.

While *salafīs* prohibit Muslims from giving Christians presents on their holidays or giving other Muslims presents on those occasions, they permit Muslims to accept presents from Christians on Christian holidays. This opinion draws from Ibn Taymiyya, who supported accepting infidel gifts based on several traditions, including the tradition according to which 'Alī b. Abī Ṭālib accepted a gift he was given on the occasion of Nayruz, the Persian New Year. The editors of Islam Question and Answer explained that the purpose of accepting gifts is to soften the hearts of the infidels and make Islam attractive to them. Citing Q. 60:8, they asserted that Muslims should be just to non-Muslims who do not fight them. At the same time, however, they cited a number of other verses (Q. 58:22, 60:1,

[105] The Permanent Committee, "It Is Not Permissible to Eat Foods that Are Prepared by the Kuffār for their Festivals," n.d., accessed July 12, 2013: http://islamqa.info/en/12666.

[106] *Ibid.*

[107] Ibn 'Uthaymīn, "al-Tahni'a bi-'īd al-Krīsmās," in *Fatāwā al-Balad al-Ḥarām* (Cairo: Dār al-Tawfīqiyya, n.d), 184. This decision was circulated in European Muslim communities as a pamphlet: "Fī Tahni'at al-Kuffār bi-A'yadihim wa-Ḥukm al-Dhahāb lahā," distributed by "Jam'iyyat Iḥyā' al-Turāth al-Islāmī" as part of Kitāb Fatāwā wa-Rasa'īl fī al-Tawḥīd Part 1 (22). For an English translation: Muḥammad b. Ṣāliḥ al-'Uthaymīn, "Ruling on Celebrating Non-Muslim Holidays and Congratulating Them," n.d., accessed July 12, 2013: http://islamqa.info/en/947.

[108] Muḥammad b. Ṣāliḥ al-'Uthaymīn, "Ruling on Celebrating Non-Muslim Holidays and Congratulating Them," n.d., accessed July 12, 2013: http://islamqa.info/en/947.

[109] Muḥammad Ṣāliḥ al-Munajjid, "Selling Greeting Cards for Christian Holidays," n.d., accessed July 12, 2013: http://islamqa.info/en/782; Islamweb.net, "Selling Christmas gifts and decorations," December 14, 2009, accessed July 11, 2013: http://www.islamweb.net/emainpage/index.php?page=articles&id=155823http://www.islamweb.net/emainpage/index.php?page=articles&id=155823.

[110] Muḥammad Ṣāliḥ Al-Munajjid, "Collecting Donations to Give Gifts to Poor Families at Christmas," n.d., accessed July 11, 2013: http://islamqa.info/en/8375.

3:110, 11:113 [mistakenly referenced in the *fatwā* as 12:113], and 5:51) to emphasize that kindness to non-Muslims should not be confused with love and friendship and that even when accepting gifts from infidels, Muslims must maintain the concept of *al-walā' wal-barā'* and educate their children according to this principle.[111]

Unlike *wasaṭīs*, *salafīs* prohibit Muslims from congratulating Christians on Christmas. Based on their understanding of *al-walā' wal-barā'*, they reject any form of good or even cordial relations between Muslims and non-Muslims. The editors of Islamweb.net proclaimed that a Muslim may not congratulate a Christian on holidays and celebrations because this would constitute approval of sins and transgressions. Further, it is the obligation of Muslims to show the infidels "dislike[,] for they oppose Allah and ascribe partners and sons to him." The editors quoted Q. 60:4, according to which Abraham and his followers told their people that there would be animosity and hatred between them until they believed in Allah alone.[112] Al-ʿUthaymīn prohibited congratulating Christians on Christmas because it constitutes recognition of infidel rituals. He explained that congratulations signify approval of the holiday and help Christians to propagate their infidel beliefs. His *fatwā* relies on Ibn al-Qayyim, who held that wishing someone "a merry Christmas" is a greater sin than congratulating him on drinking wine, committing murder, or having illicit sex.[113] A YouTube clip associated with the *salafī* al-Ṣaḥāba mosque, Berlin, argues, based on Ibn al-Qayyim, that it is not permissible and constitutes a sin to greet a non-Muslim on his holiday by wishing him, for example, "have a nice holiday" or "enjoy your holiday."[114] Not even a prison environment affects this prohibition. In a *salafī* compilation of *fatwās* for "incarcerated Muslims" published in the United States, the

[111] Islam Question and Answer, "Accepting a Gift from a Kaafir on the Day of his Festival," n.d., accessed July 11, 2013: http://islamqa.info/en/85108.

[112] Islamweb.net, "The Ruling on Congratulating Non-Muslims on their Celebrations," February 7, 2010, accessed July 12, 2013: http://www.islamweb.net/emainpage/index.php?page=articles&id=156436.

[113] Muḥammad b. Ṣāliḥ Ibn ʿUthaymīn, "al-Tahniʾa bi-ʿīd al-Krīsmās," in *Fatāwā al-Balad al-Ḥarām* (Cairo: Dār al-Tawfīqiyya, n.d), 183–85.

[114] As-Sirat Berlin, "Darf man den Kuffar zu ihren Festtagen gratulieren?" December 29, 2012, accessed August 19, 2013: http://www.youtube.com/watch?v=r2gLGyXFlFs&feature=share&list=PLE2E53D6C93165C2E.

Saudi Waṣiyyullāh b. Muḥammad 'Abbās, a professor at Umm al-Qurā University, was asked whether Muslim prisoners may congratulate Christian volunteers who distribute gifts at Christmas on their holiday. He answered that it is impermissible, and made sure to add "nor do we accept that they greet us on what is believed to be the holiday of the Prophet because neither one of them is a legislated occasion."[115] Based on the principle of *al-walā' wal-barā'*, *salafī* jurists oppose congratulating non-Muslims even on occasions that are unrelated to their holidays. Al-'Uthaymīn prohibited congratulating an infidel on his safe arrival home, quoting the tradition narrated by Abū Hurayra, according to which the Prophet forbade initiating greetings to Jews and Christians (see Chapter 2).[116]

In visits to *salafī* mosques, where imāms and attendees experience the challenges of Christmas more directly than jurists based in Saudi Arabia, I documented a consensus on the prohibition of congratulating Christians on Christmas. However, some imāms and activists offered compromises of sorts, implying that it is not wise or required that they avoid goodwill gestures, provided that these gestures do not constitute direct recognition of an infidel holiday. Nāṣir al-'Īsā, the imām of al-Nūr mosque, Berlin, stated that while a Muslim cannot offer a congratulatory greeting specifically on a non-Muslim religious holiday, it is permissible to reply to a seasonal greeting by saying "to you as well." (Al-'Īsā holds that some *fatwās* of Saudi jurists are not applicable to Europe and result from Saudi jurists' lack of visiting the Continent and learning its realities.)[117] Bilāl Davis of the Salafi Mosque and Islamic Centre of Birmingham argued that it is permissible to wish a Christian "happy holiday" so long as this greeting is followed by an explanation that while the Muslim may wish a non-Muslim to enjoy his vacation, a Muslim cannot acknowledge a non-Muslim holiday.[118] The opinion that Muslims must not benefit financially

[115] Waṣiyyullāh b. Muḥammad 'Abbās, "Questions Related to Non-Muslim Holidays," in *Islamic Rulings for Incarcerated Muslims*, vol. 1 (Dallas: Tarbiyyah Bookstore Publishing, May 2007), 90–91.

[116] Muḥammad b. Ṣāliḥ Ibn al-'Uthaymīn, "Tahni'at al-Kāfir," in *Fatāwā al-Balad al-Ḥarām* (Cairo: Dār al-Tawfīqiyya, n.d), 185.

[117] Interview at al-Nūr mosque, Berlin, August 1, 2013.

[118] Interview at the Salafi Mosque and Islamic Centre, Birmingham, England, July 19, 2013.

from anything associated with an infidel holiday is also challenged. For example, 'Umar Jāmāykī, the imām of Ibnu Taymeeyah Mosque in Brixton, London, told me he considers receipt of a Christmas bonus legitimate because it does not constitute an acknowledgment of a non-Muslim holiday.[119]

While the Saudi Arabian religious establishment has been the main center for the issuing of strict *fatwās* on non-Muslim holidays, not all members of this establishment endorse these views. Qays Āl al-Shaykh Mubārak (b. 1960), a member of the Council of Senior Scholars since 2009 and a *Mālikī*, held that a Muslim may accept an invitation to attend a non-Islamic holiday celebration because rejecting such an invitation would alienate non-Muslims from Islam.[120] Mubārak's view is liberal not only in comparison to decisions by senior Saudi jurists but also to *wasaṭī* decisions, which permit congratulating non-Muslims on their holidays but prohibit attending their festivities.

ḤARĀM IN THE WORKPLACE

Workplaces present Muslim minorities with two types of potential risks: individually breaching Islamic norms in order to meet professional duties or to satisfy a boss's whims, and assisting others—Muslims and non-Muslims alike—in breaching Islamic norms. Occasional incidents in various European and American cities—from Muslim cashiers who refuse to handle pork products to taxi drivers who refuse to carry passengers who possess alcohol—suggest that the issue is not theoretical. In some cases, businesses agree to accommodate the service they provide to the practices of Muslim employees. In 2013, for example, it was reported that Marks & Spencer, London allowed Muslim checkout staff to refuse to serve customers who want to pay for alcohol or pork.[121]

[119] Interview at Ibnu Taymeeyah Brixton Mosque, London, July 20, 2013.

[120] 'Abdallāh al-Dānī, "Ijābat al-Da'wa li-Ghayr al-Muslimīn Mubāḥ," *'Ukāẓ*, December 23, 2010.

[121] Luke Salkeld, "M & S Faces Boycott as it Lets Muslim Staff Refuse to Sell Alcohol or Pork," *The Daily Mail*, December 23, 2013, 11.

The issue involves a conflict between two core liberal norms that cannot easily be reconciled. On the one hand, individuals have a right not to be required to act against their religious beliefs; on the other hand, if religious freedom becomes an unrestricted principle in workplaces, universal service may be denied based on an ever-growing list of affiliations and biases. After all, if taxi drivers, for example, are permitted to refuse service to passengers who carry pork because of religious convictions, who is to stop them in the future from refusing service to unmarried couples, gays, or soldiers returning from a Middle Eastern frontline? There is also the practical concern of owners that their customers will not tolerate religious accommodations that cost them time. In the above-mentioned case of Marks & Spencer, customers threatened to boycott the chain after learning that when purchasing "non-*shar'ī*" items they were expected to wait until a "non-Muslim" till or cashier was available. One said: "I had one bottle of Champagne, and the lady, who was wearing a headscarf, was very apologetic but said she could not serve me. She told me to wait until another member of staff was available." Indeed, in response to the public outcry, Marks & Spencer clarified that the policy was an error and not consistent with its national policy.[122]

When accommodations in the workplace are denied, the implication for some Muslims is that they must choose between work and faith. Some who lack financial security feel they cannot be too fastidious in choosing their job, resigning from it, or insisting on specific *sharī'a*-based demands. The dilemma they face is whether making a living is a *maṣlaḥa* that justifies committing prohibited acts and assisting others in committing such acts. Their queries often suggest that they wish for jurists to offer them religio-legal legitimizations for maintaining their jobs.

As is the case in other interactions of individual Muslims with majority non-Muslim societies, *wasaṭīs* and *salafīs* presented opposing decisions in addressing this type of dilemma. While *wasaṭī fatwās* showed empathy for the special conditions of Muslim minorities and offered pragmatic accommodations that allow for the continuation of employment, *salafī fatwās* demanded minorities strictly abide by universal duties and norms.

[122] *Ibid.*

While issues pertaining to workplaces did not inspire thorough or groundbreaking deliberations, they did reveal a fundamental difference between *wasaṭīs* and *salafīs*, exposing the *wasaṭī* focus on finding practical solutions to problems faced by individual Muslims, and the *salafī* lack of interest in the practical implications their rigid, literalist interpretations may have.

Both *wasaṭīs* and *salafīs* hold that Muslims should look for another job if their occupation forces them to carry out *ḥarām* deeds, including assisting non-Muslims in committing sins. This guideline is based on a number of verses, primarily Q. 5:2, which prohibits Muslims from assisting in sins and transgression. However, in cases where quitting results in financial harm, opinions differ. *Wasaṭīs* legitimized unlawful acts based on their classification of making a living as a *maṣlaḥa*. In contrast, the majority of *salafī* decisions demanded Muslims avoid jobs that involve committing or assisting in committing *ḥarām*, regardless of the financial consequences. *Salafīs* considered an inability to find a permissible job the equivalent of an inability to manifest Islam and thus suggested that Muslims in such a position migrate to a Muslim country rather than expect their occupation to be legitimized based on *maṣlaḥa*. Alternatively, they disregarded the dilemma altogether by expressing confidence that those who follow Allah's laws would always benefit. Even when legitimizing impermissible workplaces based on *maṣlaḥa*, salafī jurists attached harsh conditions to the latter facilitation that eliminated its potential to bring financial relief.

Wasaṭīs made clear that Muslims should not voluntarily choose careers that risk breaching Islamic norms, e.g., working as a fashion model[123] or becoming partners in a restaurant that sells pizza which contains pork.[124] They also demanded that Muslims stand firmly by their constitutional rights and reject requests from employers that compromise religious

[123] Ḥusām al-Dīn b. Mūsā 'Afāna, "A Muslim Woman Working as a Fashion Model," September 22, 2002, accessed August 27, 2013: http://www.onislam.net/english/ask-the-scholar/financial-issues/earning-livelihood/175723.html.

[124] Monzer Khaf, "Selling a Pork Pizza: Lawful?" January 1, 2012, accessed September 25, 2013: http://www.onislam.net/english/ask-the-scholar/financial-issues/earning-livelihood/455220-selling-a-pork-pizza-lawful.html.

norms, such as the shaving of the beard[125] or the removing of the headscarf. The latter issue was addressed by the Canadian-based Ahmad Kutty, who is often referenced on onislam.net on issues pertaining to the workplace. He advised a woman who complained that her "narrow minded" boss did not allow her to wear the *ḥijāb* that wearing it is an important requirement mandated by the Quran. She should not obey her boss's order, he wrote, because there is no obedience to anyone who disobeys Allah. Kutty informed the woman that her right to exercise her religion is guaranteed by the Canadian Charter of Rights and her boss's demand is a discriminatory act and a violation of the laws of the land. He suggested that the intervention of the Council on American-Islamic Relations Canada might bring the boss back to his senses.[126]

When a situation arises in which an established career path is compromised by upholding religious norms, *wasaṭīs* apply *maṣlaḥa* broadly and legitimize accommodations. In 2008, Kutty addressed a query by a track runner, who asked whether it is permissible to defer fasting on practice days. After emphasizing that fasting is the third most important duty in Islam, Kutty ruled with evident caution that "it is not allowed to skip fasting because of playing for a hobby. If, however, it is a career you are pursuing, then you should do everything possible to postpone practice during Ramaḍān. You are not allowed to change the fasting month for another month. If, however, it is a question of skipping a few days, and you have no choice over it, then according to some scholars you are allowed to skip them and fast later."[127]

In another decision Kutty instructed a football (soccer) player who skipped the fast to make up for the omission on days on which he was not playing. Drawing an analogy to an elderly person who cannot fast for medical reasons, Kutty argued that if a professional player does not

[125] Ahmad Kutty, "Should a Muslim Shave his Beard to Get a Job?" July 9, 2013, accessed August 27, 2013: http://www.onislam.net/english/ask-the-scholar/financial-issues/earning-livelihood/463411-should-a-muslim-shave-my-beard-to-get-a-job.html.

[126] Ahmad Kutty, "Not Allowed to Wear Hijab at Work," October 14, 2003, accessed August 27, 2013: http://www.onislam.net/english/ask-the-scholar/financial-issues/earning-livelihood/169711.html.

[127] Ahmad Kutty, "Fasting or Sports?" August 26, 2009, accessed August 27, 2013: http://www.onislam.net/english/ask-the-scholar/acts-of-worship/fasting/fasting-rulings-and-regulations/177138.html.

expect a break that would allow him to fast, he may offer *fidya* (compensation), such as feeding a poor person for every single day of the Ramaḍān fast that he missed.[128] Kutty's rulings were supported by a decision given in 2010 by al-Azhar following a query from Germany's Central Council of Muslims (Zentralrat der Muslime in Deutschland), the Arab-dominated Muslim-German umbrella organization. This *fatwā*, which gained the immediate endorsement of the European Council for Fatwa and Research, allowed professional German-Muslim football players to break fasting on days of matches if football was their only source of income and they were obliged to play during Ramaḍān. The Zentralrat raised the issue because a year earlier a football club from the second German division, FSV Frankfurt, warned three Muslim players who fasted that they breached a clause in their contracts that forbids them from doing so.[129] Some German-Muslim players stressed that they would not pay heed to these liberal *fatwās*. ʿAbd al-ʿAzīz Ahanfouf, a German-Moroccan soccer player for SV Darmstadt 98, explained that fasting is essential for his belief because he wants to "enter heaven." Others, including the French Muslim Franck Ribery from Bayern Munich, avoid fasting when playing.[130]

Wasaṭīs stressed that Muslims should not assist even non-Muslims in committing sins. In cases where such assistance is unavoidable, they encourage Muslims to resign and look for another job. However, drawing from their concept of facilitation, they also emphasize that a Muslim may hold his or her unlawful job if an alternative is not at hand. Not incidentally, *wasaṭī fatwās* allow much room for individual discretion by not defining exactly what constitutes an adequate "alternative." For example, they do not stipulate that Muslims should settle for *any* other job that is lawful and provides a livelihood.

[128] Ahmad Kutty, "Soccer Players Skipping Fasting," August 25, 2009, accessed April 1, 2010: http://www.islamonline.net/servlet/Satellite?pagename=IslamOnline-English-Ask_Scholar/FatwāE/FatwāE&cid=1160574242997.

[129] Associated Press, "Players Allowed to Break Ramadan Fast," July 28, 2010, accessed August 1, 2013: http://espn.go.com/sports/soccer/news/_/id/5417146/muslim-soccer-players-.

[130] Johannes Aumüller, "Fußball im Fastenmonat," October 16, 2009, accessed August 27, 2013: http://www.zeit.de/online/2007/37/ramadan-fussball.

In its second session, the European Council addressed a query by an employee in a McDonalds that sells pork products who wrote that he finds it "immensely difficult" to leave his job because his wife is about to give birth. The Council ruled that the work that the Muslim is performing is prohibited because it is associated with selling an item that is *ḥarām*. The Council advised the employee that "it is upon you to try your best to find an alternative means of making a living" and that "if you fail in doing so, then you may ask your managers at McDonalds to excuse you from selling pork, or you may coordinate with another worker so that you may work at other matters which do not involve selling pork." However, "if you find difficulty in doing so, or if you realize that this may affect your work at this food vendor, then you may continue to work if you do not have another sufficient source of income. You must, in any case, remain in pursuit of another job which does not involve dealing in any *ḥarām*."[131]

Another example is a cashier who asked whether it is permissible to work in a grocery store that sells *ḥarām* meats. She was advised by Ahmad Kutty that if she has the option to get another job, then she should take it. However, if she cannot find another job, she should not worry because this is not something she has "control over." "Such [impermissible] jobs," noted Kutty, "are unavoidable while working in a predominantly non-Muslim country."[132]

Like *wasaṭīs*, *salafīs* recognize that Muslims living in majority non-Muslim countries are often ill-positioned to negotiate the terms of their employment or find another job. Yet they do not consider this reality as justifying facilitations. The majority of their decisions demand that Muslims quit jobs that force them to commit *ḥarām* deeds or assist others in committing such deeds, and suggest that Muslims who are unable to find appropriate alternatives should migrate to a Muslim country. Al-'Uthaymīn was asked which alternative is better for Muslim women who live in Western countries, where there is no gender segregation in schools and

[131] *Fatwās of European Council for Fatwa and Research*, 49–50.

[132] Ahmad Kutty, "Working as a Cashier for a Grocery Store that Sells Haram Meats," March 22, 2004, accessed August 27, 2013: http://www.onislam.net/english/ask-the-scholar/financial-issues/earning-livelihood/170030.

workplaces: to stay home, resulting in severe economic repercussions, or to cover themselves and study and work in non-segregated environments. He accepted neither. Relying on Q. 29:10, he stressed that Muslims must abide by Allah's laws even in the face of hardships or else they are hypocrites who only claim true devotion. Relying on Q. 4:97, a main *salafī* evidence against residence in non-Muslim lands, he ruled that if a workplace does not segregate men from women, it is not permissible to work there, and if another means of making a living cannot be found in the West then a new job should be sought in another country.[133]

The Ramaḍān fast further highlights *salafīs*' insistence on the literal application of the Quran and the traditions when individual hardships are deliberated. The Permanent Committee clarified that it is not permissible to stop fasting because of work. Only when a person encounters severe hardships during a workday may he break the fast to the extent needed to ward off hardship. If the person knows in advance that he will not be able to combine fasting and work, then he should take a leave of absence from work in order to be able to "perform an important pillar of Islam." If that is not possible, then he must search for another job, bearing in mind that there are many ways of earning a living and that Allah takes care of those who trust him (Q. 65:2–3). If even that is not an option, then the Muslim must migrate to another land where it will be easier for him to practice his religion.[134]

Salafīs consider most forms of professional sports impermissible; not surprisingly, they do not hold football matches to be a legitimate reason to defer the fast as *wasaṭīs* do. The editors of Islamweb.net explicitly condemned this *wasaṭī* facilitation while emphasizing the need to base decisions on Allah's book and the Prophetic traditions. Relying on Q. 2:185, they noted that only those who are sick or traveling may break their fast and that even workers involved in physical labor, rather

[133] Muḥammad b. Ṣāliḥ al-ʿUthaymīn, "al-Ikhtilāṭ fī al-Taʿlīm wal-ʿAmal," in *Fatāwā al-ʿUlamāʾ ḥawla al-Aqalliyyāt al-Muslima fī al-ʿālam* (Alexandria: Dār al-ʾīmān, 2004), 281.
[134] Islam Question and Answer, "He Works as a Bus Driver, Is it Permissible for Him Not to Fast?" n.d., accessed August 28, 2013: http://www.islam-qa.com/en/141036.

than "merely playing," are obligated to fast and may break the fast only to the extent needed to ward off severe hardship.[135]

Salafīs' prohibition on assisting others in committing transgressions includes highly indirect forms of assistance. For example, based on Q. 2:5, they hold that it is impermissible for a technician to fix refrigerators or air conditioners in pubs or gay clubs.[136] A Muslim whose job requires assisting in transgressions must find another job. *Salafī fatwās* commonly provide reassurance that another job will be found. On rare occasions, facilitations are granted but do not provide even modest financial security. A waiter who works in a restaurant that sells pork was told by the editors of Islamweb.net that he may remain at his job based on necessity while searching for another. However, the waiter was ordered not to possess or save the money he earned and, once he had found another job, to spend whatever was left from the *ḥarām* earnings on the "general interest of Muslims," like schools.[137] In a way typical of *salafī* deliberations, the authors of the *fatwā* gave no consideration to the obvious negative implications abiding by their decision could have on a low-paid employee and his family.

[135] Islamweb.net, "Is Playing Football Considered an Excuse that Allows One to Abandon Fasting?" July 16, 2013, accessed August 29, 2013: http://www.islamweb.net/emainpage/index.php?page=showfatwa&Option=FatwaId&Id=127957.

[136] Islamweb.net, "Services Cooling Systems for Beer, Wine and Gays," April 10, 2004, accessed August 27, 2013: http://www.islamweb.net/emainpage/index.php?page=showfatwa&Option=FatwaId&Id=87412.

[137] Islamweb.net, "Working as a Waiter," n.d., accessed August 27, 2013: http://www.islamweb.net/emainpage/index.php?page=showfatwa&Option=FatwaId&Id=87931.

4

Muslim Minorities and Non-Muslim States

INTRODUCTION

Wasaṭī and *salafī* religio-juristic deliberations on interactions between Muslims and non-Muslim state institutions concentrated on three issues: (a) the permissibility of becoming members of political entities that are not Muslim, (b) the permissibility of participating in the political processes of liberal states that are not governed by Allah's laws, (c) and the permissibility of abiding by laws and regulations that contradict Islamic laws. In contrast with other topics previously addressed in this work, *wasaṭīs* and *salafīs* were not at complete odds when addressing the abovementioned issues. Both adjusted laws to allow a certain measure of cooperation with non-Muslim state institutions. *Wasaṭīs* offered broader accommodations, demonstrating the importance of integration to their doctrine of *fiqh al-aqalliyyāt al-Muslima*, their determination to protect Muslim minorities from potential harm, and their belief that interacting with non-Muslims is the most effective means to convert them. *Salafī* adjustments were narrower and more reluctant, and exposed internal debates. Still, on some issues some exercised a flexibility that was lacking in their treatment of interactions between Muslims and non-state actors, and introduced justifications similar to those applied by *wasaṭīs*.

Wasaṭīs based their legitimizations on two kinds of *maṣlaḥas*: preventing Muslims from being harmed and encouraging them to impact their non-Muslim societies. The mechanism of *fiqh al-muwāzanāt* was central to their deliberations on state-related issues. They agreed that cooperation with or participation in non-Muslim state institutions potentially involves committing prohibited acts; however, they argued that these "evils" need to be balanced against potential benefits and penalties resulting from the lack of cooperation and participation. Theories of "overlap" and "neutrality" were instrumental to their reasoning. *Wasaṭīs* argued that some of the norms applied by non-Muslim state institutions are commensurate with Islamic ones. They also argued that Western governing systems are neutral in regard to religions and faiths and thus should not be treated as normative entities or as systems competing with Islam. The latter opinion contradicts a central argument of *wasaṭī* apologias authored in other contexts, which depict liberalism and secularism as counter-Christian and anti-religious movements.

Similarly, *salafīs* based their legitimizations on the *maṣlaḥas* of preventing Muslims from being harmed and encouraging them to impact their non-Muslim societies. Their deliberations lacked the energy and the theoretical depth that characterize *wasaṭī* texts on these matters. The limited flexibility they exercised on some issues derived from two aspects of their jurisprudence. First, while *salafīs* disapprove of *wasaṭīs* broad application of *maṣlaḥa,* their *fiqh* acknowledges certain *maṣlaḥas* at the rank of necessity as justification for accommodations. Second, *salafīs* in general are cautious when dealing with political authority and are relatively more inclined to invoke *maṣlaḥa* as a justification when addressing interactions between citizens and state institutions that hold coercive powers.

Wasaṭī and *salafī* legitimizations of participation in non-Muslim state institutions raise an ethical-political question. March, interpreting John Rawls, argued for the compatibility of some of these legitimizations with the interests of the liberal society, but nevertheless accepted that in terms of "grounding moral obligation to non-Muslim societies" there are obvious limitations to justifying the participation of Muslim minorities in their states' affairs based on its perception as a means to advance Islamic aims or norms. This type of justification, he wrote, "often reflects little or no interest in the rights or interests of non-Muslims. It often implicitly or explicitly sanctions illiberal social goals if they could be achieved. And importantly, it does not involve any substantive judgment that the liberal terms of social cooperation have any independent validity or moral standing..."[1] Continuing from this point, March pointed rather apologetically to what he defined as "comprehensive-qualitative" arguments invoked by some *wasaṭī* jurists with regard to the duty to coexist with non-Muslims, integrate into their societies, and respect them, which, especially in relation to the duty to proselytize, result according to March in a more comprehensive moral obligation to non-Muslim societies, one that goes beyond the judicial mode of setting boundaries between the permissible and the prohibited.[2]

March overlooks, however, the fundamental limitation to *any* grounding of participation in or commitment to liberal societies that is based on interpretations of a revelation. We should shift our focus from the interpreted to the interpreters. Given that the permissibility of any form of participation or commitment is determined by jurists as a *shar'ī* issue, jurists reserve, in theory, the ultimate authority to retract or change the terms of any legitimization they had given based on their reconsideration of circumstances. Thus, the issue is not only whether a revelation-based doctrine can legitimize recognition of, participation in, or moral obligation to liberal systems (which, Rawls indeed implies, may be the case), or the credibility in terms of liberal theory of specific utilitarian arguments, on which, as March argues, there can be no single verdict. Rather, any *shar'ī*-grounded legitimization of participation or obligation empowers jurists and challenges the liberal order by the inherent nature of the argumentations it applies and of the mechanisms it requires to employ. In this sense, the distinction March draws between different types of argumentation is artificial. Nothing in *wasaṭī* writing is external to the boundaries of Islamic law. The application of juristic mechanisms in order to evaluate the implications of actions is always required—whether the actions are associated with a narrow interest of a specific Muslim community or with the more abstract duty of Muslims to engage with (certain) non-Muslims in a way that is gentle, transparent, open-ended, just, and gradualist.

[1] Andrew March, *Islam and Liberal Citizenship: The Search for an Overlapping Consensus* (Oxford and New York: Oxford University Press, 2009), 268–69.

[2] *Ibid.*, 269–70.

The following chapter demonstrates that in the evolution of the jurisprudence of Muslim minorities, the retraction of legitimizations that are based on "overlaps" and *maṣlaḥas* has been more than theoretical. But it also demonstrates that such retractions have been the exception, and points to the limited practical effect juristic decisions have had, at least thus far, on the relations between Muslim minorities and their states' institutions.

The chapter examines four issues pertaining to Muslim relations with non-Muslim states: naturalization, electoral participation, service in non-Muslim militaries and police forces, and the banning of the *ḥijāb*. It analyzes the debates and common ground reached between *salafīs* and *wasaṭīs*, as well as a number of disagreements that emerged within the *salafī* camp, and reflects on some of the potential implications of their theorizing.

NATURALIZATION

The permissibility of naturalizing in non-Muslim states was first deliberated in the context of anti-imperialist struggles. In 1924, after the French government made it easier for Tunisians to obtain French citizenship, the Tunisian Nationalist Party asked Rashīd Riḍā's *al-Manār* whether Muslims who accept the French offer, and in so doing subject themselves to French authority and to French man-made laws, should be considered apostates. Riḍā ruled, as did a number of Tunisian jurists at the time, that Muslims who naturalize should be excommunicated because in so doing they give preference to a non-Muslim system of law and reject the fundamentals of faith.[3] In 1932, he described naturalized Tunisians as enemies of Allah and His Prophet and ruled that they should be prevented

[3] "Tajannus al-Muslim bi-Jinsiyya Tunāfī al-Islām," *al-Manār* 25, 1 (January 1924), 21–32; Umar Ryad, "A Prelude to Fiqh al-Aqalliyyāt: Rashīd Riḍā's Fatwās to Muslims under Non-Muslim Rule," in Christiane Timmerman *et al.* (eds.), *In-between Spaces: Christian and Muslim Minorities in Transition in Europe and the Middle East* (Brussels: Peter Lang: 2009), 244–45.

from marrying Muslim women or being buried in Muslim cemeteries. He made an exception for French converts to Islam.[4]

The *wasaṭī* project calls on Muslims to establish a permanent presence in the West and impact their non-Muslim societies through constructive and positive engagement. Naturalization is an important—and in the political field a crucial—aspect for the realization of these goals. Nevertheless, its permissibility was hardly addressed in the foundational *wasaṭī* texts on Muslim minorities. While al-'Alwānī mentioned that citizenship in the West was the first issue he took up in addressing *fiqh al-aqalliyyāt al-Muslima*,[5] his first systematic deliberations on the religious law of Muslim minorities hardly discussed it, and neither do al-Qaraḍāwī's. Obtaining citizenship in non-Muslim states was debated and legitimized by the European Council only in its sixteenth and seventeenth sessions (July 2006, May 2007). That is, only after almost a decade since its formation.[6] The Council based its succinct 2006 legitimization on a decision issued in June of the same year by the International Fiqh Council of the Organization of Islamic Conference permitting naturalization provided that it does not negate the necessities which the *sharī'a* safeguards and does not involve harming the Islamic identity of those attaining it.[7]

Conceivably, naturalization was not a pressing issue for *wasaṭīs* when delineating their approach because it had been thoroughly addressed in the 1980s and 1990s by other jurists and juristic panels who conditionally legitimized naturalization based on an evaluation of individual and communal *maṣlaḥas*. Some of these decisions were later incorporated in legitimizations offered by *wasaṭī* members of the European Council for

[4] Umar Ryad, "A Prelude to Fiqh al-Aqalliyyāt: Rashīd Riḍā's Fatwās to Muslims under Non-Muslim Rule," 246.

[5] Ṭaha Jābir Al-'Alwānī, "Madkhal ilā Fiqh al-Aqalliyyāt," *al-Majalla al-'Ilmiyya lil-Majlis al-'Ūrūbbī lil-Iftā' wal-Buḥūth*, no. 4–5 (June 2004), 40.

[6] Al-Majlis al-'Ūrūbbī lil-Iftā' wal-Buḥūth, "Qarār bi-Sha'n al-Muwā'ama bayna al-Taqayyud bil-Thawābit wa-bayna Muqtaḍayāt al-Muwāṭana" (decision 4/16), July 30, 2008, accessed September 5, 2013: http://www.e-cfr.org/ar/index.php?ArticleID=284; "al-Muwāṭana wa-Muqtaḍayātuhā" (decision 1/17), *al-Majalla al-'Ilmiyya lil-Majlis al-'Ūrūbbī lil-Iftā' wal-Buḥūth* 12–13 (July 2008), 498–99.

[7] Majlis Majma' al-Fiqh al-Islāmī al-Dawlī, "al-Tawfīq bayna al-Taqayyud bil-Thawābit wa-bayna Muqtaḍayāt al-Muwāṭana lil-Muslimīn Khārij al-Duwal al-Islāmiyya" (decision 155, fourth of the seventeenth session, June 24–28, 2006), accessed September 5, 2013: http://www.fiqhacademy.org.sa/qrarat/17-4.htm.

Fatwa and Research. Legitimizations were based on a balancing of benefits and harms and the conclusion that while assuming the citizenship of a non-Muslim state is unlawful in itself, it can be justified if it is required in order to protect and advance the interests of Islam, or those of individual Muslims. For example, the muftī of Tunisia, Muḥammad al-Shādhilī al-Nayfar, ruled in 1989 that willing naturalization is permissible if aimed at enhancing the spread of Islam and the protection of Muslim minorities.[8] In 1997, Sulaymān Muḥammad Tūbūlyāk distinguished between Muslims whose lands were occupied and migrants. He ruled that the former are obliged to obtain citizenship in order to protect the necessities which Islamic law safeguards. As for the latter, obtaining citizenship may be legitimized based on the existence of *maṣlaḥa*: political refugees may obtain citizenship in case of necessity, provided that they can manifest their religion; labor-migrants should in general refrain from obtaining citizenship, but may do so if working outside the realm of Islam is a necessity, the job does not involve *ḥarām*, and gaining citizenship is essential for obtaining a working permit; and proselytizers can obtain citizenship if it makes it easier for them to spread Islam. It is, however, impermissible to gain citizenship in order to promote worldly purposes that are not at the rank of necessity.[9] Muḥammad al-Kadī al-'Umrānī, a Netherlands-based jurist, concluded in a book based on the PhD dissertation he submitted to King Muḥammad I University in Morocco that naturalization is permissible because it promotes the spread of Islam and strengthens the position of Muslim minorities. He based his conclusion on al-Nayfar's determination and on determinations by pan-Islamic juristic councils, including the juristic council of the Muslim World League, which ruled in 1983 that the issue must be decided on a case-by-case basis and based on *fiqh al-muwāzanāt*.[10]

[8] Muḥammad al-Shādhilī al-Nayfar, "al-Tajannus bi-Jinsiyya Ghayr Islāmiyya," *Majallat al-Majma' al-Fiqhī al-Islāmī* 2, 4 (1989), 250.

[9] Sulaymān Muḥammad Tūbūlyāk, *al-Aḥkām al-Siyāsiyya lil-Aqalliyyāt al-Muslima fī al-Fiqh al-Islāmī* (Amman and Beirut: Dār al-Nafā'is, Dār al-Bayāriq, 1997), 76–91.

[10] Muḥammad al-Kadī al-'Umrānī, *Fiqh al-Usra al-Muslima fī al-Mahājir*, second part (Beirut: Dār al-Kutub al-'Ilmiyya, 2001), 295–304.

Comprehensive deliberations on the matter by members of the European Council only surfaced in the mid-2000s. These texts not only refuted prohibitions of naturalization, but also asserted the core ideals of the *wasaṭī* approach, specifically its views on facilitation and its narrow understanding of "loyalty and disavowal." Thus, they defended the foundations of *wasaṭīyya* against rival *salafī* views in the context of an issue on which a broad agreement emerged. Legitimizations ranged from ruling that naturalization can be authorized based on *fiqh al-muwāzanāt* to hinting that it is a religious duty. *Wasaṭī* jurists accepted that citizenship cannot be legitimized in itself, but only to the extent that it promotes certain interests of individual Muslims or of the Muslims and Islam at large. As when addressing social and financial interactions, justifications stressed the importance of removing hardship as well as of advancing proselytizing. A further objective introduced by jurists was the promotion of the political interests of Muslims and Islam in general. The difference between *jinsiyya* (citizenship) and *muwāṭana* (which translates as citizenship, but can also apply to residence and obedience to the laws of the land without full naturalization that grants political rights), was not distinguished.

Ṣalāḥ al-Dīn Sulṭān's apologetic study considered the permissibility of obtaining citizenship a logical result of the permissibility of residing in non-Muslim countries, which he justified by drawing on the *wasaṭī* foundations of juristic pragmatism and triumphal expansionism. Perhaps more than any other *wasaṭī* text, his essay on naturalization pointedly revealed the realism that motivates conceptualizations of migrants as missionaries. Muslims living as minorities, wrote Sulṭān, had migrated from their homelands because they experienced political oppression and financial weakness; even if jurists ordered them to return, they would not. Thus, there is no point in judging and scorning them and it is better to approach them as preachers and legitimize their stay and their naturalization, especially since no single state is entirely Islamic. Moreover, even if such an ideal Islamic state existed, it would not be able to absorb all the Muslims who live in non-Muslim lands, and even if at some point the ideal Muslim state would come into existence and be able to absorb all Muslim minorities, the Muslim nation with its universal message should still not isolate itself from the rest of humanity.[11] Relying on the *wasaṭī* narrow contextualization of *al-walāʾ wal-barāʾ*, Sulṭān rejected the opinion that residence and citizenship constitute extending loyalty to infidels, which is a breach of this concept.[12] Citing the 1996 opinion of the *salafī* Muḥammad b. ʿAbdallāh b. Sabīl (d. 2012, see below), a member of the Saudi Council of Senior Scholars, Sulṭān rejected the categorization of Muslims who naturalize as disloyal to Islam as excessive and imposing *ḥaraj*.[13] In his opinion, those concerned for the Islamic identity of Muslim youth in the West do not realize that times have changed. He argued that they do not appreciate the proliferation of Islamic education in the West and the proliferation of non-Islamic education in Muslim lands, nor do they recognize the new opportunities which distance education provides.[14]

Yet for Sulṭān, who cites in his legitimization Tūbūlyāk's study among others,[15] naturalizing is more than an imposed condition that has to be tolerated. He holds that if one accepts that Islam is a universal religion, one cannot settle for consistent proselytizing sojourns. Instead, Muslims should settle and naturalize in non-Muslim lands in order to allow for an essential aspect of successful *daʿwa* efforts: to sense the agonies and hopes of non-Muslims, and to convince non-Muslims that the Muslim proselytizer truly wishes prosperity for their society. Furthermore, only a Muslim who settles and naturalizes has the right to vote and, whether in the West or the East, exercising this right is the most profound way to effect change.[16]

ʿAbdallāh b. Bayyah's reflection on the permissibility of *muwāṭana* also focused on defending the limited, contextualized *wasaṭī* approach to "loyalty and disavowal" and introduced several additional justifications. One is that while loyalty to religion is the firmest of all loyalties, other loyalties—such as to one's country—are also permissible so long as they do not come at the expense of loyalty to religion or force its neglect.[17] Another is that an "overlap" exists between the requirements of

[11] Ṣalāḥ al-Dīn Sulṭān, "al-Muwāṭana fī Diyār al-Islām bayna al-Nāfīn wal-Muthbitīn," *al-Majalla al-ʿIlmiyya lil-Majlis al-ʿŪrūbbī lil-Iftāʾ wal-Buḥūth*, no. 12–13 (July 2008), 136.
[12] *Ibid.*, 141–51. [13] *Ibid.*, 145. [14] *Ibid.*, 154.
[15] *Ibid.*, 161. [16] *Ibid.*, 152–53.
[17] ʿAbdallāh Ibn Bayyah, "al-Walāʾ bayna al-Dīn wal-Muwāṭana," *al-Majalla al-ʿIlmiyya lil-Majlis al-ʿŪrūbbī lil-Iftāʾ wal-Buḥūth*, no. 12–13 (July 2008), 108.

citizenship and the requirements of Islam, including justice, equality, protection of property, social solidarity with the poor, and repelling aggressors.[18] Yet another is the neutrality of modern nation-states. Ibn Bayyah rejected the interpretation, common to *wasaṭī* apologias published in other contexts, of secularism as an ideology that regulates faiths. He argued that it is, in fact, a system that dissociates from favoring any specific religion while acknowledging personal and communal freedoms.[19]

Yūsuf al-Qaraḍāwī's discussion of the issue also focused on the narrow *wasaṭī* approach to "loyalty and disavowal," but in a different context. He wrestled with one specific opinion, Ḥasan al-Bannā's, that strongly prohibited obtaining citizenship in non-Muslim states based on the impermissibility of being loyal to the infidels and siding with them against Muslims. Al-Bannā went as far as to suggest based on Q. 4:100 that a Muslim whose presence in a non-Muslim land is conditioned on obtaining the citizenship of that non-Muslim state must migrate. Al-Qaraḍāwī, who in principle, as noted in the first chapter, does not consider himself to be bound by the teachings of al-Bannā, emphasized that the founder of the Muslim Brothers addressed a different situation than that of contemporary Muslims in the West. Al-Bannā's *fatwā*, wrote al-Qaraḍāwī, was a consequence of the time and circumstances in which it was written, and was affected by his youthful enthusiasm (the founder of the Muslim Brothers was 36 at the time). To be sure, when non-Muslims fight against Muslims, taking their citizenship constitutes betrayal, and thus Tunisian jurists were correct to excommunicate fellow countrymen who naturalized during the French occupation. However, in the contemporary world, countries are more interconnected and several colonialist powers of the past are now the allies of Muslims. By naturalizing, Muslim minorities avoid deportation (and thus protect the Islamic interest to create a presence in the West) and gain the right to vote in elections (and thus increase their ability to affect Western countries).[20]

[18] *Ibid.*, 109–10. [19] *Ibid.*, 110.

[20] Yūsuf al-Qaraḍāwī, "al-Waṭan wal-Muwāṭana fī Ḍaw' al-Uṣūl al-'Aqdiyya wal-Maqāṣid al-Shar'iyya," *al-Majalla al-'Ilmiyya lil-Majlis al-'Ūrūbbī lil-Iftā' wal-Buḥūth*, no. 12–13 (July 2008), 87–89.

Ḥusayn Ḥalāwa's legitimization of naturalization went as far as to consider it an obligation. He argued that naturalization is essential for "positive integration": acclimatizing in non-Muslim societies and affecting them without assimilating into them. By naturalizing, Muslims would gain financial strength, safeguard themselves from deportation, and possess the political rights needed for promoting their values and interests. Given these benefits, naturalization is not only permissible, but is a duty.[21]

The *salafī* understanding of "loyalty and disavowal" prohibits any extension, voluntary or coerced, of loyalty or affection to non-Muslims. A reasonable conclusion to be drawn from this is that becoming a citizen of a non-Muslim state, which implies voluntary commitment to abide by its laws and civil norms, is prohibited under all circumstances. This opinion was indeed the one advocated by a number of *salafī* panels and jurists. The Permanent Committee prohibited naturalizing in non-Muslim lands based on the argument that it constitutes a step to extending loyalty to an infidel government. In this context, the Committee stressed further that residence in non-Muslim countries is in principle prohibited based on Q. 4:97–98, the tradition according to which the Prophet said that he disavows of any Muslim who settles among the polytheists, and on other traditions and the *ijmāʿ* (consensus) regarding the duty of Muslims to migrate from lands of infidelity to Muslim lands if they are able to do so—unless they are knowledgeable in Islam, can manifest their religion, and spread their religion among the non-believers.[22] The abovementioned Muḥammad b. ʿAbdallāh b. Sabīl also strongly prohibited naturalization in non-Muslim countries while noting that residence in infidel societies is permissible for those who can manifest their religion there. He regarded naturalizing an expression of loyalty to infidels, and thus a breach of the obligation to disavow them, as well as a commitment to man-made laws

[21] Ḥusayn Ḥalāwa, "Qawāʿid al-Indimāj al-ʾĪjābī lil-Muslimīn fī ʾŪrūbbā," *al-Majalla al-ʿIlmiyya lil-Majlis al-ʾŪrūbbī lil-Iftāʾ wal-Buḥūth*, no. 12–13 (July 2008), 307.

[22] The Permanent Committee, "Ḥukm Tajannus al-Muslim bi-Jinsiyyat al-Dawla Dhāt al-Hukūma al-Kāfira," in Aḥmad b. ʿAbdallāh al-Shāfiʿī (ed.), *500 Jawāb fī al-Buyūʿ wal-Muʿāmalāt* (Cairo: Dār Ibn Ḥazm, 2010), 242–43.

at the expense of Allah's laws. Rashīd Riḍā was among the jurists referenced in his deliberation.[23]

The issue stirred debate among *salafīs*, as a number of them legitimized naturalization—some in more generous terms than others—based on evaluations of *maṣlaḥa*. Disagreements such as these expose the limitations of the *salafī* claim that through their literalist approach and limited juristic discretion uniformity in interpreting the Lawgiver's intentions is guaranteed. Legitimizations lacked theoretical depth, but their result was commensurate with a guiding principle of *salafī* jurisprudence (see Chapter 1) according to which *maṣlaḥa* at the rank of necessity may be applied, in some cases, to individuals who are helpless when faced with the coercive powers of the state (in contrast to individuals who experience hardships in social or financial spheres).

One example is 'Abdallāh b. Jibrīn, who ruled individually that in exceptional cases (about which he did not elaborate), gaining citizenship is legitimate. He wrote, "If a person is compelled to seek the nationality of a *kāfir* state because he has been forced to leave his own country and he can find no (Muslim) country to give him refuge, then this is permissible on the condition that he is able to practice his religion openly." Ibn Jibrīn emphasized, "with regard to obtaining *kāfir* nationality for purely worldly purposes, I do not think that this is permissible."[24] Similarly, the Saudi jurist Khālid b. 'Alī al-Mushayqiḥ ruled that taking the citizenship of an infidel country is permissible in cases of necessity, such as for the sake of political refuge, but only if the person seeking it can practice Islam freely.[25]

Other *salafīs* agreed. Addressing a query from a Muslim in Australia who expressed concern about affirming allegiance to Queen and Country,

[23] Muḥammad b. 'Abdallāh Ibn Sabīl, "Ḥukm al-Tajannus bi-Jinsiyyat Dawla Ghayr Islāmiyya," issued in 1996, accessed September 5, 2013: http://www.dorar.net/book_end/3384.

[24] 'Abdallāh Ibn Jibrīn, "Ruling on Obtaining Nationality of a Kaafir State," in Muhammad Saed Abdul-Rahman (ed.), *Islam: Questions and Answers—Alliance and Amity, Disavowal and Enmity* (London: MSA Publication Ltd, 2003), 105. For the Arabic version: "Ḥukm al-Ḥuṣūl 'alā al-Jinsiyya al-Kāfira," in *Fatāwā al-Balad al-Ḥarām* (Cairo: al-Maktaba al-Tawfīqiyya, n.d.), 193.

[25] Khālid b. 'Alī al-Mushayqiḥ, "al-Ḥuṣūl 'alā Jinsiyyat Dawla Kāfira min Ajl al-'amal," December 17, 2011, accessed September 5, 2013: http://ar.islamway.net/fatwa/36040.

even if not under oath, the editors of Islamweb.net opened their remarks by stressing the general impermissibility of living in non-Muslim countries while noting that naturalization offers many advantages. They offered legitimization based on restrictive conditions similar to those offered by b. Jibrīn and al-Mushayqiḥ:

> A Muslim is not permitted to apply for citizenship of non-Muslim countries except in a dire need, such as not being able to practice his religion in his own country or fear of oppression or being in danger for his life or the threat of imprisonment or torture in his homeland and there is no Islamic country where he can live. In such circumstances one can apply for citizenship of a non-Muslim country.

The editors suggested that a Muslim who must swear allegiance in order to gain citizenship should "try to allude to the words of oath [viz., create a different meaning] as much as possible to escape their intended point."[26]

Responding three years later to a query by a British Muslim who noted that "many Muslims in the UK apply for British nationality and passports" and expressed concern about swearing allegiance to Queen and Country, the editors opened a much wider door, one very close to that opened in *wasaṭī* and other decisions, by suggesting "considerable religious benefit" as grounds for permitting naturalization without defining its terms. Their *fatwā* recognized that "there is no doubt that a person who accepts the naturalization of disbelieving countries commits many religious infractions," and elaborated that "among these infractions is to utter what is not permissible to believe in or abide by, like accepting their regime which is totally different from Islam, and uttering an oath to be loyal and friendly with them," as well as being forced, subsequent to naturalization, to serve "in their army if military service is obligatory in their country, as well as fight on their side against their enemies even if these enemies are his brothers in religion and creed, not to mention many more obligations which contradict Islam." Notwithstanding these infractions, in case of "dire necessity or a considerable religious benefit" a Muslim may apply

[26] Islamweb.net, "Becoming a Citizen of Australia," January 23, 2001, accessed September 2, 2013: http://www.islamweb.net/emainpage/index.php?page=showfatwa&Option=FatwaId&lang=E&Id=8255.

for citizenship, provided that he makes sure to avoid to the fullest extent possible the forbidden matters that result from naturalization and is able to freely practice the rites of his religion.[27]

The restrictive quality of *wasaṭī* and narrower *salafī* legitimizations alike is clear. By justifying naturalization based on the application of the "jurisprudence of balances," or on the conceptualization of moral "overlaps" or the neutrality of the secular state, jurists suggest that citizenship should be sought—and thus also maintained—only to the extent that it provides benefits for the individual Muslim, for Muslim communities or for the Muslim nation, or that it can be judged to be compatible with Islamic norms. An approval that is based on religio-juristic argumentations can, logically, also be retracted or modified based on similar argumentations if circumstances change. Thus, in theory, an evaluation by a jurist that a dire individual need for political shelter no longer exists can result in a requirement to relinquish citizenship; and an evaluation that naturalization proved futile in promoting *da'wa*, or that state norms can no longer be considered to be overlapping with Islamic ones, can result in a similar demand. The broadness of a justification does not damage the potential for retraction. 'Abdallāh b. Bayyah's legitimization of naturalization, for example, which credits the liberal state with being both a champion of Islamic norms and neutral on religious affairs, is indeed, as March puts it, "a quite unmistakable endorsement of secularism and citizenship on liberal terms as a system that is beneficial for Muslim minorities and that is asserted to be compatible with Islamic commitments."[28] But justice, freedom, and other overlapping concepts are all rather vague terms, and so is neutrality. What if a certain non-Muslim state legislates or acts in a way that breaches b. Bayyah's understanding of what justice or freedom mean in Islam? Would he then still approve of gaining or maintaining its citizenship?

[27] Islamweb.net, "Oath of Allegiance in the UK," February 23, 2004, accessed September 2, 2013: http://www.islamweb.net/emainpage/index.php?page=showfatwa&Option=FatwaId&lang=E&Id=87140.

[28] Andrew March, *Islam and Liberal Citizenship: The Search for an Overlapping Consensus*, 231.

This prospect remains, however, highly hypothetical. Thus far, at least, no jurist has explicitly retracted or modified the general principled legitimization of citizenship, or a specific legitimization, based on new evaluations of the "overlap" between the nature of citizenship and Islamic norms, or its ability to promote Islamic interests. As we shall see below, this has not been suggested even in a case (the French headscarves ban) in which a state was considered to have acted on a matter of great importance to Muslims in a way that was neither just nor neutral. Moreover, there is no evidence of a single Muslim who has given up his or her citizenship and cited the disappearance of credible benefits or compatible norms as a reason for doing so.

ELECTORAL PARTICIPATION

Whereas naturalization is a prerequisite for realizing the *wasaṭī* objective of creating a permanent Muslim presence in the West, electoral participation is a key for realizing the objectives that legitimize their presence in the first place: improving the material state of Muslims, encouraging non-Muslim societies to embrace Islamic norms, protecting the interests of the Muslim nation and of Muslim communities, and expanding the opportunities to proselytize. Thus, from the late 1990s, legitimization—and even strong encouragement—of electoral participation was a focus of *wasaṭī* deliberations on Muslim minorities. While *wasaṭī* legitimizations were the broadest, and while jurists of other orientations challenged them, they did not evolve in a vacuum and were not exceptional, as a broad agreement emerged in Islamic jurisprudence that voting in elections in non-Muslim states is permissible. This broad agreement was shared also by a majority of *salafī* jurists and panels, who offered far more restrictive conditions for political participation, but nevertheless legitimized it based on justifications very similar to those introduced by *wasaṭīs*. However, other *salafīs*, as well as jurists of other orientations, argued that electoral participation is impermissible.

Dilwar Hussain was correct in arguing that the debate over electoral participation is linked to how Muslims view the relation between their religion and modernity,[29] but in the context of legitimizing and delegitimizing political participation in the West, the lines of demarcation that evolved in the 2000s are more nuanced, with *salafīs* who strongly oppose any embrace of Western norms—and especially of liberal democracy—joining the opinion that political participation is permissible if certain conditions are met. Rather than being determined by their views on "modernity" or "democracy," jurists' decisions on the matter were determined by their interpretations of *fiqh al-muwāzanāt* and the limits of applying *maṣlaḥa* in the context of the relations between Muslims and majority non-Muslim states.

Already in the mid-1990s, a number of jurists endorsed political participation in the West. Sheikh al-Azhar Jādd al-Ḥaqq 'Alī Jādd al-Ḥaqq (d. 1996) was asked in 1995 by a Muslim from Denmark whether it is permissible for Muslims in Europe to vote and become members of political parties. He based his legitimization on Q. 60: 5–8 and 4:5, which indicate the permissibility of good relations between Muslims and non-Muslims, and on the constitution of al-Madīna, which indicates the permissibility of a political entity in which Muslims and non-Muslims join together. He argued that there is no objection whatsoever to the participation of Muslims in political parties or trade unions as long as the Muslims elected do not endorse measures that are against the faith of Islam or the interests of Muslims.[30]

Tūbūlyāk offered different argumentations in 1997. Relying on the mechanisms of *fiqh al-muwāzanāt* and *ma'ālāt al-af'āl* (while not defining them as such), he provided unequivocal legitimization for Muslim minorities' political participation, provided that it was guided by the interests of Muslims and Islam and in accordance with existing Islamic norms.

[29] Dilwar Hussain, "Muslim Political Participation in Britain and the 'Europeanistation' of Fiqh," *Die Welt des Islams* 44, 3 (2004), 379–80.

[30] Wasif Shadid and Sjoerd van Koningsveld, "Loyalty to a Non-Muslim Government: An Analysis of Islamic Normative Discussions and the Views of some Contemporary Islamicists," in Wasif Shadid and Sjoerd van Koningsveld (eds.), *Political Participation and the Identities of Muslims in Non-Muslim States* (Kampen: Kok Pharos, 1996), 105–6; Wasif Shadid and P. S. van Koninsveld, "Religious Authorities of Muslims in the West: Their View on Political Participation," in Wasif Shadid and Sjoerd van Koningsveld (eds.), *Intercultural Relations and Religious Authorities: Muslims in the European Union* (Leuven: Peeters, 2002), 156–57.

Tūbūlyāk focused his discussion on encouraging Muslim minorities to establish political parties in non-Muslim countries. He suggested that in some cases establishing political parties is not only permissible but is a religious duty. The reasons, in their order as detailed by Tūbūlyāk, are as follows:

(a) In democracies, political parties are the only means to protect the rights of those parties' members, and the protection of rights is a necessity in Islam.

(b) Islam commands the believers to unite and cooperate in promoting piety and devotion. Forming political parties is a way of fulfilling that directive, because it is essential, in most countries, for the preservation of those minorities.

(c) The Quran commands Muslims to do good and forbids evil. In *dār al-kufr* (the land of infidels), Muslim minorities can only do so by uniting in political parties.

(d) Wherever they are, Muslims are obliged to spread the word of Islam, fend off the plots of its enemies, and defend Muslim rights; this is their duty, and the best way to fulfill it in democracies is through the formation of political parties. Even if one accepts that there is harm in forming political parties, greater harm would be incurred if they were not formed because the presence of Muslims in those lands would be endangered.

(e) The protection of rights and freedoms, which is given the highest importance in Islamic law, can only be achieved through the formation of political parties that will protect minorities from the oppression of the majority.

(f) The forces that are hostile to Islam organize in political parties; it does not make sense, neither from the point of view of Islamic law nor the point of view of reason, that their efforts would not be countered by Muslims.

(g) The experiences of Muslims from Britain to Bosnia Herzegovina to Turkey offer evidence of the critical role Islamic political parties can play in organizing Muslims and enhancing their renaissance.

(h) Religious laws are meant to safeguard the interests of Allah's servants, and any law that leads to a different result becomes invalid. Muslim minorities will face harm and risk if not permitted to form political parties; thus, prohibiting their formation is contradictory to the logic of *sharīʻa*.

(i) Nothing in the Quran or the Prophetic traditions prohibits establishing political parties, especially if they obey Islamic principles.[31]

Several conditions were attached to Tūbūlyāk's defense of creating political parties. To be permissible, political parties established by Muslim minorities must act in accordance with Islamic law and norms; base their activities on the Quran and the Prophetic traditions, for anything else is rejected in Islam; unite the Muslims living as minorities as much as possible regardless of their origin, race or language; and establish ties with Muslims in other countries.[32]

Tūbūlyāk further argued that, in cases in which Muslims are not permitted to form their own political party, it is permissible for them to join non-Muslim parties. Invoking the principle of choosing the lesser of two evils, he suggested that while in principle Muslims should not join organizations that are not governed by Islamic norms, a Muslim of strong faith and personality who is able to make an impact and who believes that he will benefit Muslim minorities by joining a non-Muslim political party can do so. Similarly, Tūbūlyāk legitimized the alliance of Muslim political parties with non-Muslim parties, provided that cooperation serves a *maṣlaḥa* and does not harm Islam or Muslims by, for example, limiting proselytizing activities. He also wrote that in cases where a Muslim candidate does not run for office, Muslims are required to vote for the non-Muslim candidate or party that is least hostile to Muslims.[33] Fundamental to the former legitimization was what Tūbūlyāk characterized as a scholarly consensus that cooperation with infidels is legitimate in times of peace if it serves a need of the Muslims and is even legitimized by some jurists in times of war if it serves a need.[34]

[31] Tūbūlyāk, *al-Aḥkām al-Siyāsiyya lil-Aqalliyyāt al-Muslima fī al-Fiqh al-Islāmī*, 13–17.
[32] *Ibid.*, 138–39. [33] *Ibid.*, 147. [34] *Ibid.*, 139–46.

In his conclusion, Tūbūlyāk emphasized that any necessity legitimizes concessions only to the extent required for meeting that necessity (*tuqaddiru bi-qadrihā*). Thus, Muslim politicians must do their best not to breach Islamic regulations more than is necessary. Islamic politics in non-Muslim societies must follow *sharʿī* regulations, empty promises must not be made, and personal attacks must be avoided. If elected, a Muslim member of parliament should not approve legislation that contradicts Islam or harms Muslims wherever they may be and must champion the liberties and rights of Muslims everywhere. In affirming an oath of allegiance, a Muslim member of parliament must articulate that the purpose is to serve Islam and Muslims and avoid uttering any words that contradict Islamic principles.[35]

From the early days of the formulation of *wasaṭī fiqh al-aqalliyyāt al-Muslima*, *wasaṭī* jurists and juristic panels encouraged political participation, with some going so far as to consider it a religious duty. *Wasaṭī fatwās* on the matter gave considerable attention to *fiqh al-muwāzanāt*, suggesting that while participation in infidel political systems involves harm from the religious point of view or constitutes evil, and thus cannot be legitimized in and of itself, the potential implications of abstention for Muslims and Islam should be also considered. The equation put forward in *wasaṭī* decisions was the following: whenever it is established that the benefits for the spread of Islam, the protection of Muslims rights, or the institution of Islamic values (or all of the aforementioned) are greater than the evil involved in taking part in a system that does not recognize Allah's laws, participation is permissible and is potentially even a duty.

This equation adheres to *wasaṭī* views on democracy and the jurisprudence of Muslim minorities. Because *wasaṭīs* do not reject electoral politics outright, emphasize the importance of actively promoting political change in the Muslim world, and justify participation in Muslim political systems that do not abide by the *sharīʿa* based on their belief in gradualist transformation (see Chapter 1), conditionally legitimizing participation in secular Western political systems did not require them to make a radical accommodation. One of the foundational concepts in

[35] *Ibid.*, 147–48.

wasaṭī fiqh al-aqalliyyāt al-Muslima is that promoting a permanent Muslim presence in the West and the spread of Islam there is a communal *maṣlaḥa*. A juristic balancing that gives weight to safeguarding this *maṣlaḥa* through political activism is a potential logical consequence. *Wasaṭī fiqh al-aqalliyyāt al-Muslima* demands that Muslims respect the laws of their receiving states, as well as interact with non-Muslims and work for the benefit of society as a whole. Political participation is commensurate with these objectives.

Wasaṭīs, inspired by the example of the Jewish Diaspora, argued that Muslim electoral participation in the West will benefit Islam in general. In their eyes, Jews living as minorities in various countries, first and foremost in the United States, demonstrated just how effective a lobby formed to defend the interests of a faith-based nation could be. One example is al-Qaraḍāwī's 2006 *fatwā* on the duties of Muslims living in the West. Al-Qaraḍāwī supported his demand that Muslim migrants champion the causes of oppressed Muslims around the world by stating: "Nowadays we see the Jews, from the four corners of the world, championing and backing Israel, and we call on all Muslims in all parts of the world, saying it is high time to champion the rights of their Muslim *umma*."[36]

Political participation was legitimized and encouraged by *wasaṭīs* in a number decisions and deliberations. The European Council for Fatwa and Research addressed the issue in its second session in October 1998 in response to a query about municipal elections in Europe and voting for a non-Muslim political party which "may not serve the interests of Muslims." Basing its decision on *fiqh al-muwāzanāt*, it stated that voting is lawful if it serves a *maṣlaḥa* greater than the *mafsada* incurred: "This matter is to be decided by Islamic organizations and establishments. If they see that the interests of Muslims can only be served by this participation, then it is permissible on condition that it does not involve the Muslims making more concessions or losses than gains."[37]

[36] Yūsuf al-Qaraḍāwī, "Duties of Muslims Living in the West," first published May 7, 2006 on Islamonline.net, accessed June 14, 2013: http://www.onislam.net/english/ask-the-scholar/dawah-principles/dawah-to-non-and-new-muslims/175226.html.

[37] *Fatwās of European Council for Fatwa and Research*, trans. Anas Usāma al-Tikritī and Shākir Nāṣif al-'Ubaydī (Cairo: Islamic INC, 2002), 100.

In July 1999, ʿAbdallāh b. Bayyah presented the foundations of the *wasaṭī* approach to Muslim minorities' jurisprudence while speaking at a conference in Santa Clara, California. He emphasized that the West should not be considered *dār al-ḥarb*, that good relations and justice should be maintained with non-Muslims, that the laws of receiving states should be respected, and that *taysīr* should be applied to Muslims living in the West. Echoing the Council's decision from the previous year and invoking *fiqh al-muwāzanāt*, Ibn Bayyah argued that it is important that "people are concerned with political candidates in this country [the United States]" because "if we support the candidates that are known to have positive attitudes towards the Muslims and who are supportive of Muslim causes and even those who are just better than opposing candidates" then "this will be considered taking the lesser of two evils." Explaining his utilization of *fiqh al-muwāzanāt* on this matter, Ibn Bayyah stated that in "a non-Muslim situation, voting and not voting are both not good situations," but because Muslims in the United States will be affected by politics whether they are politically active or not, "lack of participation can end up being a greater evil than the participation itself."[38]

In 1999, al-ʿAlwānī legitimized political participation in a *fatwā* that presented the foundations for his approach to the jurisprudence of Muslim minorities (see Chapter 2) and introduced the issue as a core of his project. The *fatwā* was written in response to a query by ʿAlī Ramaḍān Abū Zaʿkūk, the executive chairman of the Chicago-based American Muslim Council, regarding registering to vote in the United States. Al-ʿAlwānī ruled that political participation is not only permissible or optional but is a *duty* because it is essential for the protection of all forms of *maṣlaḥa* for Muslims in the United States—their necessities, needs, and improvements. To be able to protect their rights, support their brothers in faith wherever they may be, spread the truth of Islam and materialize its universality, Muslims must be politically involved. Thus, Muslims are encouraged to run for any public office that can benefit Muslims or protect them from harm, apply for American citizenship, register to

[38] ʿAbdallāh Ibn Bayyah, "Muslims Living in Non-Muslim Lands," n.d., accessed May 5, 2012: http://www.themodernreligion.com/world/muslims-living.html.

vote, and endorse the election of a non-Muslim candidate who helps Muslims more, or harms them less, than the other candidates.

Al-'Alwānī addressed in detail the arguments against participation invoked in Abū Za'kūk's query. His *fatwā* constituted an attack against the *salafī* interpretation of "disavowing" non-Muslims and reserving loyalty to Muslims only, as well as their unease with permanent residence in non-Muslim lands. However, as is usually the case in *wasaṭī–salafī* dialectics, he refrained from explicitly identifying the other party to the controversy. His reasoning reflected the fundamentals of his construction of *fiqh al-aqalliyyāt al-Muslima*. First, he argued that the Quranic concept of *al-walā' wal-barā'* (loyalty and disavowal) does not command Muslims to act unjustly toward infidels or to refrain from cooperating with them if it is in the interest of the Muslims. Thus, this concept cannot be invoked as a reason to ban political participation in the United States. Second, those who think that legitimizing political participation in an infidel regime constitutes neglect of the duty to establish an Islamic regime are wrong. Establishing a Muslim regime is the duty of Muslims living in Muslim majority societies. The duty of Muslims living as a minority in the United States is different: to fortify the Islamic presence in the country through participation in wider society and building a united community that will be able to bring Americans to Islam by convincing them of Islam's truthfulness. This process will lead to the eventual creation of an Islamic political order in America. According to al-'Alwānī, the gradualist method is in line with the path of the Prophet, who first established a community, then a society, and, finally, an Islamic system. Furthermore, any advancement of virtue and justice constitutes a brick in the construction of an Islamic regime. If Muslim political participation helps outlaw abortion or drugs, then it should be considered a way to support Muslim values even if it is not facilitated through Muslim political parties or slogans. Third, al-'Alwānī argued that those who believe that political participation is wrong because it contradicts the principle that Muslim presence among the infidels must be temporary are again fundamentally incorrect because their objection is based on a weak and anachronistic division of the world into *dār al-Islām* (the abode of Islam) and *dār al-ḥarb* (the abode of war). Al-'Alwānī rejected these terms, believing that the world should instead be divided between the abode of Islam and the abode of proselytizing (*dār al-daʿwa*). Both are legitimate areas for permanent Muslim residence.[39]

A year after the publication of this *fatwā*, al-ʿAlwānī asserted in his first systematization of his concept of *fiqh al-aqalliyyāt* that Muslim minorities are obligated to be politically active in their receiving societies.[40] In that book, as well as in the expanded 2004 version published by the European Council's journal, al-ʿAlwānī introduced the question of political participation as an example of the importance of reformulating queries so that juristic decisions serve the purposes of *sharīʿa* and lead to beneficial results. The question jurists need to address, he argued, is not whether it is permissible to be politically active in a non-Muslim state but whether it is permissible for Muslims *not* to be politically active, given the universality of Islam, the mutual cultural influences in our times, and the prospect of establishing institutions that will benefit society.[41]

During the 2000s, a number of *wasaṭī* jurists and panels reaffirmed the permissibility of political participation, with some contending that it is a duty and others strongly encouraging it. The continuous treatment of the issue and its often apologetic nature suggested that *wasaṭīs* were aware of the continued existence of contrary opinions and the need to refute them. To note a few examples, the closing statement of the seventeenth session of the European Council for Fatwa and Research in May 2007 described political participation as a *maṣlaḥa* in the rank of necessity.[42] A study published in 2008 by Ḥamza b. Ḥusayn al-Faʿr al-Sharīf, a member of the Council, argued that based on *fiqh al-muwāzanāt*, political participation is permissible and in fact a duty if necessary to safeguard Muslim existence in a non-Muslim society and protect Muslim rights.[43]

[39] Imām Muḥammad Imām, "al-Ḥukm al-Sharʿī fī Mushārakat al-Muslimīn fī al-Ḥayāt al-Siyāsiyya al-Amrīkiyya," *al-Sharq al-Awsaṭ* (November 13, 1999), 26.

[40] Ṭaha Jābir al-ʿAlwānī, *Fī Fiqh al-Aqalliyyāt al-Muslima* (6th October City: Nahḍat Miṣr lil-Ṭibāʿa wal-Nashr wal-Tawzīʿ, June 2000), 50.

[41] *Ibid.*, 9; Al-ʿAlwānī, "Madkhal ilā Fiqh al-Aqalliyyāt," 50–51.

[42] "al-Bayān al-Khitāmī lil-Dawra al-Sābiʿa ʿAshara," *al-Majalla al-ʿIlmiyya lil-Majlis al-ʾŪrūbbī lil-Iftāʾ wal-Buḥūth*, no. 12–13 (July 2008), 511.

[43] Ḥamza b. Ḥusayn al-Faʿr al-Sharīf, "Ḥukm Mushārakat al-Muslimīn fī Mujtamaʿāt al-Aqalliyyāt Ijtimāʿiyan wa-Siyāsiyyan," *al-Majalla al-ʿIlmiyya lil-Majlis al-ʾŪrūbbī lil-Iftāʾ wal-Buḥūth*, no. 12–13 (July 2008), 286–87.

In setting out general principles for Muslim integration in Europe, the European Muslim Charter—formulated by the Federation of Islamic Organizations in Europe, the forerunner of the European Council for Fatwa and Research, and signed in Brussels by some 400 Muslim organizations in January 2008—stated that "Muslims of Europe are encouraged to participate in the political process as active citizens. Real citizenship includes political engagement, from casting one's vote to taking part in political institutions."[44] In 2008 Yūsuf al-Qaraḍāwī legitimized obtaining the citizenship of non-Muslim states based in part on the need to provide Muslims with the ability to make an impact through electoral processes.[45] In an article he published in 2012 on "Muslim Minorities and Politics," he suggested political participation (including joining non-Muslim political parties) to be a logical consequence of Muslim presence in the West and provided a number of juristic justifications that legitimize it, including that *maṣlaḥas* in the ranks of necessities as well as needs, whether communal or individual, legitimize the prohibited. Thus, in some situations, in order to defend their rights it is permissible for Muslim minorities to do prohibited things such as swearing an oath to a constitution that contains clauses which contradict the *sharī'a*.[46] Muzammil Siddiqi argued that, indeed, by participating in a non-Islamic system, one cannot rule by what Allah commanded. However, "things do not change overnight" but rather through "patience, wisdom, and hard work." It is in the best *maṣlaḥa* of Muslims to participate in the American political system in order to safeguard their own interests as well as to promote the good in society.[47] Rāshid al-Ghannūshī (b. 1941), the leader of Tunisian Islamism, argued in an article he published in 2008 that Muslim history testifies

[44] Federation of Islamic Organizations in Europe, *European Muslim Charter* (a pamphlet, published 2008), article 21, 8.

[45] al-Qaraḍāwī, "al-Waṭan wal-Muwāṭana fī Ḍaw' al-Uṣūl al-'Aqdiyya wal-Maqāṣid al-Shar'iyya," 89.

[46] Yūsuf al-Qaraḍāwī, "Muslim Minorities and Politics," April 30, 2012, accessed June 23, 2012: http://www.onislam.net/english/shariah/contemporary-issues/critiques-and-thought/456871-muslim-minorities-and-politics.html?Thought.

[47] Muzammil Siddiqi, "Muslims Participating in the US Local Councils," n.d., accessed May 5, 2012: http://www.onislam.net/english/ask-the-scholar/shariah-based-systems/imamate-and-political-systems/175184-muslims-participating-in-the-us-local-councils.html?Political_Systems=.

that Islam spreads through proselytizing rather than the sword. The adherence of Western countries to human and civil rights improves the ability of Muslims to integrate and participate in public affairs while simultaneously maintaining their Muslim identity, as well as to spread Islam in a way that allows its values and its ability to save the West to be presented.[48] In an interview in February 2012, the secretary general of the European Council, Sheikh Ḥalāwa, made sure to correct this author and explain that it is not only the right but the duty of Muslim minorities to be politically active. He stressed that the Council does not endorse candidates but asks voters to determine for themselves which candidate best enhances *maṣlaḥa*.[49]

In contrast to other issues, a majority of leading mainstream *salafī* jurists and panels joined the *wasaṭī* opinion and legitimized Muslim political participation in the West based on similar justifications. There is a substantial difference between the two legitimizations. Unlike *wasaṭīs*, the permission *salafīs* granted did not encourage Muslims to vote and, moreover, did not oblige them to do so. However, the religio-legal result is similar in practical terms, making it possible for Muslims who adhere to the *salafī* approach to vote and compete in general and municipal elections.

This result is explained by the nuances of mainstream *salafī* attitudes toward political authority, electoral politics, and Muslim minorities and, specifically, by how mainstream *salafīs* interpret and apply *maṣlaḥa* in the context of these fields. First, because political participation is contextualized by *salafīs* as another means to protect and promote Islam and Muslim communities who are faced with the coercive power of non-Muslim regimes, rather than to ease specific hardships faced by individual Muslims in certain social spheres, legitimizing it based on a balance of benefits and harms is commensurate with the prevailing *salafī* approach to *maṣlaḥa*. Second, because mainstream *salafīs* conditionally approved of voting in unlawful political systems in Muslim countries, legitimizing

[48] Rāshid al-Ghannūshī, "Naḥnu fī ʿālam Maftūḥ," *al-Majalla al-ʿIlmiyya lil-Majlis al-ʾŪrūbbī lil-Iftāʾ wal-Buḥūth*, no. 12–13 (July 2008), 379–82.

[49] Interview by the author with Ḥusayn Ḥalāwa at the Islamic Cultural Center of Ireland, February 14, 2012.

voting in non-Muslim states does not constitute a radical break from their views. This is not to suggest that they hold sinful Muslim systems and infidel systems to be the same (see Chapter 1). Third, the contentious nature of politics reassures *salafīs* that by participating in the political arena, Muslims will not breach their concept of "loyalty and disavowal."

Salafī legitimization of electoral participation was expressed in a number of decisions. Asked whether it is permissible for Muslims to establish Islamic parties in secular states where they are officially subjected to secular laws but their objective is to practice *da'wa* secretly, the Permanent Committee replied positively: "It is prescribed for Muslims who live in non-Islamic states to unite, cooperate, and work together, whether in the name of Islamic parties or Islamic societies, for it is cooperating in righteousness and piety."[50] The Muslim World League's juristic panel, headed by Saudi Arabia's Grand Muftī, 'Abd al-'Azīz b. 'Abdallāh Āl al-Shaykh, suggested in 2007 that participation should be subject to *fiqh al-muwāzanāt*. If voting enhances *maṣlaḥas*—including presenting the truth about Islam, defending the rights of Muslims in the country, and increasing Muslim influence in government—then it is permissible provided that a Muslim votes in order to promote a *maṣlaḥa*, that the vote is effective, and that voting does not lead to neglect of religion.[51]

Responding to a query on whether it is permissible for Muslims living in non-Muslim countries to vote for infidels "who seem less evil," Muḥammad Ṣāliḥ al-Munajjid argued that in some cases it is wrong to vote. These cases include if voting will have no effect on Muslims, if Muslims have no effect on the outcome of the vote, if all candidates are equally evil, or if all candidates have the same attitude towards Muslims. However, in situations where it is in "the interests of Islam" to vote so as "to ward off greater evil and to reduce harmful effects," for example, when one candidate is less hostile towards Muslims than another and Muslim votes can impact the result, then "there is nothing wrong with Muslims casting their

[50] The Permanent Committee for Scholarly Research and Iftā', "Fatwā 5651," n.d., accessed August 23, 2013: http://www.alifta.com/Fatawa/FatawaChapters.aspx?View=Page&BookID=7&PageID=9143&back=true&languagename=en.

[51] Al-Majma' al-Fiqhī al-Islāmī, "Mushārakat al-Muslim fī Intikhābāt ma'a Ghayr al-Muslimīn," November 8, 2007, accessed May 5, 2012: http://www.themwl.org/Fatwa/default.aspx?d=1&cidi=167&l=AR&cid=17.

votes in favor of the less evil candidate." Al-Munajjid stressed that before ruling in favor of political participation jurists must be consulted and briefed in detail about the circumstances and laws in the non-Muslim country.

Al-Munajjid's *fatwā* concluded with a reaffirmation of the concept of loyalty and disavowal: "No one should imagine that anyone who says it is ok to vote is thereby expressing approval or support of *kufr*." On the contrary, voting is done "in the interests of the Muslims, not out of love for *kufr* and its people." Whoever wants to be on the safe side and refrain from voting is allowed to do so, but those who do vote can be assured from history that Muslims cooperated with non-Muslims when it served their interest. For example, "the Muslims rejoiced when the Romans defeated the Persians, as did the Muslims in Abyssinia (Ethiopia) when the Negus [the Ethiopian King] defeated those who had challenged his authority."[52] This reference by al-Munajjid is exceptional. As noted in Chapter 2, *salafī* texts on Muslim minorities ignore the first *hijra* (which is mentioned abundantly in *wasaṭī* texts) because of its potential to legitimize friendly ties with non-Muslims and integration into non-Muslim societies. In this particular discussion, the first *hijra* appeared because it lends credibility to al-Munajjid's unusual endorsement of actions that allow a measure of integration.

A legitimization of political participation based on *fiqh al-muwāzanāt* was also offered by the editors of Islamweb.net. Asked in 2005 whether it is permissible for Muslims in Europe to vote in referendums on the constitution of the European Union, the editors stated that in principle it is not because by participating one "could confirm the falsehood this constitution contains." However, if trustworthy scholars, especially those living in the country of the hesitant Muslim, see that "there is religious benefit in participating in this election, like repelling the greater of two evils and decreasing falsehood, then there is no harm in participating."[53]

[52] Muḥammad Ṣāliḥ al-Munajjid, "Is it Permissible for Muslims to Vote for Kaffirs Who Seem Less Evil?" in Muhammad Saed Abdul-Rahman (ed.), *Islam: Questions and Answers—Alliance and Amity, Disavowal and Enmity* (London: MSA Publication Ltd, 2003), 138–39.

[53] Islamweb.net, "Voting within the European Union," June 9, 2005, accessed September 16, 2013: http://www.islamweb.net/emainpage/index.php?page=showfatwa&Option=FatwaId&Id=90148.

In 2006, addressing a query by an Irish Muslim on the permissibility of joining the Irish Republican Party in order to lobby for issues concerning Muslims, the editors answered that in principle it is prohibited to join a party that is founded on convictions that contradict Islam, such as secularism or nationalism, because that constitutes a form of taking the enemies of Allah as allies and helping them in their falsehood (and therefore breaches the principle of loyalty and disavowal). However, if a Muslim community sees that "there are some religious benefits which can be achieved for the Muslims" by joining a political party, voting in elections, or nominating Muslim members, "then there is no harm." Any such action should not be taken individually, though, because by doing so one is subjecting oneself to afflictions.[54]

A legitimization offered by Haytham al-Ḥaddād, an England-based activist and jurist and a former student of b. Bāz, rejected the applicability of balancing benefits and harms, but produced a similar result. In a lecture given at the Redbridge Islamic Centre in Ilford, Essex, al-Ḥaddād drew a distinction between the impermissibility of liberal systems and the permissibility of participating in those systems. Political leaders who give voters the opportunity to choose between man-made laws and Allah's laws, rather than exercise their duty to apply Islam, commit infidelity, whereas voters who take advantage of the opportunity to cast their ballots and choose Islam are not committing *kufr*. According to al-Ḥaddād, voting for the least harmful non-Muslim political parties when no Islamic option exists, and when one of several infidel parties is certain to gain power whether Muslims vote or not, should be considered a means of selection rather than an endorsement of the infidel electoral system. Breaking from the common *salafī* and *wasaṭī* interpretation of this situation, he suggested that voting for an infidel party that is better for Muslims is permissible not because it constitutes a "lesser of two evils" but simply because, being merely an act of selection, it is not prohibited (*ḥarām*). He noted that for the foreseeable future, political

[54] Islamweb.net, "Joining Political Parties in Non-Muslim Countries," January 14, 2006, accessed September 17, 2013: http://www.islamweb.net/emainpage/index.php?page=showfatwa&Option=FatwaId&Id=91038.

participation can benefit Muslim causes, and in the long term the establishment of an Islamic state in Britain will be impossible without political involvement.[55]

My field experience in *salafī* mosques suggests that community leaders broadly accepted the legitimization of political participation. On October 17, 2012, shortly before the U.S. presidential elections, I visited the Islamic Cultural Center of New York. There, a poster on the main billboard directed viewers to the website of the "New York Muslim Voter and Information Club," an advocacy group that encourages Muslims to register to vote and become part of a "major political force." Charnor S. Jalloh, the mosque's assistant imām who vehemently rejects *wasaṭī* doctrine and considers Saudi *salafīs* a reference, explained that in his opinion voting is permissible if its serves a *maṣlaḥa*. Nevertheless, it is not obligatory because there are other means of promoting Muslim interests. The imām of the *salafī* Ibnu Taymeeyah Brixton Mosque in London, 'Umar Jāmāykī, told me that he considers voting permissible, so long as it is based on *fiqh al-muwāzanāt* and the evaluation of which of the candidates is better for Muslims.[56] At the Salafi Mosque and Islamic Centre in Birmingham, Bilāl Davis (Abū Ḥakīm) and Abū Khadīja sharply criticized democratic elections as contrary to Islam, pointing to a correlation between liberalism and social vices and the risk of allowing "idiots" to decide the fate of a country. They argued that it is not a coincidence that the world's three largest democracies—India, the United States, and Russia—have the largest suicide rates and claimed that in democracies there is, in theory, nothing to prohibit incest. That being so, they still argued that based on the jurisprudence of balances and the principle of choosing the lesser evil, the participation of Muslims in electoral processes in the West is legitimate.[57] The imām of the *salafī* al-Nūr mosque

[55] MRDF, "Political Participation from an Academic Islamic Perspective—Sheikh Haitham al-Haddad" (a three-part lecture), May 1, 2010, accessed September 13, 2013: http://www.youtube.com/watch?v=56sRaj2EkQE&feature=relmfu; http://www.youtube.com/watch?v=RYmP6yhhfHs&feature=relmfu; http://www.youtube.com/watch?v=nxKxvPP7m5c&feature=relmfu.

[56] Interview at Ibnu Taymeeyah Brixton Mosque, London, July 20, 2013.

[57] Interviews at the Salafi Mosque and Islamic Centre, Birmingham, England, July 19, 2013.

in Berlin, Nāṣir al-ʿĪsā, said he considers voting permissible, emphasizing that Muslims in Germany should vote for the candidate who promotes their rights best. However, he emphasized that voting is an option, not a duty.[58] At al-Muḥsinīn Mosque in Bonn, Germany, one of the leaders, who asked not to be identified, said that the permissibility of voting is based on the jurisprudence of balances. He noted that he judges candidates based on their approaches to issues that concern Muslims in Germany such as poverty and the wearing of headscarves, but not issues pertaining to Islam at large.[59]

Though *salafīs* widely agree on the permissibility of electoral participation in non-Muslim lands, this opinion is challenged by some, demonstrating once again the limitations of *salafī* self-declared literalism as a means to produce uniformity. The challenges highlight the importance of disavowing infidels as well as deny the applicability of the jurisprudence of balances to this particular issue. One prominent *salafī* who cautioned against it was Nāṣir al-Dīn al-Albānī. Answering a query on whether the principle of choosing the lesser of two evils legitimizes participation in the American presidential elections, he invoked Q. 2:120: "The Jews and Christians will never be pleased with you until you follow their way."[60] He went on to describe his "amazement" that voting, which implies taking the *kuffār* as allies, is even considered. He quoted Q. 11:113 to warn about the hellfire that awaits those who associate with those who do wrong.[61] His opinion is intriguing, since in the context of elections in Muslim majority countries he argued that if a number of Christian candidates are imposed upon Muslims and one of them will be elected whether the Muslims vote or not, then Muslims should participate in the elections and choose the candidate who constitutes a lesser evil.[62]

[58] Interview at al-Nūr Mosque, Berlin, August 1, 2013.

[59] Interview at the al-Muḥsinīn Mosque bookstore, Bonn, July 27, 2013.

[60] Al-Qur'an, A Contemporary Translation by Ahmed Ali (Princeton: Princeton University Press, 1993).

[61] "Voting in Non-Muslim States—Sheikh al-Albaani Rahimahullah," accessed May 5, 2012: http://www.youtube.com/watch?v=ml35FwR-Px4.

[62] Muhammad Naasiruddeen al-Albaanee, "The Reality of al-Albaanee's Position on Voting," February 9, 2007, accessed September 18, 2013: http://www.madeenah.com/article.cfm?id=1212.

A similar approach was articulated by a *salafī* preacher of far more modest juristic credentials, the former boxer Fāyiz Muḥammad (b. 1970), an Australian of Lebanese extraction who studied at the Islamic University of al-Madīna. Muḥammad, the head of an Islamic youth center in Sydney, incited outrage in Australia in 2007, a year after he had left the country for Lebanon, when a British documentary revealed that he had urged children to become martyrs and used hate-speech against unbelievers. (He has not been associated with actual *jihādi* activities.)[63] Addressing elections in Britain, he refuted the notion that electoral participation can be legitimized based on the principle of choosing the lesser of two evils. He argued that the government in Britain functions under man-made law, the law of the devil, and thus voting, which constitutes recognition of the unlawful system, is absolutely prohibited. He stressed that if Westerners would only follow the laws of Allah, their problems would be solved.[64]

At al-Ikhwa, a *salafī* mosque in Brooklyn, a number of interviewees told me during my visit on October 17, 2012, that voting is impermissible because it allows the majority to rule even when it legislates against the word of Allah. One interviewee explained his rejection of voting by noting that homosexuality, which is unlawful in Islam, was legalized in the United States. Not only that, he continued, but speaking against its evilness has become a punishable offense.

The most direct and sophisticated challenges to the legitimization of political participation originate not from *salafīs*, but from members of Ḥizb al-Taḥrīr (The Liberation Party), a movement that, as noted by Hussain, "typifies the anti-democratic antiparticipation tradition."[65] Its scholarship describes the issue as the epitome of the falsity of *wasaṭī fiqh al-aqalliyyāt al-Muslima* and its dangers.

[63] Carolyn Webb, "Sheikh Sparks Outrage," *The Age* (January 19, 2007), accessed September 18, 2013: http://www.theage.com.au/news/national/sheikh-sparks-outrage/2007/01/18/1169095914411.html?page=fullpage.

[64] BarclayAvenue, "Islam in Australia: Voting Is Commiting Polytheism Says Sheik Feiz Mohammed," June 16, 2011, accessed September 16, 2013: http://www.youtube.com/watch?v=Qfxs5qrn6wY&feature=related.

[65] Hussain, "Muslim Political Participation in Britain and the 'Europeanistation' of Fiqh," 387.

Ḥizb al-Taḥrīr was established in Eastern Jerusalem in 1953 by Muḥammad Taqī al-Dīn al-Nabhānī (d. 1977), a Palestinian al-Azhar graduate, religious teacher, and *qāḍī*, who since the 1930s had developed strong anti-imperialist sentiments. Like the Muslim Brothers, al-Nabhānī advocated a systematic agenda calling for the reconstitution of religion as a comprehensive framework for all aspects of life and the recreation of a united Muslim *umma*. Unlike the Brothers, who advocated a gradualist program in which an Islamic state and greater Muslim unity were to be achieved through bottom-up educational and welfare activities, al-Nabhānī believed that the creation of a united Islamic state led by a *khalīfa* is a prerequisite to the creation of an Islamic social order. The revolution envisioned by Ḥizb al-Taḥrīr is totalistic. The party holds that no government in the world applies Islam's laws; thus all states, including Muslim ones, are part of *dār al-kufr*. Once the party unites all Muslims under one leader in one state that state will become *dār al-Islām*. Non-Muslim countries will be invited to join Islam and, should they refuse, *jihād* will be declared against them by the Muslim state without any hesitation.[66] Ironically, while Ḥizb al-Taḥrīr's activities are banned in most Middle Eastern, Central Asian, and South Asian countries, and while the party failed to emerge as an effective revolutionary force in Muslim societies, it has operated freely since the 1960s in a number of Western states. Its branches in Europe and America preach for Muslim disengagement from Western political systems, denounce Western values, and encourage Muslim minorities to play a role in bringing about the Islamization of their societies in preparation for their eventual joining of the *Khilāfa* (Caliphate). The party calls for a literal application of Islamic law and strongly opposes *wasaṭiyya*, which it considers a deviant group that teaches, under Western influence, an idea of "compromise" which is alien to Islam. Hence, party members oppose the *wasaṭī* encouragement for conditional integration into Western societies.[67]

[66] Houriya Ahmed and Hannah Stuart, *Hizb ut-Tharir: Ideology and Strategy* (London: The Center for Social Cohesion, 2009), 21–34.
[67] *Ibid.*, 57–74.

A detailed Taḥrīrī prohibition of electoral participation was offered in 2004 by the Watford-based Asif Khan, a graduate in chemistry from Brunel University with no official juristic education who served as editor of *Khilafah* magazine, Ḥizb al-Taḥrīr's ideological pamphlet in the United Kingdom. Khan's treatise, *Fiqh of Minorities: The New Fiqh to Subvert Islam*, refuted the foundations of *wasaṭī fiqh al-aqalliyyāt al-Muslima*, as articulated by al-ʿAlwānī in particular, and focused on the falsity of the *wasaṭī* opinion regarding political participation in infidel systems. Khan did not address *salafī* legitimizations, probably because most of these were still not issued when his original text was written. The treatise no longer reflects his opinion; in 2007 Khan severed his ties with Ḥizb al-Taḥrīr, joined the Labour Party, and was elected a member of the Watford municipal council. He explained that he found that Ḥizb al-Taḥrīr's ideology "doesn't fit with reality."[68]

Khan considered *wasaṭīs* as jurists who "while sincerely looking to resolve the problems of the Muslims in the West have attempted to base their methodology on assumptions that do not stand up to reality or to the nature of Islam."[69] He rejected the *wasaṭī* conviction that *fatwās* need to accommodate changing times and locations, arguing that it is permissible to deviate only from laws that are based on custom and habit.[70] He also discredited the *wasaṭī* nullification of the term *dār al-kufr* in favor of *dār al-daʿwa*, arguing, in line with *Taḥrīrī* creed, that *dār al-kufr* is any land in which the systems of *kufr* are applied and security is maintained through any means but Islam.[71]

Khan's opposition to political participation denounced two *wasaṭī* assertions. First, he argued that the Quranic story of Prophet Yūsuf's employment in the service of Pharaoh couldn't be used to legitimize Muslim participation in non-Islamic government (Q. 12:55–56). This story was invoked by *wasaṭīs* to demonstrate the permissibility of

[68] Mike Wright, "Watford Labour Councillor, Asif Khan, Was a Member of Radical Islamic Group, Hizb ut-Tahrir," *Watford Observer* (November 13, 2012), accessed September 17, 2013: http://m.watfordobserver.co.uk/news/10044065.Watford_councillor_was_member_of_radical_Islamic_group/.

[69] Asif Khan, *The Fiqh of Minorities: The New Fiqh to Subvert Islam* (London: Khalifa Publications, 2004), 5.

[70] *Ibid.*, 13–15. [71] *Ibid.*, 33–37.

maintaining coexistence and constructive cooperation with non-Muslims in majority non-Muslim countries,[72] as well as the permissibility of political participation in non-Muslim countries.[73] Khan argued that Q. 12:55–56 can be understood only in one of two ways, neither of which imply that one of the Prophets was a high-ranking official in an un-Islamic government: either Yūsuf was "simply" put in charge of collecting and storing the harvest of Egypt, or he was placed in charge of the entire land, and thus his case cannot be likened to "the tactics of those who participate in elections in *kufr* systems."[74]

Khan's second central argument against *wasaṭī* legitimization disputed their application of *maṣlaḥa*. His refutation was both theoretical and pragmatic. First, people cannot determine what constitutes a *maṣlaḥa* because "nothing comprehends the reality of man except his Creator." Allah proscribes any human attempt to claim there is a benefit in that which has been forbidden. Thus, if infidel systems are unlawful, participation in them cannot be legitimized. Second, *fiqh al-muwāzanāt* and choosing the lesser of two evils should only be applied in cases of extreme necessities, when a Muslim has no choice but to perform an action (such as if a woman were drowning and the only way to save her would be for a man to see her *'awra*, or concealed parts of her body). Clearly, this is not the case regarding voting. Third, given the multitude of disputes between Muslims "that are open for all to see," how could they reach a consensus as to what constitutes a *maṣlaḥa*? Fourth, contrary to what *wasaṭīs* imply in their decisions, since the 1980s Muslims have been able to build mosques and schools in Western lands without political participation. Fifth, history reveals that *maṣlaḥa* can be wrongfully applied: many

[72] Ḥalāwa, "Qawā'id al-Indimāj al-'Ījābī lil-Muslimīn fī 'Ūrūbbā," 317–18.

[73] Muzammil Siddiqi, "Muslims Participating in the US Local Councils," n.d., accessed May 5, 2012: http://www.onislam.net/english/ask-the-scholar/shariah-based-systems/imamate-and-political-systems/175184-muslims-participating-in-the-us-local-councils.html?Political_Systems=; Rāshid al-Ghannūshī, "Islam and Voting" (a summary of a lecture given in Glasgow, April 27, 2003), trans. Z. 'Abd al-Hādī, April 28, 2005, accessed September 18, 2013: http://www.ummah.com/forum/showthread.php?55399-Voting-in-Non-Muslim-Lands-Collection-of-Fatawa-from-Various-Sources.

[74] Khan, *The Fiqh of Minorities: The New Fiqh to Subvert Islam*, 18–24.

American Muslims voted for George W. Bush[75] believing that he would "achieve an Islamic interest by allowing them to build institutions, help them improve their image, and win support for many issues such as Palestine," but as soon as Bush was elected he lit "the fire of a new crusader war."[76]

A similar approach to Khan's, albeit one leading to a different conclusion, was taken in an unsigned article published in *Khilafah* magazine in April 2010. The article stressed the impermissibility of parliaments that do not abide by Islamic law and rejected applying *maṣlaḥa* to legitimize participation in Western electoral systems based on a combination of juristic theory and pragmatic considerations similar to that presented by Khan. However, it did allow for the possibility of political participation by arguing that one responsibility of parliament members—holding the government to account—is acceptable if undertaken in accordance with Islamic law. Thus, a Muslim may run for a non-Muslim parliament, and other Muslims may vote for him, provided that he will not legislate, will not cooperate with those who do not abide by Islam, and will make it publicly known that he does not believe in the system and runs in order to undermine it.[77]

Another *Taḥrīrī* refutation of the *wasaṭī* view was published in Ḥizb al-Taḥrīr's British-branch 2011 agenda, "The Future for Muslims in Britain." It explained that the political system in Britain is capitalist, secular, and legislates on issues already resolved in the Quran; participating in it demands compromises which are fundamentally at odds with Islam. The document noted (without referring directly to *wasaṭīs*, who have emphasized this point) that because the conflict between Islam and democracy is inherent, the example of the Jewish political influence on Western

[75] On the relatively greater support of Muslim Americans for the Republican candidate (in comparison to the 1996 elections): Alexander Rose, "How Did Muslims Vote in 2000?" *Middle East Quarterly* 8, 3 (Summer 2001), 13–17.

[76] Khan, *The Fiqh of Minorities: The New Fiqh to Subvert Islam*, 24–29, 42.

[77] Khilafah Magazine, "Islam, Politics and Elections," *Khilafah Magazine* (April 2010), accessed September 18, 2013: http://www.khilafah.eu/kmag/article/islam-politics-and-elections.

governments, according to which "some Muslims model their thinking," is irrelevant to Muslims in Britain.[78]

Clearly, of the two opinions, legitimization of political participation provides greater prospects for integration than prohibitions, as it envisions Muslim minorities who advocate their views and interests within the framework of liberal-democratic political structures. However, as with legitimizations of naturalization, the introduction of religious jurisprudence to liberal systems raises ethical-political questions. A guiding principle of liberal democracies is that their citizens should seek the good of the republic; another guiding principle is that of majority rule; yet another is that basic freedoms and the rights of minorities should be protected. Theoretically, all three principles are to some extent challenged by *wasaṭī* and *salafī* legitimizations, which hold the benefit of Islam and of Muslims to be their primary objective, regard political participation acceptable only to the extent that it enhances Islamic interests, and are committed to norms that contradict, in part, liberal ones.

There are two ways to approach this theoretical challenge. One is to consider the terms of legitimization offered by jurists as a form of transnational politics. Jurists' focus on the need to serve the interests of Islam and Muslims challenges the liberal concept that the good of the republic or political community should serve as the objective of political action. It also challenges the traditional demand of nation-states to be the primary source of a citizen's allegiance. Yet, as suggested by March,[79] one indeed need not be a Marxist—or an Islamist for that matter—to appreciate that while political factions in liberal democracies disguise their agendas as concern for the welfare of the citizenry at large, these agendas often represent the narrow interests of sub-national social, financial, religious, ethnic, and other groups. Thus, in terms of Western political *practices*, rather than ideals, there is no novelty in Islamic jurists' calls for Muslim minorities to vote or serve in accordance with their communal interests. More specifically, transnational sentiments play an increasing

[78] Hizb ut-Tahrir Britain, "The Future for Muslims in Britain," January 22, 2011, accessed September 18, 2013: http://www.hizb.org.uk/solutions/report-the-future-for-muslims-in-britain.

[79] March, *Islam and Liberal Citizenship: The Search for an Overlapping Consensus*, 256.

role, generally regarded as acceptable by liberal thinkers, in the politics of Western countries, challenging the exclusiveness of nation-states as the ultimate source of allegiance.[80] Among American Jews, for example, a minority declares that candidates' attitudes towards Israel are their primary concern.[81] The universal nature of jurists' conceptualized Islamic *umma* presents a unique type of transnational allegiance. However, because the "Muslim nation" does not exist at present as an actual political force, identification with it can only be reduced to abstract images of Muslim unity, to traditional forms of transnational politics (e.g., support for Palestine, Pakistan, or Bosnia), or to the promotion of local ethnic-religiously based interests.

Another issue is legitimacy. Here, the restrictive dimensions of legitimizations that are based on *maṣlaḥas* are more challenging. First, by suggesting that liberal systems are in essence rebellious against God (even when recognizing that some of the norms they practice are commensurate with Islam), *wasaṭī* and *salafī* legitimizations hint that engagement with these systems is conditional rather than substantive, and is permissible only to the extent that it can be judged to promote an eventual change of regime within a *sharʿī* context. Second, while March is correct in arguing that promoting Islamic interests or norms does not necessarily resent or regret any benefits that non-Muslims also accrue,[82] legitimizations based on the evaluation that liberal systems make it possible to advance Islamic norms and interests, and even legitimizations that consider liberal systems to represent certain Islamic norms, imply a need for continuous juristic guidance. By presenting their interpretations of texts as the reference for political legitimacy, and by calling for the

[80] There is no shortage of theoretical and descriptive literature on this phenomenon. For example, Benedict Anderson, "The New World Disorder," *New left Review* 1, 193 (May–June 1992), 3–15; Zlatko Skribš, *Long Distance Nationalism: Diasporas, Homelands and Identities* (Aldershot, UK: Ashgate, 1999); José Itzigsohn *et al.*, "Mapping Dominican Transnationalism: Narrow and Broad Transnational Practices," *Ethnic and Racial Studies* 22, 2 (March 1999), 316–39; Nina Glick-Schiller and Georges Eugene Fouron, *Georges Woke Up Laughing* (Durham, NC: Duke University Press, 2001).

[81] Akiva Eldar, "American Jews Are Giving Up on Israel," *Haaretz* (November 12, 2012), accessed November 4, 2012: http://www.haaretz.com/opinion/american-jews-are-giving-up-on-israel.premium-1.476880.

[82] March, *Islam and Liberal Citizenship: The Search for an Overlapping Consensus*, 256.

application of religio-juristic mechanisms as a means to determine whether political participation is permissible and what its outcomes should be, jurists suggest that legitimization may be retracted or modified, should circumstances change, and is thus not only functional, but also potentially temporary.

As is the case with naturalization, the issue remains highly hypothetical, though. Prominent *wasaṭī* and *salafī* jurists have refrained, in large part, from applying the evaluation of benefits and harms to specific political campaigns in the West, and insisted that the decision on whether to participate and for whom to vote should be taken at the local level. Their doing so suggests, perhaps, that they are conscious of the inherent challenges their theorizing create. More importantly, no meaningful political movements were established in the West that apply the criteria set by jurists in a structured way, or that are *sharīʿa*-based in general. The few politicians of Muslim faith who rose to the national stage in Western countries strongly opposed political manifestations of Islam or, at the very least, disassociated from them. The first Islamic political party formed in a Western country, the Islamic Party of Britain, was established in 1989 and gained only paltry support among Muslim voters; its best achievement was in the 1990 Bradford North by-elections, when its candidate won 2.2 percent of the votes. The performance of a French Muslim party—Parti des musulmans de France, formed in Strasbourg in 1997—has not been more impressive, as none of the candidates who ran under its banner for Parliament in 2007 won more than 2.3 percent of the votes. It faired just as poorly the following year in municipal elections. Moreover, the banning of *ḥijābs* in French schools did not encourage or produce any signficant Islamic political mobilization (see below), and neither did the banning of minaret construction on Swiss mosques.

SERVICE IN NON-MUSLIM MILITARIES AND POLICE

The 9/11 attacks increased tensions between Muslim minorities and non-Muslim Western majorities. The plotters were "sleepers," or terrorists who disguised themselves as loyal residents of their countries, and the attacks gave rise to anti-Islamic sentiments in the United States and Europe, undermining two foundations of the *wasaṭī* approach: its call for the creation of a permanent and integrated Muslim presence in the West, and its hope that through gentle and gradualist means Westerners would come closer to Islam. Shortly after the attacks, and as the United States prepared for battle in Afghanistan, *wasaṭīs* were compelled to address a specific dilemma that was one of the most challenging their theory of jurisprudence ever dealt with: Is it permissible for a Muslim to fight with a non-Muslim military fighting against a Muslim one? The implications of a prohibition in the post 9/11 context were clear: it could boost allegations that Muslims are a "fifth column" in the West. However, making matters all the more difficult, Islamic jurisprudence offered no encouraging precedents, as a consensus of opinions described participation in a war against Muslims as impermissible under any circumstances.

Wasaṭīs responded to the challenge by issuing one of their most innovative and audacious decisions, conditionally legitimizing service in non-Muslim militaries that fight against Muslims. That decision, discussed in depth by Nafi,[83] as well as other decisions that followed, are clear examples of *wasaṭī* pragmatism and leniency. The conceptualization by *wasaṭīs* of an "overlap" between Islamic and liberal reactions to terror, their evaluation of harms and benefits, and their elevation of proselytizing to be a primary objective that should be protected in the context of 9/11, shine as *coups de maître* of accommodating strong prohibitions within a *sharʿī* framework, and exemplify the potential of the *wasaṭī* approach to enhance integration even under the most difficult circumstances. However, these decisions were not the final *wasaṭī* word on the matter. As the shock of 9/11 subsided, *wasaṭī* responses to Muslim participation in post-9/11 Western military campaigns gradually shifted to strong prohibition. This shift reveals that while *wasaṭīs* are inclined to adjust, even radically so, religious laws to the special conditions of non-Muslim societies, they do not accept the liberal nation-state as a primary source of allegiance, or majority rule as binding. Service in the United

[83] Basheer M. Nafi, "Fatwā and War: On the Allegiance of the American Muslim Soldiers in the Aftermath of September 11," *Islamic Law and Society* 11, 1 (2004), 78–116.

States military was legitimized only when *wasaṭī* jurists believed the American cause was justified, and when these jurists were concerned about the hardships that might be incurred by the Muslim community and the potential of harming the propagation of Islam if Muslim soldiers refused to fight. But legitimization was revoked when jurists decided that the American cause was not justified and Muslim participation in the war was not a necessity to safeguard the Muslim minority from harm or to spread Islam in the West.

The issue of Muslim service in non-Muslim militaries was not new to Islamic jurisprudence. In a 1907 *fatwā* relating to the Russian–Japanese War, Rashīd Riḍā ruled that it is permissible for a Muslim to fight in the ranks of a non-Muslim military. Pointing to *maṣlaḥa*, he introduced two justifications, both indicating that such service can be tolerated because it protects the interests of the Muslim minority and potentially of Muslims at large. First, a Muslim's "obedience to the state protects his brothers among the state's subjects from any oppression or evil that may befall them if the state is an oppressive, autocratic one; it makes them equal to any other citizen in rights and privileges if it is a representative, just state; and it benefits them in other ways if the state is in between." Second, the knowledge and practice of war are amongst the most important aspects of social life; if Muslims are forbidden from acquiring them, they will be weakened.[84] Riḍā's response presented criteria that would be adopted by later jurists. However, because both Russia and Japan are non-Muslim, the query he dealt with did not force him to struggle with a more problematic issue: Is it permissible for a Muslim to be part of a non-Muslim military fighting against a Muslim one?

This question was rarely deliberated during the twentieth century. One possible reason is the small number of conflicts to which it was relevant. Another is that the answer—an unequivocal no—seemed obvious to jurists. Al-Qaraḍāwī's *The Permissible and the Prohibited in Islam* from 1960 mentioned the utter impermissibility of a Muslim fighting against another Muslim. The broader context of his discussion, in a book intended

[84] "Qatla Muslimī al-Rūs fī al-Ḥarb al-Yabāniyya," *al-Manār* 10, 2 (April 13, 1907), 117–18.

first and foremost for Muslim minorities, was the sanctity of human life, not whether it is permissible for Muslims to fight alongside non-Muslims. He relied on a number of traditions, including the Prophet's words, reported by al-Aḥnaf b. Qays, that if a Muslim attacks another Muslim with a weapon, both are on the doorsteps of hell, and if one of them kills the other, both are doomed to hell. When asked why the Muslim who was killed would also go to hell, the Prophet answered: because he wanted to kill the other Muslim.[85]

Juristic deliberations written in the 1980s and the 1990s legitimized service in non-Muslim militaries based on *maṣlaḥa* while strictly prohibiting fighting against Muslim countries. The Tunisian *muftī* Muḥammad al-Shādhilī al-Nayfar ruled that in cases of extreme necessity—for example, when the penalty for desertion is execution—Muslims may fight alongside a non-Muslim military and that service in a non-Muslim military is also permissible if it serves the interests of Islam. For example, joining the Allies in fighting the Italian occupation of Libya was legitimate because it fell under the category of being assisted by non-Muslims. Al-Nayfar emphasized that Muslims must never, under any circumstances, fight against Muslims.[86]

Sulaymān Muḥammad Tūbūlyāk addressed the issue in detail in the mid-1990s. At that time, there was no concrete conflict between any Muslim and non-Muslim force. To the contrary, a Western coalition had just salvaged the author's native Muslim Bosnia. His legitimization, which partly drew on Riḍā's, invoked the safeguarding of *maṣlaḥas*. Tūbūlyāk argued that Muslims should serve in non-Muslim militaries as a means of gaining military training and military know-how in order to strengthen their standing and be prepared for *jihād*. In this context he applied the principle of the "lesser of two evils": to serve in a non-Muslim military involves harm, but the harm resulting from Muslims lacking the ability to defend their religion, their lives, their honor, and their properties is greater. Drawing on the tradition according to which the Prophet said

[85] Yūsuf al-Qaraḍāwī, *al-Ḥalāl wal-Ḥarām fī al-Islām* (Cairo: Maktabat Wahaba, 2004, first published August 1960), 282.

[86] Al-Nayfar, "al-Tajannus bi-Jinsiyya Ghayr Islāmiyya," 238–41.

"*lā ḍarar wa-lā ḍirār*," Tūbūlyāk suggested that Muslims should serve in order to avoid appearing weak, which could expose the weakness of Muslims in general, as well as to avoid depriving Muslims of equal status in society. Furthermore, Muslims should always prefer a communal *maṣlaḥa* to an individual one. Thus, while some Muslims may incur personal *mafsada* by serving, in doing so they serve the interests of Muslim communities. An example is the important role played by Muslims serving in non-Muslim militaries in the Bosnian conflict.[87]

The case of fighting against a Muslim force is different. Tūbūlyāk flatly and unequivocally ruled that whatever the circumstances, even if compelled, even if threatened with execution, Muslims who live as minorities must refrain from joining the infidels in a battle against Muslims. In his view, the issue is clear-cut because of Allah's and the Prophet's strong prohibitions on Muslims shedding one another's blood, as indicated, among other sources, by Q. 17:33, and because a consensus was reached on the matter by all schools of law. Tūbūlyāk advised that the end of not harming other Muslims justifies all means. If Muslims can buy off their dismissal from service, they should do so. If not, Muslims should avoid the battle or, as an alternative, make sure that their actions do not result in Muslim casualties, for example, by directing their fire to distant targets.[88]

Wasaṭī jurists did not treat military service in the early years of the evolution of their approach to Muslim minorities. Following the 9/11 attacks, they were encouraged to reconsider conventions. The wars launched by the United States in Afghanistan and Iraq presented a challenge to some Muslim-American soldiers, as well as to Muslim soldiers in allied armies. In the post 9/11 atmosphere, avoidance of military service based on Islamic principles risked causing not only personal hardship but also negative publicity that could intensify concerns, legitimate or not, about the "dual-loyalty" of Muslims in the West.

As the United States prepared to retaliate in Afghanistan, a Muslim chaplain in the American army, Captain Muḥammad 'Abd al-Rashīd,

[87] Tūbūlyāk, *al-Aḥkām al-Siyāsiyya lil-Aqalliyyāt al-Muslima fī al-Fiqh al-Islāmī*, 112–21.
[88] *Ibid.*, 122–27.

presented al-ʿAlwānī with a query on the permissibility of participating in a war against the perpetrators of the attacks. Al-ʿAlwānī, who in 1996 cooperated in a program with the U.S. Defense Department to train Muslim military chaplains,[89] consulted with al-Qaraḍāwī, who joined three of the most respected Egyptian proponents of *wasaṭiyya* (see Chapter 1), Ṭāriq al-Bishrī, Muḥammad Salīm al-ʿAwā, and Fahmī Huwaydī, as well as the Syrian Haytham al-Khayyāṭ, in issuing on September 27, 2001, a *fatwā* that legitimized, for the first time, such participation. Al-ʿAwā drafted the decision. Al-ʿAlwānī's unusual appeal to al-Qaraḍāwī, and al-Qaraḍāwī's consultation with a group of associates, suggests that they appreciated the gravity of the moment. In the *fatwā*'s opening lines, the jurists admit that "this question presents a very complicated and a highly sensitive situation for our Muslim brothers and sisters serving in the American army as well as other armies that face similar situations."

Al-Qaraḍāwī and his associates based their decision on two considerations. One was that the objectives of the planned American strikes "overlap" with the *sharʿī* understanding of a just war: the 9/11 operation was a terror attack and, according to Islamic law, a crime of *ḥirāba* (an act of violent piracy or, in a broader sense, waging war against society) whose perpetrators and their abettors must be brought to justice in an impartial court. Based on Q. 5:2, it is not just an option but the duty of Muslims to participate in the effort to bring the criminals to justice with all possible means. Another consideration relied on the principle of the "lesser of two evils": a Muslim resigning from his post in the American military as it prepares itself to wage war in Afghanistan would harm millions of other Muslims. Even if fighting against a Muslim country causes the Muslim soldier spiritual or psychological discomfort, he must endure this hardship for the sake of the greater public good. The *fatwā* did not ignore the tradition according to which the Prophet condemned to Hell Muslims who kill other Muslims, yet, in the best of *wasaṭī* tradition, it contextualized it to argue that the *ḥadīth* only applies to Muslims who have a choice whether to fight or not, and not to Muslims

[89] Alan Verskin, *Oppressed in the Land? Fatwās on Muslims Living under Non-Muslim Rule from the Middle Ages to the Present* (Princeton: Markus Wiener Publishers, 2013), 130.

who are citizens of a state and members of an army who have no choice but to follow orders. While for Tūbūlyāk it was obvious that a Muslim should prefer being killed to fighting other Muslims, in the aftermath of 9/11 al-Qaraḍāwī and his associates went as far as to suggest that Muslim soldiers should only appeal to serve in the back lines (where the risk of causing the death of other Muslims is smaller) if such a request would not raise doubts about their allegiance.[90]

Following the commencement of the war in Afghanistan on October 7, 2001, *wasaṭī* positions became more nuanced, but still legitimized participation. In a *fatwā* responding to a query from Zaynab on the permissibility of participating in the war, al-Qaraḍāwī authorized participation based exclusively on *maṣlaḥa* and only if the soldier does his best to avoid direct confrontation. The notion that the American cause is just from a *shar'ī* perspective was abandoned. The *fatwā* demonstrated the centrality of the "jurisprudence of balances" in *wasaṭī fatwās* relating to non-Muslim state authorities, as well as the application of proselytizing as a *maṣlaḥa* that justifies permitting the strongly prohibited.

The *fatwā* began by emphasizing that a Muslim who fights another Muslim has committed an act of *kufr*. However, a Muslim who is recruited to a non-Muslim military to fight against Muslims finds himself in a special circumstance that demands special consideration. This Muslim might be a "helpless" soldier who has "no choice" but to yield to the orders of his commanders. If that is the case, and he does not manage to be exempted, the Muslim soldier can join the rear to aid in military service while avoiding combat to the fullest extent possible. If he does participate in a war against Muslims, the soldier should have an inner feeling of resentment, which is the "least of faith." In al-Qaraḍāwī's view, the harm caused by avoiding the battle is greater than that caused by participating in it because if a Muslim soldier refuses to fight other Muslims, "the Muslim as well as the Muslim community may be accused of high treason. Such an accusation may pose a threat to the Muslim minority and this may also disrupt the course of *da'wa* that has been in

[90] Nafi, "Fatwā and War: On the Allegiance of the American Muslim Soldiers in the Aftermath of September 11," 80–82.

full swing since tens of years ago [viz., for decades], and has started to reap fruits."[91]

Fayṣal al-Mawlawī's position on the question posed by Zaynab was more ambivalent. He wrote that "the American-Muslim soldier is between the devil and the deep blue sea and he is facing a difficult situation." On the one hand, it is a basic rule in Islam that a Muslim is not allowed to fight against fellow Muslims. On the other hand, Q. 64:16 excuses a Muslim for not being able to carry out Allah's orders if he has no means to put them into effect. According to al-Mawlawī the issuance of a general *fatwā* that gives precedence to religious identity over citizenship would impose great harm on Muslims, but so would the opposite. Thus, each Muslim soldier should assess the consequences of fighting or of abstaining and reach a decision by himself; such a decision, however, should not expose him to danger that he cannot bear. Al-ʻAlwānī stated that Muslim-American soldiers, like other American citizens, have the right to become conscientious objectors if they feel that a war is unjust.[92]

Nafi's analysis of the primary *wasaṭī* legitimization argued that it reflected a "novel approach to the relationship between the individual Muslim and the modern nation-state," because its authors suggested that "the allegiance of the American Muslim soldier in a time of war is to his country, even if the war is being fought between the United States and a Muslim country."[93] However, Nafi also acknowledged that it follows from the *fatwā*'s concept of "overlap" that if the American cause "was not justified [in religio-juristic terms], the American Muslim's participation in a war launched by the US government would not be permitted," and that in this case "the *fatwā*'s implications would be restrictive rather than permissive."[94] The point overlooked by Nafi, quite similar to that overlooked by March in his discussion of political participation, is that in

[91] Group of Muftis, "Ulama's Fatwas on American Muslim Participating in US Military Campaign," *IslamOnline.net*, October 16, 2001, accessed September 12, 2013: http://www.onislam.net/english/ask-the-scholar/international-relations-and-jihad/relations-during-war/175001.html.

[92] *Ibid.*

[93] Nafi, "Fatwā and War: On the Allegiance of the American Muslim Soldiers in the Aftermath of September 11," 93.

[94] *Ibid.*, 94.

purely theoretical terms the two allegiances are in conflict. A decision that calls on soldiers to participate in war based on an evaluation of the war's compatability with Islamic norms and Islamic interests cannot be considered as one that (to use Nafi's words) recognizes the "sovereignty of the nation-state as fully legitimate"[95] or that normalizes "the presence of Muslims as a minority living under non-Islamic rule."[96]

The restrictive quality of retractable legitimizations that permit cooperation based on religio-juristic evaluations was established already in the previous discussions of naturalization and electoral participation. Yet, in the case of participation in war, it did not remain hypothetical as, over time, *wasaṭī* jurists *did* find that circumstances changed and retracted their previous legitimizations. As the war in Afghanistan continued and the war in Iraq began (March 20, 2003), they issued strong prohibitions on Muslim-American participation. Realizing that Operation Iraqi Freedom was not popular in the United States, and interpreting the war as a conspiracy against the Muslim nation, they decided that the participation of Muslim soldiers in the American military could not be justified by necessity or the prospect of proselytizing and does not overlap with Islamic norms. The war in Iraq was described by *wasaṭīs* as an illegitimate, flagrant aggression, an extension of the crusader goal to destroy the Islamic revival and to enforce American world domination. Muslims were instructed to resist the war and "defend the oppressed Iraqis."[97] On Islamonline.net, al-Qaraḍāwī's online flagship at the time, Fayṣal al-Mawlawī declared that it is not permissible for Muslim-American and Muslim-British soldiers or any other Muslim soldiers to participate in the war against the Iraqi people. He added, "It is totally prohibited for them to participate in any aggressive war against any country." 'Alī Jum'a, the Grand Muftī of Egypt, was attributed on the same *wasaṭī* flagship with making a similar prohibition, stating that "if a Muslim is compelled to go there [to Iraq] he must not participate in fighting, even if he is killed for this." The al-Azhar jurist 'Abd al-Majīd

95 *Ibid.*, 93. 96 *Ibid.*, 94.

97 Group of Muftis, "War on Iraq: New Crusade or Imperialism?" March 26, 2003, accessed September 1, 2009: http://www.islamonline.net/servlet/Satellite?pagename=IslamOnline-English-.

Ṣubḥ asked Muslim-American soldiers to follow the example of the boxer Muḥammad ʿAlī, who "abstained from participating" in the Vietnam War.[98]

The Iraq trauma resurfaced in *wasaṭī* deliberations during the 2000s on the permissibility of gaining citizenship. Sulṭān felt it was necessary to address the risk that naturalization would force Muslims to participate in unlawful military operations. His argument introduced once again the theory of overlap and exemplified once again its limitations. Hinting at the difference between the war in Afghanistan and the war in Iraq, he ruled that the religious identity of the fighting force should play no role at all: If a Muslim lives in a non-Muslim state that is attacked, it is his duty to participate in defending it whether the aggressor is a Muslim or not. If his state is the aggressor, he must not participate whether the attacked is Muslim or not, and in such a case should ask to be discharged on grounds of conscientious objection.[99]

From the *salafī* point of view, the issue is less complicated. In principle, *salafīs* hold service in non-Muslim militaries impermissible. This opinion is based on a foundation of "loyalty and disavowal," that Muslims should not help infidels become stronger. However, *salafīs* do not dismiss this option altogether, provided that the Muslim soldier is not involved, in any way, in aggressions against Muslims. Their limited legitimization, based on *maṣlaḥa*, demonstrates their inclination to apply a measure of flexibility when the relations between individuals and non-Muslim states are at stake. It also demonstrates indifference or ignorance of the potential impact religio-juristic decisions can have on the actual lives of Muslim individuals and communities in the West. In this spirit, al-ʿUthaymīn ruled that service in a non-Muslim military is "problematic" because it has the potential to help the infidels wage war against Muslims or those who have a treaty with Muslims. Even if this is not the case, a Muslim is only permitted to serve in a non-Muslim force as a spy who learns secrets, a preacher, an imām, or a *muʾadhdhin* serving Muslims and calling

[98] Group of Muftis, "Participation of Muslim Soldiers in US & its Allies Armies in War on Iraq," March 20, 2003, accessed September 1, 2009: http://www.islamonline.net/servlet/Satellite?pagename=IslamOnline-English-Ask_Scholar/FatwaE/FatwaE&cid=1119503546682.

[99] Sulṭān, "al-Muwāṭana fī Diyār al-Islām bayna al-Nāfīn wal-Muthbitīn," 153.

non-Muslims to Islam.[100] Similarly, al-Munajjid ruled that working for an infidel army helps and assists the infidels and is thus impermissible, but if it brings benefits to Muslims, such as exposing their secrets, or if the work is strictly in the field of proselytizing, including advising other Muslim soldiers against strengthening the infidels, it is legitimate.[101]

The case of serving an infidel force that fights against Muslims is different. *Salafīs* consider it impermissible under all circumstances. As noted by Nafi, the *wasaṭī* legitimization of service in Afghanistan did not provoke direct responses from leading *salafī* jurists. An exception was a refute of the abovementioned *wasaṭī fatwā* from September 27, 2001, issued by the Egyptian-born (1954) and American-based (since 1992) Ṣalāḥ al-Ṣāwī, a former lecturer at Umm al-Qurā University who in 2009 was appointed the secretary general of the Assembly of Muslim Jurists in America, an organization that in its juristic orientation is neither expressly *salafī* nor *wasaṭī*. Al-Ṣāwī rejected what he held to be that *fatwā*'s broad approach to the crime of *ḥirāba*; the American allegations against the Taliban, which he deemed had not been sufficiently proven; and the greater weight given by al-Qaraḍāwī and his associates, in their balancing between evils, to a speculated evil (the doubts that would be raised regarding the loyalty of Muslim Americans) than an almost assured one (the spilling of Muslim blood, including that of innocent Muslims).[102]

Other *salafī fatwās* published following the commencement of the war in Afghanistan were explicit in prohibiting Muslim participation. However, they did so without directly addressing that conflict or *wasaṭī fatwās*. Al-Munajjid ruled that it is not permissible to serve in any capacity in an army waging war against Muslims. He cautioned, based on Q. 5:51, that doing so constitutes major *kufr*, resulting in the

[100] Quoted in Muḥammad Ṣāliḥ al-Munajjid, "Military Service in Kaafir Armies and Working as a 'Chaplain' in those Armies," in Muhammad Saed Abdul-Rahman (ed.), *Islam: Questions and Answers—Alliance and Amity, Disavowal and Enmity* (London: MSA Publication Ltd, 2003), 137–38.

[101] Muḥammad Ṣāliḥ al-Munajjid, "It Is Not Permissible for a Muslim to Fight with Kaafirs against the Muslims at All," in Muhammad Saed Abdul-Rahman (ed.), *Islam: Questions and Answers—Alliance and Amity, Disavowal and Enmity* (London: MSA Publication Ltd, 2003), 84–85.

[102] Nafi, "Fatwā and War: On the Allegiance of the American Muslim Soldiers in the Aftermath of September 11," 111–13.

excommunication of the transgressor. Addressing what a conscripted Muslim should do "to get out of this situation," he promised that "we would ask Allah to help him" and suggested consulting Muslims with relevant knowledge or experience.[103] The conflict in Iraq galvanized similar decisions. Answering a query of a prospective medical student who wished to enlist in the military in order to finance his studies by means other than an interest-based loan but who was concerned he would be sent to Iraq, the editors of Islamweb.net explained that taking an interest-based loan is a major sin, but so is enlistment because it might lead the Muslim to engage in war against other Muslims or to die in battle "not for the sake of Allah."[104]

Salafī jurists also prohibited any form of indirect assistance to infidels fighting against Muslims. A Muslim businessman who had been "offered a golden opportunity to sell equipment" to a non-Muslim military that is "waging war against the Muslims" was advised not to sign the contract, as this would constitute *kufr*. The editors at Islam Question and Answer explained that it is not permissible to sell the infidels even a date, if that date assists them in fighting Muslims.[105] Al-Munajjid ruled that it is impermissible to donate blood to a non-Muslim who is in a state of war against other Muslims because doing so may help the infidel aggressor.[106]

Service in non-Muslim police forces potentially presents similar dilemmas to those of military service: a Muslim may be compelled to use force in a way that contravenes Islamic law. Unlike military service, joining the police is almost never compulsory. Nevertheless, *wasaṭīs* are more at ease with this type of service, possibly because it does not necessarily involve the risk of deliberately and violently targeting Muslims. A Canadian

[103] Al-Munajjid, "It Is Not Permissible for a Muslim to Fight with Kaafirs against the Muslims at All," 84–85.

[104] Islamweb.net, "Taking a Riba Loan or Taking Military Contract to Finance Medical School Costs," May 10, 2004, accessed September 15, 2013: http://www.islamweb.net/emainpage/index.php?page=showfatwa&Option=FatwaId&Id=87679.

[105] Islam Question and Answer, "Ruling on Helping the Kuffar against the Muslims," n.d., accessed September 1, 2009: http://islam-qa.com/en/ref/33691/army.

[106] Muḥammad Ṣāliḥ al-Munajjid, "Giving Blood to a Kaafir Who Is Not Hostile towards Islam and Who Is Not in a State of War with Us," in Muhammad Saed Abdul-Rahman (ed.), *Islam: Questions and Answers—Alliance and Amity, Disavowal and Enmity* (London: MSA Publication Ltd, 2003), 83–84.

Muslim police officer expressed his concern that by enforcing man-made laws he violates his religious duties. Ahmad Kutty responded by invoking "overlap" as well as the importance of contracts in Islam. He ruled that no fundamentals of Islam are violated by serving and protecting the citizens of one's country; a police officer is not making any laws but helping to protect citizens by upholding preexisting ones. Doing so is line with the teachings of Islam, which "stands for law and order and values it at all times." For Kutty, the issue is not whether Canadian laws are man-made or not. A Muslim citizen of Canada is party to a social contract that requires him to abide by the laws of his land, and Muslims should respect contracts. Kutty noted that the Muslims sent to Ethiopia in the first *hijra* were ordered by the Prophet to respect its laws and live there peacefully. Any alternate approach, he cautioned, risks encouraging lawfulness and anarchy.[107] The editors of Onislam.net, who introduced Kutty's decision, were more cautious. They suggested rather vaguely that joining a police force is "fine," so long as no injustices are committed, nobody is oppressed, and Islamic rules are upheld.[108]

Salafīs passed conflicting judgments on the permissibility of service in non-Muslim police forces, again demonstrating that their approach's self-proclaimed uniformity is not always realized. In legitimizing it, al-Munajjid invoked the potential partial overlap of Islamic norms and Western ones, albeit in a more cautious form than did *wasaṭīs*. He ruled that such service is permissible if the Muslim policeman is able to "fight evil and oppression or reduce it by using the existing laws which may contain something of justice and decency." However, if the policeman's work involves enforcing unjust laws, such as preventing women from wearing the headscarf, then it becomes impermissible.[109] In contrast, the editors of Islamweb.net ruled that it is impermissible for a Muslim to

[107] Ahmad Kutty, "Can I Work as a Police Officer?" August 19, 2008, accessed September 12, 2013: http://www.onislam.net/english/ask-the-scholar/financial-issues/earning-livelihood/177033.html.

[108] *Ibid.*

[109] Muḥammad Ṣāliḥ al-Munajjid, "Muslim Working in Law Enforcement in a non-Islamic Country," in Muhammad Saed Abdul-Rahman (ed.), *Islam: Questions and Answers—Alliance and Amity, Disavowal and Enmity* (London: MSA Publication Ltd, 2003), 156–57.

serve in the French police because it constitutes service in an unjust government. They based their decision on a tradition reported by Abū Hurayra and Abū Sa'īd, according to which the Prophet said: "Some day, your Amirs will show favor to wicked people and delay performing the prayer from its fixed times. So, whoever among you sees such a thing should not take the post of a monitor, policeman, revenue officer, or a treasurer." The editors suggested that if serving unjust Muslim regimes was prohibited, then all the more so with regard to non-Muslim ones. They noted that, as a policeman in France the inquirer would be forced to protect nightclubs, bars, brothels, and other unlawful establishments.[110]

THE *ḤIJĀB* BAN IN FRANCE

On March 15, 2004, four months after declaring his intention to do so, French President Jacques Chirac signed into law the following ban: "In public and secondary schools, wearing signs or clothes by which pupils clearly display a religious affiliation is forbidden."[111] While the language of the law was neutral and affected members of all faiths, it was initiated specifically to stop the wearing of *ḥijābs* and debated for over a decade mainly in this context. Since the Third Republic, schools have been considered pivotal to the mission of disseminating and stabilizing republicanism,[112] and the primary incubators of citizenship.[113] The ban was introduced and was perceived as part of a broader campaign against what many in the French public believed to be a creeping Islamic encroachment on the French Republic and its ideology of *laïcité* (secularism, or neutrality of the state on religious affairs). It was widely supported across the French political spectrum, uniting a curious coalition of liberals,

[110] Islamweb.net, "Muslim Wants to Take Job with French Police," April 6, 2003, accessed September 16, 2013: http://www.islamweb.net/emainpage/index.php?page=showfatwa&Option=FatwaId&Id=85727.

[111] John R.Bowen, *Why the French Don't Like Headscarves: Islam, the State and Public Space* (Princeton and Oxford: Princeton University Press, 2007), 136.

[112] Joan Wallach Scott, *The Politics of the Veil* (Princeton: Princeton University Press, 2007), 107.

[113] John R. Bowen, *Can Islam Be French? Pluralism and Pragmatism in a Secularist State* (Princeton: Princeton University Press, 2010), 193.

conservatives, populists, and feminists. To quote Ezekiel, it came to be considered a bulwark against Islamic fundamentalism and the just as intimidating threat of "American-style" multiculturalism.[114] Some in the French elite went as far as to describe the ban as a religious act. The philosopher Alain Finkielkraut called schools "temples of *laïcité*," and argued that students should remove their "headcovering in this temple" precisely to open themselves "to the great works of culture, the works that make humanity."[115]

While the ban stirred a fierce debate inside and outside France, its enforcement was met with surprisingly little opposition. In its first year, only forty-seven pupils were expelled due to their refusal to remove their *ḥijābs*, 550 incidents were resolved through dialogue and ninety-six pupils left public schools for private schools, distance learning, and other countries; most of these pupils were Muslim girls. All in all, the government concluded that there were no pernicious repercussions to its stand against headscarves, and congratulated itself on the positive outcome.[116] Though the controversy remained on the French agenda during the subsequent decade, the law did not face any serious challenges to its legality or legitimacy. Incidents that did occur revolved around specific aspects of its implementation (for example, whether mothers should be allowed to wear the headscarf when joining school trips) rather than around the prohibition on wearing headscarves in schools, which is the core of the law. Bowen offered a number of reasons for the compliance of French Muslim communities with a ban that some of them believed infringed their right to practice their religious beliefs. These include the kidnapping of two French journalists in Iraq shortly before the 2004 summer vacation ended by a group that demanded a repeal of the ban—an act that placed French Muslims in a sensitive position at a crucial point in time; calls by several French Muslim organizations on French Muslims to respect the law, and the ambiguous and cautious language of other organizations; and, most importantly, the flexible approaches

[114] Judith Ezekiel, "French Dressing: Race, Gender, and the Hijab History," *Feminist Studies*, 32, 2 (Summer 2006), 257.
[115] Quoted *Ibid.*, 267.
[116] Bowen, *Why the French Don't Like Headscarves*, 150–51.

applied by some school administrations with regard to the scope of the implementation, allowing creative solutions to circumvent the prohibition such as the wearing of bandanas.[117] To these factors should be added the opinions expressed by some jurists based in the Arab world that the ban should be obeyed. These opinions suggested that while the ban is unacceptable and should be opposed, Muslims in France can abide by it based on *sharʿī* justifications, and in doing so they are not creating a lesser, local version of Islamic religious practice.

A prerequisite for both the *wasaṭī* and the *salafī* legitimizations for Muslim residence in the West, strongly rooted in Islamic jurisprudence, is the ability to manifest Islam. Neither *wasaṭīs* nor *salafīs* precisely define what "manifest" signifies, but clearly, the implication is that the lack of ability to profess fundamental rituals and practices injures the permissibility of staying in a non-Muslim land. Most contemporary religious jurists consider the wearing of *ḥijābs* a religious duty that is beyond debate, and, moreover, across Muslim societies *ḥijābs* became a signature of religious devotion and of the return to religious values. Unlike other issues, including the abovementioned permissibility of participating in a war against Muslims, the French ban literally impacted every religious Muslim family in France with young girls, and thus could not be dismissed as a mere exception. Thus, the French legislation, and the public sentiments that motivated it, encouraged *wasaṭī* and *salafī* jurists alike to consider how Muslims should respond and whether they should be called to migrate from France at once.

The differences that emerged over time between *wasaṭīs* and *salafīs* on the matter serve as yet another demonstration of the gulf between the two approaches. While the former have sided with those who reluctantly accept the removal of headscarves, the latter strictly prohibited its removal, but neglected to offer practical solutions.

The *wasaṭī* response exemplified its pragmatic tendencies as well as its triumphalist rhetoric, and how the synthesis of the two results in facilitations that are grounded on juristic mechanisms. Prior to the French legislation, *wasaṭīs* excluded the possibility of legitimizing the removal of

[117] *Ibid.*, 143–50.

ḥijābs by young French women or simply ignored the issue. The prospective legislation was challenged based on theories of "neutrality" and "overlap" that, as demonstrated throughout this chapter, are essential to the *wasaṭī* treatment of the interactions between Muslim minorities and non-Muslim state institutions. However, once the ban was enacted and enforced successfully, *wasaṭīs* adjusted their decisions, based on *maṣlaḥa*, to conditionally legitimize the removal of *ḥijābs* in French schools. Their legitimizations were veiled in confident pronouncements of Islam's eventual victory and the ultimate Islamization of Europe, as well as by their efforts to mobilize French Muslims to peacefully oppose the ban.

Two months after it became known that President Chirac decided to endorse a ban on headscarves in public education, the editors of Islamonline.net were asked what French Muslims should do if such a law were to be passed. They sought the opinion of a number of jurists who stated either that the prospective law should not be respected, or avoided that question and called for urgent action to work against its approval. The imām of Ṭāriq b. Ziyād Mosque in Frankfurt am Main, Aḥmad Hulayl, expressed his astonishment at the proposed law and stressed that the headscarf is a duty ordained by Allah. He ruled that "Muslim women in France should not yield to such pressure" and, instead, should forcefully but peacefully protest against the law. Even if these common efforts fail, "on the individual level, the Muslim woman must stick to Almighty Allah's order of wearing *ḥijāb*. Following this order of Almighty Allah is to have priority over any other order. She is to do so and be patient regardless of the hardships she may encounter in that regard, bearing in mind that true believers are always tested."[118] Jamāl Badawī answered the same query by calling for peaceful democratic action to prevent the legislation from taking effect, including protests, contacting politicians and pressuring them, and seeking the support of other groups, including non-religious Muslims and feminists.[119]

[118] Group of Muftis, "Hijab in France: Suggested Courses of Action," February 9, 2004, accessed September 25, 2013: http://www.onislam.net/english/ask-the-scholar/dawah-principles/dawah-to-non-and-new-muslims/169899.html?New_Muslims=.
[119] *Ibid.*

Chirac's endorsement of the ban was met with outcry and fury in *wasaṭī* circles. The many *wasaṭī* condemnations and entreaties included a statement by the European Council and a letter from al-Qaraḍāwī to the French President, posted to the French Embassy in Doha on December 23, 2003. Two main arguments were invoked. First, headscarves should not be considered religious symbols; the sole purpose of a religious symbol, like a cross, is to declare one's religion, while the purpose of the *ḥijāb* is to cover a part of the body and to exercise modesty. Second, by intervening in this issue, the French state demonstrated hostility towards one specific religion and thus neglected, rather than asserted, its commitment to secularism and neutrality on religious matters. Moreover, the French broke the promises of their historic revolution for *liberté* (freedom) by prohibiting women from acting in accordance with their beliefs, for *egalité* (equality) by forbidding some women to cover themselves while not prohibiting other women from uncovering themselves, and for *fraternité* (fraternity) by treating Muslim women with prejudice.[120]

Al-Qaraḍāwī commended President Chirac in his letter for fighting against racism and intolerance against foreigners and hinted that the type of Islam the French President wishes to see in France is commensurate with the principles promoted by his *wasaṭiyya* trend (*tayyār al-wasaṭiyya*), which preaches for *taysīr* instead of *taʿsīr*, for *tabshīr* instead of *tanfīr*, for dialogue with other faiths, and for tolerance of rival opinions. In the letter, al-Qaraḍāwī presented the European Council as *the* juristic reference of Muslims in Europe,[121] an outlandish display of self-praise.

[120] For the text of the statement of the European Council see: European Council for Fatwa and Research, "France: Hijab under Attack," originally poster December 13, 2003, accessed September 25, 2013: http://www.onislam.net/english/ask-the-scholar/morals-and-manners/dress-and-adornment/169674.html. For the text of al-Qaraḍāwī's letter to President Chirac: Mawqiʿ al-Qaraḍāwī, "Risāla min al-Duktūr al-Qaraḍāwī ilā al-Raʾīs al-Faransī Shīrāk," December 25, 2003, accessed September 25, 2013: http://www.qaradawi.net/news/51-2009-12-18-20-38-58.html. Al-Qaraḍāwī presented his and his Council's views on the matter in an article on his personal website: Yūsuf al-Qaraḍāwī, "Muwāṭanat al-Muslim fī Ghayr al-Mujtamaʿ al-Islāmī," November 5, 2007, accessed September 25, 2013: http://www.qaradawi.net/articles/86-2009-12-12-10-35-10/4310-2012-01-31-013200.html.

[121] Mawqiʿ al-Qaraḍāwī, "Risāla min al-Duktūr al-Qaraḍāwī ilā al-Raʾīs al-Faransī Shīrāk," December 25, 2003, accessed September 25, 2013: http://www.qaradawi.net/news/51-2009-12-18-20-38-58.html.

The *wasaṭī* condemnation of the prospective French legislation did not reflect a consensus in the Muslim world. Specifically, Sheikh al-Azhar Muḥammad Sayyid Ṭanṭāwī distinguished between the case of *ḥijābs* in Muslim lands and outside them. He declared that the French have the right to ban *ḥijābs* in their country and that it is permissible for Muslim women who live in France to respect such a law if compelled to do so.[122]

In the months and years that followed it became clear that French authorities were resolute in imposing the ban in state schools and were able to do so with little, if any, interference. It also became clear that no vibrant political mobilization against the new policy emerged and that the policy did not injure political relations between France and Muslim countries. With the ban no longer a theoretical concern but a reality, *wasaṭī* jurists were forced to address its implications based on the foundations of their juristic approach and to decide whether respecting the ban can be legitimized and whether the ban necessitates leaving France.

Al-Qaraḍāwī's answer to these questions demonstrated the importance he assigns to facilitation and proselytizing and the prowess of his juristic approach. He ruled it is permissible for French school students to take off the headscarf when they enter school, so long as they make sure to don it before arriving there and immediately after leaving it. Al-Qaraḍāwī based this decision on two principles: (a) Necessities make the prohibited permissible and needs may be regarded as necessities. Pursuing education is a need, and as such it justifies the suspension of a religious duty. (b) The utilization of *maṣlaḥa* as a means to affect *fatwās* is limited to the extent needed for the protection of *maṣlaḥa* (*tuqaddiru bi-qadrihā*). Thus, Muslims should not take advantage of this facilitation when able to wear the *ḥijāb*.[123]

[122] Al-Bawāba, "Ṭanṭāwī Yu'akkidu 'Ḥaqq' Faransā bi-Iṣdār Qānūn Yaḥẓuru al-Ḥijāb," December 30, 2002, accessed September 20, 2013: http://www.albawaba.com/ar.

[123] Al-Qaraḍāwī elaborated on this decision in an interview with Onislam.net, in which he was asked about the banning of *niqābs* in French public spheres. I was not able to trace the original text or establish whether it was given orally or in writing. For the interview see: Essam Tallema, "Sheikh Qaradawi's First Interview with Onislam.net," October 18, 2010, accessed September 24, 2013: http://www.onislam.net/english/shariah/contemporary-issues/interviews-reviews-and-events/449388-sheikh-qaradawis-first-interview-with-onislamnet.html?Events=.

Al-Qaraḍāwī reiterated this opinion while addressing the case of Spanish schoolgirls who were asked to remove their *ḥijābs* in physical education classes. The girls were threatened that failure to comply would result in their ineligibility to graduate. He ruled, based on the principle according to which necessities permit the prohibited, that these girls should settle for covering themselves as much as possible.[124]

While al-Qaraḍāwī holds that wearing the *ḥijāb* is a religious duty, he stated that the inability to fully practice that duty does not necessitate migration to a Muslim land and invoked three justifications: First, there are 5–6 million Muslims in France, some with deep roots in the country, and it will not be easy for them to move to Muslim lands, where some may not find employment. Second, the number of Muslims in France constantly increases, and in the future they will become a majority because of the relatively low birth rates of non-Muslims. Third, Muslim presence in the West is a necessity, and there is a need to develop and strengthen Muslim educational and cultural institutions in France such as schools and clubs.[125] The latter statement implied that though al-Qaraḍāwī could no longer consider French citizenship as neutral on religion, or as overlapping with the Islamic values of freedom and justice, he still considered it legitimate for Muslims because it promoted Islamic objectives. The statement suggested that according to al-Qaraḍāwī, the duty to engage in *da'wa* legitimizes Muslim presence in the West under almost any circumstances. As such, it challenges the consensus (of the three *madhhabs* that permit residence among non-Muslims) according to which the condition for such residence is the ability to practice Islam.

Other *wasaṭī* jurists agreed with al-Qaraḍāwī. For example, Ahmad Kutty accepted that if there is no alternative then Muslim women may take off the *ḥijāb* while dressing as modestly as possible.[126] He also ruled

[124] For a transcript of his program *al-Sharī'a wal-ḥayā*t in which he articulated this idea: Aljazeera.net, "Ḥalqa Maftūḥa lil-'Allāma Yūsuf al-Qaraḍāwī," October 31, 2010, accessed September 24, 2013: http://www.aljazeera.net/programs/pages/bbc8e0d8-18a1-4e00-94a4-d6ffc51a7555.

[125] *Ibid.*

[126] Ahmad Kutty, "Lesser Hijab for French Muslim Women: Acceptable?" April 12, 2011, accessed September 2013: http://www.onislam.net/english/ask-the-scholar/morals-and-manners/dress-and-adornment/169835-lesser-hijab-for-french-muslim-women-acceptable.html?Adornment=.

that if wearing a bandana is the only legally acceptable alternative, then it is permissible because it fulfills some of the requirements of the *ḥijāb*.[127] In response to a query on the matter, he ruled that Muslims should not leave France because of the ban on headscarves. He explained that today there exists no ideal Muslim country, and therefore if Muslims were forced to abandon every country in which one or another restriction on Islam is imposed, they would be constantly on the move until they were left with no country to emigrate to. Kutty suggested Muslims treat the current situation in France as a trial while continuing to adhere to all the religious duties that can be heeded and seeking to change the situation through peaceful and democratic means.[128] He also took the opportunity of the *ḥijāb* ban to preach for the *wasaṭī* integration-minded agenda. Kutty called upon Muslims to meet the challenge by getting out of their "cocoons" and becoming part of the wider community so that others acknowledge Muslims as law-abiding citizens who "believe in freedom, dignity, and self-respect for everyone," by allowing mosques to become part of the wider community "instead of being obsessed with rituals and dogmas that have no relevance to the life of the people," and by joining hands with all peace-loving and democratic citizens for common purposes.[129]

The *wasaṭī* opinions on the French ban and its implementation raise a question: Would any type of limitations on religious freedoms by European governments lead them to call for civil disobedience, or, alternately, for a massive return of Muslim minorities to Muslim lands? After all, several of their arguments, such as the impracticability of absorbing millions of migrants, would be valid also if even harsher and absurd measures are undertaken. Clearly, no inclination for accommodation is

[127] Ahmad Kutty, "Alternative for French Muslims Girls after Hijab Ban," April 14, 2011, accessed September 25, 2013: http://www.onislam.net/english/ask-the-scholar/morals-and-manners/dress-and-adornment/169916-alternatives-for-french-muslim-girls-after-hijab-ban.html?Adornment=.

[128] Ahmad Kutty, "Should I Leave France Due to the Hijab Ban?" April 13, 2011, accessed September 27, 2013: http://www.onislam.net/english/ask-the-scholar/morals-and-manners/dress-and-adornment/170770-should-i-leave-france-due-to-hijab-ban.html?Adornment=.

[129] Ahmad Kutty, "Tips to Face the Hijab Ban in France," April 13, 2011, accessed September 2013: http://www.onislam.net/english/ask-the-scholar/morals-and-manners/dress-and-adornment/169853-tips-to-face-the-hijab-ban-in-france.html?Adornment=.

without limits. But *wasaṭī* jurisprudence has been very careful not to draw red lines and explicitly declare what kind of legislations would be considered as injuring the ability to manifest Islam to a degree that makes Muslim residence in the West impermissible. Their caution allows greater space for future negotiations and juristic discretion.

In contrast to *wasaṭīs*, the French ban provoked little attention among *salafīs*. A possible reason is that from the *salafī* point of view, which considers full-face *niqābs* as the proper covering for women and holds that women may only pursue education if strict segregation from men is observed, the idea of discarding the lesser covering, *ḥijābs*, for the purpose of pursuing education could not be a matter for serious consideration. The few *salafīs* who dealt with the new situation were nevertheless forced to evaluate the great importance they give to modesty with their emphasis on the obligation to abide by the laws of the land and avoid anarchy. Their answers were clear-cut and reasserted the condition set by *Ḥanbalīs* and others with regard to residence in non-Muslim lands: if Muslim women have no alternative but to take off their covering, they must migrate.

The editors of Islamweb.net, being cognizant of what they believe to be Western enmity towards Islam in general and to Muslim women in particular, were asked what constitutes a necessity that justifies removing the *ḥijāb*. They replied that, indeed, only a necessity or a need may justify this action, but residing in an infidel land is neither a need nor a necessity. A woman who cannot practice Islam must migrate to a Muslim land where she will be able to do so. Alluding to the Prophetic tradition that is at the heart of *salafī fiqh al-aqalliyyāt al-Muslima*, they noted that the demand to remove the *ḥijāb* demonstrates the serious challenges to the Islamic character of Muslims, particularly that of women and children, who live among the infidels. The editors noted that this danger is one of the reasons why the Prophet said he disavows Muslims who live among the polytheists.[130]

[130] Islamweb.net, "Ḥukm Khalʻ al-Marʼa al-Ḥijāb fī Bilād al-Gharb," June 5, 2004, accessed September 21, 2013: http://fatwa.islamweb.net/fatwa/index.php?page=showfatwa&Option=FatwaId&lang=A&Id=49545.

In another *fatwā*, the editors distinguished between *ḥijābs* and *niqābs*. A woman was contemplating whether she should pursue her studies in France, given that the "cursed" French prohibit *ḥijābs*. The editors commended her for pursuing education and ruled that if she would be required to uncover her face and hands only, then studies could be an option because there is a scholarly debate on whether the *niqāb* is a religious obligation. However, if she fears that she would be required to discard the *ḥijāb*, then studying in France is not an option, even if that means ceasing her studies. They advised the woman to pursue her studies in a land where Islam can be implemented.[131]

The Mauritanian *salafī* jurist Muḥammad al-Shanqīṭī (b. 1963) agreed with *wasaṭīs* that the situation is a test for Muslims in France. He did not call upon French Muslims to return to their respective homelands. But neither did he present a pragmatic solution. He suggested that the French legislation is a sign of enmity for Allah and his laws in France and that it testifies to the increasing strength of Islam in France. Al-Shanqīṭī drew his conviction that French Muslim girls would overcome the challenge and continue to wear their headscarves on his impressions from a visit to Lille during one of the days of Ramaḍān. In that visit, he was deeply affected by the vitality of Muslim life there. However, he provided no advice on how Muslim students should deal with the possible repercussions of insisting on wearing *ḥijābs* in schools.[132]

[131] Islamweb.net, "Ḥukm Khal' al-Ḥijāb min Ajl Ikmāl al-Ta'līm," August 26, 2010, accessed September 2013: http://fatwa.islamweb.net/fatwa/index.php?page=showfatwa&Option=FatwaId&Id=139510.

[132] Muḥammad al-Ḥasan al-Daddū al-Shanqīṭī, "al-Kalām 'alā Mas'alat al-Ḥijāb fī Faransā," September 7, 2008, accessed September 28, 2013: http://ar.islamway.net/fatwa/26621.

Conclusion to *Sharīʿa and Muslim Minorities*

In popular Western discourses on Muslim minorities, *sharīʿa* is often portrayed as a coherent, static body of binding standards that inherently conflict with liberal and secular standards and, thus, constitutes a threat to social cohesion and public order. If Westerners are not vigilantly on guard against the enemy within, if they insist on continuing failed multicultural experiments, so the argument goes, their world and their most revered values will be gradually encroached upon and undermined until the West is ultimately superseded by a *sharīʿa*-based society. Hardly a week goes by without a *sharīʿa*-related incident and public outcry. When, for example, a family court judge in Frankfurt am Main, identified as Christa Dazt-Winter, refused to allow fast-track divorce for a Moroccan-German woman, who was beaten by her Moroccan-German husband, invoking the argument that the Quran allows a husband to beat his wife, some in the German media jumped at the opportunity to suggest that her peculiar verdict indicated Islam's growing influence on German life, and the widely circulated tabloid *Bild* warned against verdicts being issued in the "name of the Quran" rather than in the "name of the people."[1] Similarly, when the Anglican Archbishop Rowan Williams suggested that some accommodation of Islamic family law in England is unavoidable, offering the liberal principle of the freedom of choice as justification,[2] an international firestorm was set off, with a majority of

[1] "Urteile in Namen des Volkes? Oder in Namen des Korans?" *Bild* (March 22, 2007), 2.

[2] Rowan Williams, "Civil and Religious Law in England: A Religious Perspective?" Text of a lecture delivered on February 7, 2008, in Rex Ahdar and Nicholas Aroney (eds.), *Shari'a in the West* (Oxford and New York: Oxford University Press, 2010), 293–303.

columnists denouncing his statement, and warning that England will be beset by "licensed polygamy" and "barbaric procedures."[3]

But what is, exactly, the *sharīʿa* that commentators warn about? Through its comparative analysis of the *wasaṭī* and *salafī* approaches to the religious law of Muslim minorities, this book demonstrated how far removed from reality the image of a static, coherent Islamic law in fact is. Muslim jurists, all speaking in the name of Allah's law, fiercely disagree on some of the most vital aspects of Muslim life in the West while agreeing on others. A single *sharīʿa* does not exist. Rather, there are various competing interpretations of the Lawgiver's intentions, and these interpretations evolve in ways that correspond with the pressures of reality and the personal inclinations of jurists. Some jurists encourage Muslims to create a permanent presence in the West, while others tolerate such a presence at most. Some jurists call on Muslims to forge friendly relations with non-Muslims and to integrate into their societies, while others demand that Muslims segregate and disavow from them. Some jurists believe that Muslims in the West are entitled to facilitations because, as a minority, they are in a state of weakness, while others insist that their being a minority is no reason to offer accommodations. Some jurists believe that the objective of bringing non-Muslims closer to Islam legitimizes facilitations, while others fiercely reject this idea and insist that strict adherence to Allah's book and the traditions is the best method of proselytizing. The theoretical differences result in contradictory decisions that touch on almost every aspect of life, from dinner parties to military service. When one speaks of "*Sharīʿa* in the West," one must first answer the following question: Which *sharīʿa*?

Critics of multiculturalism will, perhaps, find this book's findings encouraging. The broad application of *maṣlaḥa* by *wasaṭī* jurists and the primacy their jurisprudence gives to *taysīr* and *tabshīr* suggest that at least one dominant version of Islamic law can be accommodated to demands made by liberal states and societies, even if these infringe on religious freedoms. Moreover, the book has demonstrated that the more Western

[3] John Witte Jr., "The Future of Muslim Family Law in Western Democracies," in Rex Ahdar and Nicholas Aroney (eds.), *Shariʿa in the West* (Oxford and New York: Oxford University Press, 2010), 279.

governments and societies enforce their demands confidently and without hesitation, the more justifiable, from a *wasaṭī* point of view, it is to legitimize accommodations. The final episode discussed in Chapter 4, when French authorities banned *ḥijābs* in schools, is the most obvious example. While the consensus among Muslim jurists is that wearing headscarves is a religious duty for women, and while *wasaṭī* jurists fiercely opposed the legitimacy of the French ban, they found within the framework of Islamic law appropriate justifications for complying with the ban.

Yet there is another way to approach the implications of jurists' adaptability. If an entity by the name of "*Sharī'a* in the West" does not exist, then perhaps politicians and judiciaries should shift their focus (often unqualified) from trying to make sense of Islamic law to the simpler question of whether specific manifestations of *sharī'a*—or any other religious codes for that matter—constitute an assault on liberal values. This is not an easy change. One reason that expressions of *sharī'a* in Western public spheres trouble some Westerners so much is that they force self-reflection on the relation between state, society, and religion. Many fraught issues, which could otherwise be avoided, are involved, from whether Christmas is still a religious occasion to whether women have the right to reject gender-equality. Yet only by determining more precisely what their liberalism stands for, what room it allows for public expressions of religious norms, and whether or not a special status for Christianity should be conserved, will Western societies be able to convincingly determine which interpretations of *shar'ī* norms breach the cores of their beliefs and which should not concern them at all.

In September 2013, Germany's Federal Administrative Court ruled that a Muslim girl from the Helene-Lange high school in Frankfurt am Main would be required to participate in swimming classes with boys. The judges argued that the girl could, as a compromise, wear a *burqīnī* (a full-body swimsuit originating in Australia), so that swimming with boys would not infringe on her religious beliefs.[4] A month later, a Catholic

[4] Deutsche Welle, "Burkini Swimsuit Is Compromise Says German Court," September 11, 2013, accessed September 30, 2013: http://www.dw.de/burkini-swimsuit-is-compromise-says-german-court/a-17083545.

school in England, The Mount Carmel Roman Catholic High School in Accrington, Lancashire, banned two 14-year-old Muslim students from classes because they insisted on growing their beards for religious reasons.[5] In Germany, judges appeared to be ignorant of the fact that the permissibility of the *burqīnī* is debated and that Muslim jurists of different orientations reject mixed-gender swimming regardless of what women wear.[6] In England, school authorities expressed confidence, following their own research, that Muslims are not obligated to grow beards. In the German case, the judges were influenced in part by a belief that one can ascertain what the Islamic standard is for any matter, as if one agreed-upon religious law exists. In the British example, educators were guided by a conviction that devout Muslims can simply handpick their preferred religio-juristic interpretation from a number of contesting options. Both notions are incorrect. Self-reflection on the meaning and boundaries of liberalism would make it possible to abandon unqualified attempts to interpret the *sharīʿa* in favor of clear, unbiased policies that are grounded on expressions of the self rather than on denials of another.

The practical impact of the *wasaṭī* and *salafī* approaches to *fiqh al-aqalliyyāt al-Muslima* should not be overstated. As this book emphasized, the majority of Muslims in the West are either indifferent to *sharʿī* norms or only sporadically and unsystematically adhere to their personal interpretations of religious law. The *fatwās* issued by *wasaṭī* and *salafī* jurists, and the broader framework of identity and meaning they offered, potentially only matter to a minority that is committed to *sharīʿa* as an all-encompassing system and seeks the advice of qualified jurists when regulating different aspects of their lives. Among this minority, the *wasaṭī* and *salafī* corpuses are but two options, accepted, rejected, or mitigated based on one's education, awareness, orientation, personal inclinations,

[5] *Daily Mail* Reporter, "Muslim Pupils, 14, Banned from Classroom at Catholic School for Refusing to Shave off their Beards after Claiming their Religion Forbids It," October 3, 2013, accessed October 4, 2013: http://www.dailymail.co.uk/news/article-2442317/Muslim-pupils-14-banned-classroom-refusing-shave-beards-claiming-religion-forbids-it.html.

[6] Uriya Shavit and Ofir Winter, "Sports in Contemporary Islamic Law," *Islamic Law and Society* 18, 2 (2011), 269–73; Uriya Shavit and Frederic Wiesenbach, "An 'Integrating Enclave': The Case of al-Hayat, Germany's First Islamic Fitness Center for Women in Cologne," *Journal of Muslim Minority Affairs* 32, 1 (March 2012), 50–54.

and the specific circumstances encountered by individuals. This implies that *wasaṭī* and *salafī fatwās* should not be confused as reflecting "the realities of Muslims in the West," but rather as small mirrors, revealing challenges encountered by some Muslims living in the West, the level and scope of distress these challenges create, and the ways certain jurists and juristic panels address them.

The existence of a corpus that offers a spectrum of possibilities, some pragmatic and some restrictive, has important implications in itself. In my interviews in mosques and Islamic centers, I noted that even individuals who know little about the details of juristic debates on specific issues are aware that a spectrum of decisions exists. With the existence of this corpus in mind, Muslims who choose a *salafī* opinion are infused with a sense of pride, that they opted for the more demanding option, while Muslims who choose a *wasaṭī* opinion are satisfied that, while controversial, their selection is situated within Islamic norms and acknowledged as legitimate by senior scholars. There are, of course, limitations to these qualitative-based observations, and the next step in the study of *fiqh al-aqalliyyāt al-Muslima* should be a quantitative study on the social propagation of juristic decisions.

The implications of jurists' conceptualizations of relations with the state should also not be overstated. In grounding legitimizations of cooperation with state institutions on evaluations of *maṣlaḥas* and "overlaps" between Islamic and liberal norms, *wasaṭī* and *salafī* jurists alike suggest that their authority overrides that of "man-made" institutions. There has been a great deal of apologetics on the issue in academic writing; this book introduced the argument that even when the content of specific religious decisions does not challenge liberal-democratic norms, the application of juristic mechanisms that position jurists as the ultimate reference for political and civil actions does. It demonstrated how in one case, of Muslims serving in the US military, participation in war was first legitimized and then later retracted when circumstances changed. But the book also demonstrated that jurists have proved largely disinclined to pass judgments on specific political issues, and that Islamic-based politics that adheres to *sharʿī* norms has hardly developed in the West.

Proselytizing, possibly the most socially contentious of the various themes *fiqh al-aqalliyyāt al-Muslima* introduces, should also be put in proper context. At the core of both *wasaṭī* and *salafī* legitimizations of Muslim presence in the West is the expectation of spreading the word of Islam. Serious questions about the potential implications identity-formation of this kind may have on integration and coexistence should not be ignored. However, it is also important not to ignore the fact that very little practical effort has been invested on the part of either *wasaṭīs* or *salafīs* in proselytizing, and that few Muslims in the West have proved responsive to the call to actively proselytize. From the juristic point of view, the main implication of theorizing Muslims as missionaries has been, as demonstrated throughout this book, a means that enabled *wasaṭī* jurists to offer accommodations. By no means should the elevation of proselytizing to a primary *maṣlaḥa* be considered a pretext for legitimizing facilitations, as the notion that *daʿwa* legitimizes residence in non-Muslim lands has been strongly rooted in Islamic jurisprudence since the Middle Ages, and *wasaṭī* texts are crystal clear about their belief that the West is declining and eagerly searches for the spiritual salvation Islam offers. But the ironic, cyclical result of enhancing integration through triumphalist theology should not be overlooked.

Another issue the study of *fiqh al-aqalliyyāt al-Muslima* introduces is whether this discourse should be thought of as a temporary phase that will be abandoned over time—as Muslims in the West become more confident and secure in both their religious and civil identities—for an approach developed independently of foreign interventions. This prospect is endorsed by Tariq Ramadan, a critic of the *wasaṭī* approach, and involves two aspects. First, this book has demonstrated that while the religious law of Muslim minorities can easily be confused for an example of center–periphery relations, the center being the Arab world and the periphery being Muslim communities in the West, it is, in fact, the product of transnational contacts. True, the development of both the *wasaṭī* and *salafī* corpuses relied on the contribution, authority and prestige of jurists based in the Arab world, and as such, established a dependent relationship. However, both the *wasaṭī* and *salafī* corpuses reflect, to varying degrees, the efforts of Muslims living in the West. Both developed in response to queries issued by Muslim living in the West. Both retroactively legitimized the reality of migration to the West that jurists based in the Arab world realized they could not reverse. In both, the propagation of treatises and *fatwās* required cooperation from and efforts by Muslims living in the West. In both, the involvement of jurists based outside the West enhanced their standing in the Arab world and in the Western media. In the *wasaṭī* case, and to a much lesser extent in the *salafī* one, decisions were impacted by the level and intensity of distress expressed by *mustaftīs* and by the *maṣlaḥas* they invoked. In the *wasaṭī* case, and again to a much lesser extent in the *salafī* one, jurists based in the West played an active role in the deliberation and the dissemination of decisions.

There is, neither from a *wasaṭī* nor from a *salafī* point of view, a principled rejection of a future in which Muslims in the West serve as a primary authority and sever their dependence on juristic authorities based elsewhere. The Federation of Islamic Organizations characterized the European Council as a temporary solution until a generation of European-based jurists emerges, and its agenda describes intimate knowledge with the realities of Muslim minorities as a prerequisite for addressing their queries. Thus, the gradual "Europeanization" of the Council is not only optional, but is in line with its ideological foundations. When that time comes, the replacement of al-Qaraḍāwī, who is approaching his ninetieth birthday, by a European-based jurist, will be considered. Juristic credentials and authority, rather than the place of residence, are likely to be the main qualities sought. For *salafīs*, the core of their approach to judging the validity of *fatwās* is considering their fidelity to the teachings of the Quran and the traditions. While some *salafīs* in the West do not hide that they have more respect for decisions that originate from the land of the two holiest shrines, all declare their commitment to judge for themselves whether specific decisions are correct or false. Perhaps, with time, some Western-based *salafī* jurists will also become authorities well beyond their communities.

A more substantial aspect of Ramadan's criticism goes to the core of his rejection of *wasaṭī fiqh al-aqalliyyāt al-Muslima* as a permanent religio-juristic guide. Ramadan believes that through its definition of Muslims in the West as inherently weak, and the defensive mechanisms it applies, this approach imposes marginality, alienation, and passivity and assuages the guilty consciousness of those who choose to abide by unethical systems.[7] He argues that Muslims in the West need to adopt a new, confident approach that takes from the West concepts and practices that do not contradict Islam, while simultaneously correcting wrongful Western norms, bringing them in line with the universal teachings of Islam. As an example he cites the legitimization of mortgages. He finds it disturbing that Muslims are concerned with purchasing homes and ignore the broader implications of interest-based economic systems. As an alternative to the legitimization offered by the European Council, Ramadan calls on Muslims in the West to obtain bank credit from existing financial structures in order to establish within realistic time frames Islamic-based financial systems that abide by *shar'ī* norms.[8]

Ramadan, in other words, believes that instead of making accommodations in agreement with *wasaṭī* reasoning (let alone segregating as the *salafīs* suggest) Muslims in the West should fundamentally change their condition and that of their societies. Once that happens, the need for a unique *fiqh* for minorities will subside and a better future—for Muslims and non-Muslims alike—will be secured. It is an inspiring thought, but also one that reveals the difference between political philosophers and jurists. The latter cannot settle for presenting visions and calling on people to change the world; their role is to address dilemmas and pass clear judgments on whether particular actions are permissible or impermissible. The reality is that Muslims in the West constantly encounter conflicts between their work, education, interpersonal relations, and *shar'ī* norms—and search for solutions. This was the case when Ramadan presented his alternative, this has remained the case a decade later, and this is likely to remain the case for the foreseeable future. So long as conflicts between religious law and everyday life in the West exist, the body of *fiqh al-aqalliyyāt al-Muslima* will remain relevant.

[7] Tariq Ramadan, *Western Muslims and the Future of Islam* (Oxford and New York: Oxford University Press, 2004), 53–55, 85.
[8] *Ibid.*, 191–98.

Wasaṭīs and *salafīs* are not equal parties. The majority of Muslims in the West who regulate their entire lives, or at least significant aspects of their lives, based on religious law are inclined towards the pragmatism and integration encouraged by the *wasaṭī* approach (even if they are unfamiliar with the approach itself). The *salafīs* are, self-admittedly, a small minority even in Western cities where they have established a significant presence. They have effective media organs at their disposal and enjoy the support of one of the richest countries on earth, Saudi Arabia. But their stubborn insistence not to offer facilitations in the social, financial, and personal spheres, and their rigid, segregating concept of "loyalty and disavowal" suggest that abiding by their approach places a heavy burden upon the daily lives of adherents. Thus, it is fair to speculate that while *salafiyya* has the potential to attract more followers in the future, and while the specific concepts and decisions it promotes have the potential to gain wider recognition, the "saved sect" is also likely to remain on the fringes of Muslim life in the West.

This does not mean, however, that *wasaṭīs* do not face serious obstacles as well. One problem is a lack of funding. Another is that a number of their decisions seem even too lenient to some Muslims whose Islamic observance is far from strict. *Wasaṭīs* based the more radical of their legitimizations on three main interpretations of *maṣlaḥa*: that the essence of Islam is facilitation, and Muslim minorities, being in an inherent state of weakness, are entitled to unique facilitations; that in evaluating *maṣlaḥas*, individual needs can qualify as necessities and thus can legitimize the prohibited; and that the primary objectives of the Lawgiver should be expanded, and include the spreading Islam in the West. None of these points is entirely original in itself, but their coherent integration by *wasaṭīs* in the formulation and application of their juristic approach to Muslim minorities was innovative, and it allowed them to confidently introduce a number of radically lenient decisions. A signature of *wasaṭī* writing are the sophisticated syntheses it creates out of seemingly contradicting concepts, including tradition and modernity, authenticity and renewal, weakness and strength. By conceptualizing migrants as potential missionaries, *wasaṭīs* transformed massive movements to the West from a caveat to an opportunity. By integrating this concept in their jurisprudence, *wasaṭīs* were able to frame concessions as elements of triumphal ascendance.

While *wasaṭīs* have demonstrated the breadth of accommodation allowed by broad application of *maṣlaḥa*, they have failed to convince that such application is not, at least to a certain and unavoidable extent, whimsical. The polemics on the pages of the journal published by the European Council for Fatwa and Research demonstrate the unease even some of its members feel with the argumentations presented in several of the Council's decisions. Indeed, it may not be easy to explain why, for example, the spread of Islam necessitates that Muslims in European countries become homeowners, or how one can be assured that the evaluation of buying homes as a *maṣlaḥa* is correct.

More than once the spontaneous response of lay Muslims with whom I familiarized *wasaṭī* reasoning was that it just doesn't feel right. A young Pakistani cricket player on a London train noticed that I was reading a *fatwā* compilation and struck up a conversation. He earns his living as a professional athlete and was shocked to learn that some jurists allow him to skip the fast on a day of a match based on *maṣlaḥa*. "You cannot be 50 percent Muslim," he said, and added that when fasting, he plays just as well. A Belgian bookseller in an Islamic bookstore told me he felt closer to *wasaṭīs* than to *salafīs*. But he vehemently rejected the opinion that Muslims should congratulate Christians on Christmas and the justification of such an act as an opportunity to proselytize. "If someone becomes Muslim and then learns that in order to bring him to Islam I did something prohibited, I lied, what would he think of Islam?" he asked rhetorically. A leader of a mosque in Frankfurt, an advocate of integration and an easy-going person who despises *salafīs*, told me he couldn't consider the European Council as a reference because it legitimized mortgages. "What right do they have to permit the prohibited?" he asked. These anecdotes suggest that for *wasaṭī fiqh al-aqalliyyāt al-Muslima* to be accepted as a credible enterprise, its leaders need to tread carefully when providing innovative facilitations. Indeed, the decisions issued by the European Council since 2001, following a period of juristic audacity, suggest they understood their sensitive position.

But theoretical precedents have been set, and they open exciting opportunities with potentially far-reaching implications. This brings us to our final point. It is not a coincidence that *wasaṭīs*' most forceful and controversial decisions during the past two decades were issued with regard to Muslims living as minorities. One reason, which they favor, is that the unique conditions of Muslim minorities call for special flexibility. Another, which is perhaps just as important, is that it is easier to start revolutions in the periphery than in the center. None of the major and more controversial adjustments provided by *wasaṭīs* for Muslims in the West were applied in non-minority situations. But if in the case of Muslims in the West the objectives of facilitation and proselytizing systematically justify adjustments of rulings pertaining to usurious loans, marriages, bearing arms, fasting, and other fundamental issues, what in theory prevents invoking those two objectives to justify adjustments of rulings for Muslims living in Muslim countries?

From a historical perspective, the greatest importance of *fiqh al-aqalliyyāt al-Muslima* may lie in the precedents it established. This book has analyzed how Middle Eastern jurists strive to influence Muslims in the West. Perhaps the future will show that Muslim minorities influenced the evolution of religious law in majority Muslim societies.

Bibliography

Primary Sources

'Abbās, Waṣiyyullāh b. Muḥammad, "Questions Related to Non-Muslim Holidays," in *Islamic Rulings for Incarcerated Muslims*, vol. 1 (Dallas: Tarbiyyah Bookstore Publishing, May 2007), 90–91.

'Abd al-Fatāḥ, Nabīl (ed.), *Taqrīr al-Ḥala al-Dīniyya fī Miṣr* (Cairo: Markaz al-Dirāsāt al-Siyāsiyya wal-Istrātījiyya bil-Ahrām, 1995).

'Abd al-Fattāḥ, Nabīl (ed.) *Taqrīr al-Ḥāla al-Dīniyya fī Miṣr*, vol. 2 (Cairo: Markaz al-Dirāsāt al-Siyāsiyya wal-Istrātījiyya bil-Ahrām, 1998).

'Abdallāh, Ḥasan, "al-Ṣalāt fī al-Masjid al-Aqṣā . . . Ḥarām," first section of a series of interviews with Yūsuf al-Qaraḍāwī, *Niṣf al-Dunyā*, August 16, 1998, 45–50.

'Abdallāh, Ḥasan, "Fasaḥtu Khiṭbat Ibnatī liana Khalibha Rafaḍa 'an Ta'malu," second section of a series of interviews with al-Qaraḍāwī, *Niṣf al-Dunyā*, August 23, 1998, 106–10.

'Abd al-Qādir, Khālid Muḥammad, *Min Fiqh al-Aqalliyyāt al-Muslima* (Doha: The Ministry for Endowments and Religious Affairs, January 1998).

Abū al-Majd, Aḥmad Kamāl, *Ru'ya Islāmiyya Mu'āṣira: I'lān mabādi'* (Cairo: Dār al-Shurūq, 1991, originally written, though then unpublished, in 1981).

Abū al-Majd, Aḥmad Kamāl, "Qaḍiyyat al-Ḥijāb wal-Niqāb," *al-Wafd* (January 28, 1994), 9.

'Afāna, Ḥusām al-Dīn b. Mūsā, "A Muslim Woman Working as a Fashion Model," September 22, 2002, accessed August 27, 2013: http://www.onislam.net/english/ask-the-scholar/financial-issues/earning-livelihood/175723.html.

Al-'Afīfī, 'Abd al-Razāq, "Ḥukm al-Safar ilā Bilād al-Kufr lil-'Amal," in Aḥmad b. 'Abdallāh al-Shāfi'ī (ed.), *500 Jawāb fī al-Buyū' wal-Mu'āmalāt* (Cairo: Dār Ibn Ḥazm, 2010), 68.

Al-Akhdar, Abul-Hasan Maalik (ed.), *In Defense of Islam in Light of the Events of September 11th* (Toronto: T.R.O.I.D Publications, 2002).

Al-Albaanee, Muhammad Naasiruddeen, "The Reality of al-Albaanee's Position on Voting," February 9, 2007, accessed September 18, 2013: http://www.madeenah.com/article.cfm?id=1212.

Āl al-Shaykh, Sulaymān b. 'Abdallāh, *al-Dalā'il fī Ḥukm Muwālāt Ahl al-Ishrāk*, n.d., accessed October 28, 2013: http://www.tawhed.ws/r?i=bm4wz4za.

Āl al-Shaykh, Sulaymān b. 'Abdallāh, *Awthaq 'Urā al-'Īmān*, n.d., accessed October 28, 2013: www.tawhed.ws/r1?i=2351&x=vhymy7hu.

Al-'Alwaan, Sulaymaan, "Ruling on Visiting a Sick kaafir," in Muhammad Saed Abdul-Rahman (ed.), *Islam: Questions and Answers—Alliance and Amity, Disavowal and Enmity* (London: MSA Publication Ltd, 2003), 88–90.

Al-'Alwānī, Ṭaha Jābir, *Fī Fiqh al-Aqalliyyāt al-Muslima* (6th October City: Nahḍat Miṣr lil-Ṭibā'a wal-Nashr wal-Tawzī', 2000).

Al-Alwani, Taha Jabir, *Towards a Fiqh for Minorities*, trans. Ashur A. Shamis (London and Washington: The International Institute of Islamic Thought, 2003).

Al-'Alwānī, Ṭaha Jābir, "Madkhal ilā Fiqh al-Aqalliyyāt," *al-Majalla al-'Ilmiyya lil-Majlis al-'Ūrūbbī lil-Iftā' wal-Buḥūth*, no. 4–5 (June 2004), 17–92.

Al 'Anbari, Khālid bin 'Ali bin Muhammad, *The Impact of Man-made Laws in Determining the Judgment of an Abode as Being One of Disbelief or Islam* (Amman: Jamiah Media, 2007, originally published in Arabic in 2004).

Al-Arshānī, Murshid, *al-Walā' wal-Barā'* (Ṣan'ā': Maktabat Khālid b. al-Walīd, 2004).

Al-Bannā, Ḥasan, *al-Salām fī al-Islām* (Manshūrāt al-'Asr al-Ḥadīth, 2nd edn. June 1971).

Al-Bannā, Ḥasan, "Bayna al-Ams wal-Yawm," in *Majmū'at Rasā'īl al-Imām al-Shahīd Ḥasan al-Bannā* (Cairo: Dār al-Tawzī' wal-Nashr al-Islāmiyya, 2006), 507–30.

Al-Bannā, Ḥasan, "Risālat al-Mu'tamar al-Khāmis" (February 1939), in *Majmū'at Rasā'īl al-Imām al-Shahīd Ḥasan al-Bannā* (Cairo: Dār al-Tawzī' wal-Nashr al-Islāmiyya, 2006), 325–78.

Al-Bannā, Ḥasan, "Risālat Mu'tamar Ṭalbāt al-Ikhwān" (February 1938), in *Majmū'at Rasā'īl al-Imām al-Shahīd Ḥasan al-Bannā* (Cairo: Dār al-Tawzī' wal-Nashr al-Islāmiyya, 2006), 227–48.

Al-Bannā, Ḥasan, "Risālat naḥwa al-Nūr" (October 1936), in *Majmū'at Rasā'īl al-Imām al-Shahīd Ḥasan al-Bannā* (Cairo: Dār al-Tawzī' wal-Nashr al-Islāmiyya, 2006), 153–80.

Al-Baseerah, "Terrorism, Suicide Bombings and Hijackers," n.d., accessed June 30, 2013: http://www.albaseerah.org/forum/showthread.php?t=3338.

Al-Bawāba, "Ṭanṭāwī Yu'akkidu 'Ḥaqq' Faransā bi-Iṣdār Qānūn Yaḥẓuru al-Ḥijāb," December 30, 2002, accessed September 20, 2013: http://www.albawaba.com/ar.

Al-Bishrī, al-'Arabī, "Munṭalaqāt li-Fiqh al-Aqalliyyāt," *al-Majalla al-'Ilmiyya lil-Majlis al-'Ūrūbbī lil-Iftā' wal-Buḥūth*, no. 4–5 (June 2004), 201–18.

Al-Bishrī, al-'Arabī, "Shirā' al-Buyūt 'an Ṭarīq al-Qarḍ al-Bankī," *al-Majalla al-'Ilmiyya lil-Majlis al-'Ūrūbbī lil-Iftā' wal-Buḥūth*, no. 6 (January 2005), 157–78.

Al Bur'ee, 'Abdul 'Azeez Bin Yahyaa, *A Concise Manual for the New Muslim* (USA: Salafi Ink Publications, 2012).

Al-Būṭī, Sa'īd Ramaḍān, *Ḍawābiṭ al-Maṣlaḥa fī al-Sharī'a al-Islāmiyya* (Beirut: Mu'assasat al-Risāla, 1977).

Al-Dānī, 'Abdallāh, "Ijābat al-Da'wa li-Ghayr al-Muslimīn Mubāḥ," *'Ukāẓ* (December 23, 2010).

Al-Dusārī, Fahd b. Mubārak Muḥammad, *al-Ghuluww fī al-Dīn wa-Wasaṭiyyat al-Islām* (Riyadh: Madār al-Waṭan lil-Nashr, 2005).

Al-Haddaadee, Alee bin Yahyah (ed.), *The Book of Forty Hadeeth Regarding the Madhab of the Salaf* (Birmingham: Minhaj al-Sunnah Publications, 2005).

Al-Fauzan, Saleh Fauzan, *Rulings Pertaining to Muslim Women* (Riyadh: Darussalam, 2003).

Al-Fawzaan, Saleh, "Why Do the 'Wahhabis' Always Talk About Tawheed?" *The Ark* 21 (August 2007), 4.

Al-Fawzān, 'Abdallāh b. Ṣāliḥ, *Aḥkām al-Tashābuh bil-Kuffār*, 4, n.d., accessed November 10, 2013: http://alfuzan.islamlight.net/index.php?option=com_remository&id=&Itemid=0&limit=50&limitstart=0.

Al-Fawzān, Ṣāliḥ b. Fawzān b. Abdallāh, *Wujūb al-Taḥākum ilā mā Anzala Allāh wa-Taḥrīm al-Taḥākum ilā Ghayrihi* (Riyadh: Dār al-'āṣima, 1993).

Al-Fawzān, Ṣāliḥ b. Fawzān b. 'Abdallāh, *al-Ribā wa-Ba'ḍ Ṣuwarihā al-Mu'āṣira* (Cairo: Dār al-Imām Aḥmad, 2005).

Al-Fawzān, Ṣāliḥ b. Fawzān, *Aḥkām al-Ta'āmul ma'a Ghayr al-Muslimīn* (Riyadh: Dār Kunūz Ishbīlya lil-Nashr wal-Tawzī', 2009).

Al-Fawzān, Ṣāliḥ b. Fawzān, *Mas'ūliyyat al-'Ulamā' wal-Du'āt* (Riyadh: Dār Kunūz Ishbīlya lil-Nashr wal-Tawzī', 2009).

Al-Fawzān, Ṣāliḥ b. Fawzān, *al-Wasaṭiyya fī al-Islām* (Riyadh: Dār Kunūz Ishbīlya lil-Nashr wal-Tawzī', 2010).

Al-Fawzān, Ṣāliḥ b. Fawzān, "al-Ijtihād," n.d., accessed 10 September 2012: http://www.islamcountry.com.

Al-Fouzan, Saalih bin Fouzan, *al-Walaa' wal-Baraa': Allegiance and Association with the People of Islaam and Eeman and Disassociation and Enmity with the People of Falsehood and Disbelief in Islaam*, trans. Abū 'Abd al-Raḥman Bansfield (Ipswich: Jam'iyyat Ihyā' Minhaj al-Sunna, 1997).

Al-Ghannūshī, Rāshid, "Ḥukm Mushārakat al-Islāmiyyīn fī Niẓām Ghayr Islāmī," in 'Abdallāh al-Tamīmī, *Mushārakat al-Islāmiyyīn fī al-Sulṭa* (London: Liberty for the Muslim World, 1994), 12–24.

Al-Ghannūshī, Rāshid, "Islam and Voting" (a summary of a lecture given in Glasgow, April 27, 2003), trans. Z. 'Abd al-Hādī, April 28, 2005, accessed September 18, 2013: http://www.ummah.com/forum/showthread.php?55399-Voting-in-Non-Muslim-Lands-Collection-of-Fatawa-from-Various-Sources.

Al-Ghannūshī, Rāshid, "al-Wasaṭiyya fī al-Fikr al-Siyāsī lil-Qarāḍawī," in *Yūsuf al-Qaraḍāwī: Kalimāt fī Takrīmihi wa-Buḥūth fī Fikrihi wa-Fiqhihi* (Cairo: Dār al-Salām, 2004), 294–345.

Al-Ghannūshī, Rāshid, "Makānat al-Usra bayna al-Binā' al-Islāmī wal-Binā' al-Gharbī," al-*Majalla al-'Ilmiyya lil-Majlis al-'Ūrūbbī lil-Iftā' wal-Buḥūth*, no. 8–9 (June 2006), 17–50.

Al-Ghannūshī, Rāshid, "Naḥnu fī 'ālam Maftūḥ," al-*Majalla al-'Ilmiyya lil-Majlis al-'Ūrūbbī lil-Iftā' wal-Buḥūth*, no. 12–13 (July 2008), 371–82.

Al-Ghannūshī, Rāshid, "Ḥuqūq al-Insān fī al-Islām wa-Atharihā 'alā al-Sulūk al-Iqtiṣādī lil-Muslim," *al-Majalla al-'Ilmiyya lil-Majlis al-'Ūrūbbī lil-Iftā' wal-Buḥūth*, no. 14–15 (July 2009), 223–43.

Al-Ghazālī, Muḥammad, *Mustaqbal al-Islām Khārij Arḍihi: Kayfa Nufakkiru fīhi?* (Cairo: Dār al-Shurūq, 1997, first published 1984).

Al-Ghazālī, Muḥammad, *al-Sunna al-Nabawiyya bayna Ahl al-Fiqh wa-Ahl al-Ḥadīth* (Cairo: Dār al-Shurūq, third publication March 1989, first published January 1989).

Al-Ghazālī, Muḥammad, *Azmat al-Shūrā fī al-Mujtama'āt al-'Arabiyya wal-Islāmiyya* (Place of publication and name of publisher not mentioned, October 1990).

Al-Ghazālī, Muḥammad, "Hadhā Dīnunā," *al-Sha'b* (November 20, 1990), 14.

Al-Ghazālī, Muḥammad, *Qaḍāyā al-Mar'a bayna al-Taqālīd al-Rākida wal-Wāfida* (Cairo: Dār al-Shurūq, 1994).

Al-Ghazālī, Muḥammad, *al-Ghazw al-Thaqāfī Yamtaddu fī Farāghinā* (Cairo: Dār al-Shurūq, second printing, 1998, the writing of the book dates to the mid-1980s).

Al-Ghunaymān, 'Abdallāh, "The Kufr of Those Who Rule by Man-made Laws," in Muhammad Saed Abdul-Rahman (ed.), *Islam: Questions and Answers—Polytheism (Shirk) and its Different Forms* (London: MSA Publication Ltd, 2003), 131.

Al-Ḥarīthī, Abū Farīḥān Jamāl b. Farīḥān (ed.), *al-Fatāwā al-Muhimma fī Tabṣīr al-Umma* (Cairo: Maktabat al-Hady al-Muḥammadī, 2009).

Al-Hawārī, Muḥammad, "Usus al-Binā' al-Usarī fī al-Islām," in *al-Majalla al-'Ilmiyya lil-Majlis al-'Ūrūbbī lil-Iftā' wal-Buḥūth*, no. 7 (July 2005), 119–72.

'Alī, Abū Muntaṣir ibn Mohar (president of Jam'iyyat Ihya' Minhaj al-Sunna), "Introduction," in Saalih bin Fouzan al-Fouzan, *al-walaa' wal-baraa': Allegiance and Association With the People of Islaam and Eeman and Disassociation and Enmity with the People of Falsehood and Disbelief in Islaam*, trans. Abū 'Abd al-Raḥman Bansfield (Ipswich: Jam'iyyat Ihyā' Minhaj al-Sunna, 1997), 4–5.

Aljazeera.net, "al-Wasaṭiyya fī al-Islām" (televised interview with Yūsuf al-Qaraḍāwī moderated by Aḥmad Manṣūr, October 26, 1997), June 4, 2004, accessed November 6, 2013: http://www.aljazeera.net/home/print/0353e88a-286d-4266-82c6-6094179ea26d/f4478517-8a76-4242-9c2f-38ff3d21fece.

Aljazeera.net, "Ḥalqa Maftūḥa lil-'Allāma Yūsuf al-Qaraḍāwī," October 31, 2010, accessed September 24, 2013: http://www.aljazeera.net/programs/pages/bbc8e0d8-18a1-4e00-94a4-d6ffc51a7555.

Al-Jibrīn, 'Abdallāh b. 'Abd al-Raḥman, "al-Taqlīd al-A'mā lil-Gharb," in *Fatāwā al-Balad al-Ḥarām* (Cairo: al-Maktaba al-Tawfīqiyya, n.d.), 201.

Al-Jibrīn, 'Abdallāh b. 'Abd al-Raḥman, "Ḥukm al-Iḥtifāl bi-'ām Alfayn," in *Fatāwā al-Balad al-Ḥarām* (Cairo: al-Maktaba al-Tawfīqiyya, n.d.), 23.

Al-Juday', 'Abdallāh b. Yūsuf, "Ribā wal-'Uqūd al-Māliyya al-Fāsida fī Ghayr Bilād al-Islām," *al-Majalla al-'Ilmiyya lil-Majlis al-'ūrūbbī lil-Iftā' wal-Buḥūth*, no. 14–15 (July 2009), 279–336.

Al-Jūzū, 'Abd al-Raḥman (ed.), *al-Islām Dīn al-'Ilm wal-Madaniyya*, a collection of works by Muḥammad 'Abduh (Beirut: Manshūrāt Dār Maktabat al-Hayāt, 1989).

Al-Kawākibī, 'Abd al-Raḥman, "Ṭabā'i' al-Istibdād wa-Maṣāri' al-Isti'bād," in Muḥammad 'Imāra (ed.), al-A'māl al-Kāmila li-'Abd al-Raḥman al-Kawākibī (Cairo: al-Hay'a al-Misriyya al-'āmma lil-Ta'līf wal-Nashr, 1970), 328–438.

Al-Khuḍayr, 'Abd al-Karīm, "Is it Permissible for a Muslim to Choose the Easiest Scholarly Opinion," in Muhammad Saed Abdul-Rahman (ed.), *Islam: Questions and Answers—Basis for Jurisprudence and Islamic Rulings* (London: MSA Publication Ltd, 2007), 92–93.

Al-Kittānī, ʿAlī b. al-Muntaṣir, *al-Muslimūn fī 'ūrūbbā wa-Amricā* (Beirut: Dār al-Kutub al-ʿIlmiyya, 2005).

Al-Lāfī, Muḥammad al-Fāḍil, "al-Khiṭāb al-Dīnī al-Islāmī," *al-Majalla al-ʿIlmiyya lil-Majlis al-'Ūrūbbī lil-Iftā' wal-Buḥūth*, no. 6 (January 2005), 209–58.

Al-Lajna al-Dā'ima, "Ruling on Making Fun of the Hijab," in Muhammad Saed Abdul–Rahman (ed.), *Islam: Questions and Answers—Polytheism (Shirq) and its Different Forms* (London: MSA Publication Ltd, 2003), 75–76.

Al-Lajna al-Dā'ima, "Ḥukm Akhdh al-Qarḍ al-Ribāwī lil-Ḥāja al-Māssa," in Ṣalāḥ al-Dīn Maḥmūd al-Saʿīd (ed.), *Fatāwā al-ʿUlamā' ḥawla al-Aqalliyyāt al-Muslima fī al-ʿālam* (Alexandria: Dār al-'Īmān, 2004), 133–34.

Al-Lajna al-Dā'ima, "Celebrating Innovated Festivals," in Muhammad Saed Abdul–Rahman (ed.), *Islam: Questions and Answers—Basis for Jurisprudence and Islamic Rulings* (London: MSA Publication Ltd, 2007), 124–25.

Al-Lajna al-Dā'ima, "al-Ishtighāl bil-Mūsīqā wal-ʿIlāj bihā," in Aḥmad b. ʿAbdallāh al-Shāfiʿī (ed.), *500 Jawāb fī al-Buyūʿ wal-Muʿāmalāt* (Cairo: Dār Ibn Ḥazm, 2010), 277.

Al-Lajna al-Dā'ima, "Ḥukm Luʿbat Kurat al-Qadam wa-Musābaqāt al-Mulākama wal-Muṣāraʿa al-Mawjūda al-Āna," in Aḥmad b. ʿAbdallāh al-Shāfiʿī (ed.), *500 Jawāb fī al-Buyūʿ wal-Muʿāmalāt* (Cairo: Dār Ibn Ḥazm, 2010), 222.

Al-Lajna al-Dā'ima, "Ikhtilāf al-A'imma," in *Fatāwā al-Balad al-Ḥarām* (Cairo: al-Maktaba al-Tawfīqiyya, n.d.), 943.

Al-Lajna al-Dā'ima, "Mā Ḥukm al-Safar wal-Dirāsa fī Bilād al-Kuffār" (decision 20968), in *Fatāwā al-Balad al-Ḥarām* (Cairo: al-Maktaba al-Tawfīqiyya, n.d.), 191–92.

Al-Lajna al-Dā'ima, "al-Ṣuwar lil-Ḍarūra," in *Fatāwā al-Balad al-Ḥarām* (Cairo: al-Maktaba al-Tawfīqiyya, n.d.), 707.

Al-Lajna al-Dā'ima, "Ḥukm al-Daʿwa ilā Waḥdat al-Adyān," in *Fatāwā al-Balad al-Ḥarām* (Cairo: al-Maktaba al-Tawfīqiyya, n.d.), 16–20.

Al-Madkhali, Rabee B. Haadi, *The Necessity of Conforming to the Understanding of the Salaf* (Jedda: Miraath Publications, 2012).

Al-Madkhalī, Rabī b. Hādī, *An Advice to the Salafis Living in the West*, trans. Khadīja ʿAbd al-Waḥīd bin-Ṣāliḥ (Birmingham, United Kingdom: Salafi Publications, 2012).

Al-Majlis al-'Ūrūbbī lil-Iftā' wal-Buḥūth, "al-Bayān al-Khitāmī lil-Dawra al-ʿādiyya al-Thāniyya ʿAsahara," *al-Majalla al-ʿIlmiyya lil-Majlis al-'Ūrūbbī lil-Iftā' wal-Buḥūth*, no. 4–5 (June 2004), 455–85.

Al-Majlis al-'Ūrūbbī lil-Iftā' wal-Buḥūth, "Qarḍ min al-Bank li-Binā' Markaz Islāmī," *al-'Ūrūbbīyya* 45 (May 2006), 5.

Al-Majlis al-'Ūrūbbī lil-Iftā' wal-Buḥūth, "Ḥukm al-Qurūḍ al-Ṭullābiyya fī 'ūrūbbā" (decision 18/4), published in the concluding declaration of the eighteenth session of the European Council, July 1–5, 2008, accessed July 7, 2013: http://www.e-cfr.org/ar/index.php?ArticleID=575.

Al-Majlis al-'Ūrūbbī lil-Iftā' wal-Buḥūth, "Qarār bi-Sha'n al-Muwā'ama bayna al-Taqayyud bil-Thawābit wa-bayna Muqtaḍayāt al-Muwāṭana" (decision 4/16), July 30, 2008, accessed September 5, 2013: http://www.e-cfr.org/ar/index.php?ArticleID=284.

Al-Majlis al-'Ūrūbbī lil-Iftā' wal-Buḥūth, "al-Bayān al-Khitāmī lil-Dawra al-Sābi'a 'Ashara," *al-Majalla al-'Ilmiyya lil-Majlis al-'Ūrūbbī lil-Iftā' wal-Buḥūth*, no. 12–13 (July 2008), 489–513.

Al-Majlis al-'Ūrūbbī lil-Iftā' wal-Buḥūth, "al-Muwāṭana wa-Muqtaḍayātuhā" (decision 1/17), *al-Majalla al-'Ilmiyya lil-Majlis al-'Ūrūbbī lil-Iftā' wal-Buḥūth*, no. 12–13 (July 2008), 498–99.

Al-Majlis al-'Ūrūbbī lil-Iftā' wal-Buḥūth, "Ḥawla Ikhtilāf Sā'at al-Ṣiyām fī al-Buldān dhāt Khuṭūṭ al-'Arḍ al-'āliyya," session 20, decision 7, June 28, 2010, accessed August 19, 2013: http://www.e-cfr.org/ar/index.php?ArticleID=1039.

Al-Majlis al-'Ūrūbbī lil-Iftā' wal-Buḥūth, *Qarārāt wa-Fatāwā al-Majlis al-'Ūrūbbī lil-Iftā' wal-Buḥūth—al-Majmū'atani al-'ūlā wal-Thāniyya, fatwā* 2 (Cairo: Dār al-Tawzī' wal-Nashr al-Islāmiyya, n.d).

Al-Majlis al-'Ūrūbbī lil-Iftā' wal-Buḥūth, *Qarārāt wa-Fatāwā al-Majlis min al-Dawra al-Thāmina ilā al-Khāmisa 'Ashara*, Word file from the Council's website, n.d, accessed September 13, 2010: http://www.e-cfr.org.

Al-Majma' al-Fiqhī al-Islāmī, "Mushārakat al-Muslim fī Intikhābāt ma'a Ghayr al-Muslimīn," November 8, 2007, accessed May 5, 2012: http://www.themwl.org/Fatwa/default.aspx?d=1&cidi=167&l=AR&cid=17.

Al-Manār, "Shabha wa-Jawābuhā," 1, 37 (December 3, 1898), 730–33.

Al-Manār, "al-Wifāq al-Islāmī al-Inklīzī," 5, 14 (October 18, 1902), 545–50.

Al-Manār, "Qatla Muslimī al-Rūs fī al-Ḥarb al-Yābāniyya," 10, 2 (April 13, 1907), 117–18.

Al-Manār, "Ziyārat al-Muslim li-Ghayr al-Muslimīn," 7, 1 (March 18, 1904), 26–27.

Al-Manār, "Bāb Uṣūl al-Fiqh: Adalat al-Shar' wa-Taqdīm al-Maṣlaḥa fī al-Mu'āmalāt 'alā al-Naṣṣ," 9, 10 (October 19, 1906), 745–70.

Al-Manār, "Jamā'at al-Da'wa wal-Irshād," 14, 2 (March 1, 1911), 114–20.

Al-Manār, "al-Islām fī Inkaltra," 18, 1 (February 14, 1915), 73–79.

Al-Manār, "Tajannus al-Muslim bi-Jinsiyya Tunāfī al-Islām," 25, 1 (January 1924), 21–32.

Al-Manār, "Kitāb Yusr al-Islām wa-Uṣūl al-Tashrī' al-'āmm," 29, 1 (March 22, 1928), 63–70.

Al-Munajjid, Muḥammad Ṣāliḥ, *Muḥarramāt Istahāna bihā Kathīr min al-Nās Yajibu al-Ḥadhar Minhā* (Madīna: al-Maktab al-Ta'āwunī lil-Da'wa wal-Irshād bil-Madīna al-Munawwara, 1994).

Al-Munajjid, Muḥammad Ṣāliḥ, "Giving Blood to a Kaafir Who Is Not Hostile towards Islam and Who Is Not in a State of War with Us," in Muhammad Saed Abdul-Rahman (ed.), *Islam: Questions and Answers—Alliance and Amity, Disavowal and Enmity* (London: MSA Publication Ltd, 2003), 83–84.

Al-Munajjid, Muḥammad Ṣāliḥ, "Is it Permissible for Muslims to Vote for Kaffirs Who Seem Less Evil?" in Muhammad Saed Abdul-Rahman (ed.), *Islam:*

Questions and Answers—Alliance and Amity, Disavowal and Enmity (London: MSA Publication Ltd, 2003), 138–39.

Al-Munajjid, Muḥammad Ṣāliḥ, "It Is Not Permissible for a Muslim to Fight with Kaafirs against the Muslims at All," in Muhammad Saed Abdul-Rahman (ed.), *Islam: Questions and Answers—Alliance and Amity, Disavowal and Enmity* (London: MSA Publication Ltd, 2003), 84–85.

Al-Munajjid, Muḥammad Ṣāliḥ, "Military Service in Kaafir Armies and Working as a 'Chaplain' in those Armies," in Muhammad Saed Abdul-Rahman (ed.), *Islam: Questions and Answers—Alliance and Amity, Disavowal and Enmity* (London: MSA Publication Ltd, 2003), 137–38.

Al-Munajjid, Muḥammad Ṣāliḥ, "Muslim Working in Law Enforcement in a non-Islamic Country," in Muhammad Saed Abdul-Rahman (ed.), *Islam: Questions and Answers—Alliance and Amity, Disavowal and Enmity* (London: MSA Publication Ltd, 2003), 156–57.

Al-Munajjid, Muḥammad Ṣāliḥ, "Principles and Guidelines for Muslims' Relations with Non-Muslims," in Muhammad Saed Abdul-Rahman (ed.) *Islam: Questions and Answers—Alliance and Amity, Disavowal and Enmity* (London: MSA Publication Ltd, 2003), 70–71.

Al-Munajjid, Muḥammad Ṣāliḥ, "Ruling on Loving Non-Muslims," in Muhammad Saed Abdul-Rahman (ed.), *Islam: Questions and Answers—Alliance and Amity, Disavowal and Enmity* (London: MSA Publication Ltd, 2003), 159–61.

Al-Munajjid, Muḥammad Ṣāliḥ, "Ruling on Migrating to a Muslim Country and Staying There without a Mahram," in Muhammad Saed Abdul-Rahman (ed.), *Islam: Questions and Answers—Islamic Politics* (London: MSA Publication Ltd, 2003), 18–20.

Al-Munajjid, Muḥammad Ṣāliḥ, "Detailed Discussion of bid'ah and Shirk," in Muhammad Saed Abdul-Rahman (ed.), *Islam: Questions and Answers—Basis for Jurisprudence and Islamic Rulings* (London: MSA Publication Ltd, 2007), 265–72.

Al-Munajjid, Muḥammad Ṣāliḥ, "Does Islam Regard Men and Women as Equal?" in Muhammad Saed Abdul-Rahman (ed.), *Islam: Questions and Answers—Basis for Jurisprudence and Islamic Rulings* (London: MSA Publication Ltd, 2007), 57–67.

Al-Munajjid, Muḥammad Ṣāliḥ, "There Is No Such Thing as Bid'ah Ḥasanah in Islam," in Muhammad Saed Abdul-Rahman (ed.), *Islam: Questions and Answers—Basis for Jurisprudence and Islamic Rulings* (London: MSA Publication Ltd, 2007), 357–59.

Al-Munajjid, Muḥammad Ṣāliḥ, "Collecting Donations to Give Gifts to Poor Families at Christmas," n.d., accessed July 11, 2013: http://islamqa.info/en/8375.

Al-Munajjid, Muḥammad Ṣāliḥ, "Inheritance from a Non-Muslim," n.d., accessed November 6, 2013: http://islamqa.info/en/ref/428.

Al-Munajjid, Muḥammad Ṣāliḥ, "Selling Greeting Cards for Christian Holidays," n.d., accessed July 12, 2013: http://islamqa.info/en/782.

Al-Munajjid, Muḥammad Ṣāliḥ, "Should He Go for an Interest-based Mortgage if that Is Cheaper than Renting?" n.d., accessed June 10, 2013: http://islamqa.info/en/ref/21914.

Al-Munajjid, Muḥammad Ṣāliḥ, "Taking Part in Non-Muslim Celebrations in Order to Encourage Them to Take Part in Our Celebrations," n.d., accessed July 11, 2013: http://islamqa.com/en/3325.

Al-Mushayqiḥ, Khālid b. 'Alī, "al-Ḥuṣūl 'alā Jinsiyyat Dawla Kāfira min Ajl al-'Amal," December 17, 2011, accessed September 5, 2013: http://ar.islamway.net/fatwa/36040.

Al-Najjār, 'Abd al-Majīd, "Ma'ālāt al-Af'āl wa-Athruhā fī Fiqh al-Aqalliyyāt," *al-Majalla al-'Ilmiyya lil-Majlis al-'Ūrūbbī lil-Iftā' wal-Buḥūth*, no. 4–5 (June 2004), 147–200.

Al-Najjār, 'Abd al-Majīd, *Fiqh al-Muwāṭana lil-Muslimīn fī 'Ūrūbbā* (Beirut: al-Majlis al-'Ūrūbbī lil-Iftā' wal-Buḥūth, 2009).

Al-Najjār, 'Abd al-Majīd, "al-Dawr al-Ḥaḍārī lil-Waqf al-Islāmī bil-Gharb," *al-Majalla al-'Ilmiyya lil-Majlis al-'Ūrūbbī lil-Iftā' wal-Buḥūth*, no. 18 (July 2011), 151–82.

Al-Nayfar, Muḥammad al-Shādhilī, "al-Tajannus bi-Jinsiyya Ghayr Islāmiyya," *Majallat al-Majma' al-Fiqhī al-Islāmī* 2, 4 (1989), 177–252.

Al-Qahtani, Muhammad Saeed, *al-Wala' wal-Bara' According to the 'Aqeedah of the Salaf* (London: Al-Firdous Ltd, 1993).

Al-Qaḥṭānī, Muḥammad b. Ḥusayn (ed.), *Masā'il al-A'imā' fī Nawāzil al-Mudlahimma* (Riyadh: Dār al-Awkhiyyā' lil-Ṭibā'a wal-Nashr, 2003).

Al-Qaraḍāwī, Yūsuf, *al-Ḥalāl wal-Ḥarām fī al-Islām* (Cairo: Maktabat Wahaba, 2004, first published August 1960).

Al-Qaraḍāwī, Yūsuf, *al-Ḥulūl al-Mustawrada wa-Kayfa Jannat 'alā Ummatinā* (Mu'assasāt al-Risāla, 1974).

Al-Qaraḍāwī, Yūsuf, *al-Ṣaḥwa al-Islāmiyya wa-Humūm al-Waṭan al-'Arabī wal-Islāmī* (Cairo: Dār al-Shurūq, 2006; originally published, 1988).

Al-Qaraḍāwī, Yūsuf, *Min Ajl Ṣaḥwa Rāshida* (Cairo: Dār al-Shurūq, 1988).

Al-Qaraḍāwī, Yūsuf, *Awlawiyyāt al-Ḥaraka al-Islāmiyya* (unnumbered Word file), written on April 1990, accessed September 10, 2012: http://www.torathIkhwān.com/library/92443554.doc.

Al-Qaraḍāwī, Yūsuf, *Taysīr al-Fiqh lil-Muslim al-Mu'āṣir fī Ḍaw' al-Qur'ān wal-Sunna—Fiqh al-Ṣiyyām* (Beirut: Mu'assasāt al-Risāla, 1993).

Al-Qaraḍāwī, Yūsuf, *Fī Fiqh al-Awlawiyyāt: Dirāsa Jadīda fī Ḍaw' al-Qur'ān wal-Sunna*, September 1994, accessed November 6, 2014: http://www.al-mostafa.com/.

Al-Qaraḍāwī, Yūsuf, *al-Ijtihād fī al-Sharī'a al-Islāmiyya* (Kuwait: Dār al-Qalam, 1996).

Al-Qaraḍāwī, Yūsuf, *al-Khaṣā'iṣ al-'āma lil-Islām* (Cairo: Maktabat Wahaba, August 1997).

Al-Qaraḍāwī, Yūsuf, "Fiqh al-Muwāzanāt," *al-Rā'id*, 191 (August 8–10, 1997), 25–31.

Al-Qaraḍāwī, Yūsuf, *Min Fiqh al-Dawla fī al-Islām* (Cairo and Beirut: Dār al-Shurūq, 2001, first published 1997).

Al-Qaraḍāwī, Yūsuf, *al-Mubashshirāt bi-Intiṣār al-Islām* (Beirut: Mu'assasāt al-Risāla, 2000).

Al-Qaraḍāwī, Yūsuf, *al-Siyāsa al-Shar'iyya fī Ḍaw' Nuṣūṣ al-Sharī'a wa-Maqāṣiduhā* (Beirut: Mu'assasāt al-Risāla, 2001).

Al-Qaraḍāwī, Yūsuf, *Fī Fiqh al-Aqalliyyāt al-Muslima* (Cairo: Dār al-Shurūq, 2007, first published 2001).

Al-Qaraḍāwī, Yūsuf, "Islām al-Mar'a dūn Zawjihā Hal Yufarriqu Baynahimā?" in *Fī Fiqh al-Aqalliyyāt al-Muslima* (Cairo: Dār al-Shurūq, 2007, first published 2001), 105–25.

Al-Qaraḍāwī, Yūsuf, "Shirā' Buyūt al-Suknā fī al-Gharb 'an Ṭarīq al-Bunūk" in *Fī Fiqh al-Aqalliyyāt al-Muslima* (Cairo: Dār al-Shurūq, 2007, first published 2001), 154–91.

Al-Qaraḍāwī, Yūsuf, "Tahni'at Ahl al-Kitāb bi-A'yādihim," in *Fī Fiqh al-Aqalliyyāt al-Muslima* (Cairo: Dār al-Shurūq, 2007, first published 2001), 145–50.

Al-Qaraḍāwī, Yūsuf, "Zawāj al-Muslim bi-Ghayr al-Muslima," in *Fī Fiqh al-Aqalliyyāt al-Muslima* (Cairo: Dār al-Shurūq, 2007, first published 2001), 97–104.

Al-Qaraḍāwī, Yūsuf, *al-Ṣaḥwa al-Islāmiyya min al-Murāhaqa ilā al-Rushd* (Cairo: Dār al-Shurūq, 2008, first published 2002).

Al-Qaraḍāwī, Yūsuf, "Introduction," in *Fatwās of European Council for Fatwa and Research*, trans. Anas Usāma al-Tikritī and Shākir Nāṣif al-Ubaydī (Cairo: Islamic INCO, 2002), vii–xii.

Al-Qaraḍāwī, Yūsuf, "Taqdīm," in *Qarārāt wa-Fatāwā al-Majlis al-'Ūrūbbī lil-Iftā' wal-Buḥūth*, first and second compilations (Cairo: Dār al-Tawzī' wal-Nashr al-Islāmiyya, 2002), 5–10.

Al-Qaraḍāwī, Yūsuf, *Khiṭābunā al-Islāmī fī 'Aṣr al-'Awlama* (Cairo: Dār al-Shurūq, 2009, first published 2004).

Al-Qaraḍāwī, Yūsuf, *al-Ṣaḥwa al-Islāmiyya bayna al-Jumūd wal-Taṭarruf* (Cairo: Dār al-Shurūq, 2005).

Al-Qaraḍāwī, Yūsuf, *al-Ṣaḥwa al-Islāmiyya wa-Humūm al-Waṭan al-'Arabī wal-Islāmī* (Cairo: Dār al-Shurūq, 2006).

Al-Qaraḍāwī, Yūsuf, "Duties of Muslims Living in the West," first published May 7, 2006, on Islamonline.net, accessed June 14, 2013: http://www.onislam.net/english/ask-the-scholar/dawah-principles/dawah-to-non-and-new-muslims/175226.html.

Al-Qaraḍāwī, Yūsuf, *Naḥnu wal-Gharb: As'ila Shā'ika wa-Ajwiba Ḥāsim*a (Cairo: Dār al-Tawzī' wal-Nashr al-Islāmiyya, 2006).

Al-Qaraḍāwī, Yūsuf, "Muwāṭanat al-Muslim fī Ghayr al-Mujtama' al-Islāmī," November 5, 2007, accessed September 25, 2013: http://www.qaradawi.net/articles/86-2009-12-12-10-35-10/4310-2012-01-31-013200.html.

Al-Qaraḍāwī, Yūsuf "al-Waṭan wal-Muwāṭana fī Ḍaw' al-Uṣūl al-'Aqdiyya wal-Maqāṣid al-Shar'iyya," *al-Majalla al-'Ilmiyya lil-Majlis al-'Ūrūbbī lil-Iftā' wal-Buḥūth*, no. 12–13 (July 2008), 19–98.

Al-Qaraḍāwī, Yūsuf, *Ta'rīkhuna al-Muftarā 'alayhi* (Cairo: Dār al-Shurūq, 2008).

Al-Qaraḍāwī, Yūsuf, *Fiqh al-Wasaṭiyya al-Islāmiyya wal-Tajdīd Ma'ālim wa-Manārāt* (Cairo: Dār al-Shurūq, 2010).

Al-Qaraḍāwī, Yūsuf, "Muslim Minorities and Politics," April 30, 2012, accessed June 23, 2012: http://www.onislam.net/english/shariah/contemporary-issues/critiques-and-thought/456871-muslim-minorities-and-politics.html?Thought.

Al-Qarāfī, Shihāb al-Dīn Aḥmad b. Idrīs, *al-Dhakhīra*, vol. 1 (Dār al-Gharb al-Islāmī, 1994).

Al-Rāfi'ī, Sālim b. 'Abd al-Ghānī, *Aḥkām al-Aḥwāl al-Shakhsiyya lil-Muslimīn fī al-Gharb* (Beirut: Dār Ibn Ḥazm, 2002).

Al-Sa'īd, 'Abd al-Sattār Fatḥallāh and Al-Sharīf, 'Abd al-Khāliq Ḥasan, "Can Imam Delay a Prayer for Watching a Soccer Match," June 2, 2002, accessed November 6, 2013: http://www.onislam.net/english/ask-the-scholar/acts-of-worship/prayer/congregational-prayer/175398-can-Imām-delay-a-prayer-for-watching-a-soccer-match.html.

Al-Sa'īd, Ṣalāḥ al-Dīn Maḥmūd (ed.), *Fatāwā al-'Ulamā' ḥawla al-Aqalliyyāt al-Muslima fī al-'ālam* (Alexandria: Dār al-Imān, 2004).

Al-Saqqāf, Ḥasan b. 'Ali, *al-Salafiyya al-Wahhābiyya* (Beirut: Dār al-Mīzān, 2005).

Al-Shanqīṭī, Muḥammad al-Ḥasan al-Daddū, "al-Kalām 'alā Mas'alat al-Ḥijāb fī Faransā," September 7, 2008, accessed September 28, 2013: http://ar.islamway.net/fatwa/26621.

Al-Sharīf, Ḥamza b. Ḥusayn al-Fa'r, "Ḥukm Mushārakat al-Muslimīn fī Mujtama'āt al-Aqalliyyāt Ijtimā'iyyan wa-Siyāsiyyan," *al-Majalla al-'Ilmiyya lil-Majlis al-'Ūrūbbī lil-Iftā' wal-Buḥūth*, no. 12–13 (July 2008), 273–89.

Al-Shāṭibī, Abū Isḥāq Ibrāhīm b. Mūsā b. Muḥammad, *al-Muwāfaqāt*, vol. 2 (al-Khubar, Saudi Arabia: Dār Ibn 'Affān, 1997).

Al-Shaykhī, Sālim, "al-Qurūḍ al-Ṭullābiyya fī 'Ūrūbbā," *al-Majalla al-'Ilmiyya lil-Majlis al-'Ūrūbbī lil-Iftā' wal-Buḥuth*, no. 14–15 (July 2009), 411–58.

Al-Shithrī, Ṣāliḥ b. Muḥammad, *Ḥukm al-Lujū' wal-Iqāma fī Bilād al-Kuffār* (Riyadh: Dār al-Ḥabīb, 2001).

Al-Ṭībī, 'Ukāsha 'abd al-Manān, *Fatāwā al-Shaykh al-Albānī wa-Muqāranatuhā bi-Fatāwā al-'Ulamā'* (Beirut: Dār al-Jīl, 1995).

Al-Ubaykaan, Abdul Muhsin, "7/7: A Warning against the Extremists," *The Ark* 21 (August 2007), 3.

Al-'Umrānī, Muḥammad al-Kadī, *Fiqh al-Usra al-Muslima fī al-Mahājir* (Beirut: Dār al-Kutub al-'Ilmiyya, 2001).

Al-Uthaymeen, Muhammad Ibn Saalih, "Inviting to Allah in Communities Where There Are Muslim Minorities," in Shaykh Ibn Baz and Shaykh Uthaymeen, *Muslim Minorities* (Hounslow, United Kingdom: Message of Islam, 1998), 43–59.

Al-Uthaymeen, Muhammad Ibn Saalih, "Questions and Answers," in Shaykh Ibn Baz and Shaykh Uthaymeen, *Muslim Minorities* (Hounslow, United Kingdom: Message of Islam, 1998), 60–88.

Al-'Uthaymīn, Muḥammad b. Ṣāliḥ, "Anwā' al-Shirk," in Muḥammad Muḥammad Tāmir (ed.), *Fiqh al-'Ibādāt lil-Shaykh Muḥammad b. Ṣāliḥ al-'Utahymīn* (Cairo: Dār al-Risāla, 2003), 56–57.

Al-'Uthaymīn, Muḥammad b. Ṣāliḥ, "Benefiting from What the Kaafirs Have," in Muhammad Saed Abdul-Rahman (ed.), *Islam: Questions and Answers—Alliance and Amity, Disavowal and Enmity* (London: MSA Publication Ltd, 2003), 38–40.

Al-'Uthaymīn, Muḥammad b. Ṣāliḥ, "Doesn't the Hadeeth 'Do Not Initiate the Greeting with a Jew or a Christian' Put People off Islam?" in Muhammad Saed Abdul-Rahman (ed.), *Islam: Questions and Answers—Alliance and Amity, Disavowal and Enmity* (London: MSA Publication Ltd, 2003), 32–33.

Al-'Uthaymīn, Muḥammad b. Ṣāliḥ, "Don't be Such a Fanatic!" in Muhammad Saed Abdul-Rahman (ed.), *Islam: Questions and Answers—Islamic Politics* (London: MSA Publication Ltd, 2003), 3.

Al-'Uthaymīn, Muḥammad b. Ṣāliḥ, "Ṭūl al-Layl wal-Nahār," in Muḥammad Muḥammad Tāmir (ed.), *Fiqh al-'Ibādāt lil-Shaykh Muḥammad b. Ṣāliḥ al-'Utahymīn* (Cairo: Dār al-Risāla, 2003), 223–24.

Al-'Uthaymīn, Muḥammad b. Ṣāliḥ, "al-Ikhtilāṭ fī al-Ta'līm wal-'Amal," in Ṣalāḥ al-Dīn Maḥmūd al-Sa'īd (ed.), *Fatāwā al-'Ulamā' ḥawla al-Aqalliyyāt al-Muslima fī al-'ālam* (Alexandria: Dār al-'Īmān, 2004), 281.

Al-'Uthaymīn, Muḥammad b. Ṣāliḥ. "Turīdu al-Islām wa-lā Turīdu Tark Zawjahā al-Kāfir," in Ṣalāḥ al-Dīn Maḥmūd al-Sa'īd (ed.), *Fatāwā al-'Ulamā' ḥawla al-Aqalliyyāt al-Muslima fī al-'ālam* (Alexandria: Dār al-'Īmān, 2004), 297–99.

Al-'Uthaymīn, Muḥammad b. Ṣāliḥ, "Idhā Aslamat al-Zawja wa-Jawzuhā lam Yaslam," in Ṣalāḥ al-Dīn Maḥmūd al-Sa'īd (ed.), *Fatāwā al-'Ulamā' ḥawla al-Aqalliyyāt al-Muslima fī al-'ālam* (Alexandria: Dār al-'Īmān, 2008), 278–80.

Al-'Uthaymīn, Muhammad b. Ṣāliḥ, "Can She Attend Christmas Celebrations in Order to Greet her Relatives?" n.d., accessed July 11, 2013: http://islamqa.com/en/11650.

Al-'Uthaymīn, Muḥammad b. Ṣāliḥ, "Ruling on Celebrating non-Muslim Holidays and Congratulating Them," n.d., accessed July 12, 2013: http://islamqa.info/en/947.

Al-'Uthaymīn, Muḥammad b. Ṣāliḥ, "Ruling on Women Going to Women's Clubs," n.d., accessed November 6, 2013: http://www.islam-qa.com/en/ref/9460.

Ar-Rayyis, 'Abdul-Aziz, *The Beautiful Advice to the Noble Salafis of the West,* trans. 'Abd al-Ḥaqq Al-Ashantī (London: Jamiah Media, 2010).

As-Sihaymī, AbdusSalām, *To Be a Serious Salafī* (London: Jamiah Media, 2011).

As-Sirat Berlin, "Darf man den Kuffar zu ihren Festtagen gratulieren?" December 29, 2012, accessed August 19, 2013: http://www.youtube.com/watch?v=r2gLGyXFlFs&feature=share&list=PLE2E53D6C93165C2E.

Associated Press, "Players Allowed to Break Ramadan Fast," July 28, 2010, accessed August 1, 2013: http://espn.go.com/sports/soccer/news/_/id/5417146/muslim-soccer-players-.

Aumüller, Johannes, "Fußball im Fastenmonat," October 16, 2009, accessed August 27, 2013: http://www.zeit.de/online/2007/37/ramadan-fussball.

Badawī, Jamāl, "Our Kids & Non-Islamic Feasts" (Live Dialogue with a Jurist in IslamOnline.net), December 24, 2003, accessed July 11, 2013: http://mcadams.posc.mu.edu/blog/moslems_christmas.htm.

Badawī, Jamāl, "'Alāqat al-Muslim bi-Ghayr al-Muslim: Naẓarāt fī Kitāb Allāh Ta'ālā," *al-Majalla al-'Ilmiyya lil-Majlis al-'Ūrūbbī lil-Iftā' wal-Buḥūth*, no. 6 (January 2005), 71.

BarclayAvenue, "Islam in Australia: Voting Is Commiting Polytheism Says Sheik Feiz Mohammed," June 16, 2011, accessed September 16, 2013: http://www.youtube.com/watch?v=Qfxs5qrn6wY&feature=related.

Bild, "Urteile in Namen des Volkes? Oder in Namen des Korans?" (March 22, 2007), 2.

European Council for Fatwa and Research, *Fatwās of European Council for Fatwa and Research*, trans. Anas Usāma al-Tikritī and Shākir Nāṣif al-Ubaydī (Cairo: Islamic INC, 2002).

European Council for Fatwa and Research, "Ruling on Offering Congratulations to Non-Muslims on their Festive Occasions (decision 3/6)," in *Fatwās of European Council for Fatwa and Research*, trans. Anas Usāma al-Tikritī and Shākir Nāṣif al-Ubaydī (Cairo: Islamic INC, 2002), 177–84.

European Council for Fatwa and Research, "The Ruling on a Muslim Inheriting his non-Muslim Relatives (resolution 1/5)," in *Fatwās of European Council for Fatwa and Research*, trans. Anas Usāma al-Tikritī and Shākir Nāṣif al-Ubaydī (Cairo: Islamic INC, 2002), 148–49.

European Council for Fatwa and Research, "Participating in the Funeral of a Muslim Parent," April 1, 2003, accessed April 1, 2009: http://www.islamonline.net/servlet/Satellite?cid=1119503544150&pagename=IslamOnline-English-Ask_Scholar%2FFatwaE%2FFatwaEAskTheScholar.

European Council for Fatwa and Research, "France: Hijab under Attack," originally posted December 13, 2003, accessed September 25, 2013: http://www.onislam.net/english/ask-the-scholar/morals-and-manners/dress-and-adornment/169674.html.

European Council for Fatwa and Research, "Getting a Mortgage to Build a House," June 25, 2007, accessed July 7, 2013: http://www.onislam.net/english/ask-the-scholar/morals-and-=manners/173265.html?Manners.

European Council for Fatwa and Research, "Congratulating Non-Muslims on their Festive Occasions," May 2, 2013, accessed July 11, 2013: http://www.onislam.net/english/ask-the-scholar/dawah-principles/dawah-to-non-and-new-muslims/169282-congratulating-non-muslims-on-their-festive-occasions.html?New_Muslims=.

Faraj, Maḥmūd, "al-Qaraḍāwī fī Riwāq al-Ghazālī: al-Islām Dīn al-Taqaddum al-'Ilmī wal-Ḥaḍārī, Niẓāmunā al-Ta'līmī lā Yu'ṭī al-Furṣa li-Takhrīj al-Nawābigh wal-Mubtakirīn," *al-Wafd* (September 13, 1996), 9.

Fatāwā al-Lajna al-Dā'ima, "What Is the Ruling on Buying from the *Kuffar* When There Are Muslims around?" in Muhammad Saed Abdul-Rahman (ed.), *Islam: Questions and Answers—Alliance and Amity, Disavowal and Enmity* (London: MSA Publication Ltd, 2003), 59–60.

Federation of Islamic Organizations in Europe, "European Muslim Charter" (a pamphlet), January 2008.

Group of Muftis, "Ulama's Fatwas on American Muslim Participating in US Military Campaign," *IslamOnline.net*, October 16, 2001, accessed September 12, 2013: http://www.onislam.net/english/ask-the-scholar/international-relations-and-jihad/relations-during-war/175001.html.

Group of Muftis, "Student Loans with an Interest Rate Linked to Inflation," September 18, 2002, accessed July 6, 2013: http://www.onislam.net/english/ask-the-scholar/financial-issues/usury/174613.html.

Group of Muftis, "Participation of Muslim Soldiers in US & its Allies Armies in War on Iraq," March 20, 2003, accessed September 1, 2009: http://www.islamonline.net/servlet/Satellite?pagename=IslamOnline-English-Ask_Scholar/FatwaE/FatwaE&cid=1119503546682.

Group of Muftis, "War on Iraq: New Crusade or Imperialism?" March 26, 2003, accessed September 1, 2009: http://www.islamonline.net/servlet/Satellite?pagename=IslamOnline-English-.

Group of Muftis, "Hijab in France: Suggested Courses of Action," February 9, 2004, accessed September 25, 2013: http://www.onislam.net/english/ask-the-scholar/dawah-principles/dawah-to-non-and-new-muslims/169899.html?New_Muslims=.

Ḥalāwa, Ḥusayn, "About the European Council for Fatwa and Research," in *Fatwās of European Council for Fatwa and Research,* trans. Anas Usāma al-Tikritī and Shākir Nāṣif al-Ubaydī (Cairo: Islamic INC, 2002), 1–7.

Ḥalāwa, Ḥusayn, "Ta'rīf al-Majlis al-'Ūrūbbī lil-Iftā' wal-Buḥūth," in *Qarārāt wa-Fatāwā al-Majlis al-'Ūrūbbī lil-Iftā' wal-Buḥūth*, first and second compilations (Cairo: Dār al-Tawzī' wal-Nashr al-Islāmiyya, 2002), 11–16.

Ḥalāwa, Ḥusayn, "Qawā'id al-Indimāj al-'Ījābī lil-Muslimīn fī 'Ūrūbbā," *al-Majalla al-'Ilmiyya lil-Majlis al-'Ūrūbbī lil-Iftā' wal-Buḥūth*, no. 12–13 (July 2008), 291–340.

Ḥasana, 'Umar 'Ubayd, "Taqdīm," in Khālid Muḥammad 'Abd al-Qādir, *Min Fiqh al-Aqalliyyāt al-Muslima* (Doha: The Ministry for Endowments and Religious Affairs, January 1998), 9–38.

Hay'at Kibār al-'Ulamā', "Ṣiyām Man Yaṭālu Nahāruhum" (decision 61, 22 March 1978), *al-Mujtama'* 1769 (10 September 2007), 38.

Ḥaydar, Khalīl 'Alī, *I'tidāl am Taṭarruf? Ta'amulāt Naqdiyya fī al-Tayyār al-Wasaṭiyya al-Islāmiyya* (Kuwait: Qurtas-Publishing, 1998).

Hizb ut-Tahrir Britain, "The Future for Muslims in Britain," January 22, 2011, accessed September 18, 2013: http://www.hizb.org.uk/solutions/report-the-future-for-muslims-in-britain.

Ḥusayn, 'ādil, "Faqīh al-Wasaṭiyya al-Islāmiyya fī 'Aṣrinā," in *Yūsuf al-Qaraḍāwī: Kalimāt fī Takrīmihi wa-Buḥūth fī Fikrihi wa-Fiqhihi* (Cairo: Dār al-Salām, 2004), 376–88.

Huwaydī, Fahmī, "Risāla fī Taḥrīr al-Mar'a," *Al-Ahrām* (May 14, 1991), 7.

Huwaydī, Fahmī, *al-Islām wal-Dimūqrāṭiyya* (Cairo: Markaz al-Ahrām lil-Tarjama wal-Nashr, 1993).

Huwaydī, Fahmī, *al-Qur'ān wal-Sulṭān* (Cairo: Dār al-Shurūq, fourth printing, 1999).

Ibn 'Abd al-Khāliq, 'Abd al-Raḥman, *al-Walā' wal-Barā'* (September 1986), accessed November 6, 2013: http://www.al-mostafa.com/.

Ibn 'Abd al-Wahhāb, Muḥammad, *Kitāb al-Tawḥīd* (Riyadh: Imām Muḥammad b. Sa'ūd University, n.d.).

Ibn 'Abdul Wahhab, Muhammad, *The Best Religion for Mankind*, Explained by Saalih Ibn Fawzaan Ibn 'Abdullah Al-Fawzaan (New York: Daarul Isnaad, May 2010).

Ibn Ādam, Abū al-Ḥasan Mālik (ed.), *The Crime of Hizbiyyah against the salafi Da'wah* (Grand Rapids, MI: Sunnah Publishing, 2009).

Ibn 'Atīq, Ḥamad b. 'Alī, *Sabīl al-Najā' wal-Fikāk min Muwālāt al-Murtaddīn wal-Atrāk*, n.d., accessed 10 September 2012: www.tawhed.sw.

Ibn Baaz, 'Abdul 'Azeez, "The Importance of Muslim Minorities Adhering to Islaam," in Shaykh Ibn Baz and Shakyh Uthaymeen, *Muslim Minorities* (Hounslow, United Kingdom: Message of Islam, 1998), 4–21.

Ibn Baaz, 'Abdul 'Azeez Ibn 'Abdullah, *Words of Advice Regarding Da'wah* (Birmingham: al-Hidaayah Publishing and Distribution, 1998).

Ibn Baaz, 'Abdul 'Azeez Ibn 'Abdullah, *The Legislation of Islam*, trans. Abū Sumayya 'Aqīl Walker (Grand Prairie, Canada: Ibnul Qayyim Publications, 2006).

Ibn Bayyah, 'Abdallāh, "Muslims Living in Non-Muslim Lands," July 31, 1999, accessed November 2, 2013: www.themodernreligion.com/world/muslims-living.html.

Ibn Bayyah, 'Abdallāh, "al-Farq bayna al-Ḍarūra wal-Ḥāja Taṭbīqan 'alā ba'ḍ Aḥwāl al-Aqalliyyāt al-Muslima," *al-Majalla al-'Ilmiyya lil-Majlis al-'ūrūbbī lil-Iftā' wal-Buḥūth*, no. 4–5 (June 2004), 93–145.

Ibn Bayyah, 'Abdallāh, "al-Walā' bayna al-Dīn wal-Muwāṭana," *al-Majalla al-'Ilmiyya lil-Majlis al-'Ūrūbbī lil-Iftā' wal-Buḥūth*, no. 12–13 (July 2008), 99–113.

Ibn Bāz, 'Abd al-'Azīz b. 'Abdallāh, "Jawāz al-Hudna ma'a al-A'dā' Muṭlaqa wa-Mu'aqqita Idhā Ra'ā Walī al-Amr al-Maṣlaḥa fī Dhalika," first published in *al-Muslimūn* 516 (December 24, 1994), accessed November 6, 2013: http://www.binbaz.org.sa/mat/1943.

Ibn Bāz, 'Abd al-'Azīz b. 'Abdallāh, "al-Sulḥ ma'a al-Yahūd aw Ghayrihim min al-Kafara Lā Yalzam minhu Mawaddatahum aw Muwālātahum," first published by *al-Muslimūn* 520 (January 21, 1995), accessed October 1, 2013: http://www.binbaz.org.sa/mat/1948.

Ibn Bāz, 'Abd al-'Azīz b. 'Abdallāh, "Mā Taqtaḍīhi al-Maṣlaḥa Ya'mal bihi min al-Ṣulḥ wa-'Adamihi," first published in *al-Muslimūn*, 520 (January 21, 1995), accessed November 6, 2013: http://www.binbaz.org.sa/mat/1950.

Ibn Bāz, 'Abd al-'Azīz b. 'Abdallāh, "Ruling Concerning Listening to Radio Programs that Contain Music," in Muhammad bin Abdul-Aziz Al-Musnad (ed.), *Islamic Fatawa Regarding Women* (Riyadh: Darussalam Pubslihers & Distributers, 1996), 324–25.

Ibn Bāz, 'Abd al-'Azīz b. 'Abdallāh, *The Correct Belief and its Opposite and What Negates Al-Islam*, trans. Muḥammad 'Abd al-Raḥman Abū Ḥamza Maghribī (London: al-Firdous, 1996).

Ibn Bāz, 'Abd al-'Azīz b. 'Abdallāh, "Is It Permissible to Rebel against the Ruler," in Muhammad Saed Abdul-Rahman (ed.), *Islam: Questions and Answers—Islamic Politics* (London: MSA Publication Ltd, 2003), 89–90.

Ibn Bāz, 'Abd al-'Azīz b. 'Abdallāh, "Muslim and non-Muslim Woman Visiting One Another," in Muhammad Saed Abdul-Rahman (ed.), *Islam: Questions and Answers—Alliance and Amity, Disavowal and Enmity* (London: MSA Publication Ltd, 2003), 43–44.

Ibn Bāz, 'Abd al-'Azīz b. 'Abdallāh, "Ṣiyām Man Yaṭālu Nahāruhum Jidan wa-Kadhā Man Yaqṣuru Nahāruhum," in Ṣalāḥ al-Dīn Maḥmūd al-Sa'īd (ed.), *Fatāwā al-'Ulamā' ḥawla al-Aqalliyyāt al-Muslima fī al-'ālam* (Alexandria: Dār al-'Īmān, 2004), 95–100.

Ibn Bāz, 'Abd al-'Azīz b. 'Abdallāh, Al-Fawzān, Ṣāliḥ and the Permanent Committee, "Qiyādat al-Mar'a lil-Sayyāra," in *Fatāwā al-Mar'a al-Muslima* (Cairo: Dār Ibn Ḥazm, 2007), 528–30.

Ibn Bāz, 'Abd al-'Azīz b. 'Abdallāh, "There Are No Trivial Issues in Islam," in Muhammad Saed Abdul-Rahman (ed.), *Islam: Questions and Answer—Basis for Jurisprudence and Islamic Rulings* (London: MSA Publication Ltd, 2007), 194–96.

Ibn Bāz, 'Abdul-'Azīz b. 'Abdallāh, *The Correct Islamic Aqīdah and That Which Opposes It* (Birmingham: Daar us-Sunnah Publishers, 2008).

Ibn Bāz, 'Abd al-'Azīz b. 'Abdallāh, "Ḥukm Muṣāḥabat al-Kāfir," in Aḥmad b. 'Abdallāh al-Shāfi'ī (ed.), *500 Jawāb fī al-Buyū' wal-Mu'āmalāt* (Cairo: Dār Ibn Ḥazm, 2010), 241.

Ibn Bāz, 'Abd al-'Azīz b. 'Abdallāh, "al-Safar Khārij al-Bilād al-Islāmiyya," in *Fatāwā al-Balad al-Ḥarām* (Cairo: al-Maktaba al-Tawfīqiyya, n.d.), 187–88.

Ibn Bāz, 'Abd al-'Azīz b. 'Abdallāh, "al-walā' wal-barā' wa-Aḥkām al-Kuffār," in *Fatāwā al-Balad al-Ḥarām* (Cairo: Dār al-Tawfīqiyya, n.d.), 174–75.

Ibn Bāz, 'Abd al-'Azīz b. 'Abdallāh, "Ḥukm al-Tashkīk bi-Sha'n al-Isti'āna bi-Ghayr al-Muslimīn fī Qitāl Ṭāghiyat al-'Irāq," n.d., accessed November 6, 2013: http://www.binbaz.org.sa/mat/254.

Ibn Bāz, 'Abd al-'Azīz b. 'Abdallāh, "It Is Not Permissible to Reside at a Country Where Disbelief Is Prevalent Except for the Call of Allah," n.d., accessed September 25, 2011: http://www.alifta.org/Fatāwā/Fatāwācoeval.aspx?View=Page&HajjEntryID=0&HajjEntryName=&NodeID=4656&PageID=1327&SectionID=14&SubjectPageTitlesID=98552&MarkIndex=5&0.

Ibn Bāz, 'Abd al-'Azīz b. 'Abdallāh, "Mā Ḥukm al-Iḥtifāl bi-'Īd al-Mīlād," in *Fatāwā al-Balad al-Ḥarām* (Cairo: Matktabat al-Tawfīqiyya, n.d), 1031–32.

Ibn Bāz, 'Abd al-'Azīz b. 'Abdallāh, "Mawqif al-Muslim min al-Khilāfāt al-Madhhabiyya al-Muntashira," in *Fatāwā al-Balad al-Ḥarām* (Cairo: al-Maktaba al-Tawfīqiyya, n.d.), 941.

Ibn Jibrīn, 'Abdallāh, "Ruling on Obtaining Nationality of a Kaafir State," in Muhammad Saed Abdul-Rahman (ed.), *Islam: Questions and Answers—Alliance and Amity, Disavowal and Enmity* (London: MSA Publication Ltd, 2003), 105.

Ibn Jibrīn, 'Abdallāh, "Advise to Those Who Do Not Recognize the Salafī Scholars and Call Them Wahhābis," in Muhammad Saed Abdul-Rahman (ed.), *Islam:*

Questions and Answers—Inviting Others to Islam (London: MSA Publication Ltd, 2007), 200–202.

Ibn Jibrīn, 'Abdallāh, "Ḥukm al-Ḥuṣūl 'alā al-Jinsiyya al-Kāfira," in *Fatāwā al-Balad al-Ḥarām* (Cairo: al-Maktaba al-Tawfīqiyya, n.d.), 193.

Ibn Sabīl, Muḥammad b. 'Abdallāh, "Ḥukm al-Tajannus bi-Jinsiyyat Dawla Ghayr Islāmiyya," issued in 1996, accessed September 5, 2013: http://www.dorar.net/book_end/3384.

Ibn Taymiyya, Takī al-Dīn Aḥmad, *al-Siyāsa al-Shar'iyya fī Iṣlaḥ al-Ra'ī wal-Ra'iyya* (Dār al-Kitāb al-'Arabī bi-Miṣr, 1969).

Ibn Taymiyya, Takī al-Dīn Aḥmad, *al-Ṣirāṭ al-Mustaqīm* (Cairo: Dār al-Futūḥ al-Islāmiyya, 1995).

Ibn Taymiyya, Takī al-Dīn Aḥmad, *The Friends of Allah & The Friends of Shaytan*, trans. Abū Rumaysah (Birmingham: Daar us-Sunnah Publishers, 2005).

Ibn Taymiyya, Takī al-Dīn Aḥmad, "al-'Aqīda al-Wasaṭiyya" (text in Arabic, included in *The Creed of al-Wasaṭiyyah*, trans. Abū Rumaysah, Birmingham: Dār al-Sunnah Publishers, 2009).

Ibn 'Uthaymīn, Muḥammad b. Ṣāliḥ, "Ḥukm Ziyārat al-Naṣrānī," in Aḥmad b. 'Abbās al-Shāfi'ī (ed.), *500 Jawāb fī al-Buyū' wal-Mu'āmalāt* (Cairo: Dār Ibn Ḥazm, 2010), 238.

Ibn 'Uthaymīn, Muḥammad b. Ṣāliḥ, "al-'Amal fī al-Bunūk al-Ribāwiyya wa-Mu'āmalatihā," in *Fatāwā al-Balad al-Ḥarām* (Cairo: Dār al-Tawfīqiyya, n.d), 488.

Ibn 'Uthaymīn, Muḥammad b. Ṣāliḥ, "al-Ḍābiṭ fī Mas'alat al-Tashābuh bil-Kuffār," in *Fatāwā al-Balad al-Ḥarām* (Cairo: al-Maktaba al-Tawfīqiyya, n.d.), 182.

Ibn 'Uthaymīn, Muḥammad b. Ṣāliḥ, "al-Iqāma fī Bilād al-Kuffār," in *Fatāwā al-Balad al-Ḥarām* (Cairo: al-Maktaba al-Tawfīqiyya, n.d.), 189–91.

Ibn 'Uthaymīn, Muḥammad b. Ṣāliḥ, "Ḥukm Man Yadda'ā Anna Sabab Takhalluf al-Muslimīn Huwa Tamassukuhum bi-Dīnhim," in *Fatāwā al-Balad al-Ḥarām* (Cairo: al-Maktaba al-Tawfīqiyya, n.d.), 1069–71.

Ibn 'Uthaymīn, Muḥammad b. Ṣāliḥ, "Ḥukm Qawl Akhī aw Ṣadīqī aw al-Ḍaḥk li-Ghayr al-Muslimīn li-Ṭalb al-Mawadda," in *Fatāwā al-Balad al-Ḥarām* (Cairo: al-Maktaba al-Tawfīqiyya, n.d.), 186.

Ibn 'Uthaymīn, Muḥammad b. Ṣaliḥ, "Ḥukm Tā'at al-Ḥākim alladhī Lā yaḥkumu bi-kitāb Allāh wa-Sunnat Rasūlihi," in *Fatāwā al-Balad al-Ḥarām* (Cairo: al-Maktaba al-Tawfīqiyya, n.d.), 172–73.

Ibn 'Uthaymīn, Muḥammad b. Ṣāliḥ, "Mā Huwa al-Wasaṭ fī al-Dīn?" in *Fatāwā al-Balad al-Ḥarām* (Cairo: al-Maktaba al-Tawfīqiyya, n.d.), 1051–52.

Ibn 'Uthaymīn, Muḥammad b. Ṣāliḥ, "Mā Ma'nā al-Bid'a wa-mā Ḍabiṭuhā," in *Fatāwā al-Balad al-Ḥarām* (Cairo: al-Maktaba al-Tawfīqiyya, n.d.), 1024–25.

Ibn 'Uthaymīn, Muḥammad b. Ṣāliḥ, "al-Safar ilā Bilād al-Kuffār," in *Fatāwā al-Balad al-Ḥarām* (Cairo: al-Maktaba al-Tawfīqiyya, n.d.), 189.

Ibn 'Uthaymīn, Muḥammad b. Ṣāliḥ, "al-Tahni'a bi-'īd al-Krīsmās," in *Fatāwā al-Balad al-Ḥarām* (Cairo: al-Maktaba al-Tawfīqiyya, n.d.), 183–85.

Ibn 'Uthaymīn, Muḥammad b. Ṣāliḥ, "Tahni'at al-Kāfir," in *Fatāwā al-Balad al-Ḥarām* (Cairo: al-Maktaba al-Tawfīqiyya, n.d.), 185.

Ibn 'Uthaymīn, Muḥammad b. Ṣāliḥ, "Ta'thīr al-Zamān 'alā al-Fatāwā," in *Fatāwā al-Balad al-Ḥarām* (Cairo: al-Maktaba al-Tawfīqiyya, n.d.), 937.

Ibn 'Uthaymīn, Muḥammad b. Ṣāliḥ, "Tawḍīḥ al-Walā' wal-Barā'," in *Fatāwā al-Balad al-Ḥarām* (Cairo: al-Maktaba al-Tawfīqiyya, n.d.), 175–76.

Idrees, 'Abdul-Fattah and 'Isa, 'Isa Zaki: "Watching Sport Competitions," June 4, 2006, accessed October 1, 2013: http://www.onislam.net/english/ask-the-scholar/sports-and-games/172794.html?Games.

Imām, Imām Muḥammad, "*Fatwā* Tujīzu Shirā' al-Manāzil bi-Qarḍ Ribāwī lil-Muslimīn fī Ghayr Bilād al-Islām," *al-Sharq al-Awsaṭ* (November 3, 1999), 25.

Imām, Imām Muḥammad, "al-Ḥukm al-Shar'ī fī Mushārakat al-Muslimīn fī-al-Ḥayāt al-Siyāsiyya al-Amrīkiyya," *al-Sharq al-Awsaṭ* (November 13, 1999), 26.

'Imāra, Muḥammad, *al-A'māl al-Kāmila lil-Imām Muḥammad 'Abduh* (Beirut: al-Mu'assasa al-'Arabiyya lil-Dirāsāt wal-Nashr, 1972).

'Imāra, Muḥammad, *al-Ghazw al-Thaqāfī Wahm am Ḥaqīqa?* (Beirut and Cairo: Dār al-Shurūq, 1997, first printed 1989).

'Imāra, Muḥammad, *al-Islām wa-Ḥuqūq al-Insān Ḍarūrāt Lā Ḥuqūq* (Damascus, Cairo: Markaz al-Rāya, Dār al-Islām, 2004–5).

'Imāra, Muḥammad, *al-Istiqlāl al-Ḥaḍārī* (6th October City: Nahḍat Miṣr lil-Ṭibā'a wal-Nashr wal-Tawzī', 2007).

International Union of Muslim Scholars Project, "About Us," n.d., accessed September 10, 2012: http://www.iumsonline.net/en/default.asp?MenuID=41.

Islam Question and Answer, "Being Friends with Christians and Gays," in Muhammad Saed Abdul-Rahman (ed.), *Islam: Questions and Answers—Alliance and Amity, Disavowal and Enmity* (London: MSA Publication Ltd, 2003), 57–59.

Islam Question and Answer, "Being Friends with non-Muslims," in Muhammad Saed Abdul-Rahman (ed.), *Islam: Questions and Answers—Alliance and Amity, Disavowal and Enmity* (London: MSA Publication Ltd, 2003), 45–55.

Islam Question and Answer, "Is it Permissible in Islamic Sharee'ah for a Woman to Be a Ruler?" in Muhammad Saed Abdul-Rahman (ed.), *Islam: Questions and Answers—Islamic Politics* (London: MSA Publication Ltd, 2003), 12–18.

Islam Question and Answer, "Making Friends with a Kaafir Woman," in Muhammad Saed Abdul-Rahman (ed.), *Islam: Questions and Answers—Alliance and Amity, Disavowal and Enmity* (London: MSA Publication Ltd, 2003), 63–66.

Islam Question and Answer, "Ruling on Joining in the Kaafir Festivals," in Muhammad Saed Abdul-Rahman (ed.), *Islam: Questions and Answers—Alliance and Amity, Disavowal and Enmity* (London: MSA Publication Ltd, 2003), 80–81.

Islam Question and Answer, "What Is the True Meaning of Shirk and What Are its Types?" in Muhammad Saed Abdul-Rahman (ed.), *Islam: Questions and*

Answers—Polytheism and its Different Forms (London: MSA Publication Ltd, 2003), 22–32.

Islam Question and Answer, "Does the Ruling on Driving a Car Vary from One Country to Another?" in Muhammad Saed Abdul-Rahman (ed.), *Islam: Questions and Answers—Basis for Jurisprudence and Islamic Rulings* (London: MSA Publication Ltd, 2007), 3–13.

Islam Question and Answer, "Accepting a Gift from a Kaafir on the Day of his Festival," n.d., accessed July 11, 2013: http://islamqa.info/en/85108.

Islam Question and Answer, "Bodybuilding," n.d., accessed November 10, 2013: http://islamqa.info/en/ref/40527.

Islam Question and Answer, "Buying a Flat by Installments When There Is a Clause in the Contract that Stipulates a Penalty in the Event of Late Payment," n.d., accessed April 1, 2010: http://www.islam-qa.com/en/cat/76.

Islam Question and Answer, "Farewell Parties for Kaafirs," n.d., accessed July 12, 2013: http://islamqa.info/en/ref/32560.

Islam Question and Answer, "He Took a Loan with Riba to Buy a House under Pressure from his Father," n.d., accessed July 7, 2013: http://islamqa.info/en/ref/95005.

Islam Question and Answer, "He Works as a Bus Driver, Is It Permissible for Him Not to Fast?" n.d., accessed August 28, 2013: http://www.islam-qa.com/en/141036.

Islam Question and Answer, "His Company Gives its Employees a Christmas Bonus," n.d., accessed July 11, 2013: http://islamqa.info/en/ref/146328.

Islam Question and Answer, "His Mother Will Be Angry if He Does Not Celebrate Mother's Day," n.d., accessed September 25, 2013: http://www.islam-qa.com/en/59905.

Islam Question and Answer, "Ḥukm al-Qurūḍ allatī Tumnaḥu li-Ajl al-Dirāsa," n.d., accessed July 7, 2013: http://islamqa.info/ar/ref/181723.

Islam Question and Answer, "Is It Haram to Pay Interest Based on Inflation," n.d., accessed July 7, 2013: http://islamqa.info/en/ref/12541.

Islam Question and Answer, "Muslim Forbidding his Non-Muslim Wife to Celebrate her Religious Festivals," n.d., accessed April 1, 2009: http://islamqa.com/en/cat/2021#3019.

Islam Question and Answer, "Paying Interest because of Inflation Is Riba," n.d., accessed July 7, 2013: http://islamqa.info/en/ref/23388.

Islam Question and Answer, "Ruling on Buying a House with Riba in a Kafir Country," n.d., accessed June 30, 2013: http://www.islamqa.com/en/ref/101080/mortgages.

Islam Question and Answer, "Ruling on Dealing with Mortgages in a Non-Muslim Country," n.d., accessed July 7, 2013: http://islamqa.info/en/ref/159213.

Islam Question and Answer, "Ruling on Democracy and Elections and Participation in that System" (based on *fatwā*s by al-'Uthaymīn and the Saudi Standing Committee for Academic Studies and Issuing *fatwā*s), n.d., accessed November 6, 2013: http://islamqa.info/en/ref/107166.

Islam Question and Answer, "Ruling on Helping the Kuffar against the Muslims," n.d., accessed September 1, 2009: http://islam-qa.com/en/ref/33691/army.

Islam Question and Answer, "Ruling on Subscribing to Sports Channels," n.d., accessed November 6, 2013: http://islamqa.info/en/ref/82718.

Islam Question and Answer, "Should He Take a Riba-based Loan if He Does Not Intend to Pay the Interest," n.d., accessed July 7, 2013: http://islamqa.info/en/ref/87542.

Islamic Cultural Centre of Ireland, "Does Islam Oppress Women" (leaflet).

Islamweb.net, "Buying a House with a Bank Loan," January 30, 2000, accessed July 7, 2013: http://www.islamweb.net/emainpage/index.php?page=showfatwa&Option=FatwaId&Id=82102.

Islamweb.net, "Becoming a Citizen of Australia," January 23, 2001, accessed September 2, 2013: http://www.islamweb.net/emainpage/index.php?page=showfatwa&Option=FatwaId&lang=E&Id=82552.

Islamweb.net, "Bank Loan to Buy a House," July 14, 2002, accessed April 1, 2010: http://www.islamweb.net/emainpage/index.php?page=showfatwa&Option=FatwaId&Id=84495.

Islamweb.net, "Muslim Wants to Take Job with French Police," April 6, 2003, accessed September 16, 2013: http://www.islamweb.net/emainpage/index.php?page=showfatwa&Option=FatwaId&Id=85727.

Islamweb.net, "Oath of Allegiance in the UK," 23 February 2004, accessed September 2, 2013: http://www.islamweb.net/emainpage/index.php?page=showfatwa&Option=FatwaId&lang=E&Id=87140.

Islamweb.net, "Services Cooling Systems for Beer, Wine and Gays," April 10, 2004, accessed August 27, 2013: http://www.islamweb.net/emainpage/index.php?page=showfatwa&Option=FatwaId&Id=87412.

Islamweb.net, "Taking a Riba Loan or Taking Military Contract to Finance Medical School Costs," May 10, 2004, accessed September 15, 2013: http://www.islamweb.net/emainpage/index.php?page=showfatwa&Option=FatwaId&Id=87679.

Islamweb.net, "Ḥukm Khalʿ al-Mar'a al-Ḥijāb fī Bilād al-Gharb," June 5, 2004, accessed September 21, 2013: http://fatwa.islamweb.net/fatwa/index.php?page=showfatwa&Option=FatwaId&lang=A&Id=49545.

Islamweb.net, "Attending Funeral of Christian Parent," October 21, 2004, accessed July 12, 2013: http://www.islamweb.net/emainpage/index.php?page=showfatwa&Option=FatwaId&Id=88797.

Islamweb.net, "Voting within the European Union," June 9, 2005, accessed September 16, 2013: http://www.islamweb.net/emainpage/index.php?page=showfatwa&Option=FatwaId&Id=90148.

Islamweb.net, "Joining Political Parties in Non-Muslim Countries," January 14, 2006, accessed September 17, 2013: http://www.islamweb.net/emainpage/index.php?page=showfatwa&Option=FatwaId&Id=91038.

Islamweb.net, "Reluctant to Live in an Apartment her Husband Bought with Riba," June 23, 2009, accessed July 13, 2013: http://www.islamweb.net/emainpage/index.php?page=showfatwa&Option=FatwaId&Id=124015.

Islamweb.net, "Laʿb Kurat al-Qadam Hal Yuʿtabaru ʿUdhran Yubīḥu al-Fiṭr," October 18, 2009, accessed August 28, 2013: http://fatwa.islamweb.net/fatwa/index.php?page=showfatwa&Option=FatwaId&Id=127957.

Islamweb.net, "Selling Christmas Gifts and Decorations," December 14, 2009, accessed July 11, 2013: http://www.islamweb.net/emainpage/index.php?page=articles&id=155823http://www.islamweb.net/emainpage/index.php?page=articles&id=155823.

Islamweb.net, "A New Muslim Attending a Christmas Family Gathering," December 24, 2009, accessed July 11, 2013: http://www.islamweb.net/emainpage/index.php?page=articles&id=155840.

Islamweb.net, "Muslims Preparing a Turkey Dinner on Thanksgiving Day," December 24, 2009, accessed July 12, 2013: http://www.islamweb.net/emainpage/index.php?page=articles&id=155839.

Islamweb.net, "The Ruling on Congratulating Non-Muslims on their Celebrations," February 7, 2010, accessed July 12, 2013: http://www.islamweb.net/emainpage/index.php?page=articles&id=156436.Islamweb.net

Islamweb.net, "Ḥukm Khal' al-Ḥijāb min Ajl Ikmāl al-Ta'līm," August 26, 2010, accessed September 2013: http://fatwa.islamweb.net/fatwa/index.php?page=showfatwa&Option=FatwaId&Id=139510.

Islamweb.net, "Is Playing Football Considered an Excuse that Allows One to Abandon Fasting?" July 16, 2013, accessed August 29, 2013: http://www.islamweb.net/emainpage/index.php?page=showfatwa&Option=FatwaId&Id=127957.

Islamweb.net, "Working as a Waiter," n.d., accessed August 27, 2013: http://www.islamweb.net/emainpage/index.php?page=showfatwa&Option=FatwaId&Id=87931.

Jāballāh, Aḥmad, "al-Wasaṭiyya bayna Muqtaḍayāt al-Muwāṭana fī 'Ūrūbbā wal-Ḥifāẓ 'alā al-Huwiyya al-Islāmiyya," *al-Majalla al-'Ilmiyya lil-Majlis al-'Ūrūbbī lil-Iftā' wal-Buḥūth*, no. 12–13 (July 2008), 255–72.

Kassab, Akram, *al-Manhaj al-Da'wī 'ind al-Qaraḍāwī* (Cairo: Maktabat Wahaba, 2006).

Khaf, Monzer, "Selling a Pork Pizza: Lawful?" January 1, 2012, accessed September 25, 2013: http://www.onislam.net/english/ask-the-scholar/financial-issues/earning-livelihood/455220-selling-a-pork-pizza-lawful.html.

Khaled, Amr, *Integration im Islam: Über die Rolle der Muslime in Europa* (Karlsruhe, Andalusia Verlag, 2005).

Khan, Asif, *The Fiqh of Minorities: The New Fiqh to Subvert Islam* (London: Khalifa Publications, 2004).

Khilafah Magazine, "Islam, Politics and Elections," (April 2010), accessed September 18, 2013: http://www.khilafah.eu/kmag/article/islam-politics-and-elections.

Kutty, Ahmad, "Not Allowed to Wear Hijab at Work," October 14, 2003, accessed August 27, 2013: http://www.onislam.net/english/ask-the-scholar/financial-issues/earning-livelihood/169711.html.

Kutty, Ahmad, "Working as a Cashier for a Grocery Store that Sells Haram Meats", March 22, 2004, accessed 27 August, 2013: http://www.onislam.net/english/ask-the-scholar/financial-issues/earning-livelihood/170030.

Kutty, Ahmad, "Can I Work as a Police Officer?" August 19, 2008, accessed September 12, 2013: http://www.onislam.net/english/ask-the-scholar/financial-issues/earning-livelihood/177033.html.

Kutty, Ahmad, "Soccer Players Skipping Fasting," August 25, 2009, accessed April 1, 2010: http://www.islamonline.net/servlet/Satellite?pagename=IslamOnline-English-Ask_Scholar/*Fatwā*E/*Fatwā*E&cid=1160574242997.

Kutty, Ahmad, "Fasting or Sports?" August 26, 2009, accessed August 27, 2013: http://www.onislam.net/english/ask-the-scholar/acts-of-worship/fasting/fasting-rulings-and-regulations/177138.html.

Kutty, Ahmad, "Lesser Hijab for French Muslim Women: Acceptable?" April 12, 2011, accessed September 2013: http://www.onislam.net/english/ask-the-scholar/morals-and-manners/dress-and-adornment/169835-lesser-hijab-for-french-muslim-women-acceptable.html?Adornment=.

Kutty, Ahmad, "Should I Leave France Due to the Hijab Ban?" April 13, 2011, accessed September 27, 2013: http://www.onislam.net/english/ask-the-scholar/morals-and-manners/dress-and-adornment/170770-should-i-leave-france-due-to-hijab-ban.html?Adornment=.

Kutty, Ahmad, "Tips to Face the Hijab Ban in France," April 13, 2011, accessed September 2013: http://www.onislam.net/english/ask-the-scholar/morals-and-manners/dress-and-adornment/169853-tips-to-face-the-hijab-ban-in-france.html?Adornment=.

Kutty, Ahmad, "Alternative for French Muslims Girls after Hijab Ban," April 14, 2011, accessed September 25, 2013: http://www.onislam.net/english/ask-the-scholar/morals-and-manners/dress-and-adornment/169916-alterna tives-for-french-muslim-girls-after-hijab-ban.html?Adornment=.

Kutty, Ahmad, "May I Celebrate Christmas with My Christian Mother?" December 24, 2012, accessed July 11, 2013: http://www.onislam.net/english/ask-the-scholar/morals-and-manners/customs-and-traditions/169105-may-i-celebrate-christmas-with-my-christian-mother.html?Traditions=.

Kutty, Ahmad, "Should a Muslim Shave his Beard to Get a Job?" 9 July 2013, accessed August 27, 2013: http://www.onislam.net/english/ask-the-scholar/financial-issues/earning-livelihood/463411-should-a-muslim-shave-my-beard-to-get-a-job.html.

Mahdi, AbdurRahman, *Martyrdom in Jihad Versus Suicide Bombing* (London: Islamic Knowledge, 2010).

Majlis Majma' al-Fiqh al-Islāmī al-Dawlī, "al-Tawfīq bayna al-Taqayyud bil-Thawābit wa-bayna Muqtaḍayāt al-Muwāṭana lil-Muslimīn Khārij al-Duwal al-Islāmiyya" (decision 155, fourth of the seventeenth session, June24–28, 2006), n.d., accessed September 5, 2013: http://www.fiqhacademy.org.sa/qrarat/17-4.htm.

Malaughlu, Muṣṭafā, "al-Mabādi' al-Akhlāqiyya lil-Ta'āmul al-Mālī fī 'Ūrūbbā," *al-Majalla al-'Ilmiyya lil-Majlis al-'Ūrūbbī lil-Iftā' wal-Buḥūth*, no. 14–15 (July 2009), 235–60.

Mawlawī, Fayṣal and 'Aṭiyya, Jamāl al-Dīn, "Watching Football and Playing Professionally," June 1, 2006, accessed November 6, 2013: http://www.onislam.net/english/ask-the-scholar/sports-and-games/172792-watching-football-and-playing-professionally.html?Games=.

Mawqiʿ al-Qaraḍāwī, "Risāla min al-Duktūr al-Qaraḍāwī ilā al-Raʾīs al-Faransī Shīrāk," December 25, 2003, accessed September 25, 2013: http://www.qaradawi.net/news/51-2009-12-18-20-38-58.html.
Mawqiʿ al-Qaraḍāwī, "al-Wasaṭiyya wa-Dawr al-Iʿlām fī Ibrāzihā," October 15, 2006, accessed September 10, 2012: http://www.qaradawi.net/2010-02-01-08-43-29/4576.html.
Merenkov, Zeyd Ali, "A Muslim Perspective on Christmas," part 1, December 28, 2011, accessed July 10, 2013: http://www.islamweb.net/emainpage/index.php?page=articles&id=155792.
Moustapha, Sano Koutoub, "Can Muslims Accept Christmas Cash Bonus," December 25, 2011, accessed July 11, 2013: http://www.onislam.net/english/ask-the-scholar/ideologies-movements-and-religions/170681-can-muslims-accept-christmas-cash-bonus.html?Religions=.
MRDF, "Political Participation from an Academic Islamic Perspective—Sheikh Haitham al-Haddad" (a three-part lecture), May 1, 2010, accessed September 13, 2013: http://www.youtube.com/watch?v=56sRaj2EkQE&feature=relmfu; http://www.youtube.com/watch?v=RYmP6yhhfHs&feature=relmfu; http://www.youtube.com/watch?v=nxKxvPP7m5c&feature=relmfu.
Onislam.net, "As a New Muslim, Can My Kids Celebrate Christmas?" December 18, 2012, accessed July 11, 2013: http://www.onislam.net/english/ask-the-scholar/dawah-principles/dawah-to-non-and-new-muslims/169126-as-a-new-muslim-can-my-kids-celebrate-christmas.html?New_Muslims=.
Quṭb, Sayyid, *al-ʿAdāla al-Ijtimāʿiyya fī al-Islām* (Cairo: Dār al-Shurūq, 16th printing 2006, first published in the late 1940s).
Quṭb, Sayyid, "Amrīkā allatī Raʾaytu: fī Mizān al-Qiyam al-Insāniyya" (second part), *al-Risāla* 19, 959 (November 19, 1951), 1301–6.
Quṭb, Sayyid, *al-Salām al-ʿālamī wal-Islām* (Cairo: Dār al-Shurūq, 1974, first published 1951).
Ramadan, Tariq, *Western Muslims and the Future of Islam* (Oxford and New York: Oxford University Press, 2004).
Ramadan, Tariq, *What I Believe* (Oxford and New York: Oxford University Press, 2010).
Rawās, Muḥammad, *Mawsūʿat Fiqh Ibn Taymiyya* (Beirut: Dār al-Nafāʾis, 1998).
Riḍā, Muḥammad Rashīd, *al-Khīlafa* (Cairo: al-Zahrāʾ lil-Iʿlām al-ʿArabī, 1994, first published 1922).
Riḍā, Muḥammad Rashīd, *al-Waḥī al-Muḥammadī* (Maṭbaʿat al-Manār, 1955, first published 1933).
Ṣāliḥ, Suʾād, "Valentine's Day from an Islamic Perspective," February 13, 2013, accessed July 11, 2013: http://www.onislam.net/english/ask-the-scholar/morals-and-manners/customs-and-traditions/175209-valentines-day-from-an-islamic-perspective.html?Traditions=.
Sharlo, Yuval, "Levarech Notzri le-Ḥag Ha-Molad," December 11, 2006, accessed July 11, 2013: http://www.moreshet.co.il/web/shut/shut2.asp?id=65351.

Sharlo, Yuval, "Etz Ḥag Ha-Molad Bemekom 'Avoda," December 4, 2007, accessed July 11, 2013: http://www.moreshet.co.il/web/shut/shut2.asp?id=81513.

Sharlo, Yuval, "Ḥag Ha-Molad," December 11, 2009, accessed July 11, 2013: http://www.kipa.co.il/ask/show/168472-%D7%97%D7%92-%D7%94%D7%9E%D7%95%D7%9C%D7%93.

Siddiqi, Muḥammad Yasin Mazhar, *The Prophet Muḥammad: A Role Model for Muslim Minorities*, trans. 'Abd al-Raḥman Kidawī (Markfield: The Islamic Foundation, 2006).

Siddiqi, Muzammil, "Necessity that Allows Buying a House as on Mortgage," October 20, 2010, accessed July 5, 2013: http://www.onislam.net/english/ask-the-scholar/principles-of-islamic-jurisprudence-usul-ul-fiqh/concepts-and-term/174462-aquotnecessityaquot-that-allows-buying-a-house-on-mortgage.html?Term=.

Siddiqi, Muzammil, "Celebrating Halloween," accessed January 30, 2010, http://www.islamonline.net/servlet/Satellite?pagename=IslamOnline-English-Ask_Scholar/FatwaE/FatwaE&cid=1119503543074.

Siddiqi, Muzammil, "Muslims Participating in the US Local Councils," n.d., accessed May 5, 2012: http://www.onislam.net/english/ask-the-scholar/shariah-based-systems/imamate-and-political-systems/175184-muslims-participating-in-the-us-local-councils.html?Political_Systems=.

Siddiqi, Muzammil and Kutty, Ahmad, "Can Muslims Celebrate Christmas?" December 23, 2012, accessed July 9, 2013: http://www.onislam.net/english/ask-the-scholar/morals-and-manners/customs-and-traditions/174414-can-muslims-celebrate-christmas.html?Traditions=.

Sulṭān, Ṣalāḥ al-Dīn, "al-Muwāṭana fī Diyār al-Islām bayna al-Nāfīn wal-Muthbitīn," *al-Majalla al-'Ilmiyya lil-Majlis al-'Ūrūbbī lil-Iftā' wal-Buḥūth*, no. 12–13 (July 2008), 133–72.

Tallema, Essam, "Sheikh Qaradawi's First Interview with Onislam.net," October 18, 2010, accessed September 24, 2013: http://www.onislam.net/english/shariah/contemporary-issues/interviews-reviews-and-events/449388-sheikh-qaradawis-first-interview-with-onislamnet.html?Events=.

Tāyi', Hānī Muḥammad, "al-Shaykh al-Qaraḍāwī wa-Minhaj al-Wasaṭiyya al-Islāmiyya," in *Yūsuf al-Qaraḍāwī: Kalimāt fī Takrīmihi wa-Buḥūth fī Fikrihi wa-Fiqhihi* (Cairo: Dār al-Salām, 2004), 877–912.

The Ark, "'Wahhabis' Call for the Bad Treatment of Non-Muslims," Issue 21 (August 2007), 2.

The Ark, "Wahhabism Unveiled," Issue 21 (August 2007), 1.

The Permanent Committee, "Prohibition on Celebrating the Festivals of the Kuffar," in Muhammad Saed Abdul-Rahman (ed.), *Islam: Questions and Answers—Alliance and Amity, Disavowal and Enmity* (London: MSA Publication Ltd, 2003), 79.

The Permanent Committee, "The Keeping of Photos of Young Children," in *Islamic Fataawa Regarding the Muslim Child*, trans. Abū Ziyād Ibn Maḥmūd Ibn 'Abd al-Ghafūr (London: Invitation to Islam Publishers, 2007), 37.

The Permanent Committee, "Ḥukm Tajannus al-Muslim bi-Jinsiyyat al-Dawla Dhāt al-Hukūma al-Kāfira," in Aḥmad b. 'Abbās al-Shāfi'ī (ed.), *500 Jawāb fī al-Buyū' wal-Mu'āmalāt* (Cairo: Dār Ibn Ḥazm, 2010), 242–43.
The Permanent Committee, "Fatwā 5651," n.d., accessed August 23, 2013: http://www.alifta.com/Fatawa/FatawaChapters.aspx?View=Page&BookID=7&PageID=9143&back=true&languagename=en.
The Permanent Committee, "It Is Impermissible to Glorify the Traces of Scholars in a Manner that Leads to Exceeding the Proper Limits and Committing Shirk," n.d., accessed September 10, 2012: http://www.alifta.com.
The Permanent Committee, "It Is Not Permissible to Eat Foods that Are Prepared by the Kuffār for their Festivals," n.d., accessed July 12: http://islamqa.info/en/12666.
The Permanent Council, "The Ruling on Children's Songs," in *Islamic Fataawa Regarding the Muslim Child* (London: Invitation to Islam Publishers, 2007), 220–21.
The Standing Committee, "Pictures of any Living Creatures Are Forbidden Except Due to Necessity," in Muhammad bin Abdul-Aziz Al-Musnad (ed.), *Islamic Fatawa Regarding Women* (Riyadh: Darussalam Pubslihers & Distributers, 1996), 336–37.
The Standing Committee on Academic Research and Issuing Fatwas, "Ruling on Being a Witness to a Riba-based Loan," n.d., accessed July 7, 2013: http://islamqa.info/en/ref/10235.
Tūbūlyāk, Sulaymān Muḥammad, *al-Aḥkām al-Siyāsiyya lil-Aqalliyyāt al-Muslima fī al-Fiqh al-Islāmī* (Amman and Beirut: Dār al-Nafā'is, Dār al-Bayāriq, 1997).
Williams, Rowan, "Civil and Religious Law in England: A Religious Perspective," text of a lecture delievered on February 7, 2008, in Rex Ahdar and Nicholas Aroney, *Shari'a in the West* (Oxford and New York: Oxford University Press, 2010), 293–303.
Zayd, Muṣṭafā, *al-Maṣlaḥa fī al-Tashrī' al-Islāmī* (Master's dissertation submitted to Dār al-'Ulūm at the University of Cairo on May 1954, and published by Dār al-Yusr lil-Ṭibā'a wal-Nashr, n.d.).

Secondary Sources

Abdel-Fadil, Mona, "The Islam-Online Crisis: A Battle of Wasatiyya vs. Salafi Ideologies?" *CyberOrient* 5, 1 (2011), accessed June 27, 2013: http://www.cyberorient.net/article.do?articleId=6239.
Abdul Hakim I. al-Matroudi, *The Hanbali School of Law and Ibn Taymiyyah* (London and New York: Routledge, 2006).
Abdullah, Saeed, *Islamic Banking and Interest: A Study of the Prohibition of Riba and its Contemporary Interpretation* (Leiden: Brill, 1996).
Abou El-Fadl, Khaled, "Islamic Law and Muslim Minorities: The Juristic Discourse on Muslim Minorities from the Second/Eight to the Eleventh/Seventeenth Centuries," *Islamic Law and Society* 1, 2 (1994), 141–87.

Abou El Fadl, Khaled, "Striking a Balance: Islamic Legal Discourse on Muslim Minorities," in Yvonne Yazbeck Haddad and John L. Esposito (eds.), *Muslims on The Americanization Path?* (Oxford and New York: Oxford University Press, 2000), 47–64.

Abū al-Lawz, 'Abd al-Hakim, "al-Salafiyya al-Taqlīdiyya wal-Salafiyya al-Jihādiyya," *Majallat al-Dīmuqrāṭiyya*, no. 38 (April 2010), 35–44.

Abu Rumman, Mohammed, *Salafists and the Arab Spring: The Question of Religion and Democracy in Arab Politics* (Beirut: Markaz Dirasat al-Wahda al-'Arabiyya, 2013, in Arabic).

Abu-Sahlieh, Sami A. Aldeeb., "The Islamic Conception of Migration," *International Migration Review* 30, 1 (March 1996), 37–57.

Adamas, Charles C., *Islam and Modernism in Egypt: A Study of the Modern Reform Movement Inaugurated by Muḥammad 'Abduh* (New York: Russel & Russel, 1968, first published 1933).

Adhar, Rex and Aroney, Nicholas, *Shari'a in the West* (Oxford and New York: Oxford University Press, 2010).

Adraoui, Mohamed-Ali, "Salafism in France: Ideology, Practices and Contradictions," in Roel Meijer (ed.), *Global Salafism: Islam's New Religious Movement* (London: Hurst & Company, 2009), 364–83.

Ahmed, Houriya and Stuart, Hannah, *Hizb ut-Tahrir: Ideology and Strategy* (London: The Centre for Social Cohesion, 2009).

Al-Atawneh, Muhammad, "Is Saudi Arabia a Theocracy? Religion and Governance in Contemporary Saudi Arabia," *Middle Eastern Studies* 45, 5 (2009), 721–37.

Al-Atawneh, Muhammad, *Wahhābī Islam Facing the Challenges of Modernity: Dār Al-Iftā in the Modern Saudi State* (Leiden: Brill, 2010).

Al-Atawneh, Muhammad, "Wahhabi Self-Examination Post-9/11: Rethinking the 'Other', 'Otherness' and Tolerance," *Middle Eastern Studies* 47, 2 (2011), 255–71.

Al-Enazy, Askar H., *The Creation of Saudi Arabia* (London and New York: Routledge, 2010).

Al-Enazy, Askar H., *The Creation of Saudi Arabia: Ibn Saud and British Imperial Policy, 1914–1927* (London and New York: Routledge, 2010).

Al-Khaḍar, 'Abd al-'Azīz, *al-Sa'ūdiyya Sīrat Dawla wa-Mujtama'* (Beirut: Arab Network for Research and Publishing, 2010).

Al-Rasheed, Madawi, "The Local and the Global in Saudi Salafi Discourse," in Roel Meijer (ed.), *Global Salafism: Islam's New Religious Movement* (London: Hurst & Company, 2009), 301–20.

Al-Ṭā'ī, Hāshim 'Abd al-Razzāq Ṣāliḥ, *al-Tayyār al-Islāmī fī al-Khalīj al-'Arabī, Dirāsa Ta'rīkhiyya 1945–1991* (Beirut: Mu'assasāt al-Intishār al-'Arabī, 2010).

Anderson, Benedict, "The New World Disorder," *New Left Review* 1, 193 (May–June 1992), 3–15.

Alterman, Jon B., *New Media, New Politics? From Satellite Television to the Internet in the Arab World* (Washington, D.C.: Washington Institute for Near East Policy, 1998).

Armanios, Febe, "The Islamic Traditions of Wahhabism and Salafiyya," *Congressional Research Service Reports* (December 2003), accessed October 1, 2013:

http://www.law.umaryland.edu/marshall/crsreports/crsdocuments/RS2169 501222003.pdf.

Asad, Talal, *Genealogies of Religion: Discipline and Reasons of Power in Christianity and Islam* (Baltimore: John Hopkins University Press, 1993).

Azhar, Rauf A., *Economics of an Islamic Economy* (Brill: Leiden, 2010).

Baker, Raymond William, "Invidious Comparisons: Realism, Postmodern Globalism, and Centrist Islamic Movements in Egypt," in John L. Esposito (ed.), *Political Islam: Revolution, Radicalism or Reform?* (Boulder, London: Lynne Rienner Publishers, 1997), 115–33.

Baker, Raymond William, *Islam without Fear: Egypt and the New Islamists* (Cambridge, MA and London: Harvard University Press, 2003).

Balala, Maha-Hanaan, *Islamic Finance and Law: Theory and Practice in a Globalized World* (London and New York: I. B. Tauris, 2011).

Boehmer, Daniel A. and Murphy James P., *The Politicization of the Egyptian Salafiyya: Principled Participation and Islamist Competition in the Post-Mubarak Era* (The Institution for Middle East Studies, The Elliot School of International Affairs, George Washington University, 2012).

Bowen, John R., *Why the French Don't Like Headscarves: Islam, the State and Public Space* (Princeton and Oxford: Princeton University Press, 2007).

Bowen, John R., *Can Islam Be French? Pluralism and Pragmatism in a Secularist State* (Princeton and Oxford: Princeton University Press, 2010).

Boyd, Douglas A., *Broadcasting in the Arab World* (Ames, Iowa: Iowa State University Press, 1993).

Breuer, Mordechai, *Jüdische Orthodoxie im Deutschen Reich 1871–1918* (Jerusalem: Zalman Shazar Center for Jewish History, 1990, in Hebrew).

Brown, Jonathan, *Salafis and Sufis in Egypt* (Washington: Carnegie Endowment for International Peace, 2011).

Brown, Nathan J., "Kuwait's 2008 Parliamentary Elections: A Setback for Democratic Islamism?" *Carnegie Endowment for International Peace* (2008), accessed October 28, 2013: http://edoc.bibliothek.uni-halle.de:8080/servlets/MCRFileNodeServlet/HALCoRe_derivate_00004885/CEIP_brown_kuwait2.pdf.

Brubaker, Rogers, "The Return of Assimilation? Changing Perspectives on Immigration and its Sequels in France, Germany, and the United States," in Christian Joppke and Ewa Morawska (eds.), *Toward Assimilation and Citizenship: Immigrants in Liberal Nation-States* (Basingstoke and New York: Palgrave Macmillan, 2003) 39–58.

Bukay, David, "Can There Be an Islamic Democracy?" *Middle East Quarterly* 14, 2 (Spring 2007), 71–80.

Bunt, Gary R., *Islam in the Digital Age: E-jihad, Online Fatwas and Cyber Islamic Environment* (London, Sterling, Virginia: Pluto Press, 2003).

Caeiro, Alexandre, "The Social Construction of Sharīʿa : Bank Interest, Home Purchase and Islamic Norms in the West," *Die Welt des Islams* 44, 3 (2004), 351–75.

Caeiro, Alexandre and al-Saify Mahmoud, "Qaradawi in Europe, Europe in Qaradawi? The Global Mufti's European Politics," in Bettina Gräf and Jakob

Skovgaard-Petersen (eds.), *The Global Mufti: The Phenomenon of Yūsuf al-Qaraḍāwī* (London: Hurst & Company, 2009), 109–48.

Caeiro, Alexandre, "The Power of European Fatwas: The Minority Fiqh Project and the Making of an Islamic Counterpublic," *International Journal of Middle East Studies* 42, 3 (2010), 435–49.

Caeiro, Alexandre, "Transnational Ulama, European Fatwas and Islamic Authorities: A Case Study of the European Council for Fatwa and Research," in Martin van Bruinessen and Stefano Allievi (eds.), *Producing Islamic Knowledge: Transmission and Dissemination in Western Europe* (Abingdon and New York: Routledge: 2011), 121–41.

Castles, Stephan and Miller, Mark J., *The Age of Migration: International Population Movements in the Modern World* (New York: Palgrave, 1998).

Cohen, Robin, *Global Diasporas: An Introduction* (Seattle: University of Washington Press, 1997).

Commins, David, *The Wahhabi Mission and Saudi Arabia* (London and New York: I. B. Tauris, 2006).

Commins, David, "Contestation and Authority in Wahhābi Polemics," in Mohammad Ayoob and Hasan Kosebalaban (eds.), *Religion and Politics in Saudi Arabia* (Boulder, CO and London: Lynne Rienner Publishers, 2009), 39–53.

Cook, Michael, "On the Origins of Wahhābism," *Journal of the Royal Asiatic Society* 2, 2 (July 1992), 191–202.

Davis-Secord, Sarah, "Muslims in Noram Sicily: The Evidence of Imām al-Māzārī' *Fatwās*," *Mediterranean Studies*, no. 16 (2007), 46–66.

Dekmejian, R. Hrair, "The Rise of Political Islamism in Saudi Arabia," *Middle East Journal* 48, 4 (Autumn 1994), 627–43.

DeLorenzo, Yusuf Talal, "The Fiqh Councilor in North America," in Yvonne Yazbeck Haddad and John L. Esposito (eds.), *Muslims on the Americanization Path?* (Oxford and New York: Oxford University Press, 2000), 65–86.

Deutsche Welle, "Burkini Swimsuit Is Compromise Says German Court," September 11, 2013, accessed September 30, 2013: http://www.dw.de/burkini-swimsuit-is-compromise-says-german-court/a-17083545.

Doyle, Natalie J., "Lessons from France: Popularist Anxiety and Veiled Fears of Islam," *Islam and Christian-Muslim Relations* 22, 4 (2011), 475–89.

Elliott, Andrea, "Complications Grow for Muslims Serving in U.S. Military," *New York Times* (November 8, 2009), accessed September 12, 2013: http://www.nytimes.com/2009/11/09/us/09muslim.html?pagewanted=all&_r=0.

Esposito, John L. and Voll, John O., *Makers of Contemporary Islam* (Oxford and New York: Oxford University Press, 2001).

Fandy, Mamoun, "Information Technology, Trust and Social Change in the Arab World," *The Middle East Journal* 54, 3 (Summer 2000), 378–94.

Fandy, Mamun, *Saudi Arabia and the Politics of Dissent* (New York: Palgrave, 2001).

Fishman, Shammai, *Fiqh al-Aqalliyyat: A Legal Theory for Muslim Minorities* (Washington: Hudson Institute, 2006).

Galal, Ehab, "Yūsuf al-Qaraḍāwī and the New Islamic TV," in Bettina Gräf and Jakob Skovgaard-Petersen (eds.), *The Global Mutfi: The Phenomenon of Yūsuf al-Qaraḍāwī* (London: Hurst & Company, 2009), 149–80.

Ghadban, Ralph, "Fiqh al-Aqalliyyat and its Place in Islamic Law," *Orient* 51, 2 (2010), 56–63.

Ghareeb, Edmund, "New Media and the Information Revolution in the Arab World: An Assessment," *The Middle East Journal* 54, 3 (Summer 2000), 395–418.

Glick Schiller, Nina, Linda Basch and Cristina Blanc-Szanton, "Transnationalism: A New Analytic Framework for Understanding Migration," in Nina Glick Schiller, Linda Basch, and Cristina Blanc-Szanton (eds.), *Towards a Transnational Perspective on Migration* (New York: The New York Academy of Science, 1992), 1–24.

Glick-Schiller, Nina and Fouron, Georges Eugene, *Georges Woke Up Laughing* (Durham, NC: Duke University Press, 2001).

Gräf, Bettina, "The Concept of Wasaṭiyya in the Work of Yūsuf al-Qaraḍāwī," in Bettina Gräf and Jakob Skovgaard-Petersen (eds.), *The Global Mufti: The Phenomenon of Yūsuf al-Qaraḍāwī* (London: Hurst & Company, 2009), 213–38.

Hallaq, Wael, B., "The Primacy of the Qur'ān in Shāṭibī's Legal Theory," in Wael B. Hallaq and Donald P. Little (eds.), *Islamic Studies Presented to Charles J. Adams* (Leiden: Brill, 1991), 69–90.

Hallaq, Wael B., *A History of Islamic Legal Theories* (Cambridge: Cambridge University Press, 1997).

Hallaq, Wael B., *Authority, Continuity and Change in Islamic Law* (New York: Cambridge University Press, 2001).

Hallaq, Wael B., *The Formation of Islamic Law* (Aldershot: Ashgate, 2004).

Hallaq, Wael, B., *The Origins and Evolution of Islamic Law* (Cambridge: Cambridge University Press, 2005).

Hamid, Sadek, "The Attraction of 'Authentic Islam': Salafism and British Muslim Youth," in Roel Meijer (ed.), *Global Salafism: Islam's New Religious Movement* (London: Hurst & Company, 2009), 384–403.

Hashemi, Nader, "Why Islam (Properly Understood) Is the Solution: Reflections on the Role of Religion in Tunisia's Democratic Transition," *The American Journal of Islamic Social Sciences* 30, 4 (October 2013), 137–45.

Hatina, Meir, "The 'Other Islam': The Egyptian Wasat Party," *Critique: Critical Middle Eastern Studies* 14, 2 (Summer 2005), 171–84.

Haykel, Bernard, "On the Nature of Salafī Thought and Action," in Roel Meijer (ed.), *Global Salafism: Islam's New Religious Movement* (London: Hurst & Company, 2009), 33–57.

Hegghammer, Thomas, "Jihadi-Salafis or Revolutionaries? On Religion and Politics in the Study of Militant Islamism," in Roel Meijer (ed.), *Global Salafism: Islam's New Religious Movement* (London: Hurst & Company, 2009), 244–66.

Hendrickson, Jocelyn N., *The Islamic Obligation to Emigrate: Al-Wansharīsī's Asnā al-matājir Reconsidered* (PhD dissertation, Emory University, 2009).

Hourani, Albert, *Arabic Thought in the Liberal Age 1798–1939* (London, New York and Toronto: Oxford University Press, 1962).

Hroub, Khaled, "Salafi Formations in Palestine and the Limits of a De-Palestinised Milieu," *Holy Land Studies* 7, 2 (November 2008), 157–81.

Hussain, Dilwar, "Muslim Political Participation in Britain and the 'Europeanization' of Fiqh," *Die Welt des Islams* 44, 3 (2004), 376–401.

Itzigsohn, José *et al.*, "Mapping Dominican Transnationalism: Narrow and Broad Transnational Practices," *Ethnic and Racial Studies* 22, 2 (March 1999), 316–39.

Jacob, Walter, *Contemporary American Reform Responsa* (Pennsylvania: Central Conference of American Rabbis, 1987).

Jones, Toby Craig, "Religious Revivalism and its Challenge to the Saudi Regime," in Mohammed Ayoob and Hasan Kosebalaban (eds.), *Religion and Politics in Saudi Arabia: Wahhabism and the State* (Boulder, CO and London: Lynne Rienner Publishers, 2009), 109–20.

Jonker, Gerdien, "From 'Foreign Workers' to 'Sleepers': The Churches, the State and Germany's 'Discovery' of its Muslim Population," in Jocelyne Cesari and Seán McLoughlin (eds.), *European Muslims and the Secular State* (Ashgate: The Network of Comparative Research on Islam and Muslims in Europe, 2005), 113–26.

Joppke, Christian, *Immigration and the Nation-State: The United States, Germany, and Great Britain* (Oxford and New York: Oxford University Press, 1999).

Joppke, Christian, *Veil: Mirror of Identity* (Cambridge and Malden: Polity Press, 2009).

Kepel, Gilles, *The War for the Muslim Mind: Islam and the West* (Cambridge, MA and London: The Belknap Press of Harvard University Press, 2004).

Kerr, Malcolm H., *Islamic Reform: The Political and Legal Theories of Muḥammad 'Abduh and Rashīd Riḍā* (Berkeley and Los Angeles: University of California Press, 1966).

King, Russell and Wood, Nancy, "Media and Migration: An Overview," in Russell King and Nancy Wood (eds.), *Media and Migration: Construction of Mobility and Difference* (London and New York: Routledge, 2001), 1–22.

Kirchner, Henner, "Internet in the Arab World: A Step towards an 'Information Society'?" in Kai Hafez (ed.), *Mass Media, Politics and Society in the Middle East* (Cresskill, NJ: Hampton Press, 2001), 137–58.

Kostiner, Joseph, "State, Islam and Opposition in Saudi Arabia: The Post-Desert Storm phase," *Terrorism and Political Violence* 8, 2 (1996), 75–89.

Lacroix, Stéphane, *Sheikhs and Politicians: Inside the New Egyptian Salafism* (Brookings Doha Center, June 2012).

Lauzière, Henri, "The Construction of Salafiyya: Reconsidering Salafism from the Perspective of Conceptual History," *International Journal of Middle East Studies* 42, 3 (August 2010), 369–89.

Lewis, Mervyn and Algaoud, Latifa M., *Islamic Banking* (Northampton, MA: E. Elgar Publishing, 2001).

Lyons, David, "Legal Formalism and Instrumentalism: A Pathological Study," *Cornell Law 66, Review* 949 (June 1981), 949–72.

Malik, Iftikhar H., *Islam and Modernity: Muslims in Europe and the United States* (London: Pluto Press, 2004).

March, Andrew, "Islamic Foundations for a Social Contract in Non-Muslim Liberal Democracies," *American Political Science Review* 101, 2 (May 2007), 235–52.

March, Andrew, "Are Secularism and Neutrality Attractive to Religious Minorities? Islamic Discussions of Western Secularism in the 'Jurisprudence of Muslim Minorities' (Fiqh al-Aqalliyyat) Discourse," *Cardozo Law Review* 30, 6 (2009), 2821–54.

March, Andrew, *Islam and Liberal Citizenship: The Search for an Overlapping Consensus* (Oxford and New York: Oxford University Press, 2009).

Marks, Monica, "Youth Politics and Tunisian Salafism: Understanding the Jihadi Current," *Mediterranean Politics* 18, 1 (2013), 104–11.

Masud, Muhammad Khalid, Messick, Brinkley and Powers, David S., "Muftis, Fatwas and Islamic Legal Interpretation," in Muhammad Khalid Masud, Brinkley Messick and David S. Powers (eds.), *Islamic Legal Interpretation: Muftis and their Fatwas* (Cambridge, MA: Harvard University Press, 1996), 3–32.

Masud, Muhammad Khalid, "Islamic Law and Muslim Minorities," *ISIM Newsletter* 11 (2002), 17.

McCants, William, "The Lesser of Two Evils: The Salafi Turn to Party Politics in Egypt," *Middle East Memo* 23 (May 2012), accessed November 7, 2013: http://www.brookings.edu/~/media/Research/Files/Papers/2012/5/01%20salafi%20egypt%20mccants/0501_salafi_egypt_mccants.pdf.

Meijer, Roel, "The 'Cycle of Contention' and the Limits of Terrorism in Saudi Arabia," in Paul Aarts and Gerd Nonneman (eds.), *Saudi Arabia in the Balance: Political Economy, Society, Foreign Affairs* (New York: New York University Press, 2005), 271–311.

Meijer, Roel, "Yūsuf al-'Uyayrī and the Making of a Revolutionary Salafi Praxis," *Die Welt des Islams* 47, 3–4 (2007), 422–59.

Meijer, Roel, "Commanding Right and Forbidding Wrong as a Principle of Social Action: The Case of the Jama'a al-Islamiyya," in Roel Meijer (ed.), *Global Salafism: Islam's New Religious Movement* (London: Hurst & Company, 2009), 189–220.

Meijer, Roel, "Introduction," in Roel Meijer (ed.), *Global Salafism: Islam's New Religious Movement* (London: Hurst & Company, 2009), 1–31.

Monroe, Steve L., "Salafis in Parliament: Democratic Attitudes and Party Politics in the Gulf," *The Middle East Journal* 66, 3 (Summer 2012), 409–24.

Nachmani, Amikam, *Europe and its Muslim Minorities: Aspects of Conflict, Attempts at Accord* (Brighton: Sussex Academic Press, 2009).

Nafi, Basheer M., "*Fatwā* and War: On the Allegiance of the American Muslim Soldiers in the Aftermath of September 11," *Islamic Law and Society,* 11, 1 (2004), 78–116.

Norton, Richard, "Thwarted Politics: The Case of Egypt's Hizb al-Wasat," in Robert W. Hefner (ed.), *Remaking Muslim Politics* (Princeton and Oxford: Princeton University Press, 2004), 133–60.

Nyazee, Imran Ahsan Khan, *Theories of Islamic Law: The Methodology of Ijtihād* (Islamabad: Islamic Research Institute and International Institute of Islamic Thought, 1994).

Opwis, Felicitas, "Maṣlaḥa in Contemporary Islamic Legal Theory," *Islamic Law and Society* 12, 2 (2005), 182–223.

Opwis, Felicitas, "The Construction of Madhhab Authority: Ibn Taymiyya's Interpretation of Juristic Preference (Istiḥsān)," *Islamic Law and Society* 15, 2 (2009), 219–49.

Opwis, Felicitas, *Maṣlaḥa and the Purpose of the Law: Islamic Discourses and Legal Change from the 4th/10th to 8th/14th Century* (Leiden and Boston: Brill, 2010).

Parray, Tauseef Ahmad, "'Islamic Democracy' or Democracy in Islam: Some Key Operational Democratic Concepts and Notions," *World Journal of Islamic History and Civilization* 2, 2 (2012), 66–86.

Parray, Tauseef Ahmad, "The Legal Methodology of 'Fiqh al-Aqalliyyat' and its Critics: An Analytical Study," *Journal of Muslim Minority Affairs* 32, 1 (March 2012), 87–107.

Polka, Sagi, "The Centrist Stream in Egypt and its Role in the Public Discourse Surrounding the Shaping of the Country's Cultural Identity," *Middle Eastern Studies* 39, 3 (July 2003), 39–64.

Rapoport, Yossef, "Ibn Taymiyya's Radical Legal Thought: Rationalism, Pluralism and the Primacy of Intention," in Yossef Rapoport and Shahab Ahmed (eds.), *Ibn Taymiyya and His Times* (Oxford and New York: Oxford University Press, 2010), 191–221.

Reuveni, Gideon, "Bourgeois Lifestyle, Jewishness, and Consumer Culture in Weimar Germany" (in Hebrew), *Chidushim: Studies in the History of German and Central European Jewry* 14 (Jerusalem: Leo Baeck Institute, 2010), 53–90.

Rohe, Mathias, *Muslim Minorities and the Law in Europe* (New Delhi: Global Media Publications, 2007).

Rohe, Mathias, "Islam and the Law in Europe," *Orient* 51, 2 (2010), 23–36.

Rose, Alexander, "How Did Muslims Vote in 2000?" *Middle East Quarterly* 8, 3 (Summer 2001), 13–27.

Roy, Olivier, *The Politics of Chaos in the Middle East* (New York: Columbia University Press, 2008).

Roy, Olivier, *Holy Ignorance: When Religion and Culture Part Ways* (New York: Columbia University Press, 2010).

Rubin, Barry, "Revolutionary Salafi Islamists in Egypt: An Analysis and Guide," *Middle East Review of International Affairs* 17, 2 (Summer 2013), 37–54.

Ryad, Umar, "A Prelude to Fiqh al-Aqalliyyāt: Rashīd Riḍā's *Fatwā*s to Muslims under Non-Muslim Rule," in Christiane Timmerman et al (eds.), *In-between Spaces: Christian and Muslim Minorities in Transition in Europe and the Middle East* (Brussels: Peter Lang: 2009), 239–70.

Ryan, Curtis R., "Islamist Political Activism in Jordan: Moderation, Militancy, and Democracy," *Middle East Review of International Affairs* 12, 2 (June 2008), 1–16.

Salkeld, Luke, "M & S Faces Boycott as it Lets Muslim Staff Refuse to Sell Alcohol or Pork," *The Daily Mail* (December 23, 2013), 11.

Schacht, Joseph, *The Origins of Muhammadan Jurisprudence* (Oxford: Clarendon Press, 1959).

Scott, Joan Wallach, *The Politics of the Veil* (Princeton, NJ: Princeton University Press, 2007).

Shadid, Wasif and van Koningsveld, Sjoerd, "Loyalty to a Non-Muslim Government: An Analysis of Islamic Normative Discussions and the Views of Some Contemporary Islamicists," in Wasif A. R. Shadid and Sjoerd van Koningsveld (eds.), *Political Participation and Identities of Muslims in Non-Muslim States* (Kampen: Kok Pharos Publishing House, 1996), 84–115.

Shadid, Wasif and van Koninsveld, Sjoerd., "Religious Authorities of Muslims in the West: Their View on Political Participation," in Wasif Shadid and Sjoerd van Koningsveld (eds.), *Intercultural Relations and Religious Authorities: Muslims in the European Union* (Leuven: Peeters, 2002), 149–68.

Shavit, Uriya, *The New Imagined Community: Global Media and the Construction of National and Muslim Identities of Migrants* (Brighton: Sussex Academic Press, 2009).

Shavit, Uriya, "Is Shura a Muslim Form of Democracy?" *Middle Eastern Studies* 46, 3 (May 2010), 349–74.

Shavit, Uriya, *Islamism and the West: From 'Cultural Attack' to 'Missionary Migrant'* (London: Routledge, 2014).

Shavit, Uriya and Wiesenbach, Frederic, "An 'Integrating Enclave': The Case of al-Hayat, Germany's First Islamic Fitness Center for Women in Cologne," *Journal of Muslim Minority Affairs* 32, 1 (March 2012), 47–61.

Shavit, Uriya and Winter, Ofir, "Sports in Contemporary Islamic Law," *Islamic Law and Society* 18, 2 (2011), 250–80.

Skrbiš, Zlatko, *Long Distance Nationalism: Diasporas, Homelands and Identities* (Aldershot, UK: Ashgate, 1999).

Stemman, Juan José Escobar, "Middle East Salafism's Influence and the Radicalization of Muslim Communities in Europe," *Middle East Review of International Affairs* 10, 3 (September 2006), 1–14.

Sultany, Nimer, "Against Conceptualism: Islamic Law, Democracy, and Constitutionalism in the Aftermath of the Arab Spring," *Boston University International Law Journal* (March 31, 2013), accessed July 10, 2013: http://papers.ssrn.com/sol3/papers.cfm?abstract_id=2242464.

Taylor, Jerome, "Can a Muslim Say Happy Christmas to his Friends?" *The Independent* (November 26, 2009).

Tauber, Eliezer, "The Regime of the Muslim State According to Rashīd Riḍā," *HeMizrah HeHadash* XLI (2000), 41–50 (in Hebrew).

Teitelbaum, Joshua, "The Gulf States and the End of Dual Containment," *Middle East Review of International Affairs* 2, 3 (September 1998), 21–26.

Teitelbaum, Joshua, *Holier Than Thou: Saudi-Arabia's Islamic Opposition* (Washington: The Washington Institute for Near East Policy, 2000).

Teitelbaum, Joshua, "Dueling for Da'wa: State vs. Society on the Saudi Internet," *Middle East Journal* 56, 2 (Spring 2002), 222–39.

Teitelbaum, Joshua, "Terrorist Challenges to Saudi Arabian Internal Security," *Middle East Review of International Affairs* 9, 3 (September 2005), 1–11.

Teitelbaum, Joshua, *Saudi Arabia and the New Strategic Landscape* (Stanford: Hoover Institution Press Publication, 2010).

Torelli, Stefano M., Merone, Fabio and Cavatorta, Francesco, "Salafism in Tunisia: Challenges and Opportunities for Democratization," *Middle East Policy* 19, 4 (Winter 2012) 140–54.

Verskin, Alan, *Oppressed in the Land? Fatwās on Muslims Living under Non-Muslim Rule from the Middle Ages to the Present* (Princeton: Markus Wiener Publishers, 2013).

Vogel, Frank E., *Islamic Law and Legal System: Studies of Saudi Arabia* (Leiden: Brill, 2000).

Wagemakers, Joas, "Framing the 'Threat to Islam': *al-Wala' wal-Bara'* in Salafi Discourse," *Arab Studies Quarterly* 30, 4 (Fall 2008), 1–22.

Wagemakers, Joas, "The Transformation of a Radical Concept: *al-Wala' wal-Bara'* in the Ideology of Abu Muhammad al-Maqdisi," in Roel Meijer (ed.), *Global Salafism: Islam's New Religious Movement* (London: Hurst & Company, 2009), 81–106.

Wagemakers, Joas, "The Enduring Legacy of the Second Saudi State: Quietist and Radical Wahhabi Contestations of *al-Walā' wa-l-Barā',*" *International Journal of Middle Eastern Studies* 44, 1 (February 2012), 93–110.

Walbridge, John. "The Islamic Art of Asking Questions: 'Ilm al-Ikhtilāf and the Institutionalization of Disagreement," *Islamic Studies* 41, 1 (2002), 69–86.

Webb, Carolyn, "Sheikh Sparks Outrage," *The Age* (January 19, 2007), accessed September 18, 2013: http://www.theage.com.au/news/national/sheikh-sparks-outrage/2007/01/18/1169095914411.html?page=fullpage.

Wiedl, Nina, *The Making of a German Salafiyya* (Aarhus, Denmark: Aarhus University, Centre for Studies in Islamism and Radicalisation, October 2012).

Wiktorowicz, Quintan, "The Salafi Movement in Jordan," *International Journal of Middle East Studies* 32, 2 (May, 2000), 219–40.

Wiktorowicz, Quintan, "Civil Society as Social Control: State Power in Jordan," *Comparative Politics* 33, 1 (October 2000), 43–61.

Wiktorowicz, Quintan, *The Management of Islamic Activism: Salafis, the Muslim Brotherhood, and State Power in Jordan* (Albany: State University of New York Press, 2001).

Wiktorowicz, Quintan (ed.), *Islamic Activism: A Social Movement Theory Approach* (Bloomington: Indiana University Press, 2004).

Wiktorowicz, Quintan, "Anatomy of the Salafi Movement," *Studies in Conflict and Terrorism* 29, 3 (April–May 2006), 207–39.

Wimmer, Andreas and Glick Schiller, Nina, "Methodological Nationalism, the Social Sciences and the Study of Migration: An Essay in Historical Epistemology," *International Migration Review* 37, 3 (Fall 2003), 576–610.

Witte, John Jr., "The Future of Muslim Family Law in Western Democracies," in Rex Ahdar and Nicholas Aroney (eds), *Shari'a in the West* (Oxford and New York: Oxford University Press, 2010), 279–92.

Wolf, Anne, "An Islamist 'Renaissance'? Religion and Politics in Post-revolutionary Tunisia," *The Journal of North African Studies* 18, 4 (2013), 560–73.

Wright, Mike, "Watford Labour Councillor, Asif Khan, Was a Member of Radical Islamic Group, Hizb ut-Tahrir," *Watford Observer* (November 13, 2012), accessed September 17, 2013: http://m.watfordobserver.co.uk/news/10044065.Watford_councillor_was_member_of_radical_Islamic_group/.

Zaman, Muhammad Qasim, "The 'Ulama of Contemporary Islam and their Conception of the Common Good," in Armando Salvatore and Dale F. Eickelman (eds.), *Public Islam and the Common Good* (Leiden, Boston: Brill, 2006), 129–55.

Index

The manufacturer's authorised representative in the EU for product safety is Oxford University Press España S.A. of el Parque Empresarial San Fernando de Henares, Avenida de Castilla, 2 – 28830 Madrid (www.oup.es/en or product.safety@oup.com). OUP España S.A. also acts as importer into Spain of products made by the manufacturer.

www.ingramcontent.com/pod-product-compliance
Lightning Source LLC
LaVergne TN
LVHW011915200926
848484LV00002B/631

* 9 7 8 0 1 9 8 7 5 7 2 3 8 *